HOW TO WIN AT GAMBLING

A STEP-BY-STEP MANUAL FOR WINNING MONEY AT MORE THAN 50 GAMES VARIATIONS!

ACKNOWLEDGMENTS

I would like to thank my two editors, Dana Smith, best-selling author and co-author of multiple titles, including *Tournament Tips from the Poker Pros* and *Omaha High-Low: How to Win at the Lower Limits*, and Julian Silberstang. They greatly increased the readability of the book, catching errors in delivery and content, and making sure what was intended found its full meaning in the final prose.

ABOUT THE AUTHOR

Avery Cardoza is the foremost gambling authority in the world and best-selling author of twenty-one gambling books and advanced strategies, including the *Official World Series of Poker Strategy Guide: No-Limit Tournament Hold'em*, *Poker Talk*, *Secrets of Winning Slots*, *Casino Craps for the Winner*, and the classic, *Winning Casino Blackjack for the Non-Counter*. Through his three decades of authoritative writings and no-nonsense practical advice, millions of players have learned how to play and win money at gambling.

Cardoza began his gambling career underage in Las Vegas as a professional blackjack player beating the casinos at their own game and was soon barred from one casino after another. In 1981, when even the biggest casinos refused him play, Cardoza founded Cardoza Publishing, now the foremost and largest gaming publisher in the world. Cardoza is the home of many of the giants in the world of gambling, including Doyle Brunson, Daniel Negreanu, T.J. Cloutier, Mike Caro, Tom McEvoy, Mike Matusow and Arnold Snyder. The Cardoza library, distributed around the world and translated into more than a dozen languages, includes more than 200 gaming titles. More than ten million Cardoza books have been sold.

Though originally from Brooklyn, New York, where he is occasionally found, Cardoza has used his winnings to pursue a lifestyle of extensive traveling in exotic locales around the world, and currently makes his home in Las Vegas, Nevada.

Visit www.cardozabooks.com for a full list of Cardoza Publishing books.

HOW TO WIN AT GAMBLING

A STEP-BY-STEP MANUAL FOR WINNING MONEY AT MORE THAN 50 GAMES VARIATIONS!

AVERY CARDOZA

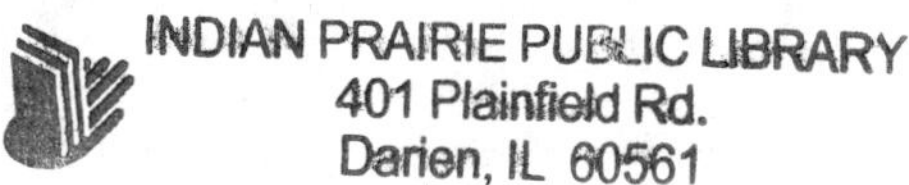

CARDOZA PUBLISHING

Dedicated to Ron Charles

Cardoza Publishing is the foremost gaming and gambling publisher in the world with a library of more than 200 up-to-date and easy-to-read books and strategies. These authoritative works are written by the top experts in their fields and with more than 10,000,000 books in print, represent the best-selling and most popular gaming books anywhere.

2010 NEW EDITION!

Library of Congress Catalog Number: 2010921139
ISBN 10: 1-58042-262-4
ISBN 13: 978-1-58042-262-8

Visit our website or write for a full list of Cardoza Publishing books and advanced strategies.

CARDOZA PUBLISHING

P.O. Box 98115, Las Vegas, NV 89193
Toll-Free Phone (800)577-WINS
email: cardozabooks@aol.com

www.cardozabooks.com

TABLE OF CONTENTS

TABLE OF CONTENTS

TABLE OF CONTENTS

INTRODUCTION

FIVE KEYS TO WINNING

1. Study and practice your favorite games before you go to a casino.
2. Protect your wins and limit your losses.
3. Make the correct strategic move on every play, every time. Losers play lame hunches–winners play smart strategy.
4. Never gamble with money you cannot afford to lose, either financially or emotionally.
5. Think like a winner–play like a winner.

You can win money at gambling! Whether you're a novice or a veteran, this brand new edition teaches you the professional approach to gambling, and gives you the best strategies for the games you play. I've updated this edition with the latest information, and have added more games, including three card poker and four card poker, a completely updated chapter on Texas hold'em and poker tournaments, and the latest winning strategies on all the popular gambling and betting games.

You'll learn everything you need to know to become a successful gambler—from the rules of the games and proper betting strategy considering the odds you face, to how each game is played not only in America, but in casinos, gambling parlors and cardrooms around the world. For every game in this book, and there are many, you'll learn the absolute best way to play with the odds in your favor.

This new expanded edition covers the most important casino gambling games as well as other popular gambling games—blackjack, craps, slots, roulette, poker, baccarat, video poker, Let it Ride, the big wheel, keno (including video keno), bingo, Spanish 21, Caribbean stud poker, three card poker and four card poker. Other popular gambling activities are covered as well, including horseracing and sports betting—football, baseball, basketball, boxing and mixed martial arts. I've also included a special bonus: Cho Dai Di, an exciting Chinese card game that originated in Southeast Asia. To my knowledge, this is the only English-language discussion of rules and strategy for this fascinating card game.

I've packed these pages with winning strategies, and even show you multiple approaches to beating your favorite games. But if you really want to win, you need more than just a basic knowledge of how to beat the game—you need to know how and when to leave with the money you've won in your pocket, and not leave it behind in the casino's coffers. That's why I also give you essential advice on money management.

This book is about gambling intelligently to increase your chances of winning. This means that you must always make the best bets possible and avoid the sucker bets—in other words, you must gamble with your head and within your means. Winning entails many things, and I'll cover them all here. Expect a straightforward discussion in this book that shows you how things *really* work at the tables and in the real world of gambling.

For me, winning is the name of the game. I play to win money. That's my personal motivation. Throughout my adult life I have supported myself strictly through my gambling activities. I've devoted a lot of thought to beating the casinos and winning at the various gambles that are available.

My goal in these pages is to impart some of this knowledge to you, to reveal the secrets of making money at gambling.

1 OVERVIEW

FIVE KEYS TO SUCCESS AT GAMBLING AND HAVING FUN

1. Play games you enjoy, but first give yourself a chance to win by learning how to beat them.
2. Always bet within your means, keeping within safe limits to make playing fun.
3. Take a few minutes before playing to brush up on your strategies.
4. Stop playing when you're not at your best to maintain your maximum edge.
5. Always aim to have fun! Unless you're gambling professionally, that's what it's all about.

Here's a quick overview of the games and gambles covered in this book.

BLACKJACK

You'll learn how to have a mathematical edge and beat the casino at blackjack. This thorough section shows how to play against any set of rules and variations and any number of decks—one, two, four, six and eight. You'll be ready to play like a pro in any game around the world, be it Las Vegas or the French Riviera. Master charts for a multitude of variations and locales are included for perfect strategy, and you'll also learn a non-counting strategy.

SPANISH 21

This relatively new casino game is an offshoot of blackjack, sharing the same basic rules but with some interesting twists. Blackjack traditionalists won't necessarily be thrilled, because the tens are removed from the deck—key cards for the player—however, casual players will love the new options. Beware though: if you're a blackjack player, you can't use your regular moves—you'll have to learn new strategies to play the casino tough.

THREE CARD POKER

Since its relatively recent introduction to the casinos, three card poker has grown into one of the most popular games on the casino floor—for a reason. Players love the option of the two games in one, and the ability to increase their wagers when they have a winning advantage over the dealer. You'll learn how the game is played, the best strategies to play, the minimum calling hands, the optimum payoff structures, and how best to profit from the ante, play and pair plus bets. You'll also learn about qualifying hands, bonus payouts and how to get the best odds at three card poker.

CRAPS

Here's a game for players who love action—and lots of it. In this chapter, you'll learn about bets that give the house no edge at all, and how to use these wagers to beat the game. I present eleven different winning strategies from a variety of approaches—single and double odds, conservative and aggressive, betting with the dice or against them. This section will make you as good as any craps player out there, for you will be playing against the minimal house edge.

FOUR CARD POKER

There are three basic bets in four card poker—ante, play and aces up—and a bonus structure for premium hands. These wagers, one of which allows you to increase your bet when you have the edge, and the fact that the game is easy to play, have contributed to the popularity of this relatively new casino game. In this section, you'll learn the basic strategy, odds of the bets, and the best way to beat the casino. The house edge is pretty low for a casino game, just 1.6% against if you follow our strategies, so you may want to get in on the action.

BACCARAT

James Bond loves this glamorous and popular European game, whose odds are so good for the player that casinos sometimes can lose money at it over a month's worth of play. There are several variations of the game and I'll show how they differ from one another. And of course, we'll discuss the winning strategies you can use to beat the casino at full-table baccarat and the mini-baccarat version as well. The house edge is very low at this game compared to the other table games—maybe you should give it a try.

ROULETTE

This chapter will show you all the basics of playing and winning, including the rules and differences for both the European and the American game, and how to make every bet possible including some little known wagers—that's over 150 bets in all! I also present three betting systems and an actual strategy for beating the wheel *with the odds.* This game is huge in Europe, but less popular in the United States—for a reason. Find out why and what will happen if the European-style game made its way to your casino.

SLOTS

Slot machines have become the most popular casino games in America, so I have expanded and rewritten this section to reflect the new changes. I'll also look at some of the new slots, show the different machines available, and tell you about the straights, the progressives, the various odds and how to improve on them, the basics of play, as well as showing you some insider insights on how to get the best slot odds possible and beat the machines.

VIDEO POKER

The video poker machines are very popular in casinos, and for good reason—with sharp play, you can win money and possibly score a big jackpot to boot! You'll learn the winning hands and payoffs at all the main variations—including jacks or better, deuces wild, bonus quads, and joker wild—how to use the various options, the best strategies to pursue for straight games and progressives, and the best way to improve your chances of winning the giant jackpot.

CHO DAI DI

As a special bonus, I'm introducing Cho Dai Di, an exciting Chinese card game that's sure to please and thrill those of you who love skill, luck and backstabbing—all in one easy-to-play package. I'll show you how to play and score, plus present some winning strategies to get you on the way. I hope you do me the honor and give this section a read—it's a great game and you'll soon be hooked.

HORSERACING

A tremendous gaming passion for many people, this section on "the ponies" shows you all about the races, from the bets available, the types of races run, the odds and the important track basics, to eleven solid winning tips to help you win money at the track. There is a lot of information in the horseracing chapter, including the five key handicapping approaches, so see if you can't use some of this knowledge to improve your play at the track.

KENO

How would you like to be $100,000 richer? A lucky catch in keno can do the trick. In this section, I'm going to show you ways to play and bet the game to give you that shot and reveal the odds involved and the payoffs on winning tickets. You'll learn how to play all the various types of tickets—including straight, split, combination, way, and the king—and how to improve your chances for a big payday along the way. We also discuss the pros and cons of video keno, and present a conclusion that may surprise you!

BINGO

This is not your grandmother's bingo! Today's bingo games are modern marvels of electronic wizardry and the foundation of a billion-dollar business. No more crayons to mark your paper ticket, there are more and more buttons to push. You'll find out how to navigate large casino bingo rooms, plus learn tips for keeping your bingo bankroll in check while having the most fun at this All-American game of chance.

SPORTS BETTING

Betting on sports is the bread and butter of many gamblers—billions of dollars are wagered on sports events every year. In this section, I'll show you how the lines are made, why they exist and how to use insider information to beat the line and make money. Betting on football, baseball, basketball, boxing and mixed martial arts are all covered—the different types of bets you can make at each, the odds and the payoffs and the best strategies to make you a winner.

THE MONEY WHEEL

You know those big wheels, reminiscent of carnival-like games you often see in casinos. I've added a small section on the Money Wheel, also called the "Big Six," where I'll show you the bets available and the odds you face.

CARIBBEAN STUD POKER

You'll learn about the significance of qualifying and non-qualifying hands, how to play the various types of hands you will be dealt including the borderline A-K hands, the hands that should always be folded, and whether or not you should take a flyer on the progressive bet. With a little luck and smart money management, you may make some profits at this game—but first you'll need to understand the best way to play. This chapter will show you how.

LET IT RIDE

This table game offers the unique—and very attractive—feature of allowing you to remove one of your three initial bets if you don't like your starting cards, and then allows you to remove a second wager if you don't like your next card! You'll learn about the odds, different payout structures, the third- and fourth-card playing strategies and, ultimately, the hands you should and shouldn't play to maximize your winning chances.

POKER

The poker section has been completely revised and expanded, and includes the super-popular game everyone is playing nowadays—hold'em, plus seven-card stud (high, low, and high-low stud) and Omaha. We cover no-limit and limit games, cash games and tournaments, online poker, and the psychology and winning principles of play that will give you the advantage over your opponents. You can make a lot of money playing poker and hopefully, the winning information here will get you started on the path to profits.

MONEY MANAGEMENT

There's more to winning than knowing the games and the odds. You must know how to handle yourself and your bankroll. Smart money management is the key to all successful gamblers, which is why I've devoted a full chapter to specifically address the psychological and emotional aspects of beating the casino. I'll tell you how to keep the game under control, how to minimize losses when you're losing, and how to turn moderate winning sessions into big winning sessions with a minimum of risk. In short, I'll show you how to walk away a winner.

THE WINNING WORD

These are my last words of advice and encouragement before I send you on your way into the betting world armed with powerful knowledge and the wherewithal to win. All right then. Let's turn some pages, learn some strategy, and get ready to put the odds on your side.

I hope you enjoy my book—and most of all, I hope it makes you a winner!

2 BLACKJACK

FIVE KEYS TO BLACKJACK

1. Learn the Basic Strategies and make the correct plays every time.
2. Make all the aggressive double down and splitting plays.
3. Don't risk busting your hand when the dealer shows a 2 through 6 (unless you have a 12 versus a 2 or 3).
4. Try to make 17 or better if the dealer's upcard is a 7 or higher.
5. Increase your advantage against the casino by learning the correct strategies in this section, and then move on to a professional card counting strategy or non-card counting strategy.

INTRODUCTION

Blackjack can be beaten! Once you've studied this section and learned the skills presented, you'll find one major difference between you and 95% of the other players at the tables—you'll be a winner at blackjack.

This section shows you how to win without the blind memorization and boring tedium usually associated with learning blackjack. These computer-tested basic strategies are carefully explained so that every play you make can be easily learned. In addition, all the winning strategies are presented in easy to read charts.

You'll learn how to beat the single deck game without counting cards. You'll also find the best way to adjust your play for multiple deck games and variations whether you're a player in the major American gambling centers—Las Vegas, Northern Nevada, Laughlin or Atlantic City—or you're heading for play on cruise ships in Europe, the Bahamas, the Caribbean or anywhere else casinos are found.

This section gives you a wealth of information. We cover the fundamentals of casino blackjack—the rules of the game, the player's options, the variations offered in casinos around the world, how to bet, casino vocabulary, how to play, and everything else you need to know about playing winning casino blackjack.

Study this section carefully and you'll be a player the casinos fear, and for good reason—you will be a consistent winner at blackjack!

BEGINNERS GUIDE TO CASINO BLACKJACK

OBJECT OF THE GAME

Your object in casino blackjack is to beat the dealer. You can beat the dealer in two ways:

1. When you have a higher total than the dealer without exceeding 21.
2. When the dealer's total exceeds 21 (assuming your total has not exceeded 21 first).

In casino blackjack, if both you and the dealer hold the same total of 21 or less, the hand is a **push** and nobody wins.

BUSTING OR BREAKING—AUTOMATIC LOSERS

If drawing additional cards to the initial two cards you're dealt causes your point total to exceed 21, your hand is **busted**—it is an automatic loss. Turn up your busted hands immediately. Once a player has busted, his hand is lost, even if the dealer busts afterwards. If the dealer busts, all remaining players automatically win their bets.

BLACKJACK—AUTOMATIC WINNER

If your original two-card hand contains an ace with any 10 or **face card** (J, Q, K), the hand is called a **blackjack** or **natural**, and is an automatic winner—you'll get paid off at 3 to 2, or, as in the case in some casinos now, 6 to 5—unless the dealer ties you with a two-card 21 as well.

If the dealer gets a blackjack, all players lose their bets. (The dealer wins only the amount bet, not the 3 to 2 or 6 to 5 payoff that you would receive for a blackjack.) If both the dealer and you are dealt a blackjack, the hand is a push. Immediately turn up your blackjack. When you can, find games paying 3 to 2, rather than the reduced 6 to 5.

PAYOFFS

All bets are paid off at **even money** ($5 bet wins $5), except in cases where you receive a blackjack, or when you exercise an option that allows you to double your bet. In these instances (doubling and splitting), the payoff is equal to the new doubled bet. Therefore, if a bet has been doubled from $5 to $10, a win pays off $10.

CARD VALUES

Each card is counted at face value. 2 = 2 points, 3 = 3 points, 10 = 10 points. The face cards—jacks, queens and kings—are counted as 10 points. The ace can be counted as 1 point or 11 points at your discretion. When you count the ace as 11 points, your hand is called **soft**, as in the hand A-7 = soft 18. All other totals, including hands where the ace counts as 1 point, are called **hard**, as in the hand 10-6-A = hard 17.

The dealer must count his ace as 11 if that gives him a hand totaling between 17 and 21; otherwise he must count the ace as 1 point. In some casinos the rules dictate that the dealer must draw on soft 17. In these casinos, the dealer's ace will count as 1 point when combined with cards totaling 6 points, and the dealer will have to draw until he forms a hand of at least hard 17.

DEALER'S RULES

The dealer must play by prescribed guidelines. He must draw to any hand 16 or below and stand on any total 17-21. As mentioned above, some casinos require the dealer to draw on soft 17. The dealer has no options and cannot deviate from these rules.

PLAYER'S OPTIONS

Unlike the dealer, players can vary their strategy. After receiving your first two cards, you have the following options:

1. **Drawing (Hitting)**
   If you're not satisfied with your two-card total, you can **draw** (**hit**) additional cards. To draw a card, scrape the felt surface with your cards, scraping toward your body. In a game where both of your cards are dealt face up, scratch the felt with your index finger or point toward the cards if you want a hit. You're not supposed to handle the cards when they're face up, so be careful not to touch them.

2. **Standing**
   When you're satisfied with your original two-card total and don't want to draw additional cards, that is, you want to **stand**, you signal this by sliding your cards face down under your bet. When the cards are dealt face up, indicate your decision to stand pat by waving your hand palm down over your cards.

3. **Doubling Down**
   Doubling down allows you to double your original bet, in which case you must draw one additional card and cannot draw any more cards thereafter. To double down, turn your cards face up, and place them in front of your bet. Then take an amount equal to your original bet and place those chips next to that bet, so that there are two equivalent bets

side by side. When the cards are dealt face up, you simply place chips equal to your original bet next to that pile. The dealer will then deal one card face down, usually slipping that card under your bet. You may look at that card if curiosity gets the best of you.

4. **Splitting Pairs**
   If you're dealt a pair of identical value cards, such as 3-3, 7-7, or 8-8 (any combination of 10, J, Q, K is considered a pair), you can **split** these cards to form two separate hands. To split a pair, turn the pair face up and separate them, putting each card in its own place in front of your bet. Then place a bet equal to the original wager behind the second hand. Each hand is played separately, using finger and hand signals to indicate hitting and standing.
   If the first card dealt to either split hand has a value identical to the original split cards, that card may be split again (resplit) into a third hand, and even additional hands, with the exception of aces. When you split aces, you can receive only one card on each ace—you are not allowed to draw again, no matter what card the dealer gives you.

5. **Doubling Down After Splitting**
   You can double down on one or both of the hands resulting from a split, called **doubling down after splitting**, if it is allowed. This option is offered in all Atlantic City casinos and in certain Nevada casinos, and is also found in Australia, Great Britain, various European and Asian casinos, and southern Africa.
   For example, if an 8-8 is split and a 3 is drawn to the first 8 to make 11, you may elect to double down on that 11. After placing an amount equal to the original bet next to the 11, you will receive only one additional card. If a 2 is drawn to the second 8, you can double down on that hand as well.

6. **Surrender (Late Surrender)**
   Players can give up their original two-card hand and lose one half of their bet after it has been determined that the dealer does not have a blackjack—an option called **surrender**. To surrender, turn both your cards face up, put them above your bet and announce, "Surrender." The dealer will collect the cards and take one half of your bet. This option is offered in only a few Nevada casinos.

7. **Insurance**
   If the dealer's upcard is an ace, he will ask everybody at the table if they want insurance. If any player exercises the **insurance** option, he is in effect betting that the dealer has a 10-value card as his hole card, thus making a blackjack. To take insurance, place one-half the amount of your bet in the area marked insurance. If the dealer does indeed have a blackjack, you'll get paid 2 to 1 on the insurance bet, while losing your original bet. In effect, the transaction is a standoff, and no money is lost. If the dealer does not have a blackjack, you'll lose the insurance bet and play continues. If you have a blackjack and take insurance on the dealer's ace, the payoff will be even money whether or not the dealer has a blackjack. Suppose a player has a $10 bet and takes insurance for $5 on his blackjack. If the dealer has a blackjack, the player wins 2 to 1 on his $5 insurance bet and ties with his own blackjack. If the dealer doesn't have a blackjack, you lose the $5 insurance bet but get paid 3 to 2 on your blackjack. Either way you win $10. To make it easy, you can just say "Even Money," and the dealer will pay you off at even money and collect the cards.

INSURANCE STRATEGY

Insurance is a bad bet because when you make an insurance wager, you're betting that the dealer has a 10 under his ace. Since the insurance payoff is 2 to 1, the wager will only be a profitable option when the ratio of tens to other cards is either equal to or less than 2 to 1.

A full deck has 36 non-tens and 16 tens, a ratio greater than 2 to 1. If the first deal off the top of the deck gives you a hand of 9-7, and the dealer shows an ace, you know three cards, all non-tens. Now the ratio is 33 to 16, still greater than 2 to 1, and still a poor bet. If you have two 10-count cards for a 20, the ratio is 35 to 14, an even worse bet.

In a multiple deck game, taking insurance is an even worse bet than in a single deck game.

INSURING A BLACKJACK

Taking insurance when you have a blackjack is also a bad bet, despite the well-intentioned advice of dealers and other players to always "insure" a blackjack. When you have a blackjack, you know three cards, your 10-count card and your ace, and the dealer's ace. The already poor starting ratio of 36 non-tens to 16 tens gets worse, becoming 34 to 15 in a single deck game. Taking insurance when you have a blackjack gives the house an 8% advantage, a poor proposition for players.

THE PLAY OF THE GAME

The dealer begins by shuffling the cards and offering the cut to one of the players. If refused, it is offered to another player. The dealer then completes the cut and removes the top card, called the **burn card**. In single and double deck games, the burn card is either put under the deck face up, where all subsequent cards will be placed, or is put face down into a plastic case (procedures vary from casino to casino) to be followed similarly by future discards.

In games dealt out of a shoe, the burn card is placed most of the way into the shoe and discards are put in the plastic case.

Players must make their bets before the cards are dealt.

The dealer deals clockwise from his left to his right, one card at a time, until each player and the dealer have received two cards. Players' cards are usually dealt face down in a single or double deck game, though it makes no difference if they are dealt face up (like the cards are dealt when using a shoe), because the dealer is bound by strict rules. The dealer deals only one of his two cards face up. This card is called an **upcard**. The face down card is known as the hole card or the **downcard**.

If the dealer's upcard is an ace, he will ask all players if they want insurance. Players that decide to take that option place a bet of one-half their wager in front of their bet in the area marked insurance. If the dealer has a blackjack, all players that did not take insurance lose their original bets. Players that took insurance break even on the play. If the dealer does not have a blackjack, he collects the lost insurance bets and play continues.

The procedures vary when the dealer shows a 10-value card. In Nevada casinos, the dealer must check his hole card for an ace. If he has a blackjack, it is an automatic winner for the house. All players lose their bets. (Players cannot insure against a 10-value card.) If the dealer doesn't have a blackjack, he will look at the first player and await that player's decision. Players that hold a blackjack push on the play.

In Atlantic City and the Bahamas, and in most European games, the dealer will only check his hole card after all players have acted.

Play begins with the bettor on the dealer's left, in the position known as **first base**. Players have the option to stand, hit, double down, split or surrender (if allowed). You can draw cards until you're satisfied with your total or until you bust (go over 21), or you can exercise one of the other options discussed previously.

Play then moves to the next player. If any player busts or receives a blackjack, he must turn over his cards immediately. If a bust, the dealer will collect the lost bet. If a blackjack, the dealer will pay the player 3 to 2 on his bet.

After the last player has acted, the dealer will turn his hole card over so that all players can view both of his cards. He must play his hand according to the strict guidelines regulating his play: drawing to 17, then standing. (In some casinos the dealer must draw to a soft 17.) If the dealer busts, all players still in the game for that round of play win automatically.

After playing his hand, the dealer will turn over each player's cards in turn, paying the winners and collecting from the losers. Once you've played your hand, you shouldn't touch your cards again. Let the dealer expose your cards, which he will do once he has played out his own hand.

When the round has been completed, you must place a new bet before the next deal if you want to continue playing.

CASINO PERSONNEL

The casino employee responsible for running the blackjack game is called the dealer. The dealer's duties are to deal the cards to the players, and play out his own hand according to the rules of the game. He converts money into chips for players entering the game or buying in for more chips during the course of the game, makes the correct payoffs for winning hands, and collects bets from the losers.

The dealer's supervisor—technically called the **floorman**, but more commonly referred to as the **pit boss**—is responsible for the supervision of between four and six tables. His job is to make sure the games run smoothly and to settle any disputes that may arise with a player. More importantly, his job is to oversee the exchange of money and correct any errors that may occur.

ENTERING A GAME

To enter a blackjack game, sit down at any unoccupied seat at the blackjack table, place the money you wish to gamble with near the betting box in front of you, and inform the dealer that you would like to get some chips for your cash. Chips may be purchased in various denominations. Let the dealer know which chips or combination of chips you want.

The dealer will take your money and call out the amount he is changing so that the pit boss is aware that a transaction is taking place and can supervise the exchange.

CONVERTING TRAVELER'S CHECKS AND MONEY ORDERS TO CASH

Dealers accept only cash or chips, so if you bring traveler's checks or money orders, you must go to the area of the casino marked Casino Cashier to get them converted to cash. Be sure to bring proper identification to ensure a smooth transaction.

CASINO CHIPS

Standard denominations of casino chips are $1, $5, $25, and $100. For the high rollers, $500 and even $1,000 chips can sometimes be obtained. Though some casinos use their own color code, the usual color scheme of chips are as shown in the following chart:

TYPICAL CHIP COLORS

Chip Value	Color	Nickname
$1	White, Blue*	Silver
$5	Red	Nickel, Redbird
$25	Green	Quarter
$100	Black	Dollar
$500	Purple	Barney
$1,000	Orange	Pumpkin

*$1 chips universally used to be silver tokens, and they can still occasionally be found, though the standard today is for the $1 chips to be white or blue in color and composed of clay or plastic.

BETTING

Casinos prefer that players use chips for betting purposes because the handling of money at the tables is cumbersome and slows the game. However, cash can be used to bet with, though all payoffs will be in chips. To bet, place your chips (or cash) in the betting box directly in front of you. All bets must be placed before the cards are dealt.

HOUSE LIMITS

Signs located at either corner of the table indicate the minimum and maximum bets allowed at a particular table. Within the same casino you will find minimums raging from $1, $2 and $5 to other tables that require players to bet at least $25 or $100 per hand. At the $1, $2 and $5 tables, the house maximum generally will not exceed $500 to $1,000, while the $25 and $100 tables may allow the players to bet as high as $3,000 a hand. (Note: In busy or higher-end casinos, it is increasingly difficult to find the $1 and $2 minimum tables.)

Some casinos will book almost any bet and give high rollers their own private table for large stakes games. If you catch the right night, you might find a whale, a high roller, making bets in $10,000 units!

CONVERTING CHIPS INTO CASH

Dealers do not convert chips into cash. When you are ready to cash in your chips, take them to the cashier's cage to exchange them for cash.

FREE DRINKS

Casinos offer their customers unlimited free drinking while playing at the table. In addition to alcoholic beverages, you can order water, milk, soft drinks, or juices. Drinks can be ordered through the cocktail waitress, who'll come by periodically to see what you might need. If a cocktail waitress doesn't appear in a timely manner, you can always ask the dealer to request one for you.

THE DECKS OF CARDS

Nevada casinos use one, two, four, six and sometimes as many as eight decks of cards in blackjack games. Within the same casino, single and multiple deck games often will be offered. When one or two decks are used, the dealer holds the cards in his hand. When more than two decks are used, the cards are dealt from a rectangular plastic or wooden device known as a shoe. The shoe is designed to hold multiple decks of cards, and allows the cards to be easily removed one at a time by the dealer. Outside of Nevada, multiple deck blackjack is the norm, and it is rare to find single-deck games.Each deck used in blackjack is a standard pack of 52 cards, consisting of four cards of each value, ace through king. Suits have no relevance in blackjack. The only thing that counts is the numerical value of the cards.

STANDEES

In some areas around the world, most notably Europe and Asia, **standees**—players not occupying a seat and betting spot at the table—are allowed to place bets in the boxes of players already seated. Standees must accept the seated player's decision and are not allowed to advise or criticize the play made.

NO-HOLE-CARD RULE

The predominant style of play in casinos outside the United States is for the dealer to take his second card after all the players have acted upon their hands. In some cases, the dealer may deal himself the card as in the U.S. casinos, but will not check a 10 or ace for blackjack until after the bettors have finished playing their hands. The disadvantage to players is that on hands that are doubled or split, the additional bet will be lost if the dealer has a blackjack. This is called the **no-hole-card rule**. A later section discusses how to adjust your strategies when playing in no-hole-card games so as to minimize the negative effect of this rule.

In Atlantic City, the game is played in this style, except that when the dealer has a blackjack, players' additional bets on doubles and splits are returned. Only the original bet will be lost. Thus, it is not a disadvantage to Atlantic City players and you don't need to adjust your playing strategies for this factor.

RULES AND VARIATIONS OF BLACKJACK

You can find blackjack games all over the world, and though basically the same wherever you play, the rules and variations vary from country to country, from casino to casino within a country, and sometimes even within a casino itself.

NEVADA RULES

The Las Vegas Strip rules are advantageous to players and give you a slight edge on the single deck game if you follow the strategies in this section. The rule exceptions noted in Downtown Las Vegas and in Northern Nevada games are slightly disadvantageous, but these can easily be overcome by using the winning techniques presented later.

LAS VEGAS STRIP RULES

- Dealer must draw on all totals of 16 or less, and stand on all totals of 17-21.
- Players may take insurance on a dealer's ace.

- Insurance payoffs are 2 to 1.
- Players receive a 3 to 2 payoff on blackjack (in some games only 6 to 5).*
- Players may double down on any initial two-card combination.
- Identical pairs may be split, resplit, and drawn to as desired with the exception of split aces, on which players are allowed only one hit on each ace.

DOWNTOWN LAS VEGAS

The same rules as the Las Vegas Strip rules with one exception:

- Dealer must draw to soft 17.

NORTHERN NEVADA

Same as Strip rules with two exceptions:

- Dealer must draw to soft 17.
- Doubling is restricted to two-card totals of 10 and 11 only.

ATLANTIC CITY RULES

The New Jersey Casino Control Commission regulates the rules and variations allowed in Atlantic City casinos, and all Atlantic City clubs must abide by the following guidelines:

- Dealer must draw to all totals 16 or less, and stand on all totals of 17-21. Many casinos now offer games where the dealer has to draw on soft 17.
- Players may take insurance on a dealer's ace. Insurance payoffs are 2 to 1.
- Players receive a 3 to 2 payoff on blackjack.*
- Players may double on any initial two-card combination.
- Identical pairs may be resplit.
- Doubling after splitting is allowed.
- Four, six and eight decks are standard. One-deck games are occasionally offered.

* Note that 6 to 5 payoffs for blackjacks are sometimes offered instead. It is a terrible rule which costs you 1.39% compared to the 3 to 2 payoff. I advise you to avoid these games.

EUROPEAN RULES

Blackjack is offered in numerous countries around Europe with the rules and variations changing slightly from place to place. However, the following conditions apply in many of these venues.

- Dealer must draw to all totals 16 or less, and stand on all totals of 17-21.
- Players may take insurance on a dealer's ace.
- Insurance payoffs are 2 to 1.
- Player receives a 3 to 2 payoff on his blackjack.
- Doubling down is allowed on two-card totals of 9, 10 or 11 only.
- Standees are permitted.
- No-hole-card rule is in place.
- 4-6 decks are standard.
- If a player draws a 2 on an A-8 double-down hand, the total counts as 11, not 21.

RULES AROUND THE WORLD

The general variations we present under the European Rules above are probably the most prevalent style of play in casinos around the world. Sometimes you may find double after split permitted, as in Great Britain, southern Africa, many European casinos, and other places. In Asian and Caribbean casinos, surrender is often allowed—just ask for the particular rules before you enter a game.

BLACKJACK IS BLACKJACK

Note that single-deck blackjack is hard to find outside the Nevada casinos. Multiple-deck blackjack is the predominant style of play in casinos around the world and the type of game you'll most likely face when you take on the casinos at blackjack. However, no matter where you play, the game of blackjack is basically the same give or take some minor options, and we'll show you how to win against any variation.

GENERAL STRATEGIC CONCEPTS

THE DEALER'S ONLY ADVANTAGE

Before we examine the correct strategies of play, let's look at a losing strategy for comparison. In this strategy, the player mimics the dealer; he draws on all totals of 16 or less, and stands on all totals 17-21.*

The player figures that, since this strategy wins for the dealer, it must be effective for players as well. After all, the dealer and the player receive the same number of good hands and the same number of poor hands. And if we draw just as the dealer draws, we must come out even, right?

No. The player will have about a 5 1/2% disadvantage to the house. The "Mimic the Dealer" strategy overlooks one important thing: The player must act upon his hand first.

The dealer's only advantage is that once the player has busted, the player automatically loses his bet regardless of the outcome of the dealer's hand. While both the dealer and the player will bust an equal number of times following these drawing-to-17 guidelines (about 28% of the time), the double bust, where both the dealer and the player bust on the same round, will occur approximately 8% of the time (28% of 28%). And since the player acted first, this 8% of the time (the double bust) will be to the advantage of the house.When we adjust for the 3 to 2 bonus that players receive on blackjacks, a bonus that the house does not receive, we find that the house has a 5 1/2% edge over a player who follows the Mimic the Dealer strategy.

OVERCOMING THE DISADVANTAGE OF ACTING FIRST

In the Mimic the Dealer strategy, we played our hands as if our goal were to get as close to 21 as reasonably possible by using 17 as a cutoff point for drawing. But this losing strategy incorrectly states the goal of the player. In blackjack, the object is to beat the dealer. Your chances of

---

* Roger Baldwin, Wilbert Cantey, Herbert Maisel, and James McDermott, in their classic book, *Playing Blackjack to Win*, originally discussed the "Mimic the Dealer" concept back in 1957.

winning are not determined by how close your total approaches 21, but on how good your total is compared to the dealer's total.

You can overcome the disadvantage of having to act first by making judicious use of the options available to you. Not only should you double down, split pairs, hit, stand and surrender (if allowed), but you can use your knowledge of the dealer's exposed upcard to fully capitalize on these options. Adjusting your strategy according to your knowledge of the dealer's upcard is a vast improvement over the "Mimic the Dealer" strategy.

Why?

Because it completely eliminates the house edge.

TO BEAT THE DEALER

Two factors affect your chances of winning—the strength of your total and the strength of the dealer's total. To beat the dealer, you must know how strong your total is compared to the dealer's total so that you'll know whether drawing additional cards or exercising one of your other options is a viable consideration. In addition, you have to be aware of the factors that influence the final outcome of these totals so that you can determine the optimal way to play your hand.

In determining the best way to play your hand, ask yourself, "How good is my total as it stands?" Do you have the expectancy of winning by standing? If so, can you increase this expectancy by drawing additional cards, or by exercising a doubling or splitting option when applicable? If you do not have the expectancy of winning by standing, will drawing additional cards or doubling or splitting increase your chances of winning?

Being able to see the dealer's upcard gives you a great deal of information about the strength of the hands the dealer is likely to make—use that information to your advantage. To determine how strong your total is—and keeping in mind that your object is to beat the dealer—ask yourself if the dealer's expectancy, judged by the information you got from his exposed card, is greater than your total.

UNDERSTANDING THE DEALER'S UPCARD

Being able to see the dealer's upcard is of great value. Two important factors—the rules governing the dealer's play of his hand, and the number of tens in a deck of cards—tell you a great deal about the potential strength of the dealer's hands, and the frequency with which those hands will bust.

THE TEN FACTOR

The most striking feature of blackjack is the dominant role that the 10-value cards (10, J, Q, K) play, what I call the **ten factor**. Each 10 and face card is counted as 10 points in blackjack. As a shortcut, let's simple refer to all tens and face cards as a 10. Thus, you are four times more likely to draw a 10 than any other value of card, since all the other cards, aces through nines, consist of only four cards each of their rank as opposed to sixteen tens. Collectively, the tens constitute slightly less than one-third of the deck (16 out of 52 cards).

Because the tens are such a dominant factor in blackjack, it is correct to think of the dealer's hand as gravitating toward a total that is 10 points greater than his exposed upcard. When I speak of a hand as gravitating toward a total, I am referring to the tendency of that hand to increase in value by 10 points as a result of the ten factor. Thus, starting out with an upcard of 9, the dealer will make a 19 hand 36% of the time, and a 19-or-better hand 52% of the time.

THE DEALER'S RULES AND THE TEN FACTOR

This strategy is based on the fact that the dealer must play by prescribed guidelines from which he cannot deviate. He must draw to all totals 16 or below, and stand on all totals 17-21 (except in casinos that require the dealer to draw to a soft 17). All hard totals that exceed a hard 21 are automatic dealer losses.

Combining our knowledge of the ten factor with the strict dealer rules gives us a natural separation of the dealer's upcard into two distinct groupings: twos through sixes, the dealer **stiff cards**; and sevens through aces, the dealer **pat cards**.

TWOS THROUGH SIXES—DEALER STIFF CARDS

Whenever the dealer shows a 2, 3, 4, 5 or 6 as an upcard, he must draw at least one additional card regardless of the value of his hole card (unless he has an ace under his 6 and is playing Las Vegas Strip, Atlantic City or European style rules which require the dealer to stand on soft 17). The high concentration of tens in the deck makes it likely that the dealer will expose a 10 as his hole card, giving him a stiff total of 12-16.

Since the dealer must draw to all hard totals 16 or below, the drawing of a 10 (and in some instances, smaller totaled cards) will bust any of these stiff totals. For example, if the dealer shows a 6 and reveals a 10 in the hole, any card higher than a 5 will bust his hand.

Thus, the high concentration of 10-value cards in the deck tells us that the dealer has a good chance of busting when his upcard is a 2, 3, 4, 5 or 6.

UNDERSTANDING THE DEALER'S STIFF CARDS	
Dealer Stiff Cards—Advantageous for Player	
2 3	4 5 6
Less Advantageous	More Advantageous

DEALER'S UPCARD OF 2 AND 3

Though it is favorable for you when the dealer shows a 2 or 3 as an upcard, you need to be cautious against these stiff cards, since the dealer will bust less often with these cards than when he shows a 4, 5 or 6.

DEALER'S UPCARD OF 4, 5 AND 6

The dealer is showing the upcards you always want him to hold. He will bust about 42% of the time with these upcards (5% more than with the 2 and 3, and about 18% more than with the pat cards). Take advantage of these weak dealer upcards by aggressively splitting and doubling.

SEVENS THROUGH ACES—DEALER PAT CARDS

Whenever the dealer shows a 7, 8, 9, 10 or ace as an upcard, we know that, because of the large number of tens, he has a high likelihood of making pat totals 17-21. Conversely, he has a smaller chance of busting than when he shows a stiff card. This high concentration of tens makes it likely that the dealer will expose a 10 for an automatic pat hand (17-21). Even when he does not have a 10 in the hole, combinations such as 8-9, A-7, 9-9 and so forth, give him an automatic pat hand as well.

UNDERSTANDING THE DEALER'S PAT CARDS	
Dealer Pat Cards—Disadvantageous for Player	
7 8	9 10 Ace
Moderately Disadvantageous	Very Disadvantageous

DEALER'S UPCARD OF 7 AND 8

While the dealer will not bust often with these upcards, they also indicate that the dealer's hands gravitate toward the weaker totals of 17 and 18. Interestingly, of all the dealer upcards including the stiff cards, the 7 will form the weakest totals.

DEALER'S UPCARD OF 9, 10 AND ACE

The 9 and 10 gravitate toward totals of 19 and 20 respectively—tough hands to beat. The ace is also a powerful dealer upcard because, in addition to forming strong hands, the dealer will bust less often with an ace than with any other upcard.

Against these powerful upcards, be very cautious in your doubling and splitting strategies.

UNDERSTANDING THE PLAYER'S HAND—HARD TOTALS

The player's totals can be divided into three distinct groupings: 11 or less, 17-21 and 12-16. Let's look at each total to see how they affect optimal strategy.

UNDERSTANDING THE PLAYER'S PAT HAND TOTALS				
17	18	19	20	21
poor	fair	good	excellent	excellent

PLAYER'S HAND OF 11 OR LESS (HARD TOTALS)

You should always draw to any hard total 11 or less (unless a doubling or splitting option is more profitable). By hitting this hand, you have no risk of busting, no matter what you draw, and drawing a card can strengthen your total. There is no question about the correct decision—drawing is a big gain.

PLAYER'S HAND OF 17-21 (HARD TOTALS)

Always stand on these hard totals (17-21) because the risk of busting is too high to make drawing worthwhile. It is obvious that the chances of improving these high totals are minimal, and the risks of busting are very probable. In addition, totals of 19, 20, 21, and to a lesser extent, 18, are already powerful hands. While a hard 17 is a poor player total, the risk of busting by drawing is far too costly to make drawing a viable option. Stand on hard totals of 17-21 against any dealer upcard.

PLAYER'S HAND OF 12-16 (HARD TOTALS)

You will make the bulk of your decisions when you're dealt these cards because there are no automatic decisions on these hard totals, as there on other player totals. Your hand is not an obvious draw (such as the 11 or less grouping) because the risk of drawing a 10 or other high card and busting is substantial. Your hand is not an obvious stand decision either (such as the 17-21 grouping), since the only times you'll win with these weak totals of 12-16 are the times that the dealer busts.

For the Cardoza Non-Counter winning strategies to be effective, you must first know the correct way to play your hands. (The same applies to any player who moves on to a professional counting or non-counting strategy.) Therefore, be sure that you understand these basic strategies before going on to the winning techniques of play.

THE OPTIMAL BASIC STRATEGIES

HITTING AND STANDING—HARD TOTALS

These strategies are applicable for single and multiple deck games in all casino centers.

GENERAL PRINCIPLES

- When the dealer shows a 7, 8, 9, 10 or A, hit all hard totals of 16 or below (unless doubling or splitting is more profitable—in any case, you will always draw a card).
- When the dealer shows a 2, 3, 4, 5 or 6, stand on all hard totals of 12 or more. Do not bust against a dealer stiff card. Exception: Hit 12 vs. 2, 3.

HITTING AND STANDING—HARD TOTALS
All Casino Centers

		DEALER'S UPCARD									
		2	3	4	5	6	7	8	9	10	A
PLAYER'S HAND	11/LESS	H	H	H	H	H	H	H	H	H	H
	12	H	H	S	S	S	H	H	H	H	H
	13	S	S	S	S	S	H	H	H	H	H
	14	S	S	S	S	S	H	H	H	H	H
	15	S	S	S	S	S	H	H	H	H	H
	16	S	S	S	S	S	H	H	H	H	H
	17-21	S	S	S	S	S	S	S	S	S	S

H = Hit S = Stand

In all of the charts, the dealer's upcard is indicated by the horizontal numbers on the top row, and the player's hand is indicted by the vertical numbers in the left column. The letters in the matrix indicate the correct strategy play.

CONCEPTUAL HITTING AND STANDING STRATEGY

In the "Understanding the Player's Hand" section, we discussed the strategy for hard totals of 11 or less, and for hard totals 17-21. Let's summarize them:

- 11 or less—Draw against all dealer upcards.
- 17-21—Stand against all dealer upcards.

HARD TOTALS 12-16

It is when you hold hard totals of 12-16 (stiffs) that your big disadvantage of having to play your hand before the dealer plays his (the only built-in house advantage) is a costly proposition. If you draw to hard totals and bust, you automatically lose. However, if you stand, you win with these weak totals only when the dealer busts.

The decision to hit or stand with hard totals 12-16 is a strategy of minimizing losses—no matter what you do, you have a potentially losing hand against any dealer upcard. Do not expect to win when you hold a stiff. However, to maximize the gain from your overall strategy, minimize your losses in disadvantageous situations like the one above, and maximize your gains in advantageous one.

PLAYER TOTALS OF 12-16 VS. DEALER PAT CARDS 7, 8, 9, 10, A

When the dealer's upcard is a 7 through an ace, you should expect the dealer to make his hand, since he will bust only about one time in four, a mere 25% of the time. If you stand on hard totals 12-16, you will win only the times that the dealer busts.

Thus, for every 100 hands where you stand with your stiff totals of 12-16 against dealer pat cards, your expectation is to lose 75 of those hands and to win only 25, a net loss of 50 hands. Not an exciting prognosis.

Conversely, drawing to your stiff totals 12-16 against the dealer pat cards gives you a big gain over standing. By drawing, you gain an average of 15%. The dealer makes too many hands showing a 7, 8, 9, 10 or ace to justify standing with your stiffs.

You will bust often when drawing to your stiffs, but don't let that dissuade you from hitting your stiffs against pat cards. The strategy on these plays is to minimize losses. You cannot afford to stand and sacrifice your hand to the 3 out of 4 hands that the dealer will make.

When the dealer shows a 7, 8, 9, 10, or ace, hit all hard totals 16 or below.

PLAYER TOTALS OF 12-16 VS. DEALER STIFF CARDS 2, 3, 4, 5, 6

The greater busting potential of the dealer stiff cards makes standing with hard totals of 12-16 a big gain over drawing. While you will win only 40% of these hands (the times that the dealer busts), standing is a far superior strategy to drawing, because you'll bust too often drawing to your own stiffs against upcards that will bust fairly often themselves. The times that you will make pat totals by drawing won't guarantee winners either, because the dealer will often make equal or better totals.

On these plays, your disadvantage of having to go first makes drawing too costly, because you automatically lose if you bust. Though the dealer will make more hands than bust, your strategy here is to minimize losses so that when you get your good hands, you'll come out an overall winner.

EXCEPTION—HIT PLAYER 12 VS. 2 OR 3

Hitting 12 vs. 2 or 3 is the only basic strategy exception to drawing with a stiff total against a dealer's stiff upcard. The double-bust factor is not as costly on these plays, since only the tens will bust your 12. Similarly, the dealer will bust less often showing a 2 or a 3 than with the other stiff cards—4, 5 and 6.

This strategy is in contrast to the play of 13 vs. 2 where the correct strategy is to stand. The additional player bust factor of the 9 makes you slightly better off by standing, even though the dealer will bust less with a 2 as an upcard. This clearly illustrates the greater importance of the player's busting factor (compared to the dealer's busting factor) when deciding whether to stand or draw with a stiff total 12-16 vs. a dealer's stiff upcard.

The combination of the player being less likely to bust (more likely to make his hand), and the dealer being more likely to make his hand (less likely to bust), makes drawing 12 vs. 2 or 3 the correct strategy play.

HITTING AND STANDING—SOFT TOTALS

The strategy for hitting and standing with soft totals in Northern Nevada and Europe is identical to the Atlantic City and Las Vegas strategies for both single and multiple deck, with one exception: In Atlantic City and Las Vegas, players can take advantage of the more liberal doubling rules and double down on hands that Northern Nevada and European Style rules players cannot.

HITTING AND STANDING—SOFT TOTALS
Northern Nevada & Europe
Single & Multiple Decks

		DEALER'S UPCARD									
		2	3	4	5	6	7	8	9	10	A
PLAYER'S HAND	A2-A6	H	H	H	H	H	H	H	H	H	H
	A7	S	S	S	S	S	S	S	H	H	H
	A8-A9	S	S	S	S	S	S	S	S	S	S

H = Hit S = Stand

HITTING AND STANDING—SOFT TOTALS Atlantic City & Las Vegas Single & Multiple Decks										
	DEALER'S UPCARD									
PLAYER'S HAND	2	3	4	5	6	7	8	9	10	A
A2-A5	H	H	D*	D	D	H	H	H	H	H
A6	D**	D	D	D	D	H	H	H	H	H
A7	S	D	D	D	D	S	S	H	H	H
A8	S	S	S	S	S	S	S	S	S	S
A9	S	S	S	S	S	S	S	S	S	S

H = Hit S = Stand D = Double

* Do not double A2 versus 4 and A3 versus 4 in a multiple-deck game.

** Do not double A6 versus 2 in a multiple-deck game.

CONCEPTUAL HITTING AND STANDING—SOFT TOTALS

For soft totals, you want to know:

- What are your chances of winning by standing?
- What are the chances of improving by drawing additional cards?

PLAYER'S HANDS OF A-2, A-3, A-4 AND A-5

Unless you're able to double down, always draw a card to these hands. Standing is a poor option, for these totals will win only when the dealer busts. You have nothing to lose by drawing (no draw can bust these totals), and may improve your total. Players that stand on these hands might just as well give the casinos their money.

Draw on A-2 to A-5 against all dealer upcards.

PLAYER'S HANDS OF A-6, A-7, A-8, AND A-9

The decision to hit or stand with soft totals 17 or higher necessitates a closer look at the strength of these totals. Unlike hard totals of 17 or more, drawing is a viable option with these soft totals. Since you have the option of counting the ace as 1 point or 11 points, drawing a 10-value card will not bust your soft totals. While you have no risk of busting, you do risk drawing a weaker total, and therefore must ask yourself the question, "How strong is my total?"

PLAYER'S HAND OF SOFT 17 (A-6)

A standing total of soft 17 is a weak hand against all dealer upcards, including the dealer stiff cards, and is a losing total in the long run. The only time you will win with this total is when the dealer busts. Otherwise, you have a push at best.

Always draw on soft 17, no matter what the dealer shows as an upcard. (In Las Vegas, Atlantic City, and other locations, the correct strategy may be to double down where it is allowed. See doubling section.) This standing total is so weak that attempting to improve your hand by drawing is always a tremendous gain against any upcard.

When a casino requires the dealer to draw to soft 17, it is disadvantageous to players. Though the dealer will sometimes bust by drawing to a soft 17, in the long run he will make more powerful totals and have more winners. Drawing to a soft 17 affects you in the same way.

PLAYER'S HAND OF SOFT 18

Against dealer stiff upcards of 2, 3, 4, 5 and 6, standing with 18 is a smart strategy move (unless you're playing Las Vegas or Atlantic City doubling rules where doubling will often be a big player gain). You have a strong total against these weak dealer upcards.

Stand against dealer upcards of 7 and 8, because an 18 is a solid hand. Against a 7, you have a winning total. And against an 8, you figure to have a potential push, as these dealer upcards gravitate toward 17 and 18 respectively. Don't risk your strong position by drawing.

Against the powerful dealer upcards of 9, 10, and ace, your standing total of 18 is a potentially losing hand. Normally you would think that hitting a soft 18 is a bad idea. However, you are not chancing a powerful total but rather attempting to improve a weak situation.

For every 100 plays at $1 a play that you draw rather than stand on soft 18 vs. 9 and 10, you will gain $9 and $4 respectively. An 18 vs. 9,

10, or ace is not a winning hand, and since your 18 is a soft total, you have a chance to minimize your losses by drawing.

PLAYER'S HAND OF SOFT 19 AND 20

These hands are strong player totals as they stand. You have no reason to draw another card.

DOUBLING DOWN

Doubling down is a valuable option that gives players a chance to double their bets in advantageous situations. The only drawback to the doubling option is that you will receive only one card, thus giving up the privilege to draw additional cards if that card is a poor draw. To determine whether the doubling option will be profitable, weigh the benefits of doubling your bet against the drawbacks of receiving only one card.

The ten factor is one of the most important considerations when contemplating the doubling option. You are more likely to draw a 10 on your double than any other card value. Thus doubling on a total of 11, where drawing a 10 will give you an unbeatable 21, is a more powerful double than an initial two-card total of 9, where drawing a 10 will give you a strong total of 19, not as powerful as the 21.

Do not double any hand of hard 12 or more, since drawing a 10 would bust your total, and you would have an automatic loser at double the bet.

The ten factor is also an important strategic consideration that affects the dealer's busting potential. Double more aggressively against the weakest of the dealer stiff cards—the 4, 5 and 6—and less aggressively against the other stiff cards, the 2 and 3. The only times you should double against the dealer pat cards are when your doubling totals of 10 and 11 are powerful.

SINGLE DECK DOUBLING STRATEGY

A. NORTHERN NEVADA SINGLE DECK DOUBLING

Players are restricted to doubling down on two-card totals of 10 and 11 only.

SINGLE DECK DOUBLING DOWN Northern Nevada										
	DEALER'S UPCARD									
PLAYER'S HAND	2	3	4	5	6	7	8	9	10	A
10	D	D	D	D	D	D	D	D		
11	D	D	D	D	D	D	D	D	D	D
D = Double Down Blank = Hit, Do Not Double Down										

B. LAS VEGAS SINGLE DECK DOUBLING

The player may double down on any initial two-card combination.

SINGLE DECK DOUBLING DOWN Las Vegas										
	DEALER'S UPCARD									
PLAYER'S HAND	2	3	4	5	6	7	8	9	10	A
62										
44/53				D	D					
9	D	D	D	D	D					
10	D	D	D	D	D	D	D	D		
11	D	D	D	D	D	D	D	D	D	D
A2			D	D	D					
A3			D	D	D					
A4			D	D	D					
A5			D	D	D					
A6	D	D	D	D	D					
A7		D	D	D	D					
A8										
A9										
D = Double Down Blank = Hit, Do Not Double Down										

MULTIPLE DECK DOUBLING STRATEGY

You'll notice that the doubling strategies for multiple-deck play are somewhat less aggressive than the single-deck game, a difference we'll discuss a little later on. First we'll discuss Northern Nevada, where there are three changes from single-deck play, then Atlantic City and Las Vegas, where there are seven differences, and finally, European style, where there are five differences in doubling strategy from single-deck play.

However, only concern yourself now with the proper play for the games you'll face, and when you encounter different conditions and rules, then make the slight adjustments necessary for that game.

A. NORTHERN NEVADA—MULTIPLE DECK DOUBLING

Players are restricted to doubling down on two-card totals of 10 and 11 only.

MULTIPLE DECK DOUBLING DOWN
Northern Nevada

PLAYER'S HAND	DEALER'S UPCARD 2	3	4	5	6	7	8	9	10	A
10	D	D	D	D	D	D	D	D		
11	D	D	D	D	D	D	D	D	D	

D = Double Down Blank = Hit, Do Not Double Down

B. LAS VEGAS, ATLANTIC CITY—MULTIPLE DECK DOUBLING

Players can double down on any initial two-card combination. These strategies are good for all multiple deck games in Atlantic City and Las Vegas.

MULTIPLE DECK DOUBLING DOWN
Las Vegas & Atlantic City

PLAYER'S HAND	DEALER'S UPCARD 2	3	4	5	6	7	8	9	10	A
8										
9		D	D	D	D					
10	D	D	D	D	D	D	D	D		
11	D	D	D	D	D	D	D	D	D	
A2				D	D					
A3				D	D					
A4			D	D	D					
A5			D	D	D					
A6		D	D	D	D					
A7		D	D	D	D					
A8										
A9										

D = Double Down Blank = Do Not Double Down

C. EUROPEAN STYLE—MULTIPLE DECK DOUBLING

Players may double down on totals of 9, 10 and 11 only. The no-hole-card rules accounts for the less frequent doubling against the dealer's 10 than you see with the Atlantic City and Nevada casinos.

MULTIPLE DECK DOUBLING DOWN European Style Rules										
	DEALER'S UPCARD									
PLAYER'S HAND	2	3	4	5	6	7	8	9	10	A
9		D	D	D	D					
10	D	D	D	D	D	D	D	D		
11	D	D	D	D	D	D	D	D		
D = Double Down Blank = Do Not Double Down										

CONCEPTUAL DOUBLING—HARD TOTALS (11, 10, 9, 8)

These strategies are applicable to single and multiple deck games in all casino centers. Where multiple deck strategies differ from the single deck, an asterisk denotes the strategy change, and that change is indicated.

DOUBLING 11*

This is the strongest doubling hand for players and should be doubled against all the dealer upcards in a single deck game. If you draw a 10-value card on your double, you will have a 21, the strongest hand you can have. At best, the dealer can tie you.

DOUBLING 10

This is the second strongest doubling hand for players and should be doubled against the dealer's 2 through 9. Your hard 10 gravitates toward a 20, an overwhelmingly strong hand against these dealer upcards.

Do not double 10 against the dealer's 10 or ace. Doubling your hard 10 against the dealer's 10 is not a potential winner, as it is against the dealer's 2 through 9, since the dealer's hand gravitates toward a 20 as well; and your possible 20 is not powerful enough to compensate for

* Do not double 11 vs. ace in multiple deck games. In no-hole-card rules games, do not double against the 10 or ace. Hit instead.

the low busting probabilities of the dealer's ace. Giving up the option to draw an additional card if the first card is a poor one is too costly on these plays.

Note: In Northern Nevada, only hard 10 and 11 can be doubled down.

DOUBLING 9

Double 9 against 2 through 6 only.* The high busting potential of the dealer stiff cards (2-6) makes the 9 a profitable double down. You cannot double down against any of the pat cards (7-ace) because your win potential when you do draw a 10 (for a total of 19) is not strong enough to compensate for the times when you draw a poor card and cannot draw again.

DOUBLING 8

Doubling 8 vs. 5 or 6 is a valid play in a single deck game.** Your 8 gravitates toward an 18, only a fair total. However, the very high busting potential of the dealer 5 and 6 makes this double a slight gain. Your 8 is not strong enough to make doubling against the other dealer upcards a good play.

CONCEPTUAL DOUBLING—SOFT TOTALS

The high concentration of tens plays a different role in soft doubling than in hard doubling. Instead of having a positive effect on your chances of making a good total, drawing a 10 will not even give you a pat hand on many of these doubles.

Doubling with soft totals is generally a gain against the weak dealer upcards. The ten factor will figure strongly in the dealer's chances of busting, while the drawing of small and medium cards will often improve your hand to a competitive total.

DOUBLING A-2, A-3, A-4, AND A-5

Double A-2, A-3, A-4 and A-5 against the dealer's 4, 5 and 6.*** The very high busting probabilities of the dealer's 4, 5 and 6 make doubling

---

* Do not double 9 vs. 2 in a multiple deck game.

** Do not double 8 against any upcard in a multiple deck game.

*** Do not double A-2 vs. 4 or A-3 vs. 4 in a multiple deck game.

with A-2 to A-5 profitable for players. Again, drawing a 10-value card does not help your total, but the high dealer busting factor gives you an edge.

Do not double against the 2 and 3 because the dealer will make too many hands with these upcards. The same is even more true with the dealer pat cards, 7 through ace.

DOUBLING A-6

Double A-6 vs. dealer 2, 3, 4, 5 and 6.* The A-6 is a more powerful double than the A-2 through A-5, as drawing a 10 to the A-6 will at least give you a pat total and a potential push against a dealer's 17. This "push" factor enables you to gain by doubling against the dealer's 2 and 3, despite the fact that a 2 or 3 will enable the dealer to make more pat totals than the weaker upcards 4, 5 and 6.

DOUBLING A-7

Double A-7 vs. 3, 4, 5 and 6. A soft 18 is only a fair total and drawing an additional card won't risk the destruction of a powerful total such as a 19 or 20. Soft 18 is a strong double against the weaker dealer stiffs 4, 5 and 6, but differs from the soft 17 in that you do not double against the 2. A standing total of 18 vs. a 2 is a stronger winning hand. You don't want to risk the weakening of this hand by doubling and having to draw a card.

DOUBLING A-8, A-9

You have two very strong totals here. Don't risk your excellent chances of winning by attempting to double.

SPLITTING PAIRS

Splitting attains two valuable goals. It can turn one poor hand into two stronger hands, such as splitting a 16 (8-8) into hands of 8 each. It also doubles the bet. The decision to split requires a closer look at your hand vs. the dealer's hand, because you must balance your hand's standing total against the two proposed split hands to see whether

---

* Do not double A6 vs. 2 in a multiple deck game.

the split and resultant doubling of your bet increases your winning expectation.

Here is the thought process:

1. **How strong is your total as it stands?**
Is the hand too powerful a total as it stands to risk breaking up? If not, consider the split.
2. **How strong are the two proposed split totals?**
Thinking in terms of the ten factor, you want to see if your split totals gravitate toward strong totals relative to the strength of the dealer's upcard, or if the split totals represent an improvement over the hard standing original hand.
3. **Does splitting either increase your chances of winning or reduce your rate of loss?**
Either one of these factors make splitting a gain over not splitting.

These three factors are your guides in determining whether a split produces a gain.

SPLITTING PAIRS—SINGLE DECK BASIC STRATEGY

These strategies are applicable to all Northern Nevada and Las Vegas single deck games.

SINGLE DECK SPLITTING PAIRS Northern Nevada & Las Vegas										
	DEALER'S UPCARD									
PLAYER'S HAND	2	3	4	5	6	7	8	9	10	A
22		spl	spl	spl	spl	spl				
33			spl	spl	spl	spl				
44										
55										
66	spl	spl	spl	spl	spl					
77	spl	spl	spl	spl	spl	spl				
88	spl	spl	spl	spl	spl	spl	spl	spl	spl	spl
99	spl	spl	spl	spl	spl		spl	spl		
1010										
AA	spl	spl	spl	spl	spl	spl	spl	spl	spl	spl
spl = Split Blank = Do Not Split										

Do not split 4-4, 5-5, or 10-10. Always split 8-8 and A-A.

SPLITTING PAIRS—MULTIPLE DECK BASIC STRATEGY

You will split slightly less aggressively against a multiple-deck game than against a single-deck game especially when the game is played with the no-hole-card rules. On the other hand, when the game offers doubling after splitting, you get more aggressive. What happens when a multiple-deck game offers doubling after splitting? Let's look at each of the possibilities in turn, showing you the best way to play no matter the situation.

A. LAS VEGAS AND NORTHERN NEVADA MULTIPLE DECK SPLITTING

The standard game allows pair splitting on any two cards, but does not allow doubling after splitting. (If the particular game allows doubling after splitting, use the Atlantic City chart.)

MULTIPLE DECK SPLITTING PAIRS
Northern Nevada & Las Vegas

PLAYER'S HAND	DEALER'S UPCARD									
	2	3	4	5	6	7	8	9	10	A
22			spl	spl	spl	spl				
33			spl	spl	spl	spl				
44										
55										
66		spl	spl	spl	spl					
77	spl	spl	spl	spl	spl	spl				
88	spl	spl	spl	spl	spl	spl	spl	spl	spl	spl
99	spl	spl	spl	spl	spl		spl	spl		
1010										
AA	spl	spl	spl	spl	spl	spl	spl	spl	spl	spl

spl = Split   Blank = Do Not Split

Do not split 4-4, 5-5, or 10-10. Always split 8-8 and A-A.

B. ATLANTIC CITY MULTIPLE DECK SPLITTING (and Nevada casinos where doubling down after splitting is permitted).

Because of the doubling after splitting rule, split pairs more aggressively to take advantage of good doubling situations that may arise as a consequence of the split.

MULTIPLE DECK SPLITTING PAIRS Atlantic City										
	DEALER'S UPCARD									
PLAYER'S HAND	2	3	4	5	6	7	8	9	10	A
22	spl	spl	spl	spl	spl	spl				
33	spl	spl	spl	spl	spl	spl				
44				spl	spl					
55										
66	spl	spl	spl	spl	spl					
77	spl	spl	spl	spl	spl	spl				
88	spl	spl	spl	spl	spl	spl	spl	spl	spl	spl
99	spl	spl	spl	spl	spl		spl	spl		
1010										
AA	spl	spl	spl	spl	spl	spl	spl	spl	spl	spl
spl = Split Blank = Do Not Split										

Do not split 5-5 or 10-10. Always split 8-8 and A-A.

C. EUROPEAN STYLE SPLITTING

Split less aggressively than in the Atlantic City (and certainly the Nevada) casinos because of the no-hole-card rule. This chart assumes that doubling after splitting is not allowed.

MULTIPLE DECK SPLITTING PAIRS
European Style Rules

PLAYER'S HAND	DEALER'S UPCARD									
	2	3	4	5	6	7	8	9	10	A
22			spl	spl	spl	spl				
33			spl	spl	spl	spl				
44										
55										
66		spl	spl	spl	spl					
77	spl	spl	spl	spl	spl	spl				
88	spl	spl	spl	spl	spl	spl	spl	spl		
99	spl	spl	spl	spl	spl		spl	spl		
1010										
AA	spl	spl	spl	spl	spl	spl	spl	spl	spl	

spl = Split Blank = Do Not Split

Do not split 4-4, 5-5, or 10-10.

D. EUROPEAN STYLE—DOUBLING AFTER SPLITTING ALLOWED

Many international casinos allow doubling after splitting. In those instances, double more aggressively than in Nevada, but less aggressively than in Atlantic City because of the no-hole-card rule.

SPLITTING PAIRS DOUBLING AFTER SPLITTING ALLOWED European Style Rules										
	DEALER'S UPCARD									
PLAYER'S HAND	2	3	4	5	6	7	8	9	10	A
22	spl	spl	spl	spl	spl	spl				
33	spl	spl	spl	spl	spl	spl				
44				spl	spl					
55										
66	spl	spl	spl	spl	spl					
77	spl	spl	spl	spl	spl	spl				
88	spl	spl	spl	spl	spl	spl	spl	spl		
99	spl	spl	spl	spl	spl		spl	spl		
1010										
AA	spl	spl	spl	spl	spl	spl	spl	spl	spl	
spl = Split Blank = Do Not Split										

Do not split 5-5 or 10-10.

CONCEPTUAL SPLITTING

Let's examine the decision to split 9-9 first—it is a good example of the thinking process involved in splitting. First of all, note that a hand totaling 18 is only a fair one, not a powerful hand like a 19 or 20.

SPLITTING 9-9—DEALER SHOWS A 2, 3, 4, 5, OR 6

Split 9-9 against these dealer stiff cards. An 18 is a winner, but splitting the hand into two halves of 9 each is a big gain. Because of the ten factor, each starting hand of 9 gravitates toward strong player totals of 19. The high busting potential of the dealer's stiff cards gives you an excellent opportunity to maximize your gain in an advantageous situation.

SPLITTING 9-9—DEALER SHOWS A 7

Stand with 9-9 vs. dealer 7. Figure the dealer for a 17. Your standing total of 18 is a stronger total and a big potential winner. While splitting nines will also produce a positive expectation of winning, risking your fairly secure 18 against the 7 for two strong but chancy totals reduces the gain. You have the dealer beat. Stand.

SPLITTING 9-9—DEALER SHOWS AN 8

Splitting 9-9 against the dealer's 8 is a big gain. Against the dealer's 8, figure your 18 to be a potential push. However, by splitting the 18 into two separate hands of 9 each, you hope to turn your potential push into two possible winners. (Each 9 gravitates toward a total of 19, one point higher than the dealer's 18.)

SPLITTING 9-9—DEALER SHOWS A 9

Splitting 9-9 vs. the dealer's 9 is also a big gain. Against the 9, an 18 is a losing total, but splitting the 18 into two totals of 9 each reduces your potential loss. Rather than one losing total of 18, you'll have two hands gravitating toward potential pushes.

SPLITTING 9-9—DEALER SHOWS A 10 OR ACE

Do not split 9-9 against the dealer's 10 or ace. Your split hands of 9 each gravitate toward good totals, but against these more powerful dealer upcards, splitting would be a poor play. Why risk making one loser into two losers?

SPLITTING 2-2 AND 3-3

Split 2-2 vs. dealer 3 through 7*

Split 3-3 vs. dealer 4 through 7**

The high busting probabilities of the dealer 4, 5 and 6 makes the 2-2 and 3-3 good splits. You should split 2-2 vs. 3, but not 3-3 vs. 3, because of the lower busting factor of your split hands of 2 each.

---

* Nevada multiple deck exception: Do not split 2-2 vs. 3.

** Atlantic City multiple deck exception (and games with doubling after splitting allowed)—split 2-2 and 3-3 vs. 2 through 7.

Drawing a 10 gives you another chance to improve on your 2, since correct basic strategy is to draw 12 vs. 3. But if you draw a 10 to your 3, you will be forced to stand.

Do not split 2-2 or 3-3 vs. the dealer's 2, because the dealer's 2 does not bust often enough to make splitting a profitable play.

Splitting 2-2 and 3-3 vs. 7 seems unusual at first glance since this play seems to exceed the normal strategic boundaries of making aggressive plays against weak dealer stiff cards. Though 7 is a pat card and will make a lot of pat hands, a 7 will also make the weakest totals, gravitating toward a total of only 17. Your starting totals of 2 and 3 will make hands of 18 or better about one-half the time. Splitting 2-2 and 3-3 against the dealer's 7 will not make money for you because of the high bust factor of your hand, but it will produce a moderate gain over drawing to these hands.

Do not split 2-2 and 3-3 against the 8, 9, 10 or ace. You do not want to turn one loser into two losers.

SPLITTING 4-4

Do not split 4-4.* The hard total of 8 gravitates toward a total of 18, a far better position than two weak starting totals of 4 each. Against dealer stiff cards 2 through 6, you'll have a big gain by drawing to an 8. While drawing a 10 will not give you an overwhelmingly strong total, an 18 is far better than drawing the same 10 to a split 4. You certainly don't want to hold two weak hands of 4 each against the dealer pat cards, especially the dealer's 7 and 8—you already have a good starting total of 8.

SPLITTING 5-5

Never split 5-5. The 5-5 by itself is an excellent starting total of 10. Why break up this powerful player total into two terrible hands of 5 each? Your 5-5 total of 10 is an excellent doubling hand against dealer upcards of 2 through 9.

---

* Atlantic City exception (and games with doubling after splitting allowed)—Split 4-4 vs. 5 and 6.

SPLITTING 6-6

Split 6-6 against dealer stiff cards 2 through 6 only.* A hard total of 12 is not very favorable, nor are the split hands of 6 and 6 very promising either. You have a losing hand either way against all dealer upcards. However, you still want to minimize your losses.

Against the dealer stiff cards 2, 3, 4, 5 and 6, your split hands of 6 and 6 will sometimes draw cards that give you some pat totals of 17 through 21.

Of course, you will often end up with stiff totals on the split pair—when you draw a 10 or other sufficiently large card—and be forced to stand. But the high dealer bust factor makes splitting 6-6 against the dealer stiffs a slight gain.

Obviously you don't split 6-6 against the dealer pat cards. You don't need two hands of 16 against a card that will bust only one time in four.

SPLITTING 7-7

Split 7-7 against dealer upcards of 2, 3, 4, 5, 6 and 7. Against the dealer stiff cards 2 through 6, two playable hands of 7 and 7 are preferable to one stiff total of 14. Splitting 7-7 is not a strong split since these totals only gravitate toward a 17, but the high bust rate of the dealer stiff cards makes this split a big gain.

Splitting 7-7 against the dealer's 7 is also an excellent split, since you are converting one losing total of 14 into two potential pushes of 17 each.

Do not split 7-7 vs. the dealer's 8, 9, 10, or ace. You definitely don't want to take one poor total of 14 and turn it into two hands that gravitate toward a second-best total of only 17.

SPLITTING 8-8

Split 8-8 against all dealer upcards.** Against the dealer's 2 through 8, you're turning one terrible hand of 16 into two playable totals of 8

---

* Nevada multiple deck exception—do not split 6-6 vs. 2.
Atlantic City multiple deck (and games with doubling after splitting allowed)—no exceptions; split 6-6 vs. dealer's upcards of 2 through 6.

** In games with the no-hole-card rule, do not split 8-8 against the dealer's 10 or ace. With the possibility of the dealer getting a blackjack, you don't want to invest more money on this hand. Hit instead.

each. You'll gain a tremendous edge on all these plays, and that's always a good thing.

Splitting 8-8 against the dealer's 9, 10, or ace is the strangest of the basic strategy plays. Using all of your intuitive knowledge, at first glance you might reason that this is a poor split because you are making two potential losers out of one. However, let's dig deeper—there's more involved in this play.

First, realize that a hand of 16 is the worst total possible for players. While splitting this 16 into two hands of 8 and 8 is not a winning situation against the strong dealer upcards of 9, 10 and ace, it is an improvement over a very weak total of hard 16. Bear with this unusual play. Why? Because computer simulations have played out the hand millions of times for both drawing and splitting, and have found that players lose less by splitting 8-8 against the dealer's 9, 10 or ace. Losing less or winning more, either way you're ahead.

The bottom line is that although the split is weak, it does produce a gain over drawing to an easily busted 16.

SPLITTING 10-10

Do not split tens. A hard total of 20 is a winning hand against all dealer upcards. Splitting tens against any dealer upcard is a terrible play—avoid it like the plague. Why turn one solid winning hand into two good but uncertain wins? Splitting tens will draw low cards all too often, in effect destroying a great hand.

SPLITTING A-A

Split A-A against all dealer upcards.* Each ace is a powerful starting total of 11 points. If you draw a 10, your 21 can't be beat. Splitting A-A is a tremendous gain against all dealer upcards.

* In no-hole-card rule games, do not split aces when the dealer is showing an ace. The high likelihood of the dealer making a blackjack when he already has an ace is too costly to double your bet. Draw instead.

THE MASTER CHARTS

MASTER CHART - SINGLE DECK Northern Nevada										
	DEALER'S UPCARD									
PLAYER'S HAND	2	3	4	5	6	7	8	9	10	A
7/less	H	H	H	H	H	H	H	H	H	H
8	H	H	H	H	H	H	H	H	H	H
9	H	H	H	H	H	H	H	H	H	H
10	D	D	D	D	D	D	D	D	H	H
11	D	D	D	D	D	D	D	D	D	D
12	H	H	S	S	S	H	H	H	H	H
13	S	S	S	S	S	H	H	H	H	H
14	S	S	S	S	S	H	H	H	H	H
15	S	S	S	S	S	H	H	H	H	H
16	S	S	S	S	S	H	H	H	H	H
A2	H	H	H	H	H	H	H	H	H	H
A3	H	H	H	H	H	H	H	H	H	H
A4	H	H	H	H	H	H	H	H	H	H
A5	H	H	H	H	H	H	H	H	H	H
A6	H	H	H	H	H	H	H	H	H	H
A7	S	S	S	S	S	S	S	H	H	H
A8	S	S	S	S	S	S	S	S	S	S
A9	S	S	S	S	S	S	S	S	S	S
22	H	spl	spl	spl	spl	spl	H	H	H	H
33	H	H	spl	spl	spl	spl	H	H	H	H
44	H	H	H	H	H	H	H	H	H	H
55	D	D	D	D	D	D	D	D	H	H
66	spl	spl	spl	spl	spl	H	H	H	H	H
77	spl	spl	spl	spl	spl	spl	H	H	H	H
88	spl	spl	spl	spl	spl	spl	spl	spl	spl	spl
99	spl	spl	spl	spl	spl	S	spl	spl	S	S
1010	S	S	S	S	S	S	S	S	S	S
AA	spl	spl	spl	spl	spl	spl	spl	spl	spl	spl
H = Hit S = Stand D = Double spl = Split										

Do not split 4-4, 5-5 and 10-10. Always split 8-8 and A-A.

MASTER CHART - SINGLE DECK Las Vegas										
	DEALER'S UPCARD									
PLAYER'S HAND	2	3	4	5	6	7	8	9	10	A
7/less	H	H	H	H	H	H	H	H	H	H
62	H	H	H	H	H	H	H	H	H	H
53	H	H	H	D	D	H	H	H	H	H
9	D	D	D	D	D	H	H	H	H	H
10	D	D	D	D	D	D	D	D	H	H
11	D	D	D	D	D	D	D	D	D	D
12	H	H	S	S	S	H	H	H	H	H
13	S	S	S	S	S	H	H	H	H	H
14	S	S	S	S	S	H	H	H	H	H
15	S	S	S	S	S	H	H	H	H	H
16	S	S	S	S	S	H	H	H	H	H
A2	H	H	D	D	D	H	H	H	H	H
A3	H	H	D	D	D	H	H	H	H	H
A4	H	H	D	D	D	H	H	H	H	H
A5	H	H	D	D	D	H	H	H	H	H
A6	D	D	D	D	D	H	H	H	H	H
A7	S	D	D	D	D	S	S	H	H	H
A8	S	S	S	S	S	S	S	S	S	S
A9	S	S	S	S	S	S	S	S	S	S
22	H	spl	spl	spl	spl	spl	H	H	H	H
33	H	H	spl	spl	spl	spl	H	H	H	H
44	H	H	H	D	D	H	H	H	H	H
55	D	D	D	D	D	D	D	D	H	H
66	spl	spl	spl	spl	spl	H	H	H	H	H
77	spl	spl	spl	spl	spl	spl	H	H	H	H
88	spl	spl	spl	spl	spl	spl	spl	spl	spl	spl
99	spl	spl	spl	spl	spl	S	spl	spl	S	S
1010	S	S	S	S	S	S	S	S	S	S
AA	spl	spl	spl	spl	spl	spl	spl	spl	spl	spl
H = Hit	S = Stand	D = Double	spl = Split							

Do not split 4-4, 5-5 and tens. Always split 8-8 and A-A.

THE DIFFERENCE BETWEEN SINGLE AND MULTIPLE DECK BLACKJACK

As we have seen, the main variations in strategy between single and multiple deck games take place with our doubling and splitting strategies—moves which entail an increased wager on the hand. Let's now see just why this is the case.

The greater number of cards used in a multiple deck game makes the removal of particular cards less important for composition change purposes—that is, they have less of an effect on your chances of getting high or low cards than if the same cards were removed in a single deck game. As a result, doubling and splitting strategies should be less aggressive.

For example, if we remove three cards in a single deck game, two fives and a 3, it creates a favorable imbalance for players and makes a 5-3 double vs. the dealer's 5 a profitable play. Not only will these cards be poor draws for a player's double, they are three cards that the dealer needs to improve his hand. The effective removal of these three cards gives you a better chance of drawing a 10 to your 8 and also increases the dealer's chance of busting. This is why, in a single deck game, 5-3 vs. 5 is a favorable double.

However, drawing this same hand (5-3 versus 5) is barely felt in a multiple-deck game. There are 29 other threes and fives in a four-deck game as compared to only five in a single deck. Thus, no favorable imbalance has been created, and doubling down is not a correct play. This lack of sensitivity to particular card removal accounts for nine strategy changes in the multiple-deck game from the single-deck strategies we just examined.

Except for these nine changes in the doubling and splitting strategies, multiple-deck basic strategy is identical to the single-deck basic strategy.

IN A MULTIPLE DECK GAME:

1. Do not double hard 8 vs. 5; hit instead
2. Do not double hard 8 vs. 6; hit instead
3. Do not double hard 9 vs. 2; hit instead
4. Do not double hard 11 vs. ace; hit instead
5. Do not double A-2 vs. 4; hit instead
6. Do not double A-3 vs. 4; hit instead
7. Do not double A-6 vs. 2; hit instead
8. Do not split 2-2 vs. 3; hit instead*
9. Do not split 6-6 vs. 2; hit instead*

---

* When doubling down is allowed after splitting, split 2-2 vs. 3 and 6-6 vs. 2.

MASTER CHART - MULTIPLE DECK Northern Nevada										
	DEALER'S UPCARD									
PLAYER'S HAND	2	3	4	5	6	7	8	9	10	A
7/less	H	H	H	H	H	H	H	H	H	H
8	H	H	H	H	H	H	H	H	H	H
9	H	H	H	H	H	H	H	H	H	H
10	D	D	D	D	D	D	D	D	H	H
11	D	D	D	D	D	D	D	D	D	H
12	H	H	S	S	S	H	H	H	H	H
13	S	S	S	S	S	H	H	H	H	H
14	S	S	S	S	S	H	H	H	H	H
15	S	S	S	S	S	H	H	H	H	H
16	S	S	S	S	S	H	H	H	H	H
A2	H	H	H	H	H	H	H	H	H	H
A3	H	H	H	H	H	H	H	H	H	H
A4	H	H	H	H	H	H	H	H	H	H
A5	H	H	H	H	H	H	H	H	H	H
A6	H	H	H	H	H	H	H	H	H	H
A7	S	S	S	S	S	S	S	H	H	H
A8	S	S	S	S	S	S	S	S	S	S
A9	S	S	S	S	S	S	S	S	S	S
22	H	H	spl	spl	spl	spl	H	H	H	H
33	H	H	spl	spl	spl	spl	H	H	H	H
44	H	H	H	H	H	H	H	H	H	H
55	D	D	D	D	D	D	D	D	H	H
66	H	spl	spl	spl	spl	H	H	H	H	H
77	spl	spl	spl	spl	spl	spl	H	H	H	H
88	spl	spl	spl	spl	spl	spl	spl	spl	spl	spl
99	spl	spl	spl	spl	spl	S	spl	spl	S	S
1010	S	S	S	S	S	S	S	S	S	S
AA	spl	spl	spl	spl	spl	spl	spl	spl	spl	spl

H = Hit S = Stand D = Double spl = Split

Do not split 4-4, 5-5, or 10-10. Always split 8-8 and A-A.

MASTER CHART - MULTIPLE DECK Las Vegas										
	DEALER'S UPCARD									
PLAYER'S HAND	2	3	4	5	6	7	8	9	10	A
7/less	H	H	H	H	H	H	H	H	H	H
8	H	H	H	H	H	H	H	H	H	H
9	H	D	D	D	D	H	H	H	H	H
10	D	D	D	D	D	D	D	D	H	H
11	D	D	D	D	D	D	D	D	D	H
12	H	H	S	S	S	H	H	H	H	H
13	S	S	S	S	S	H	H	H	H	H
14	S	S	S	S	S	H	H	H	H	H
15	S	S	S	S	S	H	H	H	H	H
16	S	S	S	S	S	H	H	H	H	H
A2	H	H	H	D	D	H	H	H	H	H
A3	H	H	H	D	D	H	H	H	H	H
A4	H	H	D	D	D	H	H	H	H	H
A5	H	H	D	D	D	H	H	H	H	H
A6	H	D	D	D	D	H	H	H	H	H
A7	S	D	D	D	D	S	S	H	H	H
A8	S	S	S	S	S	S	S	S	S	S
A9	S	S	S	S	S	S	S	S	S	S
22	H	H	spl	spl	spl	spl	H	H	H	H
33	H	H	spl	spl	spl	spl	H	H	H	H
44	H	H	H	H	H	H	H	H	H	H
55	D	D	D	D	D	D	D	D	H	H
66	H	spl	spl	spl	spl	H	H	H	H	H
77	spl	spl	spl	spl	spl	spl	H	H	H	H
88	spl	spl	spl	spl	spl	spl	spl	spl	spl	spl
99	spl	spl	spl	spl	spl	S	spl	spl	S	S
1010	S	S	S	S	S	S	S	S	S	S
AA	spl	spl	spl	spl	spl	spl	spl	spl	spl	spl
H = Hit S = Stand D = Double spl = Split										

Do not split 4-4, 5-5, or 10-10. Always split 8-8 and A-A.

ATLANTIC CITY MULTIPLE DECK

The blackjack games offered in Atlantic City differ from the Nevada games in several ways. For one thing, most Atlantic City games are dealt from either a 4-, 6- or 8-deck shoe. In recent years, single-deck games have become available, but with a caveat—blackjacks are paid off at 6 to 5, which makes it a terrible game (that rule costs you 1.39%) and the dealer hits on soft 17 (which costs you another .20%). You should avoid any game where blackjacks only pay off at 6 to 5 (as opposed to the standard 3 to 2).

Doubling allowed after splitting is standard in Atlantic City as opposed to Nevada, where only a few casinos offer this option. Resplitting of pairs is now allowed in Atlantic City, which is a change from the past.

To protect against collusion between a player and the dealer, the dealer does not check his hole card for a blackjack (as is standard in Nevada) until all players have finished playing their hands. This safeguard does not affect your chances of winning because, if the dealer does indeed have a blackjack, any additional money you have wagered on a doubled or split hand will be returned. Only the original bet loses.

Another difference is that all player hands are dealt face up in Atlantic City. No casinos allow players to physically handle the cards. Players must use hand signals to convey their strategy intentions to the dealer.

The Atlantic City basic strategy is the same as Nevada multiple-deck strategy except for more frequent pair splitting, since players are allowed to double after splitting.

MASTER CHART - MULTIPLE DECK Atlantic City										
	DEALER'S UPCARD									
PLAYER'S HAND	2	3	4	5	6	7	8	9	10	A
7/ LESS	H	H	H	H	H	H	H	H	H	H
8	H	H	H	H	H	H	H	H	H	H
9	H	D	D	D	D	H	H	H	H	H
10	D	D	D	D	D	D	D	D	H	H
11	D	D	D	D	D	D	D	D	D	H
12	H	H	S	S	S	H	H	H	H	H
13	S	S	S	S	S	H	H	H	H	H
14	S	S	S	S	S	H	H	H	H	H
15	S	S	S	S	S	H	H	H	H	H
16	S	S	S	S	S	H	H	H	H	H
A2	H	H	H	D	D	H	H	H	H	H
A3	H	H	H	D	D	H	H	H	H	H
A4	H	H	D	D	D	H	H	H	H	H
A5	H	H	D	D	D	H	H	H	H	H
A6	H	D	D	D	D	H	H	H	H	H
A7	S	D	D	D	D	S	S	H	H	H
A8	S	S	S	S	S	S	S	S	S	S
A9	S	S	S	S	S	S	S	S	S	S
22	spl	spl	spl	spl	spl	spl	H	H	H	H
33	spl	spl	spl	spl	spl	spl	H	H	H	H
44	H	H	H	spl	spl	H	H	H	H	H
55	D	D	D	D	D	D	D	D	H	H
66	H	spl	spl	spl	spl	H	H	H	H	H
77	spl	spl	spl	spl	spl	spl	H	H	H	H
88	spl	spl	spl	spl	spl	spl	spl	spl	spl	spl
99	spl	spl	spl	spl	spl	S	spl	spl	S	S
1010	S	S	S	S	S	S	S	S	S	S
AA	spl	spl	spl	spl	spl	spl	spl	spl	spl	spl
H = Hit S = Stand D = Double spl = Split										

Do not split 5-5 or 10-10. Always split 8-8 and A-A.

EUROPEAN NO-HOLE-CARD RULES

These strategies are for multiple-deck play. They take into account that you may double only on totals of 9, 10 and 11—and that you also will double and split less aggressively when the dealer shows a 10 or ace because of the no-hole-card rule. In games that allow doubling after splitting, split more aggressively to take advantage of this favorable option. Take a look at that strategy in this master chart.

MASTER CHART - MULTIPLE DECK European No-Hole-Card Style										
PLAYER'S HAND	DEALER'S UPCARD									
	2	3	4	5	6	7	8	9	10	A
7/less	H	H	H	H	H	H	H	H	H	H
8	H	H	H	H	H	H	H	H	H	H
9	H	D	D	D	D	H	H	H	H	H
10	D	D	D	D	D	D	D	D	H	H
11	D	D	D	D	D	D	D	D	H	H
12	H	H	S	S	S	H	H	H	H	H
13	S	S	S	S	S	H	H	H	H	H
14	S	S	S	S	S	H	H	H	H	H
15	S	S	S	S	S	H	H	H	H	H
16	S	S	S	S	S	H	H	H	H	H
A2	H	H	H	H	H	H	H	H	H	H
A3	H	H	H	H	H	H	H	H	H	H
A4	H	H	H	H	H	H	H	H	H	H
A5	H	H	H	H	H	H	H	H	H	H
A6	H	H	H	H	H	H	H	H	H	H
A7	S	S	S	S	S	S	S	H	H	H
A8	S	S	S	S	S	S	S	S	S	S
A9	S	S	S	S	S	S	S	S	S	S
22	H	H	spl	spl	spl	spl	H	H	H	H
33	H	H	spl	spl	spl	spl	H	H	H	H
44	H	H	H	H	H	H	H	H	H	H
55	D	D	D	D	D	D	D	D	H	H
66	H	spl	spl	spl	spl	H	H	H	H	H
77	spl	spl	spl	spl	spl	spl	H	H	H	H
88	spl	spl	spl	spl	spl	spl	spl	spl	H	H
99	spl	spl	spl	spl	spl	S	spl	spl	S	S
1010	S	S	S	S	S	S	S	S	S	S
AA	spl	spl	spl	spl	spl	spl	spl	spl	spl	H
H = Hit S = Stand D = Double spl = Split										

Do not split 4-4, 5-5 or 10-10.

MASTER CHART - MULTIPLE DECK European No-Hole-Card Style Doubling After Splitting Allowed										
	DEALER'S UPCARD									
PLAYER'S HAND	2	3	4	5	6	7	8	9	10	A
7/less	H	H	H	H	H	H	H	H	H	H
8	H	H	H	H	H	H	H	H	H	H
9	H	D	D	D	D	H	H	H	H	H
10	D	D	D	D	D	D	D	D	H	H
11	D	D	D	D	D	D	D	D	H	H
12	H	H	S	S	S	H	H	H	H	H
13	S	S	S	S	S	H	H	H	H	H
14	S	S	S	S	S	H	H	H	H	H
15	S	S	S	S	S	H	H	H	H	H
16	S	S	S	S	S	H	H	H	H	H
A2	H	H	H	H	H	H	H	H	H	H
A3	H	H	H	H	H	H	H	H	H	H
A4	H	H	H	H	H	H	H	H	H	H
A5	H	H	H	H	H	H	H	H	H	H
A6	H	H	H	H	H	H	H	H	H	H
A7	S	S	S	S	S	S	S	H	H	H
A8	S	S	S	S	S	S	S	S	S	S
A9	S	S	S	S	S	S	S	S	S	S
22	spl	spl	spl	spl	spl	spl	H	H	H	H
33	spl	spl	spl	spl	spl	spl	H	H	H	H
44	H	H	H	spl	spl	H	H	H	H	H
55	D	D	D	D	D	D	D	D	H	H
66	spl	spl	spl	spl	spl	H	H	H	H	H
77	spl	spl	spl	spl	spl	spl	H	H	H	H
88	spl	spl	spl	spl	spl	spl	spl	spl	H	H
99	spl	spl	spl	spl	spl	S	spl	spl	S	S
1010	S	S	S	S	S	S	S	S	S	S
AA	spl	spl	spl	spl	spl	spl	spl	spl	spl	H
H = Hit S = Stand D = Double spl = Split										

Do not split 5-5 or 10-10.

PLAYER'S OPTIONS

Use these strategies where the following variations are permitted.

DOUBLING DOWN PERMITTED AFTER SPLITTING

This is a standard option in Atlantic City, Great Britain and in other casinos around the world, but it is offered in only a few Nevada casinos. This option allows you to double down on one or more of the hands resulting from a split, according to the standard doubling rules of the casino. Since doubling down after splitting is favorable to players, split more aggressively to take advantage of good doubling situations when you're playing in a casino that offers you this option.

DOUBLING DOWN PERMITTED AFTER SPLITTING

Player's Hand		Single Deck	Multiple Deck
22	split against	2-7	2-7
33	split against	2-7	2-7
44	split against	4-6	5-6
66	split against	2-7	2-6
77	split against	2-8	2-7

LATE SURRENDER

This is a player option to forfeit your hand and lose half your bet after it has been determined that the dealer does not have a blackjack. It's a favorable option for players.

LATE SURRENDER (SURRENDER)

Player's Hand		Single Deck	Multiple Deck
16*	surrender against	10, A	9,10, A
15	surrender against	10	10
77	surrender against	10	-

Do not surrender soft totals. *Do not surrender 8-8. Split instead.

EARLY SURRENDER

Early surrender is an extremely valuable player option that allows you to forfeit your hand and lose half your bet before the dealer checks for a blackjack. This option is no longer offered in Atlantic City, but if it reappears in a casino, these are the strategies to follow:

EARLY SURRENDER SINGLE AND MULTIPLE DECK GAMES		
Dealer's Upcard		**Player's Totals**
A	early surrender with	5-7, 12-17
10	early surrender with	14-16
9	early surrender with	16*

Do not surrender soft totals. *Do not early surrender 8-8. Split instead.

THE WINNING EDGE

The removal of cards during play—that is, cards that have been dealt and are no longer available—and the continued dealing from a deck that is depleted of these used cards creates a situation in blackjack where the odds of receiving particular cards or combinations of cards constantly change during the course of the game. Computer studies have found that the removal of certain cards during play gives players an advantage over the house, while the removal of others gives the house an advantage over players.

Therefore, as cards are dealt, your chances of winning constantly change. Sometimes the depleted deck of cards will favor the house and sometimes it will favor players. By learning to analyze a depleted deck of cards for favorability, and by capitalizing on this situation by betting more when the remaining cards are in your favor, you can actually gain an edge over the casino.

The heart of all winning blackjack systems is based on this principle: Bet more when you have the advantage, bet less when the house has the advantage. This way, when you win, you win more. And when you lose, you lose less. Beginning with an even game (playing accurate basic strategy), this "maximize gain, minimize loss" betting strategy will give you an overall edge on the house.

So how do you determine when you have the edge?

UNDERSTANDING THE VALUE OF CARDS

Computer studies have determined that tens and aces are the most valuable cards for players, while small cards 2 through 7, are the most valuable cards for the house, with eights and nines being relatively neutral. Off the top of the deck, with all cards still in play, you have an even game with the house—neither side enjoys an advantage.*

The odds shift in favor of players when there is a higher ratio than normal of nines, tens and aces in the deck, and they shift in favor of the house when there is a higher than normal ratio of small cards 2 through 7. All counting systems base their winning strategies on keeping track of the ratio of high cards to low cards. The systems vary in complexity from the very simple to the very complicated, all being based on the same principle—betting more when a higher proportion of high cards is in the deck.

However, a lot of blackjack players want to have an edge over the house, but they are loath to learn counting systems. If you want to win without counting cards, the Cardoza School of Blackjack has developed some simple but effective techniques. Let's take a look at them.

THE CARDOZA NON-COUNTER STRATEGY—FIVE EASY GUIDELINES

The system is simple. All you need to know is that high cards favor us and small cards favor the house. When more high cards than normal are in the deck, you will bet more. But you need not count

* Assuming the player plays perfect basic strategy as we've shown, and that the game is a single-deck game with the favorable Las Vegas Strip rules. If the particular game has less liberal rules (Northern Nevada) or is a multiple-deck game, the house enjoys a slight initial edge.

cards—that's the good news. All you need to do is to keep your eyes open and watch the cards, just as you probably do anyway.

Here are five easy guidelines that will give non-counters an edge over the house:

FIVE EASY GUIDELINES

1. When a great many small cards have been played in the first round, it is to your advantage. Bet 3 or 4 units instead of your normal 1 or 2 unit bet. (If $5 is your standard bet, $15 is considered a 3-unit bet.) For example, suppose the following cards have been played: You had 8-5-6, one player had 10-6-2, another player had 10-6-5 and the dealer had 10-7. A disproportionate number of small cards have been played, meaning that the remaining deck is richer in high cards—and that's to your advantage. So you bet more.
2. In succeeding rounds, if you estimate that a disproportionate number of high cards are still remaining in the deck, continue to bet at a higher level than your minimum or neutral bet. Through practical experience, you will be able to improve on your ability to estimate these numbers.
3. If the cumulative distribution of cards seems to be fairly normal after a round of play, bet your neutral or minimum bet (1 or 2 units). However, if you notice that no aces have appeared, increase your bet by one unit. Your potential to get a blackjack has increased—exactly the hand you want to hit and beat the dealer. While the dealer's chances of getting a blackjack have increased as well, he only gets paid even money—you get paid 3 to 2.
4. Conversely, if a disproportionate number of high cards are dealt in the first round, place your minimum 1-unit bet—the house has an edge. On succeeding rounds, if you judge that a disproportionate number of small cards still remain, continue to place your minimum bets.
5. If the cumulative distribution of the cards appears to be normal, and you notice that more aces have appeared than

what you usually would expect—one ace for every 13 cards is the normal composition—downgrade your bet to one unit if you have been making 2-unit bets.

QUICK SUMMARY OF THE FIVE WINNING PRINCIPLES

To sum up, when there are more tens and aces remaining in the deck than normal, increase your bet. When there are fewer tens and aces than normal (meaning more small cards), decrease your bet. Every time the deck is shuffled, start your estimation of favorability over again.

BET RANGE

I recommend a bet range of 1 to 4 units. Thus, if $5 is your standard bet, your maximum bet should not exceed $20. This is an important guideline to follow for several reasons:

1. Your advantage will rarely be large enough to warrant a bet larger than 4 units. Consider your bankroll limitations and don't let greed to be your downfall. Keep in mind that blackjack is a slow grind for good players.
2. Raising your bets in advantageous situations to a range greater than 1-4 will attract undue attention to you as a skillful player. The casino may begin to shuffle every time you make a large bet, in effect shuffling away advantageous situations.
3. You don't want one extremely large losing bet to destroy an otherwise good session at the table.
4. Losing a huge bet can have a detrimental effect on your confidence, your concentration and your ability to think clearly. It's surprising how fast a big loss can negatively affect your otherwise positive frame of mind.
5. Varying your bets from 1 unit in disadvantageous situations to 4 units in highly advantageous situations is a wide

enough bet spread to maximize your gains and minimize your risk.

THE POWER OF YOUR ADVANTAGE

The Cardoza Non-Counter strategy gives you a powerful enough advantage to give you close to a $100 profit expectancy during a heavy weekend of play in a single deck game if you're a $5-$20 bettor, and a $500 profit expectancy if you're a $25-$100 bettor playing perfect basic strategy. When you have the winning edge on the house, time works to your advantage. The longer you play, the more money you can expect to make.

The Cardoza Non-Counter strategy is most effective in single deck games, and less so in double decks, because of the fewer number of cards in single deck games compared to four-or-more-deck games. The advantage of this strategy is that you can win with much less mental effort than counting systems require. Obviously you cannot win as much without counting cards, but you can win.

Though this strategy is less effective in four, six and eight deck games where the overall number of the cards is less susceptible to composition changes from a few cards being removed, the news isn't all bad for multiple deck players—the basic strategies presented in this book will bring you very close to an even game against the casino. If you want to improve your game further by learning a professional strategy, you must first learn these basic strategies. They are the absolute best available, and are 100% accurate for single and multiple deck games. All professional strategies assume you play a perfect basic strategy.

However, if you want to further your edge over the house and make even more money playing blackjack, you must learn a professional counting or non-counting system. See the back of the book for information on how to obtain the highly effective, but simple to use Cardoza Base Count Strategy, the full Home Instruction Course, or the Cardoza 1, 2, 3 Multiple-Deck Non-Counter—only available through Cardoza Publishing.

GETTING THE MOST OUT OF THE CARDOZA NON-COUNTER STRATEGY

If you will be playing in Nevada or other areas where you have the choice to play either a single deck or multiple deck game, it will be to your advantage to play in a single deck game for two reasons:

1. The single deck game is inherently more favorable to players.
2. The Cardoza Non-Counter strategy is most effective in a single deck game because the single deck game is highly sensitive to composition changes.

If you only have access to playing in multiple-deck games, you have two choices if you want to have the advantage over a multiple-deck game.

Choice number one is that you can purchase the simple-to-use *Cardoza 1, 2, 3 Multiple Deck Non-Counter.* This will give you an edge of about 1/2 to 1% depending upon the particular conditions of the game and your skills. The *Cardoza 1, 2, 3 Multiple Deck Non-Counter* strategy was developed for players who are intimidated by counting cards and it actually gives non-counting players the mathematical edge over the casino in multiple-deck games. This strategy is the result of our own research (more than 15 years in development).

However, you must learn the material in this book before you advance further into your blackjack studies. These basic strategies are the foundation for any winning approach—they give you what you need to know to beat the dealer. You bought this book to learn how to win—so learn the strategies.

TIPPING

Tipping, or toking as it is called in casino parlance, is a gratuitous gesture you make to a dealer who has given good service. Toking is completely at your discretion, and in no way should be considered an obligation. It is not your duty to support casino employees.

If you toke, toke only when you're winning and only those dealers that are friendly and helpful. Do not toke dealers you don't like or ones that try to make you feel guilty about not tipping. Dealers that make playing an unpleasant experience for you deserve nothing.

The best way to tip is to place a bet for the dealer in front of your own bet, so that his chances of winning that toke are tied in with your hand. If you win the hand, you both win together; if you lose the hand, you lose together. By being "partners" on the hand, you establish camaraderie with the dealer. Naturally, he or she will be rooting for you to win. When you win, the dealer wins double—the tip amount you bet plus the winnings from that bet.

CHEATING

It is my belief that cheating is not a problem in the major American gambling centers, though I would not totally eliminate the possibility. If you ever feel uncomfortable about the honesty of a game, stop playing. Though you probably are being dealt an honest game, feeling anxious or uncomfortable is not worth it.

Don't confuse bad luck with being cheated, or a dealer's mistake as chicanery. Dealers have a difficult job and work hard, but they are bound to make honest mistakes. If you find yourself shorted on a payoff, immediately bring it to the dealer's attention and the mistake will be corrected.

BANKROLLING

The following bankroll requirements give you enough capital to survive any reasonable losing streak and be able to bounce back on top. In this table, **flat betting** refers to betting the same amount every time. When ranging bets from 1 unit to 4 units, you'll need a larger bankroll because you're betting more money.

TOTAL BANKROLL REQUIREMENTS		
Hours to Play	**Bet Range**	**Bankroll Needed**
10	Flat	50 units
20+	Flat	100 units
10	1-4	150 units
20+	1-4	200 units

If you plan to play for an extended weekend (20 hours or more) at \$5-\$20 a hand, you should bring \$1,000 with you. If you are only planning to play 10 hours at those stakes, \$750 will give you a fairly safe margin. This does not mean that you will lose this money playing \$5-\$20. Using the Cardoza Non-Counter betting strategy, you will have an edge on the house in a single deck game and can expect to win money every time you play.* However, just because you have an edge in any game, doesn't mean that you're going to win. Losing streaks do occur, and a loss of \$500 to \$600 in a session playing \$5-\$20 is a real possibility. If the thought of losing amounts comparable to this during a downswing scares you, you should not play \$5-\$20 a hand—you're betting over your head.

Bet within your financial and emotional means, and you'll never regret a single session at the tables.

If you have a definite amount of money to play with and want to figure out how much your unit size bet should be, simply take your gambling stake and divide it by the amount of units you need to have.

Suppose you bring \$500 with you and plan to play for 10 hours ranging your bets from 1-4 units. Divide \$500 by 150 units (see chart: "Bankroll Needed" column) to calculate how much your unit size bet should be. Using this method, your average wager should be about \$3 a hand. Betting more than \$3 as a unit would be overbetting, leaving you vulnerable to the risk of getting put out of action by one losing streak.

* Assuming the favorable Las Vegas Strip rules in a single deck game. In a multiple deck game, the casino has a slight initial edge.

TABLE BANKROLL

How much money should you bring to the table?

My recommendation is that you bring 30 units to the table each time you play. If you play $5 units, bring $150; if $2 units, bring $60. $25 bettors should bring $750. A $100 bettor should sit down with $3,000.

You can bring less if you want to. If you're flat betting, 15 units will suffice. If 1-4 is your bet range, 20 units will do the trick. Do not bring more money to the table—30 units is enough to cover normal swings. You never want to lose more than that in any one sitting.

PARTING THOUGHTS

Blackjack is a game of skill that can be beat. However, to win, you must learn how to play the game properly. Take your time studying this section and then practice your skills at home. When you're fully armed and comfortable, then you're ready to put your money on the line in a casino and be a winner.

In a nutshell, here's the winning formula: Learn your basic strategies perfectly, apply the Cardoza Non-Counter betting strategy, and pay careful attention to the advice in the money management section. Then you'll have the knowledge and skills to be a consistent winner at the blackjack tables, plus the basic strategy skills needed to move on to the professional level strategies offered in the back of this book—strategies that will make the casinos fear your play.

But first, get the basic strategies down cold—then get ready to win the casino's money!

3 SPANISH 21

FIVE KEYS TO SPANISH 21

1. Though Spanish 21 is similar to blackjack, it is not blackjack, so be sure to learn the proper strategies for this game.
2. Be aware of the situations where you are eligible for a five-, six-, or seven-card bonus.
3. Always make the aggressive doubling and splitting plays when it is correct to make those moves, regardless of what happened the last time you put the extra money on the felt. Playing scared will hurt your chances of winning.
4. Remember that you can surrender your extra chips even after doubling down—but do so only when it is the right play.
5. Surrender is a valuable player option, not just on doubling down, as listed above, but on our original two-card total. Always surrender when it is correct to do so.

INTRODUCTION

Spanish 21 was introduced to Nevada casinos as a way to spice up the traditional blackjack game and get more action to the tables. At first glance, this blackjack variant looks like the same game except with a host of attractive and favorable options. It is played on a standard blackjack table in the same type of setting and is typically dealt out of a six or eight deck shoe.

But there's a rub: All the tens have been removed from the deck! After the aces, the ten cards are the most valuable cards in the deck for a player. The other 10-value cards—the jacks, queens, and kings—are still there, but taking four tens out of every fifty-two cards is a tremendous disadvantage to the player that is only partially compensated for by the favorable player options.

THE BASICS

Spanish 21 is played like regular blackjack. Each player gets dealt two cards to start and has the following options:

Stand: Take no more cards

Hit: Draw additional cards one at a time

Split: Take two cards of equal value into two hands that are played separately, with an additional bet of equal value to the original bet placed on the new hand. Hands may also be resplit, even aces. If you split A-A and get a third ace, you can split the hand one more time, playing each of the hands separately.

Double down: Double the bet on a hand and receive one, and only one, additional card.

The dealer also gets two cards, one face down and hidden from the players, the other face up and exposed. Players make decisions based on their two cards and information they glean from the dealer's upcard.

All cards are counted at face value. For example, a two of clubs is equal to 2 points and a nine of hearts is equal to 9 points. The picture cards are equal to 10 points. Aces can count as 1 point or 11. A hand of A-5 is called *soft 16* since the ace can count as 11 points or 1 point. If a king is drawn, the ace would count as 1 point giving the player a hard 16. If a player gets more than 21 points, he busts and is an automatic loser, even if the dealer busts out afterward.

So, if one more king or jack or even a 6 is drawn to the 16, the hand would bust and be an automatic loser.

When players have finished taking their turns, it is the dealer's turn to play. He must take cards according to the prescribed rules of the game: Draw cards up to a hand of 17 points and then stand. In most jurisdictions, if the dealer makes a soft 17—that is, when the ace is used as an 11 to make 17—the dealer must continue drawing to get to at least a hard 17 points. For example, if the dealer has an ace and a 6 for a soft 17, he would have to draw when the rules of the table require it. If a queen is then drawn, he must stand as he has a hard 17.

If the dealer busts, all players left in the hand automatically win.

If both the player and the dealer have the same total, the hand is a push—a tie—and the player gets to keep his bet. There is one exception to this rule, and it works in favor of the player: If both the player and the dealer have a multiple-card 21, the player wins. A blackjack is an automatic winner for the dealer at even money or for the player at 3 to 2. However, if both the player and the dealer hold a natural, the player will win and still gets the 3 to 2 payoff. (In regular blackjack, the hand would be a push instead.).

Won bets are paid at even money, 1 to 1; for every $1 bet, the player wins $1. Or, if the hand is lost, a player loses only what was bet.

BONUS OPTIONS

There are some great options in Spanish 21 that make it exciting for regular blackjack converts. First, you can double down on any number of cards, not only on your first two cards. For example, if you start out with a 5 and a 3 and get dealt another 3, you can double down! Or if you're dealt a 3 and a 2, get dealt another 2 and then a 4, you can still double down. You can also double down after splitting. For example, if you've split 8-8 and get dealt a 2 on your first 8 for a total of 10, you can put additional chips on the felt and double down on that split hand. You can also double down on the other split hand if you so choose.

An additional attractive feature is the late surrender option. You not only can surrender your hand and forfeit half your bet if you don't like your initial two cards, you also can surrender after doubling down!

Let's say that you double down on an 11 and receive a 5. You may exercise the surrender option by forfeiting your hand and taking back your doubled bet, thus losing only the original wager.

BONUSES

In addition to the favorable options shown above, you'll receive bonus payouts for five, six, and seven-card 21s. Most of the bonuses are on high-risk hands, ones where the player can bust with a draw.

Following are the extra payouts in Spanish 21.

SPANISH 21: EXTRA PAYOUTS

Bonus Hand	Payout
Five-Card 21 *	3 to 2
Six-Card Hand*	2 to 1
Seven-Card 21 *	3 to 1
6-7-8 Same Suit	2 to 1
6-7-8- All Spades	3 to 1
6-7-8 Mixed Suits	3 to 2
Three Sevens Same Suit	2 to 1
Three Sevens All Spades	3 to 1
Three Sevens Mixed Suits	3 to 2

*Bonuses are not paid if the hand was doubled down.

SUPER BONUS

There is also a **Super Bonus** if you get a 7-7-7 hand all of the same suit and the dealer also holds a 7 (provided that it is not reached through a split or doubled play). The super bonus will be $1,000 if the original bet is $5 up to $24.50 and $5,000 if the original bet is $25 or more. In both cases, other players at the table who placed a bet that round will receive an envy bonus of $50. Some casinos have a different super bonus—they pay $1,000 for every $5 bet up to a $25 bet ($5,000 maximum).

STRATEGY

With perfect play, you can reduce the house advantage to between 0.4% and 0.8%, depending upon the particular rules in play. When the dealer stands on all 17s, the house edge will be closer to the .4%; and when he hits soft 17 (which is unfavorable for the player—you would rather he stands), it is closer to 0.8%. However, unless you really dig into a complicated playing strategy, you should figure the house to have an edge of around 1%.

In this chapter, I recommend a simplified strategy because the full-on correct strategy is very complicated, well beyond what an average player will want to digest just to play a good game against the house. The problem is that the correct strategy varies depending upon the number of cards drawn. Further, it gets so complicated that few players would want to make all that effort just to get the edge down an additional few tenths of a percentage point. For example, with a two-card soft 17, you would double down against a dealer's 4, but if it's a three-card 17, correct strategy would be to only hit.

These kinds of complexities occur for all sorts of hitting, standing, doubling, splitting, and surrender situations and would make the entire task of memorization complicated. If you're going to put in all that effort, you may as well do it at blackjack and learn a card counting strategy that can actually give you the edge.

Keeping that in mind, here is a simplified strategy to give you a relatively solid game against Spanish 21.

THE SIMPLIFIED STRATEGY

The removal of the four tens from the deck makes it a lot harder to draw a card valued at 10 points. Rather than sixteen 10-value cards per deck (four each of the 10 through king), there are only twelve of them, 25% fewer than a regular deck. Because of the altered balance of tens—which are good cards for players to have in the deck—the strategy you use in regular blackjack games does not apply to Spanish 21.

As a result of fewer tens, basic strategy calls for less aggressive play in doubling down and splitting situations than you would exercise in standard blackjack games. But at the same time, with fewer tens to bust hands, you'll be more aggressive with stiff hands (hard 12-16).

Note that fewer blackjacks are drawn in Spanish 21 than in blackjack (one in every 24 hands as opposed to one in every 21 hands).

There are some similarities in strategy between Spanish 21 and blackjack, but you'll have to learn the specific ones that apply to this game.

Following is the simplified strategy:

SPANISH 21: SIMPLIFIED STRATEGY

Hitting and Standing

Draw on hard 5 to 9
Hit on 10 and 11 vs. 9 through ace
Hit 12, 13, 14 vs. all upcards
Hit 15 and 16 vs. 7 through ace
Stand on 15 and 16 vs. 2 through 6
Stand on hard 17 through 21
Stand on 14 to 16 vs. 2 through 6, hit against 7 and higher

Double Down Hard Totals

Double down on 10 and 11 vs. 2 through 8

Soft Totals (when the ace counts as 1 point)

Hit on all soft hands 17 or less
Stand on all soft hands 18 to 21

Splitting

Always split A-A and 8-8
Never split 4-4, 5-5 or 10-cards
Split 2-2, 3-3, 6-6, and 7-7 vs. 2 through 7
Split nines versus 2 through 9

Surrender

Surrender hard 16 and 17 vs. ace
Surrender after doubling with 12 to 16 vs. the dealer's 8 to ace

Special Plays

Hit suited sevens against all upcards (go for the big bonus)
Never take insurance

Five-or-More Card Hands

Hit five-card 14s and 15s against all cards
Hit five-card soft 17s and 18s against all cards

MASTER CHART - SIMPLIFIED SPANISH 21 STRATEGY										
	DEALER'S UPCARD									
	2	3	4	5	6	7	8	9	10	A
PLAYER'S HAND: HARD HANDS										
5-9	H	H	H	H	H	H	H	H	H	H
10-11	D	D	D	D	D	D	D	H	H	H
12-14	H	H	H	H	H	H	H	H	H	H
15	S	S	S	S	S	H	H	H	H	H
16	S	S	S	S	S	H	H	H	H	X
17	S	S	S	S	S	S	S	S	S	X
18-21	S	S	S	S	S	S	S	S	S	S
SOFT HANDS										
A2-A6	H	H	H	H	H	H	H	H	H	H
A7-A9	S	S	S	S	S	S	S	S	S	S
SPLITTING										
22-33	spl	spl	spl	spl	spl	spl	H	H	H	H
66-77	spl	spl	spl	spl	spl	spl	H	H	H	H
88	spl	spl	spl	spl	spl	spl	spl	spl	spl	spl
99	spl	spl	spl	spl	spl	spl	spl	spl	S	S
AA	spl	spl	spl	spl	spl	spl	spl	spl	spl	spl
AFTER DOUBLING										
12-16	S	S	S	S	S	S	X	X	X	X
H = Hit	S = Stand	D = Double	spl = Split	X = Surrender						

Never split 4-4, 5-5, 10-10 (play as hard hands). Always split 8-8 and A-A.

PARTING THOUGHTS

Remember that Spanish 21 is not traditional blackjack; you have to take into account the missing tens and play a different strategy than you may be used to. However, you'll love the new options. If you get on a roll with Spanish 21, you can build your chip stack quickly—just remember to walk away with profits!

4 THREE CARD POKER

FIVE KEYS TO THREE CARD POKER
1. Always call with a hand that is Q-6-4 or higher; fold lesser hands.
2. Avoid games with bad payout structures.
3. You only have to beat the dealer, not the other players.
4. Memorize the ranking of three card poker hands, which is different from standard poker.
5. Always use smart money management.

INTRODUCTION

Three card poker is one of the most popular new table games. It's being offered in more and more casinos and judging by its prevalence, the game is gaining in popularity, or at least maintaining a foothold in the casinos. Invented by Derek Webb, three card poker was originally called brit-brag (being a derivation of an old game called "brag") and was later sold to Shuffle Master in 1999. Shuffle Master licenses the game around the world along with their other popular games: Caribbean stud poker, Let it Ride, and four card poker.

One of the attractions of three card poker is that it's easy to play. Another is that players have a whole lot of fun trying to beat it.

While "three card poker" suggests a poker variation, don't let the name fool you. Although there are a few similarities, three card poker is not poker, just as four card poker and Caribbean stud poker are not poker either. They just borrow a few ideas and use the name "poker" so that players feel more comfortable stepping in and trying their hand. Although it is played with a standard 52-card deck and uses some of the hand rankings, three card poker has little else in common with poker. For one, you're playing against the house, not against the other players at the table; and like blackjack, it's you against the dealer. Unlike real poker, you make hands from three cards instead of five, the hand rankings are different, and there is no bluffing or psychology, which forms the heart of traditional poker games.

Anyway, enough of what the game is *not*—let's see what the game *is about* and how to best play and win.

Three card poker is a fast-action game with lots of thrills and a fairly low house advantage—as long as you play optimum strategy, avoid bad payout schedules, and practice sound money management.

Let's get on with the basics and put the cards in the air.

THE BASICS

THE LAYOUT

A three card poker table looks similar to a blackjack table, with players on one side seated around an oval shape and the dealer opposite them on the flat side, with racks of casino chips in front of him. There is also a Shuffle Master automatic shuffling machine, which shuffles the cards and dispenses them in packets of three. There are three betting circles in front of each seat. The top betting circle is labeled "Pair Plus," the middle circle labeled "Ante" and the bottom circle, closest to the player, labeled "Play."

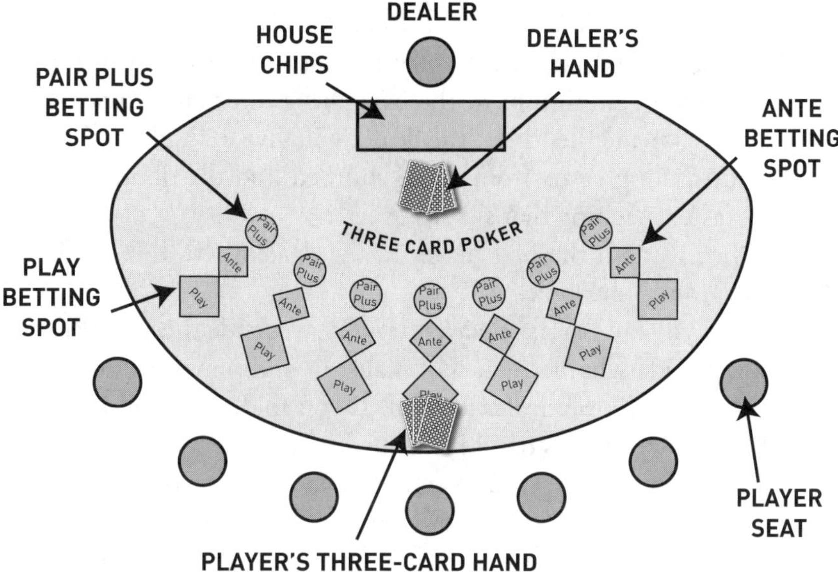

BASIC BETS

There are two bets you can make, the ante bet and pair plus bet, and they are separate wagers, independent of one another. You can just bet one of them, or you can bet both, at your discretion. You may bet as much as you like or as little on either bet, within the casino's minimum and maximum limit.

The **ante bet** is a wager that you will have a better hand than the dealer. If you think you might, you **play** and increase that wager (essentially, you **call** or **raise**), or you **fold** and forfeit your original bet. The **pair plus bet** is independent of whether or not you have a better hand than the dealer—it is a wager that your three-card hand will have a pair or higher in it. You will lose your pair plus wager if you have less than a pair, and you will win if you have a pair or better. It's as simple as that.

So, you see, three card poker is actually two games in one—the **ante/play game** and the **pair plus game**.

PLAY OF THE GAME

Before any cards are dealt, players must make a wager that is equal to the table minimum in the pair plus and/or ante circle. After everybody has made their bets, the dealer will give each player a three-card hand, pulling cards from those shuffled and distributed by the Shuffle Master machine that sits to his left.

Play begins with the first player to the dealer's left and continues clockwise around the table.

Let's say you are that first player. If you have made the ante bet, you must now decide whether you will make an additional bet that your hand is better than the dealer, or fold. If you fold, you lose your ante bet and your play on this hand is finished.

If you decide to play your hand after looking at your cards, you place a bet equal to the amount of your ante bet in the "Play" spot on the table. (This is the spot closest to you.) Play then moves on to the next player, who makes the same decisions you did. He either folds, or he calls and places an additional bet in the "Play" spot.

After everybody at the table has made their decisions, the dealer turns up his three-card hand. The way play proceeds from here depends on whether or not the dealer's hand qualifies.

Let's look at both.

DEALER'S HAND DOESN'T QUALIFY

The dealer must have at least a queen-high hand or better for play to proceed. For example, J-10-7 and 10-8-5 are hands that do not qualify.

Lowest Dealer Qualifying Hand

If the dealer's hand doesn't meet this minimum standard, he doesn't "qualify" and players who are still active in the hand—that is, they haven't forfeited their ante bet—are paid 1 to 1 on their ante bet.

Any bets that were made in the "Play" spot will be returned to the players; they are neither won nor lost when the dealer does not qualify. In casino parlance, the bet is a push, neither the player nor the house wins.

But what happens when the dealer's hand *does* qualify?

DEALER'S HAND QUALIFIES

If the dealer's hand qualifies—that is, he has a hand of at least Q-x-x—he will compare his hand against each player to determine the winner. For example, Q-8-3 and Q-4-2 are both qualifying hands. So too are A-K-3, 2-2-9 and straight and flush hands.

If you have a better hand than the dealer, or one of equal strength (Q-9-8 vs. Q-9-8 is a winner for the player), you win and will get paid 1 to 1 on your ante and play bets. For example, if you have A-K-3 and the dealer A-J-9, and you have a $10 bet on each spot, you'll win $20. Similarly, if you have a pair of sixes and the dealer has a pair of twos, you'll win as well. If the dealer has a better hand than you, you lose both bets.

If you have a really strong hand, a straight or higher, that's even better—you will win a bonus on top of the standard payout for your ante bet. We'll talk about that in the Ante Bonus section.

Let's now look at the winning hands so that you can better understand which hands win and which ones qualify for the bonus payouts.

WINNING HANDS

Because you are only dealt three cards, the hand rankings are a little different from traditional five-card hands. The rankings, like regular poker, are based on the mathematical likelihood of making certain hands. Because the hands contain only three cards—as opposed to five cards as in standard poker games—you will see hand strengths that are a little different than you might expect.

Here are the hand rankings, starting with the highest and going down to the lowest:

THREE CARD POKER: HAND RANKINGS	
Straight Flush:	Three cards of the same suit in sequence, such as the 4-5-6 of hearts.
Three of a Kind:	Three cards of equal rank, such as 9-9-9 or K-K-K.
Straight:	Three cards of mixed suits in sequence, such as 4-5-6 or 10-J-Q.
Flush:	Three cards of the same suit, such as Q-7-4 all diamonds.
Pair:	Two cards of equal rank and one card of another rank, such as J-J-6 or Q-Q-2.
High Card:	None of the above–no pair, flush, straight, three of a kind or straight flush. J-8-5, for example, is a jack-high hand.

Notice that, unlike regular poker, three of a kind beats a straight, and a straight beats a flush in three card poker. (Of course, there is no possibility of having a two-pair hand, which requires four cards, since you're only dealt three cards.) Keep these differences in mind when deciding whether to continue playing.

Hands that do not contain at least a pair are valued according to the highest card in the hand, then the second, then the third, and so on. So, Q-7-3 would beat Q-6-4, which is the minimum hand the dealer needs to qualify and continue to play. Since the queens are a tie, the second-highest card is used to break the tie; in this example, the 7 beats the 6. The rank of the third card doesn't matter because the second card, the 7, resolved the tie.

What if you have a Q-6-5 and the dealer has a Q-6-3? In that case, the third card determines the winner. In this example, you win since your 5 is higher than the dealer's 3.

What is the best hand you can make in three card poker?

It's an A-K-Q straight flush.

ANTE BONUS

If you have a straight, three of a kind, or a straight flush, you will be paid a bonus on your ante bet. You get this bonus even if the dealer's hand doesn't qualify and even if he has a stronger hand than yours—the only requirement for you to win the bonus is that you have one of the qualifying hands. For example, if you have a straight and the dealer has three of a kind (remember, three of a kinds are better than straights!), you still get the bonus. And if he has J-10-8 and doesn't qualify, but you have a 2-3-4 for a straight, you also get the bonus payout.

The bonus payout for the ante bonus is paid based on the payout schedule posted at the table. This payout structure varies from casino to casino. The range of payouts found is as follows: for a straight flush, you will be paid 5 to 1 or 4 to 1; for three of a kind, you will be paid 4 to 1 or 3 to 1; for a straight, you will receive 1 to 1 for your ante bet.

The payout structure for the ante bonus affects the overall house edge on the ante/play portion of the game. In the next section, you'll see how that affects you.

Let's look at a sample hand so that you fully understand how the bonus payout works. Let's say you have a $20 bet on the ante and you call for an additional $20 when you see you've been dealt a three of a kind. You also have a $20 bet on the pair plus.

Lo and behold, the dealer turns over a straight flush, and you lose the ante and play bets, $40 down the toilet with a very strong hand. However, your three of a kind qualifies for a bonus paid at 4 to 1, so you win $80 on the bonus. So even though you lost on you main hand, with the bonus, you ended up winning an overall $40 on the hand!

WINNING STRATEGIES

WINNING STRATEGY: ANTE/PLAY BET

The strategy for the ante portion of three card poker is quite simple. You either forfeit your ante bet and play stops there, or you play on and make an additional bet in the "Play" spot. There is only one decision you need to make, and that decision is straightforward: If you have a hand Q-6-4 or better, you call, and continue playing your hand. If you have a lower hand than that, you fold. For example, you would fold hands such as Q-5-3, J-8-6 and 9-6-5.

Lowest Player Hand to Make Additional Bet

Here's an easy way to determine if your hand is better than Q-6-4. First, look at your highest card. If it is a king or ace, just ignore your other two cards and continue playing. If you have a queen in your hand, just make sure your other two cards are at least as high as a 6 and a 4. If not, fold.

If you play optimal basic strategy, the house enjoys a 2.02% edge with perfect play on the ante and play bet, as long as you are playing at a casino using the following bonus payouts on the ante: straight flush 5 to 1; three of a kind, 4 to 1; and straight, 3 to 1. This is a **full ante bet bonus payout schedule** and the one you would like at your table.

There are other payout schedules you may encounter, and the reductions in these payouts affect your winning chances. The following table shows how it affects the house edge:

ANTE BET BONUS				
HAND	A	B	C	D
STRAIGHT FLUSH	5 to 1	4 to 1	3 to 1	5 to 1
THREE OF A KIND	4 to 1	3 to 1	2 to 1	3 to 1
STRAIGHT	1 to 1	1 to 1	1 to 1	1 to 1
HOUSE EDGE	**2.02%**	**2.28%**	**2.56%**	**2.16%**

If there were no bonus on the ante bets, you would be playing at a 3.4% disadvantage. However, by being able to increase your bet when you have hands that will give you a bonus payout, the overall house edge on the bet drops, which is to your benefit. As you see from the above table, you would like to play in a casino that offers Paytable A, the full payout schedule.

WINNING STRATEGY: PAIR PLUS

There is no strategy to the pair plus wager except whether to make the bet at all. Once your money is in the betting spot, you have no more decisions to make. You'll either be dealt a winner—which is a hand of a pair or better—or you won't, and your bet will be lost. It doesn't matter if the dealer qualifies or even beats you, as it does with the ante bet—if your hand has a pair or better, you win. If it does not have at least a pair, you lose.

Once you place your pair plus bet, there is no strategy to consider. In that sense, the game is like slots. There is another similarity to slots in that your strategy is to play games that have better paytables and thus give you improved chances of winning, rather than games with poorer structures. For example, you'd rather play a slot machine set for a 98% return in a player's area than machines situated by the buffet, which usually offer lousy returns.

The pair plus bet is paid based on the casino's paytable. Let's take a look at some pair plus payout schedules that are being offered in casinos.

PAIR PLUS PAYOUT
COMMON PAY STRUCTURES

HAND	A	B	C	D
STRAIGHT FLUSH	40 to 1	40 to 1	40 to 1	40 to 1
THREE OF A KIND	30 to 1	25 to 1	30 to 1	30 to 1
STRAIGHT	6 to 1	6 to 1	5 to 1	6 to 1
FLUSH	4 to 1	4 to 1	4 to 1	3 to 1
PAIR	1 to 1	1 to 1	1 to 1	1 to 1
HOUSE EDGE	**2.32%**	**3.49%**	**5.90%**	**7.28%**

PAYTABLES

The original paytable, as developed by inventor Derek Webb, is shown in column A. This paytable gives the house a 2.32% edge. Many casinos only offer a paytable as shown in column D, which is much worse for the player. While the only difference is a 3 to 1 payout on flushes as opposed to the 4 to 1 in the original paytable, it's s significant one.

How much?

When the less favorable payout schedule is used—paying only 3 to 1 on a flush, as opposed to 4 to 1—the house enjoys a whopping 7.28% edge. Flushes come often enough with three cards, so while the change from 3 to 1 to 4 to 1 doesn't seem like much, it makes a big difference in your chances of winning, and turns an otherwise playable game into a very unplayable one. Flushes come about once in twenty hands, which is frequent enough to expect at least two to four per hour (depending upon the speed of play at your table). That "small" change in payout increases your percentage disadvantage against the house considerably, as you can see.

You shouldn't even consider a payout schedule with a house advantage that steep. It's greedy on the part of the casino, and playing against an edge that large, you'll very quickly see your bankroll dissipate.

So, the strategy on this bet is to make sure that the paytable on the pair plus bet gives you a 4 to 1 payout on the flush, with the other payouts being in line. Otherwise, avoid this wager.

PARTING THOUGHTS

You want to play three card poker at casinos that have the best payout structures. You have two bets to choose from, the ante/play and the pair plus. The common ante/play schedules for the bonus bet are within about 1/2% of each other, so they are not as critical as the payouts you'll find on the pair plus. On the pair plus, there is a large disparity in payouts to the point where you need to avoid the bet altogether if the casino offers the greedier version of the schedule.

If you find the full payout version, which features 4 to 1 on the flush and gives the house about a 2.3% edge, you have a reasonable game. However, if the casino only pays 3 to 1 on the flush, which means that you're playing at about a 7.3% disadvantage, you should avoid that bet altogether. That's way too high for a table game. You may as well flush your money down the toilet because it will get lost almost as fast.

Remember that three card poker, like many casino games, is a negative expectation contest, which means that you can't expect to win over the long run because the odds are against you. They eventually will take their toll, so you don't want to be betting big money in the expectation of being a professional player at this game—because you simply can't. However, this is not to say that you can't have some fun playing three card poker, seeing how the cards fall for you, and enjoy riding a good hot streak. Just make sure to limit your losses by always playing the best strategy and cutting sessions short when luck is against you. And, alternately, when the cards are going your way, make sure you walk away a winner.

5 CRAPS

FIVE KEYS TO CRAPS

1. Understand completely all the different bets that you can make at the craps table.
2. Avoid all of the proposition bets in the center of the table–the odds are awful and can quickly devour your chips.
3. Stick to the best bets in the house–the pass, don't pass, come, don't come, and free odds bets.
4. Protect yourself by always betting sensibly. Craps is a fast game and you can lose money at a dizzying pace.
5. Practice good money management. Protect your wins when you're ahead by pocketing your profits, and restrict your losses by betting less or leaving the table when the dice are against you.

INTRODUCTION

Craps is the most exciting of the casino games, one perfectly tuned to the temperament of action players. The game offers you opportunities to win large sums of money quickly. However, you can lose big money just as fast unless you are familiar with the best bets available and know how to use them in a coordinated strategy. This chapter gives you everything you need to know about craps—from the rules of the game to how to bet and play, to the possible combinations of the dice and craps lingo. You'll learn the best percentage bets to make and how to use them in winning strategies, plus how to bankroll and manage your money like a pro.

We present winning strategies for players betting with the dice, and for players betting against the dice. You'll learn the best ways to bet your money—whether you're a conservative or an aggressive player—to keep losing streaks to the bare minimum and take your winning streaks all the way to the bank!

You'll learn 11 winning strategies in all, enough to keep your excitement level high and profits rolling in when things are going right. Whether you're a beginner or an experienced player with decades of experience under your belt, you'll find this chapter to be an indispensable guide on how to play and win at craps.

Now let's get on with it and let the dice roll!

BEGINNER'S GUIDE TO CASINO CRAPS

THE TABLE

The standard casino craps table is rectangular, with curved corners, and accommodates between 15 and 24 players. The sides of the table are several feet above the layout where the bets are made, giving the dice walls to carom off and players a ledge to lean on.

THE LAYOUT

The craps layout is divided into three distinct sections. The two end sections, which are identical, are areas around which the players cluster and are where the majority of bets are made. Each end area is run by a dealer who stands in the middle area of the table. The middle area is flanked on either side by a boxman and a stickman. This area contains the **proposition**, or **center bets**, and is completely under the jurisdiction of the stickman.

The layout is a large piece of green felt with various imprints marking the plethora of bets possible. All action is centered on the layout. Bets are placed, paid off, and collected on this felt surface. And, of course, the dice are thrown onto the layout.

Layouts around the world are basically the same, though some venues may have slight variations. None of these need concern you, since the game of craps is basically the same whatever casino you play in. The minor variations that do occur concern bets whose odds are so poor that you wouldn't want to make them anyway.

Following is a standard craps layout.

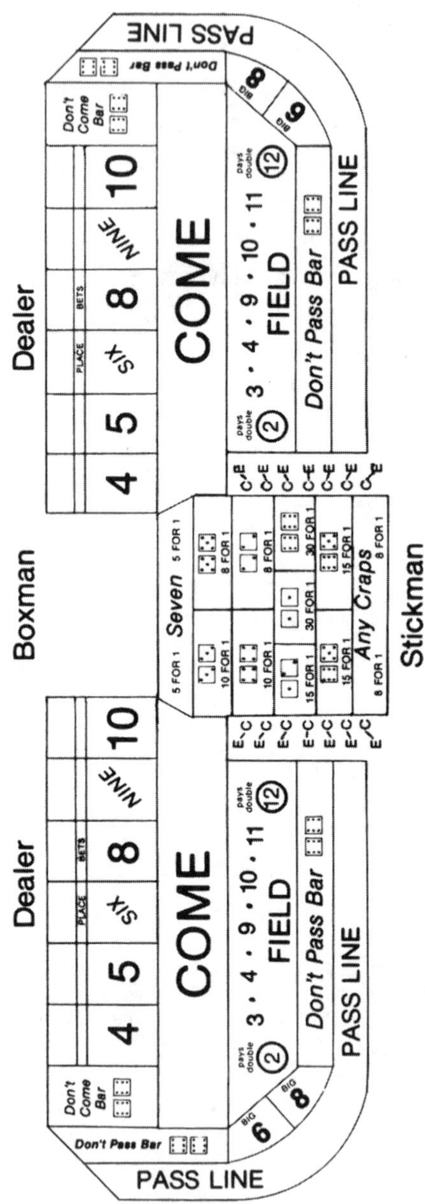
Dealer
Boxman
Dealer
Stickman
PASS LINE
Don't Pass Bar
Don't Come Bar
PLACE BETS
4
5
SIX
8
NINE
10
COME
pays double
2
3 · 4 · 9 · 10 · 11
12
FIELD
Don't Pass Bar
PASS LINE
BIG 6
BIG 8
Seven 5 FOR 1
10 FOR 1
8 FOR 1
30 FOR 1
15 FOR 1
Any Craps 8 FOR 1
C-E
E-C

The Layout

THE PIT

Craps tables are arranged on the casino floor in a pattern so that a central area, known as the **pit**, is formed in the middle. The tables are arranged around the pit so that the employees working the tables have their backs to the pit area, and so that the supervisors, standing inside the pit, can easily watch over all of the craps tables.

THE DICE

The game of craps is played with two standard six-sided dice, with each die numbered from 1 to 6. The dice are manufactured so that they fall as randomly as possible, with a 5 being just as likely to fall on one die as a 3. However, combining two dice creates some combinations that are more likely to appear than others—this is the basis of the odds in craps.

PLAYERS

Only one player is needed to play craps, while as many players as can fit around a craps table is the maximum. When the action is hot and heavy, bettors are often lined up shoulder-to-shoulder screaming, yelling and cajoling for the dice to come through and make them winners.

CASINO PERSONNEL

The average craps table is manned by a crew of four casino employees—one stickman, who stands at the center of the table; two dealers, who stand on the opposite side of the stickman at either end of the table; and a boxman, who is seated between the two standing dealers and directly across from the stickman.

Let's look at the function of each crewman in turn.

THE STICKMAN

The **stickman's** main responsibility is the handling of the dice, a task he performs with a flexible, hooked stick. When a new shooter is coming out, the stickman offers him a cache of dice to choose from. After the shooter has selected two of them, the stickman returns the remaining dice to his box.

After each roll of the dice, the stickman announces the number thrown and brings the dice back to the center of the table. He usually also supplies additional information about its consequences.

If a 7 is thrown on the come-out roll, he may announce, "7, winner on the pass line." If a 2, 3 or 12 is rolled on the come-out, he may say, "Craps, line away." When a shooter sevens-out, the stickman announces, "7 out, line away."

A good stickman is a show all by himself. By the excitement he generates, he makes the game more lively and colorful for players and dealers alike. From the casino's standpoint, happy players tend to bet heavier and wilder than they normally would.

The stickman is also responsible for the proposition, or center bets, made in the middle of the layout. He places all proposition bets directed his way into their proper location on the layout. If these bets are winners, the stickman directs the dealers to pay off the winning players. If the bets are losers, he collects the lost bet's and pushes them over to the boxman.

The dice are returned to the shooter after the dealers have finished making payoffs.

THE DEALERS

A **dealer** stands on either side of the boxman. A dealer's main responsibility is to handle all the monetary transactions and betting on his end of the table. He pays off winning bets and collects losing ones, converts cash into chips, and changes chips into higher or lower denominations for the players.

Though a player can make many of the bets himself, wagers such as the place bets and certain free-odds bets must be given to the dealer to be placed.

Each standing dealer has a **marker buck**, a plastic disk used to indicate the established point. If a player is coming out, beginning his roll, the marker buck will be lying on its black side, labeled **"off."** If a point is established, the dealer will flip the marker buck to the white side, marked **"on,"** and place it in the appropriately numbered box to indicate the point. It is with the dealers that you will have most of your contact and to whom you can address your questions.

THE BOXMAN

The **boxman** sits between the two dealers and across from the stickman, and supervises the running of the craps table from this central position. His job is to watch over the casino's bankroll, most of which sits right in front of him in huge stacks, and make sure that the dealers make the correct payoffs so that neither a player nor the house gets shorted.

He is responsible for settling any disputes that may arise between the players and the dealers. Generally, the benefit of the doubt will be given to the player on any disputed call. If the dice leave the table for any reason, the returned dice are brought directly to the boxman for inspection. He checks the logo and coded numbers on the dice to make sure that they haven't been switched, and inspects the surfaces for imperfections that may influence the game. If the boxman is suspicious of the returned dice for any reason, he will remove them from play and have the stickman offer the shooter a new pair.

When one boxman is on duty, he supervises one end of the table while the stickman watches the other.

However, when the action is fast and stacks of chips are riding on each roll of the dice, a second boxman is often added to the crew to help watch the table. In these cases, the boxmen will sit next to each other behind the chips, each being responsible for one end of the table.

In addition to the boxmen, other supervisors, called floormen and pit bosses, watch over the action from behind the boxman.

FLOORMEN

The **floormen** spend their entire shift on their feet, and are responsible for supervising a particular table or group of tables in the pit. In addition to these supervisory capacities, they deal with players that have established credit lines. If you request credit, the floorman checks to see if your credit is good and if your credit is verified, he authorizes the dealer to give you the chips that you requested. At the same time, or soon after, he brings you an IOU to sign, acknowledging the credit transaction.

PIT BOSS

The **pit boss**, under whose authority the floormen work, is in the charge of the entire craps pit. He is rarely in contact with the players unless a high roller is playing, in which case he may introduce himself to the high roller or offer him some comps.

ENTERING A GAME

To enter a craps game, slip into a space on the rail of the craps table. After catching the dealer's attention, place your cash on the layout and tell him the denomination of chips you want to play. The dealer will take your money and give it to the boxman, who will supervise the exchange.

CONVERTING TRAVELER'S CHECKS AND MONEY ORDERS TO CASH

Dealers will accept only cash or chips at the table, so if you bring traveler's checks or money orders, you must go to the area of the casino marked **Casino Cashier** to get them converted to cash. Be sure to bring proper identification to ensure a smooth transaction.

BETTING

Casinos prefer that players use chips for betting purposes, because handling money at the tables is cumbersome and slows the game. Though cash can be used to bet with, all payoffs will be in chips.

CASINO CHIPS

Chip denominations are in $1, $5, $25, $100 and $500 units. $1 chips are generally referred to as **silver**, $5 chips as **nickels**, $25 chips as **quarters**, and $100 chips as **dollars**. Unless playing at a 25¢ minimum craps table, $1 chips are the minimum currency available.

HOUSE LIMITS

The house limits are posted at every table. They indicate the minimum bet required to play, as well as the maximum bet allowed. Minimum bets may range from $1 and $5 per bet, to a maximum of $500, $1,000 or $2,000 a bet. Occasionally, 25¢ minimum craps tables may be found as well. If special arrangements are made, a player can bet as much as he can muster in certain casinos. In 1981, a man walked into the old Binion's Horseshoe Casino in Las Vegas when it was being run by the late Benny Binion, who allowed unlimited wagers in craps. The man placed a bet for $777,777 on the don't pass line—and walked out two rolls later with $1.5 million in cash!

CONVERTING CHIPS INTO CASH

Dealers do not convert your chips into cash. Once you've bought chips at the table, that cash is dropped into a drop box, and thereafter is unobtainable at the table. When you are ready to convert your chips, take them to the cashier's cage to exchange them for cash.

FREE DRINKS

Casinos offer their customers unlimited free drinking while gambling at the tables. In addition to alcoholic beverages, a player can order juices or any other beverages from a cocktail server.

TIPPING

Tipping, or **toking** as it is called in casinos, is a gratuitous gesture that you make to the crew of dealers if you feel that they have given you good service. Tipping is totally at your discretion, and in no way should be considered an obligation. If you toke, toke only when you're winning, and only if the crew is friendly and helpful to you. Do not toke dealers that you don't like or ones that try to make you feel guilty about not tipping. Dealers that make playing an unpleasant experience for you deserve nothing.

The crewmen working at the craps table share the tips. Though the usual tip is to make a proposition bet by saying "One for the boys," a better way to toke the crew is to make a line bet for them so that they can have a good chance of winning the bet. Dealers prefer this type of tip since they too are aware of how poor the proposition bets are. This is also better than just handing over the toke because if you win the bet, the dealer wins double for the tip—the amount you bet for him plus the winnings from that bet.

THE PLAY OF THE GAME AND THE COME-OUT ROLL

When a new player is ready to throw the dice, the stickman will empty his box of dice and push them across the layout with his stick. After this player, known as the **shooter**, selects two dice of his choice, the stickman will retrieve the remaining dice and return them to his box. In a new game, the player closest to the boxman's left side will receive the dice first, and the rotation of the dice will go clockwise from player to player around the craps table.

The shooter has no advantage over the other players except perhaps the psychological edge that he may get from throwing the dice himself. He is required to make either a pass or don't pass bet as the shooter, and can also make any other bets allowed.

You can make a wide variety of bets, and these bets should be placed before the shooter throws the dice. You can bet with the dice or against them at your preference, but in either case, the casino will book all wagers.

Play is ready to begin. The shooter is supposed to throw the dice so that they bounce off the far wall of the table. If the throw does not reach the far wall, the shooter will be requested to toss harder on his next throw. If he persists in underthrowing the dice, the boxman may disallow him from throwing further. This policy protects against cheaters who can manipulate unobstructed throws of the dice.

The first throw is called the **come-out roll**—it is the most significant roll in craps. The come-out roll marks the first roll of a **shoot**, and can either become an automatic winner or loser for players betting with the dice, called **right bettors**, or those betting against the dice, called **wrong bettors**—or it can establish a point with which the shooter hopes to repeat before a 7 is thrown.

The come-out roll works as follows. The throw of a 7 or 11 on the come-out roll is an automatic winner for the pass line bettors, players betting that the dice will win, or *pass*. The throw of a **craps**—a 2, 3 or 12—is an automatic loser. For the don't pass bettors, those betting against the dice, the come-out roll works almost exactly opposite to the pass line bet. A come-out roll of a 7 or an 11 is an automatic loser, a 2 or a 3 an automatic winner, while the 12 (in some casinos a 2 instead) is a standoff.

If the come-out roll is an automatic decision—a 2, 3, 7, 11 or 12—the affected players will have their bets paid or collected, and the following roll will be a new come-out roll. Any other number thrown—a 4, 5, 6, 8, 9 or 10—becomes the **point**, and the dealers will indicate this by flipping their respective marker bucks to the white side marked "on," and will move the disk into the rectangular numbered boxes corresponding to the point number thrown.

The shoot will continue until either the point is repeated, which is a winner for the pass line bettors and a loser for the don't pass bettors, or until a seven is thrown, known as **sevening-out**, which is a loser on the pass line and a winner on the don't pass. In either case, the shoot will have been completed, and the following roll will be a new come-out roll, the start of a new shoot.

Once a point is established, only the 7 and the point are consequential rolls for the pass and don't pass bettors, also called **line bettors**. All other rolls are neutral throws for these bets.

Many other bets are available to players (we will discuss them later), some that can be made only after a point is established, and others that can be made at any time during a shoot. Therefore, while the line bettors may not be affected by a particular throw, the dealers may be paying off or collecting chips on other affected wagers while the shoot is in progress.

A shooter can continue throwing the dice until he sevens-out, whereupon, after all the bets are settled on the layout, the stickman will present the collection of dice to the next player in a clockwise rotation. Even though the shooter may **crap-out** (the throw of a 2, 3 or 12) on his come-out roll, a losing roll for the pass line bettors, the shooter does not have to yield the dice. It is only when he throws a 7 before his point repeats (sevens-out) that he must relinquish the dice.

THE COME-OUT ROLL IN A NUTSHELL

The come-out roll occurs when:

1. A new shooter takes the dice.
2. The shooter throws a 2, 3, 7, 11 or 12 on the come-out roll, an automatic winner or loser for the line bettors.
3. After a point is established, the shooter either repeats that point or sevens-out.

BETTING RIGHT OR WRONG

Betting right or wrong are casino terms used to designate whether a player is betting with the dice, **betting right**, or betting against the dice, **betting wrong**. The words right and wrong are in no way indicative of a correct or incorrect way of playing. Both ways of betting are equally valid.

UNDERSTANDING THE ODDS

Knowing how to figure the possible combinations that can occur when two dice are thrown is essential to understanding the basics of craps—the bets, the odds, and the payoffs. You may be surprised at how simple the odds really are. Playing craps will be a more rewarding experience once you learn these fundamentals.

Each one of the two dice has six equally possible outcomes when thrown—numbers one through six. When the two dice are thrown together, they have a total of 36 possible outcomes—the six combinations of one die multiplied by the six combinations of the other die. The chart below shows these combinations. Notice that certain totals have more possibilities of being thrown; that is, they are more probable of occurring by the random throw of the two dice.

COMBINATIONS OF THE DICE

NUMBER THROWN	COMBINATIONS	NUMBER OF COMBINATIONS
2	1-1	1
3	1-2, 2-1	2
4	1-3, 3-1, 2-2	3
5	1-4, 4-1, 2-3, 3-2	4
6	1-5, 5-1, 2-4, 4-2, 3-3	5
7	1-6, 6-1, 2-5, 5-2, 3-4, 4-3	6
8	2-6, 6-2, 3-5, 5-3, 4-4	5
9	3-6, 6-3, 4-5, 5-4	4
10	4-6, 6-4, 5-5	3
11	5-6, 6-5	2
12	6-6	1

By looking at the chart, you can see that the 7 is more likely to be thrown than any other number, as it has six possible combinations. Next in frequency are the 6 and the 8 with five outcomes each; then the 5 and the 9 with four outcomes; the 4 and the 10, three outcomes apiece; the 3 and the 11, two outcomes; and finally, the 2 and the 12, which have only one combination each.

A SHORTCUT TO REMEMBERING THE ODDS

Notice the symmetry of combinations on either side of the 7. The 6 and 8 have equal possibilities of being thrown, just as the 5 and 9, 4 and 10, 3 and 11, and 2 and 12 do. If you take rolls of 7 and below and subtract one from that number, you arrive at the correct number of combinations for that roll. Thus, there are four ways to roll a 5 (5-1), six ways to roll a 7 (7-1) and one way to roll a 2 (2-1).

For numbers greater than the 7, match that number with the corresponding symmetrical number on the other side of the 7, and subtract one. Thus, to find the combinations of the 8, you match it with the 6 (which has an equal likelihood of occurring), and subtracting one, you get five combinations.

FIGURING THE ODDS OF ROLLING A SPECIFIC NUMBER

To figure the odds of rolling any particular number, divide the number of combinations for that particular number into 36, the total number of combinations possible. For example, there are six ways to roll a 7. Dividing the six combinations into 36, which is the total number of possible combinations, we find that the odds of rolling a 7 on any one roll is one in six (6/36 reduced to 1/6), or equivalently, 5 to 1. The chart below shows the odds of rolling a number on any one roll.

ODDS OF ROLLING THE NUMBERS

	Combinations	Chance of Being Rolled	Expressed in Odds
2 or 12	1	1/36	35 to 1
3 or 11	2	2/36	17 to 1
4 or 10	3	3/36	11 to 1
5 or 9	4	4/36	8 to 1
6 or 8	5	5/36	6.2 to 1
7	6	6/36	5 to 1

The listing of two numbers together such as the 5 or 9 is done to abbreviate. The odds apply to either the 5 or the 9, not to both together.

UNDERSTANDING THE TERMINOLOGY—CORRECT ODDS, HOUSE PAYOFF AND EDGE

The house advantage, or edge, is the difference between your chances of winning the bet, called the **correct odds**, and the casino's actual payoff, called the **house payoff** or simply, the **payoff**. For example, the correct odds of rolling a 7 are 5 to 1. Since the house will pay only 4 to 1 when 7 is thrown, it maintains an edge of 16.67% on this wager.

To play craps intelligently and better understand the choices available, first and foremost you must be aware of the house advantage on every bet you'll ever make. Why? Because the house edge determines your chances of winning at craps over the long run.

FIVE FOR ONE, FIVE TO ONE

On a layout, you sometimes will see payoffs represented as "for" instead of the usual "to," such as "9 *for* 1." This means that the payoff will be a total of 9 units, 8 winning chips along with your original bet, which is a house subterfuge to increase its edge over players. The usual 9 to 1 payoff means that 9 winning chips and your original bet will be returned to you, for a total of 10 units.

Beware of any payoffs with the wording "for." As a rule, these types of bet have poor odds to begin with, and are bets that you wouldn't want to make anyway, with either the "to" or the "for."

THE BETS

Craps offers you a wide variety of possible wagers, with each bet having its own characteristics and inherent odds. Some bets, which are referred to as **sequence bets**, may require a series of rolls before the outcome is determined, while the outcome of others, called **one-roll bets**, are determined on the very next roll.

The house pays off some bets at even money—for every dollar wagered, you win a dollar—while other bets have payoffs as high as 30 to 1. In general, however, the higher the house payoff, the worse the odds are for players. And the odds of the bet, that is, the mathematical house return on every dollar wagered, is your most important concern as a player. To have the best chances of winning, you must avoid all the sucker bets, and make only the best bets available to you.

MOST ADVANTAGEOUS BETS

The bets presented in this section have the lowest built-in house edge of all the bets in craps. One bet, the free-odds bet, gives the house no advantage whatsoever. The pass, don't pass, come, don't come and the free-odds bets are the most important bets you can make, and are the foundation of these winning strategies.

THE LINE BETS—PASS AND DON'T PASS

These even-money bets can only be made on a come-out roll, before a point is established, and give the house an edge of only 1.4%. When backed by the free-odds wagers, the overall house edge drops to 0.8% in a single odds game, and to 0.6% in a double odds game.

PASS LINE

Players making pass line bets are wagering that the dice will pass, or win, and are called right bettors. Pass line bets are also referred to as **front line bets**, and are made by placing a wager in the area marked pass line.

On the come-out roll, a throw of a 7 or 11 is an automatic winner for pass line bettors while the throw of a craps (a 2, 3 or 12) is an automatic loser. If any other number is thrown—the 4, 5, 6, 8, 9 or 10—that number is established as the point. The shooter must repeat rolling the point before a 7 is thrown for pass line bettors to win. The throw of a 7 before the point repeats is a loser for pass line bettors, called sevening-out, and the dealers will collect all lost bets.

Once the point is established, only the 7 and the point number affect the pass line bettor. All other numbers have no bearing on the bet and can be considered neutral throws.

Let's look at three progressions to see how the pass line bet works.

1. The come-out roll is a 5, establishing 5 as the point. The following roll is a 2, a neutral throw, since a point has already been established. An 8 is then thrown, still having no bearing on the outcome, and then a 5. The point was repeated, or made, before the seven was thrown, and the pass line bettors win their bets.

2. The come-out roll is a 7, an automatic winner for the pass line bettors, who are paid off by the dealers. Since the progression has been completed, the following roll will be another come-out roll.
3. Here is a losing proposition. The come-out roll is a 9, establishing 9 as the point. The shooter then rolls a 6, then a 12, and then an 11. All three rolls are neutral since a point is already established. The following roll is a 7. Since a 7 was rolled before a 9 (the shooter's point) repeated, pass line bettors lose and the dealer collects their bets. A new come-out roll will ensue.

PASS LINE IN A NUTSHELL	
Payoff:	Even-Money
House Edge:	1.4%
Automatic Winners:	7 or 11 on the come-out roll
Automatic Losers:	2, 3, or 12 on the come-out roll

If a point is established on the come-out roll, pass line bettors:
Win when the point repeats before the 7 is thrown.
Lose when a 7 is thrown before the point repeats.

DON'T PASS

Players betting don't pass are called wrong bettors, and are betting against the dice. Don't pass bets are also called **back line bets** and are made by placing the wager in the area marked don't pass.

On the come-out roll, a throw of a 2 or 3 is an automatic winner for don't-pass bettors, while a 7 or an 11 is an automatic loser. The 12 is a standoff between a back line bettor and the house. (In some casinos, 2 is the standoff and 12 is the automatic winner. It makes no difference either way, since there is only one way to throw the 2 or the 12.)

Once the point is established, don't pass bettors win if a 7 is thrown before the shooter repeats his point, and they lose when the point is repeated before the shooter sevens-out.

Here are some progressions to illustrate the don't-pass wager.

1. The come-out roll is a 6, establishing 6 as the point. The following rolls are a 5 (no bearing on the outcome), then a 12 (still no bearing), and then a 7. Since a 7 was rolled before the 6 repeated, don't-pass bettors win.
2. The come-out roll is a 3, an automatic winner for don't-pass bettors.
3. The come-out roll is a 4, establishing 4 as the point. A 3 is then rolled (neutral), and then a 4, a loss for back line bettors since the point repeated before the 7 was rolled.

DON'T PASS LINE IN A NUTSHELL	
Payoff	Even-Money
House Edge:	1.4%
Automatic Winners:	2 (or 12) and 3 on the come-out roll
Automatic Losers:	7 or 11 on the come-out roll
Standoff:	12 (or 2 in some casinos) on the come-out roll

If a point is established on the come-out roll,
don't-pass bettors:
Win when a 7 is thrown before the point repeats.
Lose when the point repeats before the 7 is thrown.

COME AND DON'T COME BETS

The come and don't come bets work according to the same rules as the pass and don't pass bets, except that the come and don't come bets can only be made *after* a point is established. The line bets, however, can only be placed on a come-out roll *before* a point is established.

The advantage of these bets is that they allow you to cover more points as a right or wrong bettor at the same low 1.4% house edge. And like the line bets, the overall house edge drops to 0.8% when backed by single odds, and 0.6% when backed by double odds.

Come bets are made by putting chips into the area marked come, while don't come bets are placed in the don't-come box. Won bets are paid at even money.

COME BETS

You follow the play of the come bets just as you do with the pass line bets. A 7 or 11 on the first throw following the placing of the bet is an automatic winner, while a 2, 3 or 12 is an automatic loser.

Any other number thrown (a 4, 5, 6, 8, 9 or 10) becomes the point for that come bet, called a **come point**. The dealer will move the bet from the come box into the large rectangular numbered boxes located at the top of the layout to mark the come point. Once the come point is established, the bet is won if the come point repeats before the shooter sevens-out, and is lost if the 7 is rolled before the point repeats. All other throws are inconsequential on this bet. Won bets will be paid off and removed from the layout.

You can make continuous come bets until all the points are covered if you want to. Thus, it is possible for the throw of a 7 to simultaneously wipe out several established come bets. On the other hand, a hot shooter rolling point numbers can give the aggressive come bettor a lot of winners.

Let's follow a progression where the right bettor makes both pass line and come bets.

Player Bets: $5 on the pass line.
The come-out roll is a 5, establishing 5 as the point.

Player Bets: $5 on the come.
The roll is an 8, establishing 8 as the come point. The dealer moves the $5 come bet to the rectangular box marked 8 to indicate that 8 is the point for that come bet. In effect, the player has two points working, the 5 and the 8, and decides to make another come bet.

Player Bets: $5 on the come.

The roll is a 6. The dealer moves this new come bet to the 6, the come point for this bet. The other two points are not affected by this roll.

Player Bets: The player has three points established, the 5, 6, and 8, and makes no more bets at this time.

The roll is a 5, a $5 winner on the pass line. It is paid off and removed from the layout, leaving the player with two come points, the 6 and 8.

Player Bets: $5 on the pass line. Since the next roll is a come-out roll and the player wants to cover another point, he bets the pass.

The roll is a 10, establishing 10 as the point.

Player Bets: No additional bets at this time.

The roll is a 2 (neutral on all established bets), then an 8 is thrown, a $5 winner on the come point of 8, and that bet is paid off and removed. The following roll is not a come-out roll, because the come point was made, not the pass line point, the 10.

Player Bets: Wishing to establish a third point, $5 is bet on the come.

The roll is a 7. While the 7 is a $5 winner for the new come bet, it is a loser for the two established points, and they are removed from the layout by the dealer. The roll of the 7 cleared the layout, and the following roll will be a new come-out roll.

DON'T COME BETS

Like the don't-pass wager, a 7 or 11 on the first roll following a don't-come bet is an automatic loser, and 2 and 3 are automatic winners, 12 being a standoff. (In casinos where 2 is a standoff and the 12 a winner on the don't pass, the same holds true for the don't come bets.)

If a 4, 5, 6, 8, 9 or 10 is thrown, establishing a point for the don't-come bet, the dealer will move the chips behind the appropriate point box to mark the don't come point. Don't come bettors will win if the 7 is thrown before that point is made. Other numbers, as with the don't-pass bets, are neutral rolls. Only a 7 and the come point determine the bet.

Let's follow a progression where the wrong bettor makes both don't pass and don't come bets.

Player Bets: $5 on the don't pass.
The roll is a 10, establishing 10 as the point.

Player Bets: Continuing to bet against the dice, he now makes a $5 bet on the don't come.
The roll is a 2, a $5 winner on the new don't come bet, and that bet is paid off and removed.

Player Bets: $5 on the don't come.
The roll is a 6. The dealer moves the bet from the don't come area to the upper section of the box numbered 6 to indicate that 6 is the point for this don't come bet. The player now has two points working, the 10 and 6, and decides to establish a third point.

Player Bets: $5 on the don't come.
The roll is a 10, a $5 loser on the don't pass since the point repeated before a 7 was thrown. The don't come point of 6 is unaffected, and the new don't come bet is moved to the 10 box, since 10 is the come point for the new don't come wager.

Player Bets: The player decides not to make any more bets, being content with his bets on points 6 and 10, unwilling to place more bets on the layout. If he were to make another bet against the dice, he would bet don't pass because the next throw is a come-out roll.
The roll is 7, winner on both established come points; they are paid off and removed. The next roll will be a new come-out.

FREE-ODDS BETS

Though not designated anywhere on the layout, the *free-odds bets* are the best bets you can make at craps, and are an indispensable part of winning strategies. Unlike the other bets at craps, the house has no advantage over players in free-odds bets.

However, to make a free-odds bet, you must first have placed a pass, don't pass, come or don't come wager and, in a sense, you are backing those bets since you can only make a free-odds bet in conjunction with these wagers. When backed by single odds, the overall odds of the pass, don't pass, come and don't come bets drop to 0.8%. Where double odds are allowed and utilized, the overall odds drop to only 0.6% against the player. The house edge is even lower when 10x or even 100x free odds are allowed.

The free odds bets are the best odds you can get at craps.

FREE-ODDS—PASS LINE

Once a point is established on the come-out roll, a pass line bettor is allowed to make an additional bet, called a **free-odds bet**, that his point will be repeated before a 7 is thrown. A free-odds bet is made by placing chips behind the pass line wager and just outside the pass line area. This bet pays you off at the correct odds, giving the house no edge.

PASS LINE AND FREE-ODDS BET

When single odds are allowed, you can bet up to the amount that you wagered on your pass line bet and in certain instances, you can bet more. When double odds are allowed, you can bet twice the amount of your pass line bet as a free-odds wager.

You can bet less than the permissible amount on the free-odds wager, and are allowed to reduce or remove this bet at any time. But you should never do that because the free-odds bets are the most advantageous bets in craps, and you want to take full advantage of them.

Here is a table that shows the correct odds of the point repeating before a 7 is thrown, and the house payoff. Note that the house takes no percentage advantage on these bets, since the payoff is identical to the correct odds.

ODDS OF POINT REPEATING BEFORE A SEVEN

Point Number	Correct Odds	House Payoff
4 or 10	2 to 1	2 to 1
5 or 9	3 to 2	3 to 2
6 or 8	6 to 5	6 to 5

The odds presented in this table are easy to figure since the only numbers that affect the free-odds bet are the point number, which is a winner, and 7, which is a loser. All other throws are inconsequential.

There are three ways to roll a winning 4 or 10, and six ways to roll a losing 7—thus 2 to 1 is the correct odds on points 4 or 10. A 5 or 9 can be rolled four ways each against the same six ways of rolling a 7, so the correct odds are 3 to 2 against a 5 or 9. A 6 or 8 can be made with five combinations. Again, since there are six ways to roll a losing 7, the correct odds are 6 to 5 against rolling a 6 or 8.

SPECIAL ALLOWANCES—SINGLE ODDS GAME

To make the payoffs easier, most casinos will allow you to make a single odds bet that is greater than your pass line (or come) bet in the following instances:

1. With a pass line bet such as $5 or $25 and the point being a 5 or 9, casinos allow you to make an odds bet of $6 and $30 respectively behind the line. If you win your bet, the 3 to 2 payoff on the $6 free-odds bet would be $9, and on the $30 bet, $45.
   If you had not been allowed this special allowance, you would have been unable to get the full correct odds on your $5 or $25 free-odds bet, since the $1-or-more minimum craps tables do not deal in half-dollars.
2. With a three-unit bet such as $3 or $15, and the point being a 6 or 8, casinos allow a five-unit free-odds bet behind the line. This allows players to take full advantage of the 6 to 5 payoff on points 6 and 8. In the above examples, $5 and $25 free-odds bets are permitted, and pay players $6 and $30 respectively if they win.

A three-unit bet is $3 for a $1 bettor, $15 for a $5 bettor, $30 for a $10 bettor, and so on. Any bet that is divisible by three is considered a three-unit bet and can be backed by the special allowance single odds bets.

A $30 bet on the pass line can be backed by only $30 if the point is a 5 or 9, since the 3 to 2 payoff can be made on this amount, but if the point is a 6 or an 8, it can be backed by $50 (five unit special allowance).

If uncertain about the amounts you are allowed to back your pass line bet with, check with the dealer, who will tell you the permissible wager.

THREE UNIT BET • SINGLE ODDS
SPECIAL ALLOWANCE

Basic Three Unit Bet	6 or 8 as Point
$3	$5 ($6)
$15	$25 ($30)
$30	$50 ($60)
$45	$75 ($90)
$75	$125 ($150)
$300	$500 ($600)

The first column, Basic Three Unit Bet, is what our standard pass and come bet is, while the second column shows the special allowance permitted when the point is 6 or 8. Numbers in parenthesis indicate the amount paid if the single odds bet is won.

Note that this is only a partial listing of the basic three-unit bets, and many more are possible if you want to bet in different ranges than these.

No special allowances are allowed when a 4 or 10 are points because they are easily paid off at 2 to 1, no matter what the amount of the wager.

On bets smaller than $5 with the point being a 6 or 8, single odds bets will not be able to receive the full 6 to 5 payoff, and will be paid off at even money only because craps tables do not stock units smaller than $1 chips.

On bets larger than $5 but in unequal multiples of $5, the free-odds bet will be paid to the highest multiple of $5 at 6 to 5, and the remainder will be paid at even money. Thus, a $12 odds bet on the 8 will yield a payoff of only $14, $12 on the first $10 (at 6 to 5), and even money on the unequal remainder of $2.

When free-odds bets do not receive their full payoff, the bet works to your disadvantage. Therefore, I recommend that you make pass and come wagers in multiples of $3, because $3 multiples allow you to take full advantage of the special allowances, and they lower the overall house edge for the single odds game to below 0.8%.

DOUBLE ODDS—PASS LINE

Double odds work just like single odds except that players are allowed to bet double their pass line bet as a free-odds wager. If $10 is bet on the pass line and a 5 is established as the point, the double odds game allows a player to bet $20 as a free-odds wager and receive the same correct 3 to 2 odds on that point, instead of only being allowed a $10 free-odds bet, as in the single odds game.

When combined with the pass line bet, double odds brings the overall house edge down to only 0.6%, the best odds you can get at craps. Therefore, when you have the choice of playing a single or double odds game, choose the double odds game to take advantage of every favorable option allowed.

If you're uncertain whether double odds are allowed, just ask the dealer.

SPECIAL ALLOWANCES—DOUBLE ODDS GAME

There is one special allowance to keep in mind on the double odds game. With a two-unit bet on the pass line and the point a 6 or 8, double odds casinos allow players to wager five units as a free-odds bet. Thus, with a $10 bet (two $5 unit chips), and the point a 6 or 8, a $25 double odds bet would be allowed. If you win, the 6 to 5 payoff will give you $30 in winnings (six $5 chips, an easier payoff for the casino).

I recommend that you bet in multiples of two because it permits you to take advantage of the special five-unit allowance when the point is a 6 or an 8. Any bet that can be divided by two can be considered a two-unit bet and can be backed by the special five-unit allowance if the point is a 6 or an 8.

TWO UNIT BET • DOUBLE ODDS SPECIAL ALLOWANCE		
Basic 2-Unit Bet*	**6 or 8 as Point**	**4,5,9 or 10 as Point**
$2	$5 ($6)	$4
$10	$25 ($30)	$20
$20	$50 ($60)	$40
$30	$75 ($90)	$60
$50	$125 ($150)	$100
$200	$500 ($600)	$400

*The Basic Two Unit Bet is our standard pass and come bet. The third column is the normal double odds allowance for points 4, 5, 9 and 10.

Numbers in parenthesis indicate the amount paid if the double odds bet is won at 6 to 5 payoff. Two-unit bets other than the ones shown in this chart are also possible.

Note that other two unit bets than those shown in the chart are possible.

Let's see how the free-odds bet works in a single odds game. You make a $15 bet on the pass line, and the come-out roll is a 6. Taking advantage of the special five-unit allowance, $25 is wagered as a free-odds bet behind the line. If the shooter throws a 7 before the point repeats, you lose your $15 pass bet and the $25 free-odds bet, but if the point is rolled before the 7, you will win $15 on the pass line bet and $30 on the odds bet ($25 paid at 6 to 5).

If the game had been a double odds game, you could have backed your $15 pass bet with a $30 free-odds bet. And if the point had been a 6, the free-odds bet would pay you $36 if won ($30 at 6 to 5 = $30).

FREE-ODDS—DON'T PASS

Once the point is established, don't-pass bettors are allowed to make a free-odds bet that a 7 will be rolled before the point repeats. The bet is paid off at correct odds, the house enjoying no edge, and is made by placing the free-odds bet next to the don't pass wager in the don't pass box.

DON'T PASS AND FREE-ODDS BET

Since the odds favor don't pass bettors once the point is established (there being more ways to roll a winning 7 than any point number), don't pass bettors must **lay odds**; that is, they must put more money on the free-odds bet than they will win.

Let's say the point is a 4. A don't-pass bettor's chances of winning the bet are 2 to 1 in his favor. There are only three ways to roll a 4, a loser, against the six combinations of a 7, a winner. Therefore, a don't-pass bettor must bet $20 to win $10 when the point is a 4 (or 10). On the other side of the bet, pass line bettors are receiving 2 to 1 odds, since their bet is the underdog, having only three winning chances against six losing combinations.

To lay odds as a don't-pass bettor, the allowable free-odds bet is determined by the *payoff*, not the original bet. Using the above example of a $10 bet on the don't pass with 4 established as the point, a don't pass bettor in a single odds game is allowed up to a $10 win on the free-odds bet. Since the odds are 2 to 1 in his favor, the don't-pass bettor must lay $20 to win $10. In a double odds game (meaning that a player can win $20 on his original $10 bet) at 1 to 2 odds, $40 would have to be staked for a potential win of $20.

The odds that don't-pass bettors must lay are exactly opposite to the odds that pass-line bettors take on the same points.

Below is a table showing the free-odds bets from the wrong bettor's position.

ODDS OF ROLLING A SEVEN BEFORE POINT REPEATS

Point Number	Correct Odds	House Payoff
4 or 10	1 to 2	1 to 2
5 or 9	2 to 3	2 to 3
6 or 8	5 to 6	5 to 6

Note that the house has no percentage advantage on these bets since the payoff is identical to the correct odds.

Like the free-odds bets for right bettors, don't pass free-odds wagers can be removed or reduced at any time, but since these are your best bets, you should not remove or reduce them.

Let's look at a quick example to see how the free-odds bet works for don't-pass bettors.

$10 is bet on the don't pass, and the come-out roll is a 9. The wrong bettor bets $15 behind the line as a free-odds bet, the maximum allowed in a single odds game. He stands to win $10 on the free-odds bet if a 7 is rolled before a 9 repeats, in addition to $10 on his don't pass bet. If the point is rolled before a 7, he will lose the $15 free-odds bet and the $10 don't pass bet. If double odds were allowed, $20 would be the maximum allowable free-odds win. At 2 to 3 odds, the don't-pass bettor would have to lay $30 to win $20.

WRONG BETTORS SPECIAL ALLOWANCES: SINGLE ODDS GAME

The casino makes a special provision for don't-pass bettors when the point is a 5 or 9, and an odd figure such as $5 is wagered. Since craps tables do not deal in half dollars, players are allowed to make a free-odds bet of $9 behind the line in this instance, and if the bet is won, they will get paid $6 ($9 at 2 to 3).

Whenever the point is 5 or 9 and the original bet is an unequal amount, the house allows players to bet more than the straight single odds. Ask the dealer the exact amount allowed in those instances, as the rules may vary from casino to casino.

FREE-ODDS: COME AND DON'T COME

Once a come point is established, you can take odds (or lay odds for don't come bettors) and get the same advantageous payoffs: 2-1 on points 4 and 10 (1-2 for wrong bettors); 3-2 on the 5 and 9 (2-3 for wrong bettors); and 6-5 on the 6 and 8 (5-6 for wrong bettors). The house has no advantage on these free-odds wagers and, like the line bets, the overall house edge on the come or don't come bets, teamed with single odds, drops to 0.8%; and with double odds, it drops to 0.6%.

The same special allowances apply for the come bets. In a single odds game, a three-unit bet can be backed by five units if the point is 6 or 8, while a free-odds bet on points 5 and 9 can be backed by additional chips if the original come bet is uneven. In the double odds game, players can back a two-unit wager with five units if the point is a 6 or 8.

However, the odds bets on the come and don't come bets are placed differently from line bets. Rather than being made by players, the odds bets are given to the dealer with the instruction, "Odds on the come," or "Odds on the don't come." The dealer will place the odds bet in the appropriate box atop the come point, but slightly offset, so that the odds bet can be differentiated from the come bet.

COME, DON'T COME AND FREE-ODDS BETS

The only other difference is with the come bet. While the come bet is working on the come-out roll, the odds bet on that come bet is not. Let's say that you placed a $15 bet on the come point of 6 and backed that bet with a $25 free-odds bet. A come-out roll of a 7 would, of course, be a loser for the $15 come bet, as that bet is always working; but since the free-odds bet was off, the $25 single odds wager would be returned to you.

If a 6 were rolled instead, which is a winner for the come bet, you would only win the $15, and be returned the $25 odds bet.

Though it is standard procedure for the free-odds bet that backs the come wager to be "off" on the come-out roll, you can request the odds bet to be "on" by informing the dealer, "Odds are on for the come bet." In that case, of course, the odds bet is subject to the normal rules.

The odds on don't come bets, as with pass and don't pass wagers, are always working.

Let's look at some betting sequences to illustrate how the free-odds bets on come and don't come wagers work in conjunction with the line bets.

RIGHT BETTORS (PASS AND COME BETS)

Player R is a right bettor who likes betting with the dice. His standard betting unit is $15 (3 units of $5), which allows him to take advantage of the special free-odds allowances when the points are 5 and 9, and 6 and 8.

SINGLE ODDS GAME

Player R Bets: $15 on the pass line.

The come-out roll is an 8, establishing 8 as the point.

Player R Bets: $25 odds bet behind the 8 (5 unit special allowance bet). He also bets $15 on the come line.

The roll is a 4, establishing the 4 as a come point. Dealer moves Player R's come bet from the come line to the box marked 4. (His $15 pass line and $25 odds bet on the 8 stay where they are.)

Player R Bets: $15 odds bet on the 4. The dealer places the wager on the come bet, but at a tilt to show it's an odds bet. Player R decides to make another $15 come bet.

The roll is an 11. The new come bet is an automatic winner for $15. The other bets are unaffected.

Player R Bets: $15 more on the come.

The roll is a 4, a winner on that come point. Player R wins $15 on the come bet and $30 (2 to 1 payoff) on the free-odds bet. The new $15 come bet is moved to the place box of 4 to indicate that it's a come point.

Player R Bets: $15 odds on the come point of 4. And he bets $15 more on the come.

Player R now has a $15 pass line bet backed by $25 odds on the point of 8, a $15 come bet backed by $15 odds on the point of 4, and a new $15 come wager.

The roll is an 8, a winner on the pass line. Player R gets paid $15 on the pass line bet and $30 on his odds bet (6 to 5 odds) and these bets are removed from the layout. The new come bet is moved to the 8 box, the come point for that last bet. A new come-out roll will follow since the point was made.

Player R Bets: $15 on the passline. and he places a $25 odds bet on his come point of 8.

The roll is a 7, a $15 winner on the new pass line bet, but a loser for the two come points of 4 and 8. Since the odds bets were off on the come-out roll, the $15 odds on the 4 and $25 odds on the 8 are returned to the player, leaving him with only a $30 loss on the come points, but a $15 winner on the pass line bet.

Player R wins $120 in bets and loses only $30 for a net win of $90.

WRONG BETTORS (DON'T PASS AND DON'T COME BETS)

Player W is a wrong bettor who prefers to bet against the dice. His standard betting unit is $20 because it's easier to figure the laying of odds with bets in multiples of $10.

SINGLE ODDS GAME

Player W Bets: $20 on the don't pass.

The come-out roll is a 6, establishing 6 as the point.

Player W Bets: $24 free-odds bet behind the 6 (laying 5 to 6 odds). He also bets $20 on the don't come.

The roll is a 3, craps, a winner on the new don't come bet. The other bets are unaffected. The winning bet is removed from the layout.

Player W Bets: $20 on the don't come.

The roll is a 10, and the dealer moves the don't come bet above the box marked 10 to indicate the come point for the don't come bet.

Player W Bets: $40 free-odds on the come point of 10, (laying 1 to 2 odds). The dealer places the odds bet atop the original bet, but at a tilt so the bet can be a distinguished from the don't come bet. He also places a $20 bet in the don't come box.

The roll is a 9, establishing 9 as the come point for the new don't come bet. Player W now has bets against three points, the 6, 9, and 10. The roll of any of those point numbers is a loss for Player B on that particular number rolled, while the throw of a 7 will be a winner on all.

Player W Bets: $30 free-odds on the 9, and decides not to make any more don't come bets.

The roll is a 6, a loser on the don't pass. Player W loses that $20 bet and the $24 odds bet behind it. Since the point has been made, the next roll is a new come-out roll. All bets for Player W and other wrong bettors will be working.

Player W Bets: $20 on the don't pass.

The roll is an 8, establishing 8 as the come point on the new don't pass bet.

Player W Bets: $24 odds on the come point of 8, and decides not to make any further bets at this time.

The roll is a 7, a simultaneous winner on all of the don't pass, don't come, and odds bets. Player W wins $20 per wrong bet plus the $20 odds behind each bet, for a $40 win per point. With three points covered, his total win on that 7 was $120.

Player W wins $140 in bets and lost only $44, for a net win of $96.

THE REST OF THE BETS

With the exception of the place bet of 6 and 8, I do not recommend any of the bets presented in this next section, which include the remainder of the bets possible at craps. The house edge over players on these bets is too large to be incorporated into a winning strategy. If you make these bets, you will soon find your pockets drained of significant portions of your bankroll.

In fact, the majority of bets listed here are sucker bets, wagers that give the house an edge so exorbitant that players stand no more than a slim chance of winning. Just because a bet looks exotic and is available doesn't mean that you should make it. To do well at craps, avoid all bets with prohibitive odds.

The bets listed in this section are discussed to give you a full understanding of all the bets possible at craps—and so that you will never be tempted to make these poor wagers.

PLACE BETS

Place bets are among the most popular wagers in craps. They are bets that a particular point number—the 4, 5, 6, 8, 9 or 10—will be rolled before a 7 is thrown. Players can make as many place bets as they want, and some players do, covering all the numbers with place bets.

However, this is not recommended strategy because, with the exception of the place bets of 6 and 8, the other place bets—4, 5, 9 and 10—are poor wagers that have no role in your winning strategies.

A player makes a place bet by giving the dealer the desired wager, and telling him what to do with it. For example "Place the 9," which indicates that the player wants to make a place bet on the 9.

Though place bets can be made at any time, they are not working—they are "off"—on the come-out roll unless the player requests them to be "on" (working). Players can also request their place bets to be off for a limited series of throws, and they may increase, reduce or remove them at any time prior to a roll.

HOUSE PAYOFFS ON PLACE BETS

Bet	Payoff	Correct Odds	House Advantage
4 or 10	9 to 5	2 to 1	6.67%
5 or 9	7 to 5	3 to 2	4.00%
6 or 8	7 to 6	6 to 5	1.52%

To get the full payoffs on the place bets, make your bets in the proper multiples. On place bets of 4 and 10, and 5 and 9, bets should be made in multiples of $5 since the payoffs are 9 to 5 and 7 to 5 respectively. On the 6 and 8, the bet should be in multiples of $6 (7 to 6 payoff).

Excess bets in unequal multiples are paid off at even money only, and thus work to the disadvantage of players. For example, a $10 bet on the 6 will be paid as follows: The first $6 will get the full 7 to 6 odds for $7, while the remaining $4 gets paid at even-money, or $4, for a total win of $11. The last $4, paid off at only even money, is a terrible payoff and makes the entire bet a poor one.

Unless you make the place bets of 6 or 8 in multiples of $6 to ensure full payoffs, you should not make the bet. Also, bets that are less than $5 on the 4, 5, 9 and 10, and less than $6 on the 6 and 8, will be paid off at only even money.

To summarize, do not make place bets of 4 or 10, or 5 and 9, because the house edge is too high.

The place bets of 6 and 8 have playable odds of 1.52% and can be used in an aggressive, maximize-gains strategy, though some players may prefer to stick with the line, come, and don't come bets backed by free-odds, since they are the best bets of all.

BIG 6 AND BIG 8

The **Big 6** and **Big 8** are bets that a particular number, the 6 or 8, will be thrown before a 7 is rolled. These bets can be made at any time, and are made by putting the wager into the box marked Big 6 or Big 8.

These bets work just like the place bets of 6 and 8 except that the house only pays the bettor even-money on a winning bet, as opposed to the 7 to 6 payoff the bettor would receive if he had made the superior place bet on 6 or 8 instead.

Let's look at the correct odds. There are five ways to throw a winning 6 (or 8, if that is bet), and six ways to throw a losing 7, making the correct odds 6 to 5. The house pays only even money on a won bet in Nevada, giving casinos a whopping 9.90% advantage. This makes the Big 6 and Big 8 terrible bets in Nevada, especially when they are compared to the 1.52% odds of the 6 and 8 place bets.

(The Big 6 and Big 8 bets were formerly offered in Atlantic City and were paid off at 7 to 6, like the place bets of 6 and 8. However, the New Jersey gaming commission approved the removal of the Big 6 and Big 8 wager, and they are no longer offered there.)

BUY BETS

BUYING THE 4 OR 10

The **buy bet** is an option the casino gives players when they bet on a place number, and though it reduces the odds on the 4 or 10 from 6.67% to 4.76%, the buy bet is still a poor one that should not be made.

Just for informative purposes, here's how it works.

To buy the 4 or 10, you must give the house a 5% commission on your bet. Once you've bought a number, the house will pay off the bet at the correct odds. Thus, your payoff will be 2 to 1, the correct odds, rather than 9 to 5 like the payoff usually is for these place bets.

A 5% commission on $20 is $1. For any bet smaller than $20, the commission is still $1 since craps tables generally carry no smaller units. In these cases, the house edge on your buy bet would be much larger than 4.76%. If you buy the 4 and 10 at $10 each, for a total of $20, the commission would only be 5% of the two-bet total, or $1.

Like the place bets, buy bets are not working on the come-out roll, unless you instruct the dealer that the bet is on. They are also similar to the place bets in that they can be increased, reduced or removed at any time prior to the roll. Note that an increased buy bet is subject to the 5% commission on the additional wager.

Some casinos will keep the 5% commission if you decide to remove an established bet, or charge an additional 5% if you win the bet and decide to let it ride.

BUYING THE 5, 6, 8, 9

Theoretically, you can buy these numbers as well, but since the commission is 5% and the house edge on all these place bets is less than that, there is no advantage in buying these numbers.

LAY BETS

The **lay bet** is the opposite of a buy bet, and is used by wrong bettors who are wagering that the 7 will be thrown before the point (or points) they are betting against is rolled. While the bet is paid off at correct odds, it costs bettors 5% commission on the projected win to get this payoff; therefore, it is a poor bet.

Lay bets, which can be bet at any time, can be made by giving the dealer your chips along with the required 5% commission on the projected win. The dealer places the bet above the point number covered (in the area where the don't come bets are placed) and places a buy button on top to designate the lay bet.

To receive the full value on the lay bet of 4 or 10, you would have to wager at least $40 to win $20 (1 to 2 odds). The 5% commission on the projected win of $20 would be $1. Any bet smaller than the $40 lay bet on the 4 or 10 would still be charged the minimum $1 commission (craps tables do not generally deal in currency smaller than $1 chips) making the house edge greater than the 2.44% advantage already built into this wager.

The 5 and 9 lay bets would require a minimum wager of $30 for you to get the maximum value. The potential $20 win (laying odds at 2 to 3) would be charged a $1 commission. Again, a bet smaller than the projected win of $20 would still be charged the minimum $1 commission, and raise the overall house edge on the bet.

The 6 and 8 bets would require a wager of $24 at 5 to 6 odds on a projected win of $20 to get full value from the commission.

HOUSE ALLOWANCE ON LAY BETS

Points	House Advantage
4 or 10	2.44%
5 or 9	3.23%
6 or 8	4.00%

The lay bet can be added to, reduced, or removed altogether at any time. I advise you to not make lay bets. You get much better odds with the wagers in the previous section, "The Most Advantageous Bets."

FIELD BET

The **field bet** is a one-roll wager that the next throw of the dice will be a number listed in the field box—the 2, 3, 4, 9, 10, 11 or 12. If one of the numbers not listed is rolled—a 5, 6, 7 or 8—the bet is lost. The field bet can be made at any time and is done by placing the wager in the area marked "Field".

At first glance, this bet looks attractive. There are seven winning numbers listed in the field box, and two of them, the 2 and the 12, pay double if they are rolled. In some casinos, the 2 or 12 pays triple. The other winning numbers—the 3, 4, 9, 10 and 11—pay even-money. But let's look closer.

The losing numbers (the 5, 6, 7 and 8) are the most frequently rolled numbers, and make up a total of 20 losing combinations. There are four ways to roll a 5, five ways to roll a 6, fives ways to make an 8, and six ways to roll a 7 for a total of 20. Adding up all the other numbers gives us a total of only 16 winning combinations. The 2 to 1 bonus on the 2 and the 12 is actually worth one more combination each for a total of 18 winning units; and where the 12 (or 2) is paid at 3 to 1, we get a total of 19 winners.

However, there are 20 combinations that will beat you, giving the house an edge of 5.55% when the 2 and 12 are paid at 2 to 1, and 2.7% when one is paid at 2 to 1 and the other at 3 to 1.

In either case, the house advantage is much larger than other bets available at craps, which is why you should not make field bets.

PROPOSITION BETS (CENTER BETS)

The proposition, or center bets as they are sometimes called, are located at the center of the layout, and are made by either giving the chips to the dealer, who passes them along to the stickman; or can sometimes be tossed directly to the stickman, as with the hardway or craps-eleven bets.

The central area of the layout is under the complete domain of the stickman. Although he physically handles the placing and removing of bets in this area, players generally make their bets and receive their payoffs from the dealer.

The proposition bets are the worst bets you can make at craps, and you should never make them. The house advantage rages as high as 16.67% on some of these wagers. However, these bets are listed and their odds are explained so that you will be completely familiar with all the wagers possible at craps.

ANY SEVEN

With this bet, the **any seven**, you are betting that the following roll of the dice will be a 7. It is paid off by the house at 4 to 1 (5 for 1), which makes among the worst bets you can make.

Out of 36 possible combinations, there are six ways to throw a 7, making the odds one in six of throwing a 7 on any one roll (5 to

1). Since players are paid off at only 4 to 1, the house maintains an exorbitant edge of 16.67% over players.

Don't make this bet even in your wildest dreams.

ANY CRAPS

The **any craps** bet, located at the bottom of the center layout and along its sides, is a bet that the following roll will be a craps—a 2, 3 or 12.

There are four ways to roll a winner. The 2 and 12 account for one way each, and there are two ways to roll a three. The other 32 combinations are losers, making the correct odds 8 to 1. The house only pays 7 to 1, an 11.1% house edge.

2 OR 12

The **2 or 12** is a bet that the next roll of the dice will be a 2, or a 12 if you bet that number, and is paid off by the house at 30 to 1.

Of the 36 possible combinations of the dice, there is only one way of rolling a 2 or a 12, making the correct odds 35 to 1 against rolling either number. With only a 30 to 1 payoff, the house enjoys a hefty 13.69% advantage.

Sometimes a casino may only pay off at 30 for 1 (29 to 1), giving the house an edge of 16.67%. This should make no difference to you since you won't go near that bet in either case.

3 OR 11

The **3 or 11** is a wager that the following roll will be a 3 or an 11, whichever number you place your money on, with a house payoff of 15 to 1.

Since there are only two ways to roll either number, out of a possible 36 combinations, the correct odds are 17 to 1 (34 losers, 2 winners). The house edge is 11.1%. Where the payoff is 15 for 1 (14 to 1), this edge jumps to a whopping 16.67%.

HORN BET

It takes four chips, or multiples thereof, to make a **horn bet**. The horn bet is a four-way bet that the next roll will be a 2, 3, 11 or 12—in effect combining four poor bets together. The house pays off the winning number at the normal payoffs (15 to 1 for the 3 or 11, and 30 to 1 for the 2 or 12), and deducts the other three losing chips from the payoff.

This sucker bet combines four losing wagers for a combined house edge of 11.1%, or 16.67% with the poorer payoffs discussed earlier. The bottom line: Never make this bet.

HORN HIGH BET

The **horn high bet** is a five-chip wager that the next roll of the dice will hit one of the horn numbers—2, 3, 11, or 12. The "extra" fifth chip in the wager is assigned by the player to the number he chooses, in effect, making that part of the horn a two unit wager.

This bet is indicated by handing the dealer five chips, and saying, for example, "horn high 12," or "horn high 3." Winning wagers are paid as in a regular horn wager except the "high horn" wager which will collect double.

HOP BET

This one-roll wager, the **hop bet**, which does not appear on the layout, is generally made on a combination of the dice not otherwise offered on the one-roll bets, such as 2-3. If the bet is a pair such as 5-5, a player will get the same payoff as the casino gives on the 2 or 12 bet (30 to 1, or 29 to 1). If the bet is a non-pair such as 4-5, which has two ways to win (4-5 and 5-4), the payoff will be the same as for the 3 or 11 bet (15 to 1, or 14 to 1).

To make a hop bet, give your bet to the dealer or stickman, and call out "Hop 54," for example, if the 5-4 is the hop bet you wish to make.

With the more generous payoff, hop bets give the casino an edge of 13.39%; otherwise the edge is 16.67%. In either case, consider the bet a donation to the casino.

CRAPS-ELEVEN (C-E)

Stickmen constantly exhort players to make the horrendous **craps-eleven** bet, which is an appeal to bet the Any Craps and 11 bet simultaneously—the circles with the "C" and "E" on the layout. Don't go near either bet by itself, let alone both together.

Save your money for the show.

HARDWAYS

When the numbers 4, 6, 8 or 10 are rolled as doubles, the roll is said to be thrown **hardways** or **hard**. A throw of 2-2 is often called "4, the hardway," or "hard 4;" and similarly with 3-3 for hard 6, 4-4 for hard 8, and 5-5 for hard 10.

Rolling the 4, 6, 8 and 10 in other combinations is called **easy**; for example, 6-4 is "10, the easy way."

Betting hardways is betting that the particular number you choose comes up hard before it comes up easy, or before a 7 is thrown.

Let's look at the odds involved in this bet.

HARD 4 AND HARD 10

There is only one way to throw a hard 4 (2-2) or hard 10 (5-5), and eight ways to lose—six ways to roll a seven, and two ways to throw a 4 or 10 the easy way (1-3, 3-1, 6-4 and 4-6).

The correct odds should be 8 to 1, but the house only pays 7 to 1 for an advantage of 11.1%. As with the other center bets, this bet is greatly disadvantageous to players and should never be made.

HARD 6 AND HARD 8

There are a total of ten losing combinations—the six ways to roll a 7, and four ways to roll a 6 or an 8 the easy way. (There are a total of five ways to throw the 6 or 8; subtracting the hardway leaves four other combinations). There is only one way to throw the 6 or 8 the hardway.

The correct odds of this hardway bet is 10 to 1, but the house only pays 9 to 1, giving it a commanding edge of 9.09% over players. Skip this bet.

BETS PLAY AS THEY LAY

When you hand the dealer your chips to make a center bet, it is important that you watch and make sure that he gets your wager in the proper area, for the casino rule is that bets "play as they lay." Misunderstandings do occur, but it is ultimately your responsibility to make sure your wager is in its desired place.

HOUSE EDGE: THE BETS		
BET	**PAYOUT**	**HOUSE EDGE**
Pass Line	1 to 1	1.41%
Don't Pass Line	1 to 1	1.40%
Come Bet	1 to 1	1.41%
Don't Come Bet	1 to 1	1.40%
Pass Line (1x odds)	1 to 1	0.85%
Pass Line (2x odds)	1 to 1	0.61%
Don't Pass Line (1x odds)	1 to 1	0.68%
Don't Pass Line (2x odds)	1 to 1	0.46%
Field: 2 or 12 (pays 2x)	2 to 1	5.56%
Field: 2 or 12 (pays 3x)	3 to 1	2.78%
Any 7	5 to 1	16.67%
Any craps (2, 3, or 12)	7 to 1	11.11%
Any 2 or 12	30 to 1	13.89%
Any 3 or 11	15 to 1	11.11%
Any 3 or 11	15 for 1	16.67%
Horn Bet (2, 3, 11, 12)	2/12: 30 to 1 3/11: 15 to 1	12.50%
Horn Bet (2, 3, 11, 12)	2/12: 30 for 1 3/11: 15 for 1	16.67%
Big 6 or Big 8	1 to 1	9.09%
Hardways 6 or 8	9 to 1	9.09%
Hardways 4 or 10	7 to 1	11.11%
Place 4	9 to 5	6.67%
Place 5	7 to 5	4.00%
Place 6	7 to 6	1.52%
Place 8	7 to 6	1.52%
Place 9	7 to 5	4.00%
Place 10	9 to 5	6.67%
Lay 4 (5% vig)	1 to 2	2.44%
Lay 5 (5% vig)	2 to 3	3.23%
Lay 6 (5% vig)	5 to 6	4.00%
Lay 8(5% vig)	5 to 6	4.00%
Lay 9 (5% vig)	2 to 3	3.23%
Lay 10 (5% vig)	1 to 2	2.44%

WINNING STRATEGIES

The underlying principle of all our winning strategies is to make only the best bets available, those with the lowest odds, to have the best chances of winning. When you use the strategies in this book, the overall house edge will be only 0.8% in a single odds game and 0.6% in a double odds game. As players, we will never make any bet that gives the house an advantage greater than 1.52%. We will place the majority of our money on bets where the house has no advantage whatsoever!

We'll play aggressively when winning, so that our winning sessions will be big. But when the dice go against us, we'll reduce our bets, or even stop betting altogether. This will maximize our profits and minimize our losses, a smart money management technique that can put money in our pockets. And we'll follow the guidelines in the money management chapter, so that once we're winning big, we'll leave big winners.

This winning strategies chapter is divided into two main sections, one for right bettors, and one for wrong bettors. Remember that betting right or wrong are equally valid approaches to winning, with equivalent odds. Choosing either method is merely a matter of personal style.

Within each approach, right and wrong betting, you will find the best strategies for the single and double odds game, and also the best methods for conservative and aggressive bettors to follow.

The **Basic-Conservative Methods** presented are formulated for cautious bettors who want to get the best odds possible, but not risk substantial sums. The **Aggressive Methods** are more suited to heavier bettors who are willing to risk more to win more.

The two methods, Basic-Conservative and Aggressive, are equally effective. Choosing one or the other depends solely on your bankroll considerations and financial temperament.

WINNING STRATEGIES: BETTING WITH THE DICE

This section explains how the right bettor, using sound principles of play, can lower the house edge to the lowest possible figure, 0.8%

in a single odds game and 0.6% in a double odds one. Using these methods, the right bettor makes the majority of his wagers the free-odds bets, wagers where the house not only has no advantage, but also pays winners more than they have wagered.

As right bettors, we'll use only the best bets in our basic strategies—the pass line, come and free-odds wagers, bets that give us the best chances of winning. Built into these strategies are methods to turn winning sessions into big winning sessions without risking big losses.

BASIC-CONSERVATIVE METHOD—RIGHT BETTORS/SINGLE ODDS STRATEGY

Make your standard bet in increments of three units so that you can take advantage of the special free-odds allowances when the points are 6 or 8, whereupon you can back your pass line or come bet by five units. Or if the points are 5 or 9, you can bet extra units if your original bet is uneven, such as $15, where $20 would be permitted as a free-odds wager.

This strategy allows maximum use of the free-odds bets, wagers on which the house has no edge, and brings the overall house advantage down to the bare minimum possible in a single odds game.

These are the three guidelines of the Basic-Conservative Strategy:

1. Make three-unit pass line and come bets until you have two points established, and back both those bets with the maximum single odds allowed.
2. Every time a point repeats, whether as a come or pass line point, make another three-unit pass line or come bet so that you continue to have two points working for you. If a 2, 3, 11 or 12 declares a winner or a loser on the new pass line or come bet, follow with another bet until you get that second point established and take the maximum single odds allowed on that point.
3. If the shooter sevens-out, clearing the board of all bets, begin the progression again with a new pass line bet.

AGGRESSIVE METHOD— RIGHT BETTORS/SINGLE ODDS STRATEGY

Rather than playing only two points as in the Basic-Conservative method, this strategy attempts to establish three points immediately. Otherwise, the strategies are equivalent.

1. Begin by making a pass line bet. After a point is established, make a free-odds bet behind the pass line and a three-unit come bet. When the come point is established, back that point with the maximum single odds allowed, and place yet another come bet backing it with free-odds. Once three points have been established, it's time to stop betting.
2. Every time a point repeats and is paid off, make another bet, so that at all times during a shoot, you will have three points working. If the come point is made, place another come bet. If it's the pass line, make another pass line bet. As always, back all your bets with the maximum single odds allowed.
3. If the shooter sevens-out, start the sequence all over again.

With three points covered, you can make a lot of money using this Aggressive method when the shooter starts rolling numbers, especially when you also use optimal strategy for maximizing your winning sessions.

MAXIMIZING PROFITS—METHODS FOR RIGHT BETTORS

The way to win big at craps is to play winning streaks aggressively so that when points start repeating, your profits will mount quickly. The beauty of these strategies is that, while you give yourself the opportunity to make huge profits, you never risk taking a devastating loss, since you only increase your bets when winning.

Don't start playing more aggressively until you're ahead by at least 20 units as a Basic-Conservative players, and 25 units as an Aggressive player. For $1 bettors making standard bets of $3, that means $20 and $25 respectively; for $5 bettors making standard bets of $15, that means $100 and $125; and for $25-chip players betting $75 a play, it means $500 and $625 respectively.

Theoretically, you could increase your bet size before this time, but that would leave your bankroll vulnerable to bad runs of luck. The concept is to play aggressively on the casino's money, not yours. Wait until all your points are established and working before increasing your bets.

Let's say that you're betting $15 as your basic three-unit bet ($5 units), and have already established the pass line point with single odds on the 8, and two come points with single odds on the 5 and 10. You now have three points working for you, the basic plan for the Aggressive Method, and find that you're already ahead 27 units.

Your strategy should now work as follows. Every time a point repeats and you get paid off, instead of re-establishing an additional come or pass line point at the basic three-unit bet, increase that bet by three units to six units, and back the new bet with maximum single odds. Thus, on a six-unit bet, points 4 and 10 can be backed by six units, 5 and 9 by six units, and 6 and 8 by ten units.

(If the bet is uneven on points 5 and 9, more than six units can be bet as a free-odds wager; however, if the bet is even and can be paid at 3 to 2, the special allowance wouldn't apply.)

Let's say that points 8 and 10 have repeated and you've made six-unit bets on the new pass and come wagers. The new points thrown are 9 on the come bet and 10 on the pass line. As it stands, you have six-unit bets on the 9 and 10—both bets backed by the full odds—and three units on the come point of 5. If the 10, your pass line point, repeats, your new bet would be six units, since your other point, the 5, still has only a three-unit bet on it. Do not increase bets to higher levels (in this example, above 6 units) until all the points have been brought up to the same bet size.

If the streak continues and all the basic pass and come bets have been brought up to six unit bets, begin to reestablish won points by making pass and come bets in units of nine and, of course, backing all these bets with the maximum single odds allowed. Increase bets in this fashion for as long as the streak continues.

This steady progressive increase of bets allows you to maximize the profits resulting from a hot roll while protecting you against a sudden seven-out making serious inroads into your winnings.

MAXIMIZING PROFITS: THE TEXAS ROLL METHOD

As an alternate and more aggressive way of increasing won bets, you could increase each won bet by three units regardless of how many units you've already placed on the other points. Thus, a bet that repeated twice in a row could have a nine-unit bet on it with the other points covered by only three units each.

Your bet increases should be in units of three so that you can continue to take advantage of the special three-unit single odds allowances.

Do not begin new progressions (once a shooter sevens-out) at a level higher than three units. This is very important. A bettor that continues to bet in amounts higher than his initial standard three-unit wager is susceptible to a short losing streak wiping out his gains in a few bad shoots. Therefore, only bet more aggressively during a hot streak, and never try to anticipate that one will occur.

Once you've had your one great shoot, never give the casino a chance to get your winnings back. Simply return to your basic three-unit bet. If things go poorly, call it quits soon thereafter, leaving you with a huge win. If the shooter gets hot again, you can start increasing your bets and winnings, always ready for the next big kill.

This is smart money management—the key to success for winners.

DOUBLE ODDS STRATEGIES

When you have a choice, you should always choose a double odds game over a single odds game, because the additional allowance of the free-odds bet drops the overall house edge from 0.8% to 0.6% using these methods.

The playing strategies you will pursue in the double odds game are identical to the single odds game except that you bet in units of two instead of three, as recommended in the single odds game, to take advantage of the special five-unit free-odds allowance when the point is 6 or 8. Basic-Conservative bettors should establish two points with maximum double odds on each, while Aggressive bettors will want to cover three points.

Follow the procedures for the single odds methods, substituting only the two-unit basic bet for the three-unit bets, and making double odds bets instead of single odds.

MAXIMIZING PROFITS—DOUBLE ODDS GAME

Again, your strategy will follow that of the single odds game except that you increase your bets by two units instead of three. Basic-Conservative bettors should not begin increasing bets until they have accumulated 20 units in profits, while Aggressive bettors will need to accumulate 25 units.

Remember to take advantage of the special allowances when the point is a 6 or 8. You can back a four-unit bet by 10 units in the double odds game, and a six-unit bet by 15 units.

When the shooter eventually sevens-out, ending your winning streak, you start the next progression again at two units, ready to capitalize on another hot roll if one develops.

WINNING STRATEGIES: BETTING AGAINST THE DICE

Though the odds of winning are equivalent to the right betting strategies, 0.8% in a single odds game and 0.6% in a double odds game, very few craps players bet against the dice. Many bettors feel uncomfortable about having to lay odds, putting more money on their free-odds bet than they will win if they win their bet. However, whether you're betting right or wrong, the free-odds wagers give the house no edge.

Players that bet wrong don't mind giving the odds, since the roll of a 7, a winner for wrong bettors, occurs more often than any point number, and they will have frequent winners. In addition, if a point is repeated, a losing roll for wrong bettors, only one bet will be lost. The other points covered by the wrong bettor are still in play.

On the other side of the dice, the right bettors fear the 7, because all their established points and free-odds bets are lost when it is thrown.

As a wrong bettor, apply the same principles of play as right bettors. Make only the best bets available, those that reduce the house edge to the lowest possible figure—the don't pass, the don't come, and free-odds bets.

BASIC-CONSERVATIVE METHOD— WRONG BETTORS/SINGLE ODDS STRATEGY

Make your standard bet in even increments of two units. Bets such as $15 or $25 are difficult to work with when the point is a 5 or 9 where 2 to 3 odds should be laid. Betting in other unit sizes is equally valid, but you will find it easiest to work in multiples of $10.

These are the guidelines of the Basic-Conservative Strategy:

1. Make two-unit don't pass and don't come bets until you have established bets against two points, and back both those bets with maximum free-odds.
2. If a point repeats, a loser for you, make another don't come or don't pass bet so that you can continue to have bets working against two points. If a 2, 3, 11 or 12 determines a winner or loser on a new don't pass or don't come bet, follow with another bet until you get a second point established—and then play the maximum single odds against that point.
3. If a second point repeats, stop establishing don't pass and don't come bets. This is an important safeguard that protects you against bad losing streaks.
4. If a 7 is thrown, a winner on all your bets, begin the progression again with your two-unit don't pass bet.
5. Follow the recommendations in the Maximizing Profits section for advice on how to increase your winnings when the dice are going your way.

As cautious bettors, limit yourself to covering only two points and strictly follow the safeguard recommended in step three.

AGGRESSIVE METHOD— WRONG BETTORS/SINGLE ODDS STRATEGY

The Aggressive strategy follows the same guidelines as the Basic-Conservative method except that you cover three points during a shoot instead of two, and you stop making additional don't pass and don't come bets if three points repeat (instead of two as advised in the Basic-Conservative method). Use the same bets—the don't pass, don't come and free-odds bets—and enjoy the same low 0.8% house edge in a single odds game.

Begin by making a don't pass bet, and backing that with the maximum single odds once the point is established. Then make two successive don't come wagers, or as many as necessary, until two points are established, and back those bets with maximum single odds as well. Once you have bets established against three points, stop betting.

If a 2, 3, 11 or 12 is rolled before all the points are established, make another don't come bet until that third point is set. Strictly adhere to your safeguard. That is, if a third point repeats, stop making additional bets during the cycle; just ride out the unlucky streak. Never bet into a losing streak.

When the shooter sevens-out, a winner on all your bets, start the cycle again, establishing three points with the maximum single odds.

MAXIMIZING PROFITS—METHODS FOR WRONG BETTORS

The safest and most effective way of winning big at craps is to increase bets only during cold runs (hot run for you), when the dice are going your way. The concept is to parlay average winnings into big winnings. You do this by increasing your bets only during a winning cycle when the dice have already won for you, never after a losing bet. Players and systems that attempt to regain lost money by increasing their bets court disaster. This type of desperate betting leaves you vulnerable to huge losses, and that's just plain bad money management.

Do not start playing more aggressively until you're ahead by at least 20 units as a Basic-Conservative player, and 25 units as an Aggressive player. This gives you the opportunity to make big profits when the dice are with you, while protecting you against getting hurt by a bad run. In fact, if you strictly follow the basic wrong betting safeguards and the stop-loss advice in the money management section, you'll never take a crippling loss—but you'll always be ready to win big.

Unlike the right bettor strategies where bets are increased during a cycle, wait until the shooter sevens-out, a winner for you, before you begin to play more aggressively. Once you're ahead by the recommended amounts, and the previous betting cycle was a winning one, increase your basic bet by two units.

If all your points were covered by two-unit basic bets, you now cover the points by four-unit basic bets. And if you emerge as a winner again after the shooter sevens-out, continue to bet into the winning streak by upping your bet by another two units to six units. Continue to increase your bets by two units as long as the streak continues, all the time backing the bets with the maximum single odds allowed.

If the basic bet is $10 (two units of $5), the next basic bet will be $20, and then $30 and so on.

Anytime a sequence has been a losing one, begin the following shoot at the original two-unit basic bet. In the example above, you would begin again at $10. Smart money management dictates that you only increase bets during a winning streak.

All the time during a shoot, follow the safeguards outlined in these strategies. In you're a Basic-Conservative bettor, stop establishing points if two points repeat. If you're an Aggressive bettor, hold your bets if a third point repeats.

DOUBLE ODDS STRATEGY—WRONG BETTORS

If you're a wrong bettor, you should play a double odds game over a single odds game whenever possible, because it lowers the overall house edge from 0.8% to 0.6%. And you always want to play with the best odds you can get—the lower the house edge, the greater your chances of winning.

By nature, the double odds strategies are more aggressive than the single odds games, and are more in tune for a player whose temperament demands hotter action. For example, if the point is a 4 and $10 is bet on the don't pass, the single odds bettor would wager $20 (laying 1 to 2) as a free odds bet, while the double odds bettor covers that some point with a $40 wager (also laying 1 to 2). Double odds bettors lay more to win more, and therefore need a larger bankroll than single odds bettors. Therefore, if you're a double odds bettor, you must feel comfortable with the larger bet levels to play this strategy.

These double odds strategies are identical to the single odds methods, except that you're playing double odds instead of single odds. You begin by making a two-unit don't pass bet, and backing that bet by double odds once a point is established. If $10 is the line bet, $40 will be the double odds bet if the point is 4 or 10 (laying 1 to 2), $30 if the point is 5 or 9 (laying 2 to 3), and $24 if the point is 6 or 8 (laying 5 to 6).

Basic-Conservative bettors will follow with a don't come bet and lay double odds on both points, while Aggressive bettors will make two more don't come bets backed by the full double odds, or as many don't pass or don't come bets as needed until three points are covered and then backed by free odds bets.

Like the single odds strategies, Basic-Conservative players attempt to keep two points working at all times while Aggressive players strive for three working points. When points repeat, new don't pass or don't come bets are made to reestablish another. However, if you're a Basic-Conservative player and a second point repeats, or if you're an Aggressive player and a third point repeats, curtail all new betting until the shooter sevens-out, a winner on your remaining bets.

You use this stop-loss as a safeguard to protect yourself against betting wiped out by one really bad shoot. However, if the dice start blowing profits in your direction, be ready to capitalize on the situation.

Start the next come-out roll fresh, with a two-unit don't pass wager, always ready for a streak that will mint chips for your bankroll.

DOUBLE ODDS STRATEGY—MAXIMIZING GAINS

I recommend that you increase your wagers cautiously when you're playing a double odds game. The mushrooming effect of double odds can rapidly increase your outlay of money on the table, so you want to be conservative in your increases. For example, a $10 bettor may want to increase bets by only $5, since each $5 increase could call for an additional double odds bet of $20 if the point were a 4 or 10. Use your own discretion for bet increases, possibly one unit per winning cycle.

Use the same principles outlined in the single odds Basic-Conservative strategy for increasing bets. Increase your wagers only during a winning streak and not before you're up at least 20 units. If you use the Aggressive strategy, leave yourself a cushion of 25 units before increasing your wagers.

BANKROLLING

The amount of money necessary to withstand the normal fluctuations common to craps varies according to the type of strategy you play (right or wrong betting), the aggressiveness of your approach (Basic-Conservative or Aggressive), and how long you expect to play.

Let's discuss the single session bankroll first for the various strategies, and then talk about the type of bankroll you will need for longer sessions at the craps table.

SINGLE SESSION BANKROLL • RIGHT BETTORS		
Approach (Points Covered)	**Units Needed for a Single Cycle**	**Table Bankroll Needed**
Single & Double Odds Game		
Basic-Cons. (2 Points)	14	100
Aggressive (3 points)	21	150

BANKROLL NEEDED: BASIC-CONSERVATIVE STRATEGY

In the single odds game, Basic-Conservative bettors will cover two points through pass and come bets and back both points with the maximum single odds allowed. Since the standard line bet will be three units, and the single odds bet backing the pass and come wagers will be between three and five units, you can expect each point to require a total of six to eight units to be fully covered, or about 14 units to fully cover each cycle of two points.

In the double odds game, a standard line bet of two units will be backed with the maximum double odds allowed, or about four to five units, for a total of six to seven units per point. Fully covering a cycle of two points will require about 14 units, the same as the single odds game.

BANKROLL NEEDED: AGGRESSIVE STRATEGY

Aggressive strategy bettors will need roughly 21 units to fully cover their three points in a single or double odds game. To play safe and give yourself sufficient funds, you should have a big enough table stake for about seven betting cycles. The "Table Bankroll Needed" columns in the above charts were computed by multiplying the units needed for a single cycle by seven, and then adding a few units as extra padding.

SINGLE SESSION BANKROLL • WRONG BETTORS		
Approach (Points Covered)	**Units Needed for a Single Cycle**	**Table Bankroll Needed**
Single Odds Game		
Basic-Cons. (2 Points)	10	75
Aggressive (3 points)	15	115
Double Odds Game		
Basic-Cons. (2 Points)	16	125
Aggressive (3 points)	24	175

BANKROLL NEEDED: SINGLE ODDS GAME—WRONG BETTORS

The standard bet size for both Basic-Conservative players and Aggressive players is two units in our strategies.* Our free odds wager in the single odds game will be two units on the 6 or 8 (laying 5 to 6); three units on the 5 or 9 (laying 2 to 3); and four units on the 4 or 10 (laying 1 to 2), for an average of about three units per single odds bet.

* If you bet in unit sizes other than two units, you can figure the table stake needed by estimating the number of units needed for one full cycle of play and multiplying that number by seven.

In addition to the two-unit don't pass or don't come bets, this adds up to five units per point.

Basic-Conservative bettors will need 10 units, two points times five units, for each betting cycle. Aggressive bettors will need 15 units for a round, three points each covered by approximately five betting units.

BANKROLL NEEDED: DOUBLE ODDS GAME—WRONG BETTORS

The standard betting size for either strategy is two units, and you'll back each point by about six units, for a total of about eight units that you'll need to fully cover each point in a double odds game. Basic-Conservative bettors playing two points will need 16 units for a betting cycle, while Aggressive players, who cover three points, will need about 24 betting units.

In a double odds game, a two-unit bet on the 4 or 10 gets backed by eight units; on the 5 and 9, it gets backed by six units; and on the 6 or 8, it gets backed by a little under five units, for an average of six units per double odds bet.

TOTAL BANKROLL

The longer you plan on playing craps in a single session, the larger your bankroll must be to cover the inevitable fluctuations. The following bankroll requirements have been formulated to give you enough capital to survive any reasonable losing streak and be able to bounce back on top.

TOTAL BANKROLL REQUIREMENTS
RIGHT BETTORS

Approach (Points Covered)	Single Session Stake	One Day Bankroll	Weekend Bankroll
Single and Double Odds Games			
Basic-Cons. (2 pts)	100	300	500
Aggressive (3 pts)	150	450	750

TOTAL BANKROLL REQUIREMENTS WRONG BETTORS			
Approach (Points Covered)	**Single Session Stake**	**One Day Bankroll**	**Weekend Bankroll**
Single Odds Games			
Basic-Cons. (2 pts)	75	225	375
Aggressive (3 pts)	115	350	675
Double Odds Games			
Basic-Cons. (2 pts)	125	375	625
Aggressive (3 pts)	175	525	875

The bankroll you need for a full day's session should be about three times that of a single session; and a weekend's bankroll should be about five times that of a single session. Never dip into your pockets past these levels—remember, you never want to get badly beaten at the tables. These bankroll levels give you sufficient room to take some losses and still have enough of a bankroll to play confidently, while waiting for a hot streak to turn the tables on the casino and make a profit.

This does not mean that you must have all your money on the table when you're playing, but that the money should be readily available in case you need it.

Never use your entire table stake in any one session; restrict your losses if luck goes against you. This way, you'll never get hurt by an unlucky session.

If you arrive at the casino with a definite amount of money to gamble with, and want to figure out how much your unit size bet should be, simply take your gambling stake and divide it by the amount of units you need to have for the particular strategy you want to play.

If you bring $1,000 with you and were to spend a day using the right bettors Basic-Conservative strategy in a single odds game, you would divide $1,000 by 300 units, the number in the Total Bankroll column, for a basic unit bet of roughly $3 ($3.33). Since right bettors wager in units of three in our single odds strategy, the standard pass or come bet would be about $10.

If you plan to play the Aggressive strategy, you would divide $1,000 by 450 units, for a basic unit bet of $2 ($2.22). Three-unit bets would come out to the rough equivalent of betting $5 or $6 on the pass line or come bet. A good choice in the single odds game would be $5 since you could use the special odds bet allowance when the point is a 6 or an 8.

Similarly, if you like to bet against the dice and have brought $1,500 for a single day of gambling, bet in $10 units if you're playing the Aggressive strategy in a single odds game. You simply divide $1,500 by 350 for the rough equivalent of $5 ($4.29). Since your strategies call for bets in increments of two units, the standard don't come or don't pass wager would be $10.

I strongly advise you not to overdo things at the craps tables. Although these strategies reduce the house edge to the lowest possible amount and give you the best chances of winning, one bad run can pound your bankroll down. Of course, one good run will makes lots of money, but in gambling, you must always protect against bad-case scenarios. We'll look at that next.

MINIMIZING LOSSES

Here are three simple guidelines that will save you a lot of money. You'll notice that the stop-loss limits are less than the recommended single session table stakes.

1. **Set Stop-Loss Limits**
   Right bettors: Limit your table losses to 70 units if you're a Basic-Conservative bettor, and 100 units if you're an Aggressive bettor. If you're betting $5 chips ($15 standard line bet), never lose more than $350 and $500 respectively in any one session. If you're betting $1 chips ($3 standard line bet), don't lose more than $70 if you're a Basic-Conservative bettor, and $100 if you're an Aggressive bettor.
   Wrong bettors: Wrong bettors should limit their table losses to the same levels as right bettors in single and double odds games.

If you never dig into your pocket for more money, you can never be a big loser. Take a break and try again later. Never put yourself into a position where losing too much in one session totally demoralizes you.

2. **Bet Within Your Means**
   Never increase your bet range beyond your bankroll capabilities. Always bet within your means.
3. **Do Not Increase Your Bets When Losing**
   Never increase your bet size in an attempt to catch up and break even. Betting more money will not change the odds of the game, nor will it change your luck. What it will do is increase your chances of taking a terrible beating to frightening heights. Don't get into a position where losing so much in one session destroys any reasonable chance of coming out even. You can't win all the time. Rest for a while; you can get them later.

PARTING THOUGHTS

Once you're a winner, the most important thing in craps is to walk away with money in your pocket. Craps is a very fast game, perfect for action players who love to go for monster wins. Just make sure to give yourself the best chances of hitting it big by making the smart bets we've discussed in this chapter. Also, study the money management section carefully so that you can maximize the complete potential of your winning strategies..

6 FOUR CARD POKER

FIVE KEYS TO FOUR CARD POKER
1. Never bet two times your ante bet; bet either 1x or 3x.
2. Learn the hand rankings for four card poker before you sit down to play; they differ from regular poker.
3. Realize that the odds are much better on the ante/play wager than the aces up wager.
4. You fold deuces, bet 1x on threes to nines, and 3x on tens or better.
5. Always play optimal strategy and adhere to good money management principles.

INTRODUCTION

Four card poker is another relatively new casino offering that's gained a foothold in the casinos because of its ease of play and the option to increase your bet when you have a good hand. Like its cousin, three card poker, four card poker uses poker-based rankings for its hands (though the rankings are different) and combines two games in one—or, to look at it another way, you have two distinct bets you can make, each one independent of the other.

There is the basic *ante bet* where you compete against the dealer for the highest hand. Then there's the *aces up bet*, which is similar to the pair plus bet in three card poker: You're betting only you'll be dealt a hand of a certain strength, in this case, a pair of aces or better.

But don't let the name fool you—four card poker is not a poker variation. Licensed by Shuffle Master and using their automatic shuffling machine, it is simply a game that borrows a few elements from poker, like the hand rankings and the use of its name. But the similarity to real poker ends there. For one, you're playing against the house, not the other players at the table—there is no competition to have a higher hand than your fellow players, no bluffing, and no complex strategies for outwitting opponents and getting their money. Also, unlike real poker, you only play four of the five cards you're dealt instead of getting to play all five cards—which is why they named the game *four card poker.*

Further, the hand rankings are different from standard poker games. In fact, they're significantly different because of the four-card hands. Let's take a look at them now.

HAND RANKINGS

The hand rankings are based on the mathematical frequency of four-card hands being dealt and, as you can see, are markedly different from the standard high poker rankings. Four-card straights and flushes come more frequently than three-of-a-kind hands, which is why three of a kind is ranked higher on the chart and is a more valuable hand to hold. Also note that, unlike poker, four of a kind beats a straight flush in four card poker.

In the unlikely event that you are dealt a royal flush, your four-card hand would only be an ace-high straight flush, which would lose if the dealer makes four of a kind! A-A-A-A is the best hand in four card poker.

In order from strongest to weakest, the best four card poker hands are:

FOUR CARD POKER: HAND RANKINGS	
Four of a Kind:	Four cards of the same rank, such as 9-9-9-9.
Straight Flush:	Four cards of the same suit in sequence, such as the 10-9-8-7, all diamonds.
Three of a Kind:	Three cards of the same rank, such as 5-5-5-4.
Flush:	Four cards of the same suit, such as K-7-6-2 all hearts.
Straight:	Four cards of mixed suits in sequence, such as J-10-9-8.
Two Pair:	Two cards of equal value and two other cards of equal value, such as 8-8-3-3.
One Pair:	One pair of equally ranked cards, such as J-J-9-2.
High Card:	None of the above hands, such as Q-7-3-2 in different suits.

BASICS OF FOUR CARD POKER

Four card poker is played with a standard 52-card deck on a blackjack-type table. You'll find the game nestled on the casino floor among other table games, such as Let it Ride, three card poker, blackjack, and Caribbean stud.

There are three betting circles in front of each player. They are marked: "Aces Up," "Ante," and "1x to 3x Ante." Note that "1x ante" means one times your ante bet, in other words, an equal amount, and "3x ante" means three times your ante bet. These are the three betting spots where you will place your bets.

Play begins with each player putting chips in the corresponding betting circles on either the **ante bet** or **aces up bet**. You can also make wagers, as many do, on both these bets, or just choose the wager that suits you best. You may bet as much as you like or as little on either bet, within the casino's minimum and maximum limits.

As in blackjack, your only opponent is the dealer. You don't have to worry about beating the other players and there are no qualifying hands for the dealer to make—your only goal is to make an equal or better four card poker hand than the dealer makes. If you do, your hand is a winner. If not, the dealer will collect your bets.

Each player is dealt five cards. The dealer, however, gets six cards, one of which he displays face up. The extra card that the dealer receives works to the house advantage in this game.

Let's look at how each of the two bets work.

THE BETS

ANTE BET

After seeing your cards and the dealer's face-up card, you have one important decision to make: You can either fold, or you can play. If you fold, you will lose your ante and/or aces up bet. If you decide to play, you make an additional bet, called the **play bet**, which you place in the "1x to 3x Ante" area.

The play bet must be at least equal to your original wager, though you can elect to make a bet that is up to three times the amount of that bet. For example, if you have a $25 bet in the ante circle and decide to play (not fold), you could place $25 more in the "1x to 3x Ante" betting spot. You could also bet as much as $75, which would be three times the ante bet. You may bet amounts in between; for example, you could make it $50, but as you'll see, the best strategy is to make either the minimum bet or the maximum—nothing in between. Let's say you make it $75 more. That makes it $100 total on the ante and play bets.

You then discard one card by putting it face down; you now have your final four-card hand. Each player, starting with the one closest to the dealer's left and continuing clockwise to the last player on his right, will do the same.

After all players have completed their actions, the dealer turns over his downcards, revealing his six cards. He selects the best four-card poker hand to play and discards the other two cards.

Position by position, the dealer then compares each player's hand to his, declaring winners and losers as he makes his way around the table.

If the dealer's hand is higher, players lose their ante and play bets. If a player's hand is equal to or better than the dealer's hand, he'll win 1 to 1 on the ante and additional play bet. Note that ties are based on four cards only—the fifth card is never used to break a tie.

So, following the example along, you would win $25 on the ante bet and $75 on the play bet for $100 total in winnings on this hand. Winning ante and play bets are paid at even money: For every $1 bet, you win $1. So, if you bet $100 and win, you will receive $200 back—your original $100 wager plus the $100 in winnings.

ANTE BET: BONUS PAYOUTS

If your hand is three of a kind or better, you will receive an **ante bet bonus payout**, even if the dealer's hand beats yours. This is in addition to whatever you might win with the ante and play bet. If you have three of a kind, the bonus amount is 2 to 1. For a straight flush, you'll win a bonus of 20 to 1. If you make four of a kind, you'll win a 25 to 1 bonus.

These are the standard bonus payouts and they will be posted in a prominent place at the table, typically imprinted on the layout itself.

ANTE BET: BONUS PAYOUTS	
Hand	**Payout**
Four of a Kind	25-1
Straight Flush	20-1
Three of a Kind	2-1

ACES UP BET

Like the pair plus bet in three card poker, the aces up bet is an entirely independent wager that is not tied in to the dealer's hand. You either win the aces up bet because you've been dealt a good enough hand, or you lose because your hand doesn't qualify for the minimum payout. In other words, even if the dealer has a better hand than yours and you lose your ante bet, you can still collect on your aces up bet.

The minimum winning hand needed to get a payout, as stated by the bet itself, is aces up. If you have a pair of aces or better, you will be paid for the aces up bet based on the payout schedule posted on the table. The pay schedule can vary from casino to casino, so if there is a variance among casinos, look to play where you get the best payouts on winning hands.

The optimal payout schedule is pictured below.

ACES UP PAY SCHEDULES	
HAND	PAYOUT
FOUR OF A KIND	50 to 1
STRAIGHT FLUSH	40 to 1
THREE OF A KIND	8 to 1
FLUSH	5 to 1
STRAIGHT	4 to 1
TWO PAIR	3 to 1
PAIR OF ACES	1 to 1
HOUSE EDGE	**3.9%**

WINNING STRATEGY

The basic strategy for whether to fold or play your hand on your initial ante bet can be summed up in three easy rules.

1. With a pair of twos or less (including all no-pair hands without straights or flushes), fold.
2. With threes through nines, make a bet equal to your ante bet.
3. With tens or better, bet three times the size of your ante.

The following chart displays this strategy for you.

FOUR CARD POKER BASIC STRATEGY		
HAND	ACTION	BET AMOUNT
PAIR OF TWOS OR LESS	Fold	None
THREES THROUGHS NINES	Play	Equal to Ante
TENS OR BETTER	Play	Three Times Ante

For example, if you had $10 bet and were dealt J-J-3-4-5 (discard the 3), you would play for $30. Similarly, if you had 7-7-7-A-K (discard the king), 4-5-6-7-10 (discard the 10), or four flush cards (discard the unsuited card), you would play for a 3x bet. If you had 4-4-Q-3-9 (discard the 3) or 8-8-4-J-5 (discard the 4), you would make a bet equal to your ante bet.

However, if your hand was weak, like 2-2-9-J-Q, 3-4-7-8-K or 4-K-A-10-7, you would simply fold your hand—you don't want to put more chips on the table with these cards.

Even though it is allowed, you never bet two times your ante bet.

Why?

Because when you have the advantage, you want to wager as much money as possible. That's why you go for the maximum three-unit bet. And when you don't have an advantage, you want to make the minimum bet possible, which is one unit.

If you decide to continue playing, bet either one time your ante bet or three times your ante bet.

PARTING THOUGHTS

In four card poker, you will be folding your hands almost half the time, because you'll be dealt a pair of twos or less. Obviously, you automatically lose your ante bet when you fold, but that is the best strategy to maximize your chances against the dealer. You won't win chips this way, but you're minimizing your chip exposure with weaker hands, the same philosophy blackjack players follow when dealt poor starting cards.

However, you will be dealt good cards too. Around 30% of the time, you will be dealt a hand of tens or better. With three times your ante bet placed on the play bet, you'll maximize your chips on these hands. These are very profitable situations for you.

The hands in between, threes through nines, where you will be making play bets equal (1x) to the size of your original ante bet, will help offset the losses on the overall ante bets on those hands.

So what is the final expectation you have at four card poker?

Following the simple strategy presented here, you will face a 1.6% house edge on the ante/play bet, which is pretty good for a casino table game. (Note the house edge on the ante bet by itself is 3.4%, but when the extra bets for the play wager are figured in, the total combined house edge is 1.6%.) On the aces up bet, given the paytable shown in this chapter, the house edge is 3.9%. This house edge will vary if different paytables than the one shown here are used.

My recommendation is to always get the best odds you can in any game you play, and that goes for four card poker as well. Given that the house edge on the ante/play bet is significantly better than on the aces up bet (1.6% compared to 3.9%), you are much better off concentrating your betting action on the ante/play portion of the game only.

The way I look at it, why give up all those extra percentages when you don't have to?

If you feel compelled to make the aces up bet, bet it in smaller amounts than the superior ante/play bet. You want the bulk of your money on the bets that give you better percentages. It not only makes the most sense, it gives you the best chance of being a winner at four-card poker.

7 BACCARAT

FIVE KEYS TO BACCARAT

1. Don't be intimidated by the tuxedos. The game has a "classy" veneer, but in reality, anyone can play.
2. For average players, the house edge at baccarat is one of the best in the casino whether betting Player or Banker.
3. Become familiar with the third card drawing rules. Baccarat will be more fun if you know the rules as well as the dealer knows them.
4. Do not make the Tie bet. This terrible bet gives the casino a big 14.1% edge.
5. You can use professional card-counting strategies to take advantage of altered decks at baccarat.

INTRODUCTION

This glamorous game is steeped in centuries of European tradition and, of course, was the main game of James Bond. While it is a mainstay and important game on the continent, baccarat has not quite caught on as much over in America. Bettors are attracted to baccarat's leisurely style of play and the very low casino odds the game offers the player. Serious players also like the "new" winning approach, card counting, that has proved so successful for blackjack players.

In its different varieties, baccarat can be found in casinos around the world. The version played in the United States originated in Cuba in the 1950s and is called **American** or **Nevada-style baccarat** though U.S. casinos simply refer to it as **baccarat**. Elsewhere in the world, this version is known as **punto banco**.

In Europe, **chemin de fer** and **baccarat banque** are quite popular, while **mini-baccarat**, a smaller version of *punto banco*, is found more and more in casinos in the U.S. and around the world.

Baccarat is a simple game to play, even for beginners, since the dealer or croupier directs all the action according to fixed rules. As you'll see, the game is quite easy to learn. So let's move right ahead and find out what this fun game is all about!

THE BASICS OF BACCARAT

THE LAYOUT

Baccarat is played on a specially constructed layout that allows players to choose either of the two betting spots, **Banker** or **Player**, to make their wagers. Regulation tables normally have betting spots for 12 to 14 players, with each player having a corresponding number spot, 1 through 12 or 14, to place his or her bets.

Bets on the Player position can be placed immediately in front of the player, in the numbered area. Bets on the Banker position go in the numbered slots labeled "**bank**."

The mini-baccarat layout has space for about seven players. As on the regulation table, each spot is numbered, and bets on either of the betting positions are placed in front of the bettor.

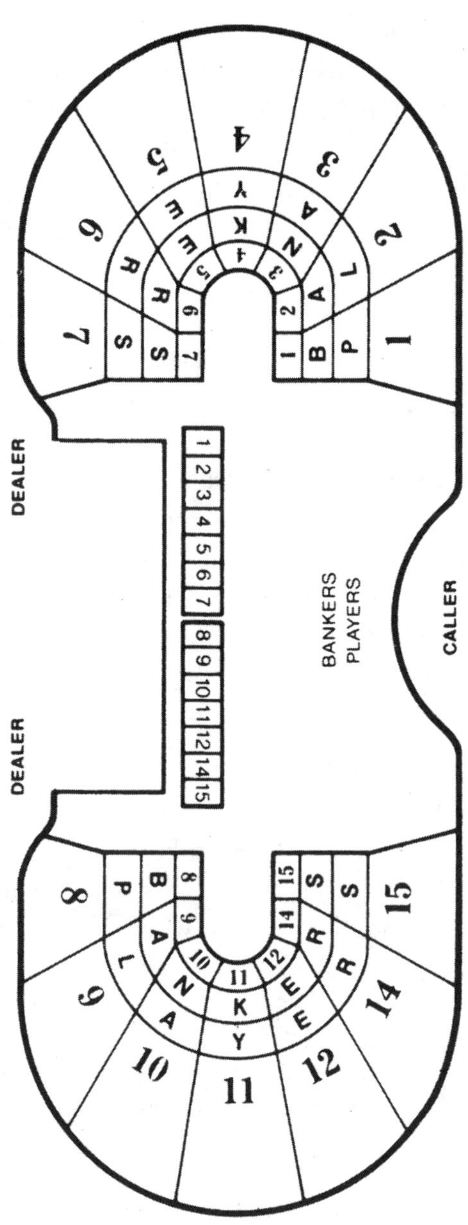

The Baccarat Layout

CASINO PERSONNEL

Three dealers usually work the baccarat game. One dealer is in charge of the game. His function is to direct the play, telling players what to do—when they need a draw and when the cards should be dealt. The other two dealers handle the betting, collect lost bets from the losers, make payoffs on won hands and keep track of the commissions owed.

CARD VALUES

Cards valued 2 to 9 are counted according to their face value, a 2 equals 2 points, an ace equals one point, and a 7 equals 7 points. The 10, jack, queen, and king, have a value of 0 points. They have no effect when adding up the points in a hand. Points are counted by adding up the value of the cards. However, hands totaling 10 or more points have the first digit dropped so that no hand contains a total of greater than 9 points. For example, two nines (18) is a hand of 8 points and a 7-5 (12) is a hand of 2 points. A hand of a 3 and a 4 would simply be valued at 7 points.

The suits have no value in baccarat.

THE OBJECT OF BACCARAT

Players have the choice of betting Banker or Player. The object of the game is for the position chosen to beat the other hand; the hand closer to the total of 9 is the winner. The worst score is zero, called *baccarat.* A tie is a standoff or push in which neither hand wins.

BETTING LIMITS

The casino limits on minimum and maximum bets are posted beside the table. As long as these guidelines are followed, a player may bet whatever he desires. Higher limits than those posted can often be arranged.

TABLE DE BANQUE CARD

Like roulette, serious baccarat players like to keep track of the winning progressions and can do so on cards provided by the casino called a **Table de Banque card**. These cards provide a convenient place to record wins by either the Banker or Player position, and keep the systems players on track for the game.

THE PLAY OF THE GAME

Baccarat is normally played with eight decks of cards dealt from a shoe, though a mini-baccarat table may use only six decks. Each deck is a standard 52-card deck containing thirteen cards, ace through king in each of the four suits. The suits, however, are irrelevant and have no bearing on the game.

There are two opposing sides, the Player and the Banker. No matter how many players are betting in a game, only two hands are dealt: one for the Banker position and one for the Player position, except in the baccarat banque version, where there are two Player positions instead of one.

You may choose either Banker or Player to bet on. You do so by placing your wager in either the Banker or Player's position that corresponds with your numbered seat. After the betting is done, each side is dealt two cards.

In Nevada style baccarat (punto banco), the players deal the cards. The shoe rotates counterclockwise around the table with each player having his or her turn at it. There is no advantage in dealing and a player may refuse the deal, in which case the shoe will be offered to the next player in turn.

The player acting as dealer slides the first card face down to the **caller**, the dealer who controls the pace and runs the game, and slips the second card, also face down, under the front corner of the shoe. Likewise, the third card will go face down to the caller, and the fourth one, like the second, goes face down under the shoe.

Each side now has two cards—the Player position represented by the caller's cards, and the Banker position, represented by the two cards under the shoe.

The caller then passes the two cards dealt to him to the bettor with the highest wager on the Player's position. After examining the cards, the bettor flips them back to the caller, who announces the total.

Then the dealer takes the Banker's cards from under the shoe and passes them along to the caller, who announces their total as well.

HAND VALUES

A dealt total of 8 or 9 points is called a **natural**, and no additional cards will be drawn. It is an automatic win unless the opposing hand has a higher natural (a 9 vs. an 8), or the hand is a tie. A natural of 8 points is called **le petit**; a total of nine is called **le grande**.

On all other totals, 0 through 7, the drawing of an additional card depends strictly on the established rules of play. In any case, there is never more than one card drawn to a hand. You do not need to be familiar with these rules because the caller will direct the action and request that a third card be drawn if the rules require it. Just follow the caller's instructions—it's as easy as that!

The Player's hand will be acted upon first, and then the Banker's. Despite the different variations of baccarat, the third card rules for draw are consistent for games around the world.

The two-card total of the Player's hand determines whether a third card should be drawn, and is regulated by the following rules:

PLAYER RULES	
TWO CARD TOTAL	**PLAYER'S ACTION**
0-5*	Draw a Card
6 OR 7	Stand
8 OR 9	Natural. Banker cannot draw.

*In chemin de fer and baccarat banque, the player has the option to stand or draw on a point total of 5 points only.

After a player has acted upon his hand, it is the Banker's turn to act. Whether the Banker position receives a card depends upon two variables. In some cases, it depends upon his two-card total; at other times, it depends upon the card that the Player position has drawn.

If the Banker hand is 0, 1 or 2, a card is drawn, while with hands of 7, 8 and 9, no cards are drawn. Whether Banker totals of 3, 4, 5 and 6 are drawn upon depends on which card the Player position has drawn.

Rules for drawing or standing can be broken up as follows.

Situation 1—Either the Player or the Banker has a natural 8 or 9. It is an automatic win for the hand with the natural. If both hands have naturals, the higher natural wins. (A natural 9 beats a natural 8.) If the naturals are equal, the hand is a tie.

Situation 2—If the Player has a 0-5, Player must draw another card; if a 6 or 7, the Player must stand.

Situation 3—If Player stands, the Banker hand follows the same rules as the Player—he must draw on totals of 0-5, and stand on 6 and 7.

Situation 4—If Player draws, Banker must draw or stand according to the value of the third card dealt as shown below in the Banker Rules chart. (Note that the banker always draws on totals of 0-2, unless, of course, the Player has a natural.)

BANKER RULES		
BANKER TOTAL	**BANK DRAWS WHEN GIVING PLAYER THIS CARD**	**BANK DOES NOT DRAW WHEN GIVING PLAYER THIS CARD**
0-2	0-9	
3	0-7, 9*	8
4	2-7	0-1, 8-9
5	4*, 5-7	0-3, 8-9
6	6-7	0-5, 8-9
7	Banker Always Stands	
8-9	A Natural; Player Can't Draw	

**In punto banco and mini-baccarat, the drawing of a third card is mandatory. In chemin de fer, it is an optional draw or stand

PAYOFFS AND ODDS

The winning hand in baccarat is paid at 1 to 1, even money, except in the case of the Banker's position, where a 5% commission is charged on a winning hand. Commission is charged because of the inherent edge that the Banker position has over the Player position.

During actual play, this commission is kept track of on the side by the use of chips, and won bets at the Banker position are paid off at even money. This avoids the cumbersome 5% change-giving on every hand. The commission is collected at the end of every shoe or before the player departs from the game.

With the commission, the average Banker edge over the bettor is only 1.17%, quite low by casino standards. The average house edge over the Player position is only slightly more, 1.36%. However, these percentages can vary as cards are removed during the course of play.

BACCARAT AROUND THE WORLD

Now let's look at the differences in the main versions of baccarat as played around the world.

AMERICAN OR NEVADA STYLE BACCARAT (PUNTO BANCO)

In this version of play, usually referred to simply as baccarat in U.S. casinos, the bettor has a choice of betting the Player (Punto) or the Banker (Banco). He plays against the house, which books all bets and pays winning hands. No third-card drawing options are available for either the Banker (Banco) or Player (Punto) position.

You may wager on a **tie bet**—a poor wager that pays off at 9 for 1 (8 to 1) and gives the casino an edge of 14.10%. (This bet is not offered in chemin de fer and baccarat banque.)

In this variation of baccarat, the only decisions a player makes are whether to bet Banker or Player, and how much to bet.

CHEMIN DE FER

The bettor who plays the Banker position deals the cards and books all bets. The other players oppose the Banker. The Player position has one third-card drawing option, and is controlled by the bettor with the highest bet placed. The Banker has two drawing options and plays the hand himself. (See Player and Banker Rules charts.) No tie bet is offered.

The casino acts only in a supervisory capacity and collects its fee as a percentage levy or as an hourly rate charged to the players.

The Banker is decided in one of three ways: by **auction**, where the highest bidder takes the Banker position and puts up his or her bid as the bank; by lot; or by acceptance, as the bank moves its way around the table.

A bettor plays Banker until he loses a hand or voluntarily gives it up. The next player, clockwise or counterclockwise according to the house rules, can play Banker and set his own limit on the bets he will book. A bettor may refuse the bank and pass it on to the next player.

The total amount of money bet against the Banker in a hand is limited by the amount of money in the bank. Any player who wishes to bet against the entire bank calls out "**banco**," thus nullifying the other bets.

BACCARAT BANQUE

The casino deals all cards and books all bets. There are two player (punto) positions on this two-sided layout. These spots are manned by bettors who oppose the banker (banco) position, which is always taken by the house. Bettors may wager on either Player position or both. The Player has one third-card drawing option.

The Banker is not bound by third-card drawing restrictions as in other variations, and may stand or draw one card. (Some casinos apply restrictions on the banker.)

BACCARAT A TOUT VA

Everything goes baccarat in the two-sided style of Baccarat banque for high rollers. That is, there is no maximum limit on bets.

MINI-BACCARAT

The same game as Nevada Style/Punto Banco except that it is played on a miniature blackjack-type table, and the casino deals the cards.

GAME COMPARISONS

The following chart shows the positions that a bettor may wager in the various versions of baccarat.

PLAYERS BETTING GUIDE		
GAME	PLAYER	BANKER
PUNTO BANCO	Yes	Yes
MINI-BACCARAT	Yes	Yes
CHEMIN DE FER	Yes	Only the bettor playing the Banker may bet Banker
BACCARAT BANQUE	Yes*	No

*Can wager on either or both of the player hands.

Yes–Indicates a player may bet the position. No–Indicates a player may not bet the position.

The odds vary slightly among the different versions of baccarat. The following chart outlines these variances.

HOUSE EDGE AT BACCARAT		
NEVADA STYLE/PUNTO BANCO		
WAGER	PAYOFF	HOUSE EDGE
PLAYER	1 to 1	1.36%
BANKER	1 to 1	1.17%
TIE	9 for 1	14.10%
CHEMIN DE FER		
WAGER	PAYOFF	HOUSE EDGE
PLAYER	1 to 1	1.23%
BANKER	1 to 1	1.067%
BACCARAT BANQUE		
WAGER	PAYOFF	HOUSE EDGE
AVERAGE EDGE		0.92%%

WINNING STRATEGIES

TRADITIONAL BETTING STRATEGIES

You don't need to make many decisions in baccarat because winning strategies have traditionally been confined to betting systems and money management techniques. These strategies are based on winning streaks and won/lost trends, going with the positions that are hot and adjusting bets according to whether the last hand won or lost.

Many interesting approaches are available for players who enjoy betting systems. Just keep in mind that these systems don't change the odds of the games they attempt to defeat.

WINNING WITH CARD COUNTING

Card counting techniques, which proved so effective at winning at blackjack, have attracted a lot of study as a winning method at baccarat. Here's how they work. In baccarat, just like blackjack, the removal of cards from play creates situations where the chances of receiving particular cards or combinations of cards change. The removal of certain types of cards favors the Player, while others favor the Banker.

A good count strategy shows you how to recognize situations that favor betting Banker, and other situations where Player is the better bet. By judiciously altering bets with the count, a card counter can improve his or her chances at the table and win money at baccarat.

The basic theory is that low cards favor the Player position and high cards favor the Banker. Certain cards have little effect and are considered neutral. Counters track the removal of these cards, betting the Player position when a higher ratio of low cards remains in the deck, and the Banker position when a higher ratio of high cards remains in the deck.

For players interested in winning with card counting methods, we recommend the excellent advanced strategy, the Baccarat Master Card Counter, described at the end of this book.

PARTING THOUGHTS

Baccarat combines the allure and glamour of European tradition with relatively low house odds for the average player—1.17% in the Banker's position and 1.36% in the Player's spot.

One advantage of baccarat, especially for high rollers, is that you cannot make mental mistakes that give the casino an added edge. Compare this to games such as blackjack, craps or poker, where poor decisions in the heat of the game can cause you to make costly errors, and you can understand one of the allures of baccarat.

Despite the exclusive look of the game, anyone can play baccarat. You don't need to bet mini-fortunes to play. Baccarat is a leisurely game, and in the version played in the American casinos, an easy one as well. There are no decisions to make except how much to bet and which position, Player or Banker, to back.

The low casino edge and the exciting winning possibilities available make baccarat a perfect place to wager in style, surrounded by elegant decor, playing this centuries-old game in the grand tradition.

8 ROULETTE

FIVE KEYS TO ROULETTE
1. Always play a single zero game rather than a double zero game when possible. The better house odds in a single zero game makes your chances of winning much greater.
2. Get familiar with all the bets and payouts so that you have the full arsenal at your command.
3. Have fun with betting systems, but realize that roulette is a negative expectation game and no betting system will overcome the house edge.
4. Except for the 5-number bet, all bets in American roulette offer equal odds.
5. Money management is essential. Be smart with your money.

INTRODUCTION

Roulette offers you a huge variety of bets, more than any other casino table game. The constant possibilities of winning and the different payoffs of the wagers, ranging from even-money payoffs to returns of 35 to 1, keeps the game exciting and suspenseful.

The game is set up for systems players: It is not unusual to find tables full of bettors armed with pencil and pad playing their favorite winning systems. Systems sometimes fail and sometimes win. We will discuss the virtues and shortcomings of systems so that you will be able to approach the game fully prepared to play the best way possible.

The attraction of making fortunes with the spin of the wheel has made roulette the oldest, most famous, and most popular gambling game in European casinos, where roulette is king—it is favored by royalty and celebrities, as well as regular gamblers looking for the thrill of action. Roulette is much less popular in America and, as opposed to the crowded and noisy tables prevalent on the other side of the Atlantic, tables in U.S. casinos are comparatively quiet.

This section explains how the two styles of play differ, American and European, and why roulette games are so popular in Europe yet play second fiddle to the other table games in American casinos.

It also shows you how to make all the different bets possible, their designations in French and in English, and the odds involved so that you'll be ready to play roulette anywhere in the world fully prepared to have the best chances of winning. Winning—that's how you get the most fun out of any gambling game.

THE BASICS OF ROULETTE

THE ROULETTE SETTING

Roulette is played with a circular **wheel** containing 36 grooved slots numbered from 1 to 36, and slots for a 0 and 00. (In some casinos, there is only a single zero for 37 slots, as opposed to wheels containing the 00 also, which have 38 total slots.) Half the 1–36 numbers on the wheel are black and the other half red. A tiny ball is used in conjunction with the wheel, and a betting layout where players can place their wagers is situated on a table beside the wheel.

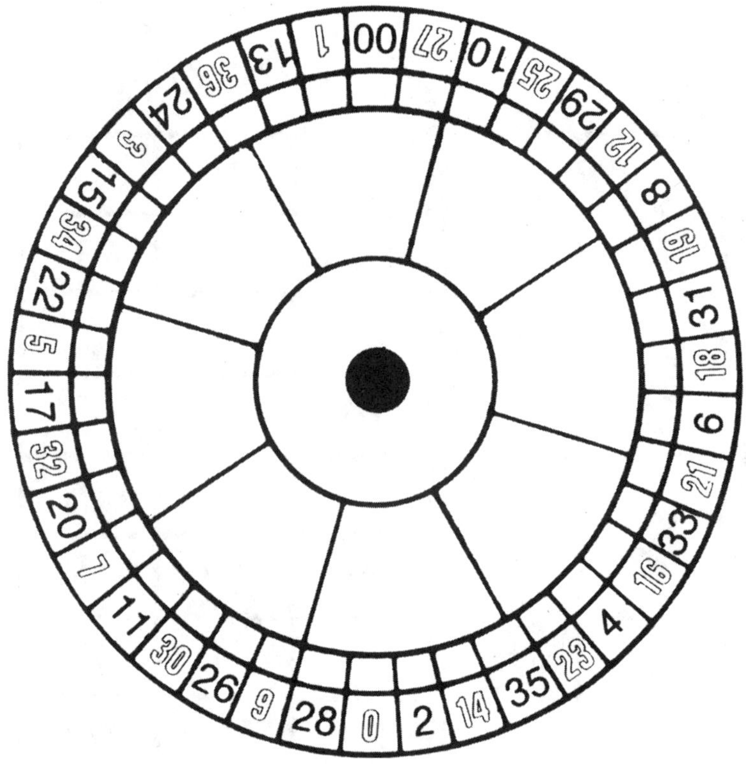

The American Wheel

In addition to the 36 numbers on the roulette wheel, the American game has a 0 and 00, while the European game has only one 0. The zero slots are neither red nor black, as are the other numbers; they are green.

The wheel is cut into tiny pockets, one for each number—37 total on a European wheel and 38 on an American—so that the ball, when spun around the wheel, will eventually fall into one of these slots, that number being the winning spin.

The European game generally has the wheel flanked on two sides by a betting layout, so that the busy tables can accommodate players on both sides of the wheel, while the less popular American games typically use but one layout to the side.

		0		00
1to18	1st 12	1	2	3
		4	5	6
EVEN		7	8	9
		10	11	12
◇	2nd 12	13	14	15
		16	17	18
◆		19	20	21
		22	23	24
ODD	3rd 12	25	26	27
		28	29	30
19to36		31	32	33
		34	35	36
		2-1	2-1	2-1

The Layout

THE DEALER

The American game typically employs only one dealer, who handles all the functions at the table. He changes money into chips, spins the wheel, collects losing bets, and pays off the winners. In between these duties, he finds time to stack and restack collected chips from the layout into neat piles, so that payoffs from the next spin can proceed smoothly and rapidly. If a table is exceptionally busy, the dealer may have an assistant to help run the game.

European style games have one to as many as three or four **croupiers**, the French term for dealers, paying and collecting bets on the two adjacent layouts; and a **tourneur**, whose main responsibility is to spin the wheel and call the result. Often, a supervisor is also present.

Thus, when things get rolling and the tables crowded, there might be as many as six casino personnel manning a roulette game—a tourneur, four croupiers and a supervisor.

THE PLAY OF THE GAME

Once players have placed their bets on the layout, choosing from the myriad possibilities available in front of them, the game is officially ready to begin. The dealer or tourneur spins the roulette wheel and then immediately throws the ball in the opposite direction from which the wheel is spinning so that both ball and wheel are racing in opposite directions on the wheel itself.

Players must then place their last-minute wagers, because when the ball is about to leave the track, the dealer will announce that bets are no longer permitted. The call of "Faites vos jeux, messieurs" (Make your bets gentlemen), or "Rien ne va plus" (Nothing more goes) are classic in French casinos.

Once the ball has stopped, the dealer or tourneur will call out the outcome, and a marker will be placed on the number just spun so that all players and dealers can clearly see the winning number.

Then the dealers (croupiers) settle the wagers. After they have collected all of the lost bets, they pay off all of the winning bets.

THE CHIPS

Keeping track of your bets is easy in American roulette games, since each player is issued special chips applicable only to the roulette game at that casino. These chips are colored, a different color for each player. Ten different players may be represented by yellow, red, pink, blue, green, black, white, beige, purple or gray chips, for example.

The colored chips are valid and can be used only at the roulette table that issues them. If the table is crowded and no more colors are available, a player may use regular casino chips for his or her bets.

Color coding makes life easy at roulette tables: There is no confusion about ownership of the chips. When a player approaches the roulette table, he exchanges cash or casino chips for an equivalent value in the colored chips, called **wheel checks** in roulette parlance. The value assigned to the colored chips is set by the player, and could be 25¢, $1.00, $5.00 or whatever. Thus, if the player wants to value the chips at 25¢, more chips will be issued from the dealer than if the chips were valued at $1.00.

The dealer will place a coin or **marker button** on top of the colored chips, and then place these on the stationary outer rim of the wheel so that the value of that wheel check is clearly marked. When a player is ready to leave, he converts his wheel checks into regular casino checks with the dealer at that table.

Life is a bit more complicated in the European style game where color coding is not used, and bettors simply use casino chips or cash to make their bets. Sometimes, in the confusion of a crowded game, vociferous arguments ensue as players lay identical claim to chips on the felt.

THE BASIC ODDS

The primary difference in the popularity of European and American roulette lies in the simple fact that the European game gives players much better odds of winning—this is where the 0, 00 difference of the two wheels comes into play.

Let's see how the odds are figured. The slots on a roulette wheel are numbered from 1 to 36—a total of 36. There is only one way to win for each number chosen. That leaves 35 other numbers that are losers for the bettor if they come up. True odds of 35 to 1 against—35 ways to lose, one way to win. And that is exactly what the casino will pay on a single number bet.

So where is the casino's profit?

It is the *zeros* added to the wheel that give casinos their edge. With the zeroes, there are 37 possibilities on a European wheel (single zero added), and 38 possibilities on an American wheel (single and double zero added). The casino's payoff is still 35 to 1, being based on the true odds of a 36-number wheel. However, with the added zeros, the true odds on a single number bet are 36 to 1 on a single zero wheel (the European game), and 37 to 1 on a double zero wheel (the American game).

Those zeros give the casino its edge on all bets made. The spin of either on the wheel causes all other wagers to lose, unless the zero (and in American roulette the 00 also) is bet directly.

The sole exceptions are the even-money bets in a European style game (and Atlantic City). In those venues, the spin of a zero gives the red-black (rouge-noir), high-low (passe-manque) and odd-even (impair-pair) bettors a second chance, and reduces the house edge on these bets to 1.35% (2.63% in Atlantic City)—the best odds a player can receive in roulette.

The zeros represent the house advantage, which is why the 00 in American roulette makes that game a much worse gamble for the player than its European counterpart. Atlantic City makes up for this a little by offering surrender on even-money bets, reducing the casino's edge on these wagers to 2.63%.

Let's sum up the odds in chart form so that you can clearly see them in one spot.

CASINO EDGE IN ROUETTE	
AMERICAN ROULETTE (DOUBLE ZERO)	
BET	**HOUSE EDGE**
5-NUMBER BET	7.89%
ALL OTHER BETS	5.26%
ATLANTIC CITY–EVEN MONEY BETS	2.63%
EUROPEAN ROULETTE (ONE ZERO)	
BET	**HOUSE EDGE**
EVEN-MONEY BETS–EN PRISON RULE	1.35%
ALL OTHER BETS	2.70%

The difference between the 1.35% of European style roulette and the 5.26% of the American style is significant as it is almost a four-fold increase, which calculates directly to a loss rate that is four times as fast.

Now you can see why roulette with a single zero and en prison rule is the rage of Europe, while double zero American roulette is not popular.

THE BETS

Roulette offers you a multitude of possible wagers, more than any other casino table game. All in all, there are over 150 possible combinations to bet. And you can make as many bets in any combinations you want as long as the bets fit within the minimum and maximum limit of the casino.

Let's examine the bets one by one.

COMBINATION OR INSIDE BETS

These bets are made within the numbers on the layout, and hence, are termed **inside bets**.

SINGLE NUMBER BET

A **single number bet** can be made on any number on the layout including the 0 and 00. To make this wager, place your chip within the lines of the number chosen, being careful not to touch the lines. Otherwise you may have another bet altogether.

The winning payoff is 35 to 1.

The Single Number Bet

SPLIT BET

Place the chip on the line adjoining two numbers for a **split bet** If either number comes up, the payoff is 17 to 1.

Split Bet

TRIO BET

The chip is placed on the outside vertical line alongside any line of numbers for a **trio bet**. If any of the three are hit, the payoff is 11 to 1.

Trio Bet

4-NUMBER BET

A **4-number bet** is also called a **square** or **corner bet**. Place the chip on the spot marking the intersection of four numbers. If any of the four come in, it is an 8 to 1 payoff.

4-Number Bet

QUATRE PREMIERE

The **quatre premiere** is available only in European roulette. This is a bet covering the 0, 1, 2 and 3, with an 8 to 1 payoff.

5-NUMBER BET

The **5-number bet** is available only in American roulette. Place the chip at the end of the intersection where the 0 and 1 overlap to cover the 0, 00, 1, 2, and 3. If any of these five comes home, the payoff is 6 to 1. In American roulette, it is the only bet not giving the house an edge of 5.26%. It's worse—7.89%!

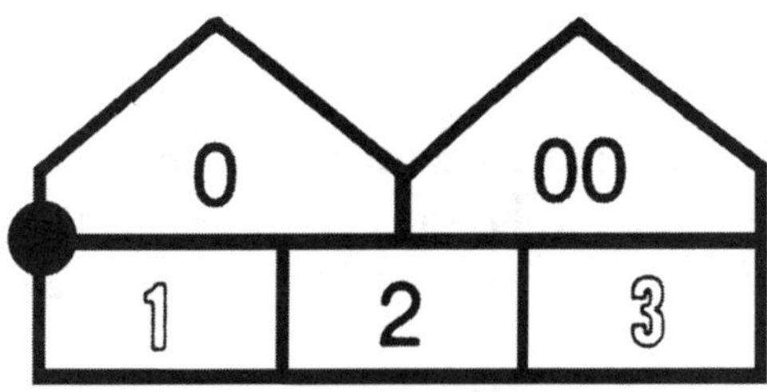

5-Number Bet

6-NUMBER BET

The **6 number bet** is also called a **block bet**. Place the chip on the outside line of the layout, while intersecting the line separating the sets of numbers chosen. The payoff is 5 to 1.

6-Number Bet

OUTSIDE BETS

The **outside bets** are outside the 36 numbers on the layout. They include the columns, dozens and even-money bets—red-black, high-low and odd-even.

1st 12		2nd 12		3rd 12	
1to18	EVEN	◇	◆	ODD	19to36

Outside Bets

COLUMNS BET

A chip placed at the head of a column, on the far side from the zero or zeros, covers all 12 numbers in the column and has a winning payoff of 2 to 1. This is called a **columns bet**. The 0 and 00 are not included in this bet and would make this bet a loser if they come up.

1	2	3
4	5	6
7	8	9
10	11	12
13	14	15
16	17	18
19	20	21
22	23	24
25	26	27
28	29	30
31	32	33
34	35	36
2-1	2-1	2-1

Columns Bet

DOZENS BET

A **dozens bet** is another way to bet 12 numbers: either numbers 1 to 12, 13 to 24 or 25 to 36. On the American layout, they are called the **first dozen**, **second dozen** and **third dozen** respectively; on the

French layout, they are known as **P12**, **M12** and **D12**. The winning payoff is 2 to 1.

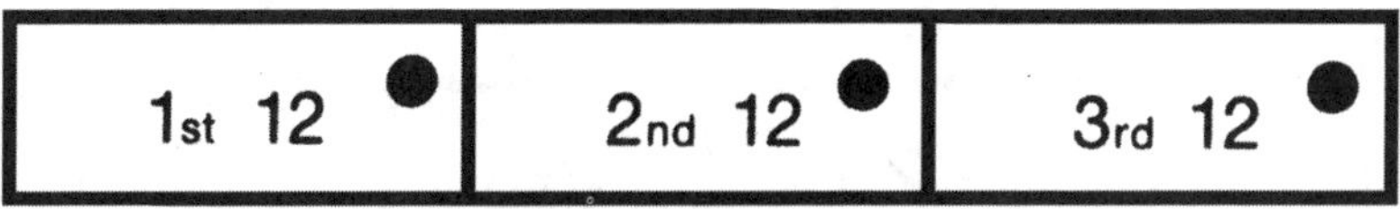

Dozens Bet

EVEN-MONEY BETS

There is one final type of bet, the **even-money bets**: **Red-Black**, **High-Low**, and **Odd-Even**. Spots for these bets are found outside the numbers, thus these bets are classified as **outside wagers**. These wagers are clearly marked in large boxes.

In Atlantic City and European style roulette, these are the best bets at the roulette table because they offer you additional features that are greatly advantageous to players. In Europe, these features are called *en prison* and *partage*; and in Atlantic City, they are called *surrender.*

First we'll go over the bets, and then we'll examine how the en prison, partage and surrender rules work and how they affect the player.

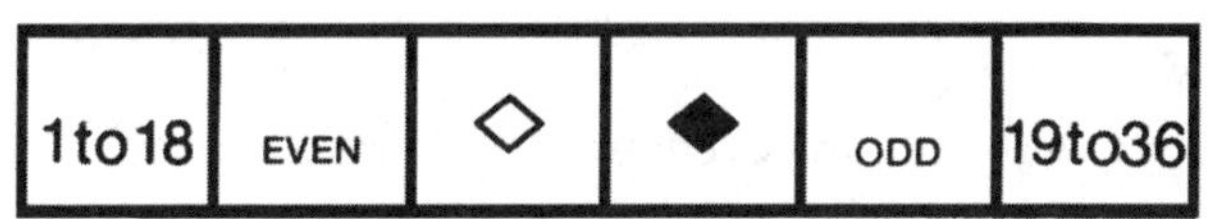

Even-Money Bets

RED-BLACK

There are 18 black and 18 red numbers. You may bet either the **red** or the **black** and will be paid off at 1 to 1 on a winning spin.

Red-Black

HIGH-LOW

Numbers 1-18 may be bet (**low**) or 19-36 (**high**). Bets are paid off at 1 to 1.

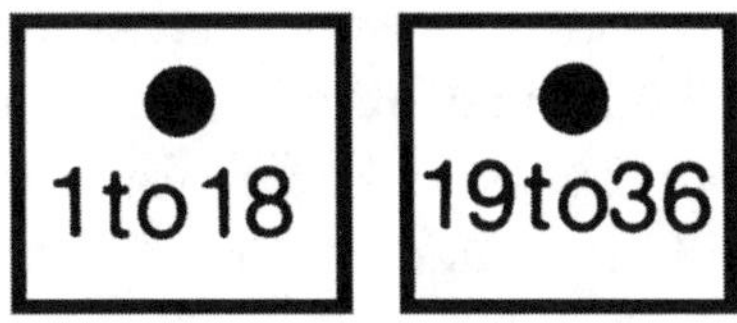

High-Low

ODD-EVEN

You may bet on the 18 even numbers, **even**; or **odd**, the 18 odd numbers. Winning bets are paid at 1 to 1.

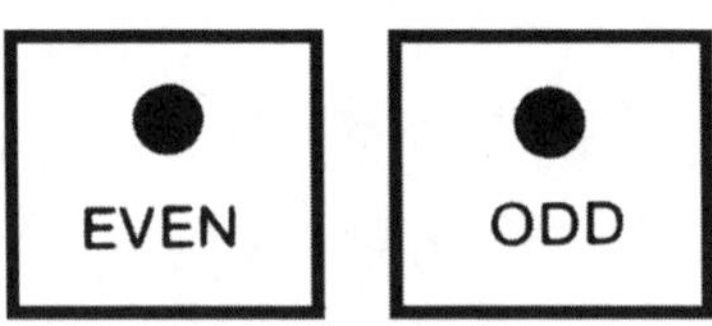

Odd-Even

EN PRISON AND PARTAGE

It is on these even number bets (above) where the American and European games really differ. In American roulette, the house automatically wins on these bets when the 0 or 00 is spun (except in Atlantic City).

However in Europe, if the 0 is spun, the **en prison** rule comes into effect. The player then has two choices. He or she can either surrender half the bet, called **partage**, or elect to allow the bet to be "imprisoned" one more spin. If the spin is won, the bet stays intact and is "**released**" for the player to do what he or she will. If the spin is lost, so is the bet.

This rule is greatly advantageous to the player, and reduces the odds on these bets to 1.35% in favor of the casino as opposed to the 2.70% on the rest of the bets in the single-zero game.

SURRENDER

In an attempt to get more gamblers to play roulette, the game in Atlantic City helps make up for the 00 of the American wheel by offering **surrender**, which actually is partage by another name. When a 0 or 00 is spun, players with bets on any of the even-money propositions lose only half the bet, "surrendering it," and keep the other half. This brings the house edge down to 2.63% on these bets.

AMERICAN AND EUROPEAN ROULETTE DIFFERENCES

The European and American game is pretty much the same except for the use of the French terms in Europe, and the American terms in U.S. casinos. However, there are three significant differences.

1. In addition to the 36 numbers on the roulette wheel, the American game has a 0 and 00, while the European game has only one 0.
2. The European game offers en prison and partage, rules greatly beneficial to the player. En prison and partage are not offered in American casinos, with the exception of Atlantic City where surrender (partage) is used.

3. The casino edge in the European game is only 1.35% as opposed to American roulette where the player has to overcome a hefty 5.26% house edge (or 2.63% on even-money bets in Atlantic City).

ROULETTE PAYOFF CHART BETS IN ROULETTE			
AMERICAN NAME	**#**	**FRENCH NAME**	**PAYOFF**
Single Number	1	En Plein	35-1
Split Bet	2	A Cheval	17-1
Trio	3	Transversale	11-1
4-Number (Corner)	4	Carré	8-1
(Not Applicable)	4	Quatre Premiere	8-1
5-Number	5	(Not Applicable)	6-1
6-Number or Block-6	6	Sixaine	5-1
Columns Bet	12	Colonne	2-1
Dozens Bet	12	Douzaine	2-1
Red or Black	18	Rouge ou Noir	1-1
High or Low	18	Passe ou Manque	1-1
Odd or Even	18	Impair ou Pair	1-1

column is the amount of numbers covered by the bet.

THE WINNING STRATEGIES

Let's start off by clearly stating that, like most other casino games, the casino has the mathematical edge over the player, and that no betting strategy or playing system can overcome those odds unless the wheel is biased—which we'll cover. That edge is 5.26% in American roulette, with the exception of even-money bets in Atlantic City where the edge is 2.63%; and 2.70% in European roulette, unless the even-money wagers are made, where the house edge drops to 1.35%.

Based on the above facts, you must develop a clear picture on how to approach a winning strategy. The key words here are *casino edge.*

You must understand that in the long haul, the casino's edge will grind out the players—but that doesn't mean that you can't show a profit in the short run. Fluctuations are normal to gambling, whatever the game, and with a little luck, you can ride a hot streak into some healthy profits.

Many betting systems have been devised to overcome the casino's edge in roulette, but you must keep these systems in perspective. Systems cannot alter or change the reality of the house edge any more than constantly calling a tree a river will change that tree to a river. Irrefutable facts are cemented in reality and only a distortion or departure from that reality will change the appearance of what one perceives—but it will not change the reality.

This is not to say that some of the betting strategies don't look good—some of them are brilliant in concept so that they *appear* to be nearly foolproof. (Note the key word "appear.") However, these systems don't change the short or long term house edge at roulette, so you should view them as no more than a fun approach.

The beauty of these systems is that they entrance some people with such beautiful, though tainted logic, that one actually sees how they can work and how they can beat the odds. And they can work—in the short run—and provide the player with that age-old smoke cloud attempt that makes him feel like he's beating the odds. But again, don't become deluded—the house edge *is* the house edge.

Man will never give up attempting to overcome the odds; that is one of the beauties of life. And that is why we are so attracted to gambling.

Most betting systems rely on the even-money wagers—red-black, odd-even, and high-low—as the heart of their progressions. You either bet one way, or the other. The idea is to bet the situations that have an "even" chance of winning, as opposed to the longer payoffs of wagers that are harder to hit, such as a columns bet or a six-number bet, for example.

Let's look at one of the most classic systems first, the Martingale.

MARTINGALE

This dangerous system can dig you into a deep hole quickly if you suffer a long string of losses—if not, like other systems, you'll be sitting pretty.

The **Martingale** is easy. You attempt to win $1.00 on every sequence, a sequence being defined as either one spin when you have won, or a number of spins, ending when there is a winner.

Your first bet is $1.00. If the bet is won, you start again, betting $1.00. If you lose, the bet is doubled to $2.00. If that bet wins, you have won $1.00 on the sequence—a $1.00 loss on the first spin but a $2.00 win on the second spin. If the second bet is lost, the next bet is again doubled, making it $4.00. A winner here again brings a $1.00 profit, $1.00 plus $2.00 in losers for $3.00, and a $4.00 winner—still $1.00 over the top.

And so the system works. Every won bet is followed by a $1.00 wager, the beginning of a fresh cycle. Every lost bet is followed by doubling that bet. Here is the danger of the Martingale: As consecutive losses mount, so does the size of your bet, where the end result is only a $1.00 win!

This is what happens if you lose seven in a row.

MARTINGALE PROGRESSION		
LOSS	INITIAL BET	TOTAL LOSS
1st	$1.00	$1.00
2nd	$2.00	$3.00
3rd	$4.00	$7.00
4th	$8.00	$15.00
5th	$16.00	$31.00
6th	$32.00	$63.00
7th	$64.00	$127.00
8th	$128.00	–

Suddenly, you are faced with a $128.00 bet with $127.00 worth of losses behind you. That's a lot of sweat and aggravation just to win $1.00 on the sequence. And seven losses in a row is not that strange an occurrence.

What happens on the next spin?

Surely you're due for a winner after seven consecutive losses. If you are pregnant or are expecting a raise or some such thing, you may be due. In gambling, you're never due for anything. There are expectations based on the odds, but the fact that seven times the wheel spun black when you've been betting red, has no bearing on the eighth spin. The odds don't change—it's still an 18 out of 37 (European wheel) or 38 (American wheel) shot for your winning red on the next spin, roughly one out of two.

Remember, it's only a wheel. It has no memory, no brain. It doesn't know who you are, what you're betting, or that black has come up seven times in a row. It really doesn't.

Back to the game—heaven forbid that two more spins go against you, because then you will be faced with the following:

MARTINGALE PROGRESSION CONTINUED		
LOSS	INITIAL BET	TOTAL LOSS
8th	$128.00	$255.00
9th	$256.00	$511.00
10th	$512.00	–

Add up these numbers, and then get out the Pepto-Bismol. Think twice before using this classic system. Do you really want to risk a situation where you'll need to bet over $500 just to win $1.00?

THE GRAND MARTINGALE

If you liked the above system, you'll love this one. The rallying point of the **Grand Martingale** is to attempt to win more than $1.00 on a losing progression by adding $1.00 to the bet after each loss. We'll spare ourselves the anguish of adding up these numbers, but you can see that they'll add up even faster than the Martingale. And seriously, who needs that?

THE PYRAMID SYSTEM

This system is far more appealing to some players because its winning approach doesn't entail the kind of deep ditch digging that the Martingale and Grand Martingale require.

Let's look at each bet in the **Pyramid System**, also called the **D'Alembert**, in terms of units. To make life easy, we'll use $1.00 as our unit bet. The first bet is $1.00. If we win, the sequence is ended, and we'll begin a new one.

If the bet is lost, our next bet becomes $2.00. Each subsequent loss adds $1.00 to the bet, so that five consecutive losses would produce a $6.00 bet on the following play. (Compare this to the Martingale, where after five losses you'd be watching a $32.00 bet gracing the tables for your $1.00 win, and the first tinges of a headache beginning to pound your skull.)

This system is interesting because after every win, you decrease your bet by one unit. The end result is that every win (as opposed to every progression) produces a win of $1.00; or if you prefer to think in terms of units, every win produces a one-unit gain.

Every won bet is $1.00 more than the previous lost bet. Let's follow a progression to see how this works.

PYRAMID PROGRESSION		
BET	RESULT	TOTAL
$1.00	Win	+$1.00
$1.00	Loss	$0.00
$2.00	Loss	-$2.00
$3.00	Win	+$1.00
$2.00	Win	+$3.00
$1.00	Loss	+$2.00
$2.00	Loss	$0.00
$3.00	Loss	-$3.00
$4.00	Loss	-$7.00
$5.00	Loss	-$12.00
$6.00	Win	-$6.00
$5.00	Loss	-$11.00
$6.00	Win	-$5.00
$5.00	Win	$0.00
TOTAL—14 PLAYS: 6 WINS, 8 LOSSES		

You can see the attraction of this system: Despite sustaining five straight losses, and eight overall against only six wins, the sequence where we left off shows us as being dead even. A win on the next play would forge a profit of $4.00, with the next bet being $3.00, so the bettor's position looks pretty good overall.

This is all well and good in the short run. However, like all other systems that try to fight a game where the house has an edge, the pyramid system will ultimately lose in the long run. As the progression continues, there will be more losses than wins and the downward dips will be deeper and more frequent than wins.

As long as you keep the immovable house edge in mind, you might play this system with great enjoyment and maybe even some profit in the short run.

BIASED WHEELS

There is a way to beat the casino at roulette. It involves finding an unbalanced wheel, one that is presumably old and rickety, which is more likely in a smaller casino or perhaps at a fair where the mechanics of the wheel are far from state of the art.

It is impossible to make a perfectly balanced wheel, one where each number has exactly the same chance of coming up as any other number. A slight imperfection in the material, normal wear and tear, a warp, a tiny tilt, a floor that is not level, or a slightly larger or shorter slot—these possibilities and any number of others can cause the imbalance of a wheel and favor some numbers to be spun more often than others.

Wheels are made with such tremendous precision nowadays that it is extremely unlikely to find a wheel with a bias significant enough to make this theory interesting. However, you may find an older wheel in use, one that's been subjected to enough wear and tear that a bias is created, or one with faulty mechanics. Until the casino has figured out that you've got something going on and shuts down the wheel, you can make a lot of money—with the odds.

First you must determine if the wheel is biased and how large the bias is. To do this requires a lot of work and patience, but if indeed you're hunch is right and the wheel is significantly biased, you will have made the effort worthwhile. There are many stories of dedicated players patiently clocking wheels, finding a bias, and winning enormous sums of money until the game is shut down on them.

To properly track a wheel, you'll need a partner or an associate or two because every spin of the wheel will need to be recorded for at least 24 hours and, ideally, two or three times that much time to get a fair sampling. A sampling taken for less than 24 hours will only show short-run deviations (unless the wheel is incredibly biased) and will not be an accurate account of numbers that may be biased.

The expectation of any single number being spun is 1 in 38 on an American wheel (1 in 37 on a European one).

For a strategy to be effective and show profits, a single number's bias must not only be greater than the 1/38 (1/37 in Europe) expected result, but be sufficient enough to overcome the casino's inherent edge of 5.26% on an American wheel and 2.70% on a European one for single-zero betting.

You may find one number or several that stand out on a wheel as being biased and base your winning strategy on those numbers (or number). The superior odds inherent in single-zero roulette make those games much better to track since, if a bias is found, the smaller house edge is easier to overcome and profits will be greater.

PARTING THOUGHTS

Roulette is a fun way to relax and try your luck at calling and betting the numbers that will come up winners on the wheel. We've presented some basic winning systems for beginning players that you can try at the tables, plus the interesting biased-wheel strategy.

All sorts of betting systems are available—different number parlays, single and multiple number cycle plays, alternate betting systems, jump plays and more. Many of these systems are quite creative, and some are very good.*

With a run of luck, you can make money at roulette if your numbers come up winners and your other wagers ride a streak. However, no matter what bets you make or what system you use, always keep sound money management principles in mind. That is the key to winning at roulette.

Good Luck!

---

* For serious players, Gambling Research Institute has developed advanced winning systems designed for winning at roulette (including advanced multiple number cycle plays and other systems). These are available through our mail order catalog in the back.

9 SLOTS

FIVE KEYS TO SLOTS

1. Play in casinos that cater to slots players. They are likely to have the loosest machines and give you the best chances of winning.
2. Join slot clubs in every casino where you play.
3. Avoid mega-progressives. The "one in a million" payday is remote, and these machines tend to grind you down with low payoffs and few wins.
4. Find the better paying machines to play.
5. Don't play adjacent machines. Loose slots are rarely placed next to each other.

INTRODUCTION

More casino space is devoted to slots than any other gambling game for good reasons: Slot machines are easy to play, they're fun, and best of all, if you get a lucky spin on the reels, you could win a jackpot worth thousands or even millions of dollars. Further, casinos make more profit on slots than any other games they offer.

Playing slot machines is easy—no more complicated than putting your money in a machine and pressing the play button to activate the reels. Of course, there are more aspects to playing the slots successfully, which we will cover later in this chapter.

Your goal is quite simple. You want the symbols on the reels to line up directly behind the payline in one of the winning combinations listed on the machine. The higher ranked the combination, the greater the payout.

Bing! Bing! Bing! Jackpot! That's what you want to hear. Let's look at how you can increase your chances of winning at slots.

BASICS OF SLOTS

The old term for slot machines was **one armed bandits**, so named because the reels were activated by a handle on the side of the machine. But that name is no longer appropriate. For one, most players don't even use the handles anymore—that is, if the machine even has a handle. Simply pressing a button gets everything going.

For another, the modern slot machine is essentially a fancy computer device. Where the reels will stop is not a mechanical function, as it previously was, but is calculated by computer chips that use **random number generators** (RNG) to ensure that each pull has an equal chance of hitting the jackpot. Essentially, as soon as the slot machine is turned on, the random number generator starts spitting out whole numbers (usually between one and several billion) hundreds of times per second. The instant you press the play button, the computer records the next few numbers from the RNG, and then feeds them through a program to determine where the reels stop. The function of the device that spins the reels is simply to display the result calculated by the computer, not to determine it.

But that's not the only change brought by modernization. Inserting coins into a slot machine has become a relic of the past. While there are a few machines that can still be played with coins, the models being manufactured nowadays take only paper money or paper tickets that you have cashed out from a ticket-in, ticket-out machine. **Ticket-in, ticket-out machines** pay you with bar-coded paper tickets that denote the amount of money you have earned at cash-out time. These tickets can be inserted into another machine for their cash value, or can be converted into actual cash at the casino cashier cage. You'll find them in all modern casinos.

PLAYING THE SLOTS

The easiest way to play the slots is by inserting bills or tickets directly into the machine and playing the credits chalked up on the machine according to how much money you have inserted. The device that accepts your money is called a **bill acceptor**. Machines normally accept $1, $5, $20, $50 and $100 bills, which are converted directly into credits on the machine and allow you to play carefree for as long as you still have credits available.

Let's take a closer look at playing by credits.

PLAYING YOUR CREDITS

Once you have credits, playing slots couldn't be easier. On every machine, you'll see a play button marked "Play Max Credits," "Play Three Credits," "Play Five Credits," or similar buttons. Pressing the play button automatically spins the reels if you have credits available. That's it! Unlike the older generations of slot machines, you don't have to constantly put in coins or pull handles. Once you have established credits on a machine, all you need is one finger to play.

Its ease of play and speed make the play button similar to a speed dial. You can make multiple plays faster than a player on an old machine could make even one spin of the reels. Casinos love this feature because it allows gamblers nonstop play at speeds not previously possible, which means more action per hour for the house.

The play button, which is large and easily visible, is typically found on the right side of the machine, the area most convenient for easy play.

COIN DENOMINATIONS

You can risk various amounts on each spin of the reels. Slot machines come in a variety of coin denominations. The most popular machines are the 25¢ and $1 machines that are found in most venues. Casinos also feature 5¢ and 10¢ machines, plus the increasingly popular 1¢ machines, called **penny slots**. These penny slots can cost players a bundle, though, and are not necessarily good for budget-minded players since they often feature options that allows multiple plays at once—in other words, for aggressive players, they are not exactly penny slots!

High-roller casinos such as Caesar's Palace, Bellagio, and the Venetian in Las Vegas feature $5, $25, $100 and even $500 slot machines.

MULTI-DENOMINATION MACHINES

As the title infers, multi-denomination machines allow you to play at various stakes by choosing the value of each credit you wager from the options listed on the machine. For example, one multi-denomination machine may allow you to bet quarters, dimes, nickels or pennies, while another may allow you to bet in denominations of 50¢, $1, $2 or $5. After you insert your bill or ticket, you select the denomination you wish to play and the slot machine automatically calculates the number of credits you will receive in exchange for the amount of money you inserted.

MULTI-GAME MACHINES

Multi-game slot machines are quite popular because you can switch from one game to another on the same machine without having to change machines each time you want to change games. One multi-game mix may offer you the choice of playing video keno, video slots, video blackjack or video poker—all on the same machine.

Multi-game machines often offer multi-denomination choices as well. For example, you might start off playing video keno in nickel denominations, and then switch your play to video blackjack for quarters by simply pressing a few buttons.

TOUCH-SCREEN MACHINES

Many modern machines don't even require that you press buttons. Instead, you touch the options you want to activate by simply pressing a finger on the appropriate symbol on the machine's video screen. **Touch-screen machines**, such as video keno and video poker, are quite popular, especially those that offer flat-top machines where the video monitor is embedded into a shelf that allows you to look down at the monitor and provides a place to rest your arms during play.

THE SLOT MACHINE

Slot machines are comprised of various components. Let's take a look at them.

REEL SLOT MACHINES

The symbols on a slot machine are displayed on spinning mechanisms called **reels**. Typical reel machines contain three reels or five reels, though there are also many novelty slots with as many as eight or ten reels, and monster machines often referred to as Big Berthas.

Reels contain 20-24 **steps** or **stops**. Each step is a place where the reel can land when it is spun. This step usually contains a **symbol** such as a cherry or a bar, or a **blank**, which is a step with no symbol.

VIDEO SLOT MACHINES

Video slot machines have become the standard in most modern casinos. Unlike the three to five paylines in reel slots, **video slot machines** may have 9, 15, 25 or even 100 different paylines. Video slot machines have no moving parts at all, as they are essentially computer games with graphic representations of reels that are spinning. Many video slot machines have a theme based on a popular TV game or show and feature vivid graphics and catchy music. They also usually offer a "bonus" round that is activated when certain symbols line up in a winning combination.

Examples of video reel slot machine themes include Monopoly, Addams Family, Elvis Presley, and Beverly Hillbillies.

PAYLINES

The glass window in front of a slot machine's reels is marked by one or more horizontal or diagonal lines called **paylines**. Essentially, this is the visual display that shows whether or not you have scored a winning spin. Winning combinations must line up directly behind a payline to be a winner.

When there are three paylines on a machine, they will generally be lined up as three horizontals, one in the middle, and one each above and below the middle line.

Usually, it takes one coin for each payline to be activated. Thus, on a three-payline machine, you'll need to play three coins to activate all three paylines, one coin for each line. If you only put in one coin on a three-payline machine, it will probably count for the middle payline only. If you hit a winning combination on the bottom line with only one coin played, it won't be a winner, since a coin for that line wasn't inserted. You would have needed to insert additional coins.

Machines with five paylines generally add two diagonal paylines, so you have five directions that can win. Again, you need to play five coins for all these paylines to be active.

Video reel machines usually feature a lot more paylines, which often are marked by "stripes" of various colors that indicate winning combinations.

WINNING HINT

When playing a progressive reel slot machine such as Megabucks or Wheel of Fortune, insert the maximum coins so that the jackpot gets activated. Otherwise, you will lose out on the huge jackpot even if you line up the winning combination.

SYMBOLS

Cherries, bars, 7's, and liberty bells—shades of the past! Although these were the basic slot machine symbols for more than 50 years, you're more likely to find unicorns, princesses, frogs, pots of gold, and a host of other new symbols on today's modern video reel games. While you'll see a wide variety of symbols and pictorials on the many new slot machines, the most successful machines always come back to the basics.

WILD SYMBOLS

Some machines designate a particular symbol as **wild**. The "WILD" symbol acts as a substitute for any other symbol on the machine to create a winning combination. For example, if you spin BAR-BAR-

WILD or 7-7-WILD on a classic slots machine, you will be paid out the same amount as for three bars or three sevens.

Some machines use symbols to multiply a payout line. For example, the diamond on IGT's traditional Double Diamond machine will double the payout when it is lined up to form a winning combination. Two diamonds on the same line are even better, as they double each other to give you four times the payout.

You sometimes see a winning combination noted as Any Bar, which means that any one of the single, double or triple bar symbols on the reels can work as a paying symbol for the combination listed. Thus, you might have DOUBLE BAR-DOUBLE BAR-ANY BAR as the three symbols needed for a winner.

A wild symbol on a video reel slot may be a picture of a gold coin, a sparkling tiara or a moneybag.

WINNING TIP

Never leave a machine that owes you money. Hit the "cash out" button to receive your winning voucher, or wait for a slot attendant to pay you, no matter how long it takes. You might as well leave your wallet on a New York City street corner as to walk away from a machine with winning credits still on it.

DIFFERENT TYPES OF MACHINES

There are basically two types of slot machines. The first type, **straight slots**, pays winning combinations according to the schedule listed on the machine itself. These payoffs never vary. The second type, **progressive slots**, features a jackpot that gets progressively larger as each coin is played. The jackpot total is posted above the machine and can rise to enormous sums of money.

SLOT DISPLAYS

Various displays on the machine give you information about what is happening on your machine. Let's take a brief look at some of the more relevant ones.

PAYOUT DISPLAY

This is the most important display on the machine because it shows you what combinations are needed to have a winning spin and how much each of these winners will pay. On a straight slot machine, all winning amounts are posted on the display itself. These are typically expressed in number of credits that can be won as opposed to dollar amounts. However, some displays post a dollar amount that can be won for a specific combination.

For example, a winning combination might show a payment of 50 credits or 100 credits.

On progressive machines, "Progressive" might be indicated next to the payout for the big jackpot hand. The progressive jackpot total is posted on a lighted display above the bank of machines. The amount of the progressive jackpot constantly rises when machines in a bank of progressive slots are getting play.

CREDITS PLAYED OR COINS PLAYED

Credits Played or **Coins Played** (on older machines) shows how many credits or coins are being wagered on the current spin. If three credits are played, the display indicates the number "3" in the area provided.

CREDITS

The **Credits** indicator shows how many credits you have accumulated either through winning spins or through money you have put into the machine. For example, placing a $20 bill into a 25¢ machine will enter eighty 25¢ credits into your account. The credits indicator will display the number "80."

Pushing the PLAY ONE CREDIT button automatically deducts one credit from your remaining credits, while PLAY MAX CREDITS deducts the maximum amount of credits you are allowed to wager on any one spin. You can use your credits by either playing them until the total is down to 0 (which means you've lost them all), or by hitting the CASH OUT button, which will convert your credits into a paper voucher, called a **ticket**, for the actual dollar amount you have won. Older machines send coins tumbling into the well below.

WINNER PAID

The **Winner Paid** indicator displays the amount won on the current spin. For example, if three bars align for a winning combination that pays 40 credits, the Winner Paid area will display the number "40."

PLAY BUTTONS

There are a few buttons that you will interact with at the machine. We'll take a brief look at them here.

PLAY MAX CREDITS/BET MAX COINS

Pressing the PLAY MAX CREDITS button bets the maximum amount of coins allowed and automatically spins the reels. Thus, if the machine accepts five coins as a maximum bet, pressing PLAY MAX CREDITS will deduct five coins from your credits. Similarly, if three coins is the maximum bet, three coins will be played and that amount will be deducted.

This button may also read BET MAX COINS or it may have a similar designation that means the same thing. Of course, the PLAY MAX CREDITS button only activates the reels if you have credits available.

PLAY ONE CREDIT

You can also play one credit at a time by depressing the PLAY ONE CREDIT button. In this case, the reels will not spin until you press the Spin Reels button or pull the handle. You can also play two credits by pressing the PLAY ONE CREDIT button twice, or three coins by pressing it three times, or the maximum number of credits by pressing the button until the full allowance of coins is reached.

CASH OUT BUTTON

When you press the CASH OUT button, the machine cashes out your credits and gives you a voucher for the amount of money you have won. Older machines deposit coins into a well below the machine, but if you have more credits than the machine is able to pay out, you will have to wait for an attendant to pay out the rest of them.

CHANGE BUTTON

When you press the CHANGE or SERVICE button on a machine, a red light flashes atop the machine to signal a casino slots attendant to give you service.

HOUSE PERCENTAGES ON SLOTS

Slots is the only game offered in the casino where you can't figure out the house edge. The payback percentage could be 93%, 99%, 96%, or any other percentage, but you have no way of knowing this as a player. The percentages on machines are neither posted nor is the frequency of occurrence of any one symbol made available. So how do you figure out the casino's edge on a particular slot machine?

You don't.

You may see a casino advertise a 99% return on slots, but that doesn't mean that each slot machine pays out the maximum 99%. The question is: Which machine or machines have that return? There is no way to know for certain where a good machine might be located.

However, in the strategy section, we'll show you ways to locate the better-paying machines and avoid the ones where the house loads up on its edge.

SLOT CLUBS

A **slot club** is a casino marketing program that allows you to earn rewards not just for your slot and video poker machine play, but for all the games. Programs vary from casino to casino, but almost all of them give you a chance to earn comps for buffets and restaurant meals, rooms, shows, and sometimes, cash rebates. Slot clubs that offer rebates are usually referred to as **cash back clubs**.

Slot clubs have greatly added to the popularity of the slots and have given players more ways to win. Best of all, there is no charge to become a member. The concept is simple. Once enrolled as a member, the casino issues you a card with your name and your unique card number. By inserting your slot card into the machines prior to playing, your card automatically tracks your betting action. The more action you give the casino, the greater the benefits you enjoy just for playing the machines.

Each casino has its own slots program, some with greater benefits than others. But all are worth joining if you like to play slots at various casinos.

JOINING A SLOT CLUB

To become a slot club member, you first have to register at the slots club booth. The application process is simple and takes only a few minutes. Casinos require a valid ID to complete the application. Keep in mind that this application is simply a formality—you will not get turned down. Casino slot clubs have no interest in your credit history or how much money you make. They just want you to play slots in their casino.

MEMBERSHIP CARD

When you join a slots club, you receive a plastic membership card right there at the club booth. Your card identifies you as a player and allows you to immediately earn promotional credits at the machines, now that the casino has you on file in its system. Armed with this card, you'll earn reward credits every time you play. In fact, you'll generally get bonus credits just for signing up!

Just make sure to insert your card into the card reader on the machine before you begin playing.

The card is programmed to identify you and register the action you give the machine. Note that you cannot earn credits if your card is not in the machine. Every slot and video poker machine in the casino will have a card reader for this purpose. Card readers are typically found on the front of the machines.

AWARDS PROGRAM

Casinos typically let you know up front how much action you need to generate for their awards programs to kick in. Action is usually defined by a points system, with each point amounting to one dollar wagered. (However, some casinos keep their rewards programs a mystery, for equally mysterious reasons.)

Casinos that offer cash-back incentives to slot club members generally tell you how many points you must earn to receive each dollar in cash rewards. In Las Vegas, for example, one cash-back players club may award one dollar for each 1,000 points earned, while another may offer one dollar for each 800 earned or, in rare cases, for each 600 points you post on your club card. You can either cash in your points at the cashier's cage for real money, or use them to pay for food in the casino's restaurants or merchandise at the casino's gift shop.

The critical element that casinos are looking for is the amount of action and how much money you wager at the machines, not how long you sit in front of a machine warming a chair. The casinos want action. When you give it to them, they will reward you with incentives.

The more money per hour you play—not how much you win or lose—the faster you will accumulate the points required by a casino to reach various levels of rewards.

WINNING STRATEGIES AT SLOTS

Surprisingly, there are lots of strategies you can pursue for such a simple game. By following the advice in this section, you'll do much better than the average player. At times and under the right conditions, you may actually find yourself with an edge.

We'll briefly touch upon a few ideas here, but if you're serious about your slots play, I recommend my book, *Secrets of Winning Slots* (available from our website at www.cardozabooks.com), which is loaded with information about slots strategies and the machines in general.

CONCENTRATE YOUR ACTION

The first rule is to concentrate your action at casinos that cater to serious slots players. If a casino wants to attract serious slots business, it must give you something to whoop about to keep you as a steady player. In the old days, this meant having machines with good paybacks. Nowadays, it also means having an aggressive slots club rich with rewards for faithful players. With all else equal, you would much rather play at a casino with a more aggressive slots club program, one that gives you quicker slots rewards. And of course, you would rather play at a casino that has better paying machines.

CHOOSING PROFITABLE CASINOS

So how do you get a sense of when a casino is good for slots players? If the casino is buzzing with slots players, that's a good sign. On the other hand, an empty mausoleum-like atmosphere doesn't bode well. Regular players return to places where they win and avoid places that suck their bankrolls dry.

Another principle is true as well. Play in places that cater to slot players and avoid places that do not. Do not play slots in places where the slots business is incidental to the main business. Why? Because the customers that play slots in these establishments are there to do something else. These places can get away with horrific odds because their customers did not come to play slots and won't be the most demanding of clients. This is another way of saying that they are not sophisticated players needing the best odds possible.

What kinds of places are these? If you want to get good odds, avoid playing slot machines in laundromats, bars, grocery and convenience stores, gas stations and the like, because these venues usually have slots that swallow your money as fast as you can feed them.

AVOIDING BAD MACHINES

Choosing the right location within a casino is often important as well. For example, slots situated along a restaurant wall or buffet line are generally set with lower percentages to catch the impulse coins that go into these machines. So you want to avoid machines in these locations.

CHECKING PAYOUT SCHEDULES

One of the main differences between video slot machines and reel machines is the way that payouts are calculated. With reel machines, the only way to win the maximum jackpot is to play the maximum number of coins, usually three and sometimes five. In other words, it is to your advantage to bet the maximum allowed. This is particularly true of big-money three-reel progressives such as Megabucks and Wheel of Fortune because you could miss a huge payday by not betting the maximum.

On video reel machines, the fixed payout values are multiplied by the number of coins you bet per line. So, if you bet one coin per line, you may win 100 coins, for example, whereas if you bet five coins per line, you would win five times that amount or 500. It all depends on how much money you want to invest.

On non-progressive reel machines, there is also a payout difference on the amount of money you are paid when you hit winning combinations. For example, one coin might pay you 800, two coins 1,600, and three coins, 4,000. That's a big difference.

FINDING THE LOOSEST AND TIGHTEST SLOTS IN A CASINO

The placement of loose and tight slot machines, and the actual paybacks of a casino's slot machines are two of the closest kept secrets in a casino. While the slots hosts and the slots manager will not *know* the percentages that any of the machines pay, or where the best ones are located, the slots girls who work the area will notice which machines have been paying the most often. Ask one of them nicely and she may give you a tip that will put you close to a 99% payback. That really is the best way to find a good slot machine.

WINNING TIP

Rarely will loose machines be situated side by side. Casinos are aware that slot players often play in pairs, and know that the excitement from one machine can carry over to the player in the adjacent machine. Thus, machines adjacent to loose machines tend to be tighter. When you discover a loose machine, you'll want to avoid the machines on either side of it.

PARTING THOUGHTS

Here's one last tip: Don't leave a winning machine! Unless you've had enough play for a day, or you need to go elsewhere, don't leave a winning machine. When your machine is hot, ride it for all it's worth. But once it stops paying well, back off and take a break—with all your profits in your pocket.

10 VIDEO POKER

FIVE KEYS TO WINNING AT VIDEO POKER
1. Shop around to find the best paying machines, and the highest jackpot on progressives. 2. Learn the correct playing strategies and never deviate from them. 3. Make sure you hold all five cards when dealt a pat winning hand. You don't want to lose a big payoff because of carelessness. 4. Never leave the machine while waiting for an attendant to pay a big winner. 5. Always play maximum credits on a standard video poker machine. The royal only pays the big jackpot when you play maximum coins.

INTRODUCTION

Since video poker was originally introduced to the casinos, it has caught on like wildfire. Players love the fact that they play the game at their leisure, just themselves and the video poker machine, and that decision-making and skill are involved.

Video poker is loosely based on draw poker. The machine deals five cards to start and you can keep or exchange any or all of these cards to form a new five-card hand. Your goal is to make a five-card poker hand in the combinations listed on the front of the machine. The higher ranked the poker hand, the greater the payout.

Video poker is simple to play, but you must make the right decisions on which cards to hold to maximize your winning chances. That is the skill element in video poker. The fun element comes in when your good play turns into winnings.

You have a wide variety of games to choose among, from the standard jacks-or-better machines found in most places, and the popular deuces wild games, to a wide choice of spin-offs and variations of the original jacks-or-better game. These variations include bonus poker, double bonus, double-double bonus, triple-double bonus, All-American poker, joker wild, bonus deuces and others.

GETTING STARTED

The typical video poker game uses a 52-card deck that is dealt fresh after each hand. To start, you need to insert money into the machine so that you have credits to play on. All modern machines have **bill acceptors** that accept $1, $5, $10, $20, $50, and $100 bills. Once the bills are accepted into the machine, the equivalent amount of **credits** will be posted on the machine for your bankroll. For example, if you insert a $20 bill into the bill acceptor on a quarter machine, 80 credits will be posted.

Wins and losses will be added or deducted from your credits. If you start out with 80 credits and bet five coins, five credits will be deducted from your total credits and the machine will show “75” credits. A win of 45 credits will boost your total to 120 credits and “120” will appear in the credits area.

PLAYING YOUR CREDITS

With credits on the machine, getting your cards dealt is as easy as hitting a button. On every machine, you’ll see a button marked **Play Max Coins**, **Play Five Credits**, or a similar play button. Pressing this button deals five cards to you and deducts five credits from your credit total. Thus, if you had 100 credits to start, pressing Play Five Credits would reduce your total to 95 credits. You now have your initial five-card hand.

There is also a button on the machine that allows you to play one credit at a time. This button may be marked **Play One Credit**, **Play One Coin**, or the like. Since the maximum number of coins is not being played, you also have to hit the **Draw/Deal** button for the cards to be dealt.

YOUR INITIAL FIVE-CARD HAND

You start out with a five-card hand. You may keep one, some, all, or none of these cards. It's your decision. There are five hold buttons, one underneath each card. To keep a card, press the button marked **Hold** underneath the corresponding card you wish to keep. Or simply press the face of the cards you want to hold on touch-screen machines.

Held will appear on the screen underneath each card or cards so chosen. The machine will not keep the other cards, the ones you wish to discard.

What happens if you press the wrong hold button by accident or change your mind? No problem. Simply press the corresponding button again, or touch the card again on touch-screen machines. The "Held" signal will disappear and the card will not be held by the computer. If you change your mind, press the button one more time, and "Held" will appear on the screen again indicating that the card will be kept on the draw.

Until you press the draw button, it is not too late to change your strategy decision.

KEEPING/DISCARDING ALL FIVE CARDS

You may keep all five original cards by pushing the hold button under each card, or discard all five original cards by pressing the Draw/Deal button without having pressed any of the hold buttons.

Discarding all your cards is often the correct strategy in video poker. We'll discuss when to do so in the winning strategies section.

THE FINAL HAND

To discard the cards you don't want to keep and receive your new ones, you must press the Draw/Deal button again. Cards with "Held" underneath them will remain on the screen, while all other cards will be replaced by new ones. This set of cards is your final hand.

MULTI-LINE VIDEO POKER MACHINES

Multi-line video poker machines that feature three lines, five lines, ten lines (and even 100 lines) are quite popular in modern casinos.

On multi-line machines, usually called **triple-play**, **five-play** or **ten-play** machines, you bet on each line of play. For example, the maximum bet on a triple-play machine is usually 15, five coins for each line. Or, if you prefer to bet only six coins per play, the machine automatically places a two-coin bet on each line. If you have a winner, each line pays you off in the same way that a single-line machine does.

The machine initially deals the same five cards on each line. You indicate the cards you want held on the bottom line only, at which point the machine automatically holds the same cards on every line. After you hit the Deal button, a set of new cards will be displayed on each line of play to replace the ones that you did not hold. Different cards usually are dealt to each line, so you'll make three to ten different hands (100 different hands on 100-line machines), one per line. Sometimes, you may make the same hand on two or more lines. For example, you might hold ace-ace on the bottom line and get dealt the remaining two aces in the deck on that line and on one other line for a double payoff. This is good news!

WINNING HINT

If you get dealt a great five-card hand that you want to keep, such as a straight or even a royal flush, you must press the hold button or touch the screen for each and every one of the cards before pressing the Deal/Draw button. If you don't hold all of them, you will lose the hand on the card exchange! If your hand is a winner, the machine will flash **"Winner"** at the bottom of the screen.

THE CASH OUT BUTTON

When you are finished playing and want to leave the machine, you can retrieve your credits at any time by pressing the **Cash Out** button. The machine will issue you a ticket equivalent to the amount of money you have remaining to your credit.

IMPORTANT TIP

If you have won more money than the machine is capable of paying out, sit tight and do not leave the machine until an attendant comes to pay you. Press the call button and an attendant should make his or her way over to your machine.

THE WINNING HANDS

Typically, the minimum winning hand in video poker is a pair of jacks or better, though that varies by machine type. For example, deuces wild machines require at least three of a kind for a payout and Pick Five machines pay out for hands as low as a pair of sixes.

The chart below describes the winning hands for the jacks-or-better variations. Hands are listed from weakest to strongest.

WINNING VIDEO POKER HANDS	
Jacks or Better:	Two cards of equal value are called a pair. Jacks or better refers to a pair of jacks, queens, kings or aces.
Two Pair:	Two sets of paired cards, such as 3-3 and 10-10.
Three of a Kind:	Three cards of equal value, such as 9-9-9.
Straight:	Five cards in numerical sequence, such as 3-4-5-6-7 or 10-J-Q-K-A. The ace can be counted as the highest card or the lowest card in a straight.
Flush:	Any five cards of the same suit, such as five hearts.
Full House:	Three of a kind and a pair together, such as 2-2-2-J-J.
Four of a Kind:	Four cards of equal value, such as K-K-K-K.
Straight Flush:	A straight all in the same suit, such as 7-8-9-10-J, all spades.
Royal Flush:	10-J-Q-K-A, all in the same suit.

On wild card machines, you will see additional listings for five-of-a-kind hands (made possible because of the wild cards), and two types of royal flushes. The more valuable royal flush is the **natural royal flush**, which doesn't use any wild cards to form it. The other type of royal flush is the **wild royal**, which uses at least one wild card to form the five-card royal flush. The natural royal is harder to get and pays far more than a royal formed with one or more deuces.

There are also payouts for other types of hands, such as the bonus quad machines where specified four-of-a-kind hands receive a higher payout amount than other types of four-of-a-kind hands. These payouts are clearly listed on the machines themselves.

TYPES OF VIDEO POKER MACHINES

PROGRESSIVES/NON-PROGRESSIVES

Video poker machines can be played as either **Flat-Top** (**Straight**) machines, with set payoffs on all the hands won, or as **Progressives**, where the progressive jackpot constantly increases until someone hits the royal flush.

On both types of machines, all the payoffs are proportionate for the winning hands. Thus, a winning payoff on two coins played will be exactly double that for the same winning hand with one coin played.

The one exception is the royal flush. One, two, three and four coins pay 200, 400, 600 and 800 coins respectively for the royal, a progression normally would give a 1,000-coin payoff. But when you play all five coins, you receive a bonus payout of 4,000 coins. Progressive machines work the same way: To get the full benefit of the royal flush jackpot, you need to play five coins.

WINNING HINT

Always insert the full five coins to get the best odds at single-line video poker.

FOUR VIDEO POKER CATEGORIES

Following are four general categories of video poker machines that you may find.

1. **Jacks or Better**—The original of the video poker machines, these games are based on the player receiving a hand of two jacks or better to get the minimum payout.
2. **Tens or Better and Two Pair**—Tens or better is similar to jacks or better except that the minimum payout on a hand is two tens, not two jacks. On the two-pair machines, two pair is the minimum payout.

3. **Wild Card**—Wild card machines add the element of a wild card that can be used as any card to form the most valuable hand possible.
4. **Specialty**—Video poker machines that don't quite fit into the other categories.

JACKS OR BETTER

The minimum hand needed to win in **jacks or better** is a pair of jacks; any lesser pair or lesser hand pays nothing. Of course, the greater the strength of the hand, the larger the payout will be. For example, as you can see in the 9-6 paytable below, a flush will pay 30 coins when you play five coins as opposed to a payout of five coins for a pair of queens.

The following chart shows typical payoffs for video poker on a jacks-or-better machine in a competitive market such as Las Vegas. I use the term *competitive*, since there are locations where video poker games are offered where the payout tables are so horrific, I wouldn't advise anyone to play them.

Machines using the paytable below are known as **9-6 machines**, so named for the 9-coin payoff on the full house and the 6-coin payoff for the flush. Experienced video poker players call machines with these payoffs **full-pay machines**; that is, they pay the maximum for a full house and a flush. Note that full-pay machines are becoming hard to find in most U.S. casinos. Las Vegas casinos usually have only one or two banks (rows) of full-pay jacks-or-better machines.

PAYTABLE ON JACKS OR BETTER 9-6 MACHINE					
HAND	COINS PLAYED				
	1	2	3	4	5
ROYAL FLUSH	250	500	750	1000	4000
STRAIGHT FLUSH	50	100	150	200	250
FOUR OF A KIND	25	50	75	100	125
FULL HOUSE	9	18	27	36	45
FLUSH	6	12	18	24	30
STRAIGHT	4	8	12	16	20
THREE OF A KIND	3	6	9	12	15
TWO PAIR	2	4	6	8	10
JACKS OR BETTER	1	2	3	4	5

BONUS QUADS

Bonus quads jacks-or-better variations, which come in a number of flavors, offer bonus payouts for specified four-of–a-kind hands, called **quads**. For example, a bonus quad machine may pay more for quad twos, threes and fours than they pay for other quads.

There are many types of games that offer higher payouts when you make quads, but with a few tweaks in strategy, they all work according to the same principles as jacks-or-better. The allure of getting paid extra for quads has made the bonus quads games popular among players. Examples of these bonus games include bonus poker, double bonus, double-double bonus and aces-bonus.

DEUCES WILD AND JOKER WILD

Some video poker games are played with wild cards that can be given any value or suit with the machine interpreting those cards in the most advantageous way for the player. In **deuces wild**, each of the four deuces are wild cards. And in **joker wild**, an added joker is the wild card. For example, the hand 2-2-5-6-8 in deuces wild would be a straight. One 2 would be used as a 7 and the other as either a 9 or 4. The deuces could also be used as eights to give three of a kind, but since the straight is more valuable, the machine will interpret it as a straight.

Wild card machines have different minimum payouts than jacks-or-better machines. For example, in deuces wild, minimum payoffs start with three-of-a-kind (trips). A pair of jacks wins nothing in deuces wild.

As with jacks-or-better, deuces wild full-pay machines are increasingly difficult to find in U.S. casinos. Seasoned players refer to full-pay deuces wild as **9-5 machines** because the payoff schedule awards 9 times your bet (45 coins when you play 5 coins) for a straight flush, and 5 times your bet (25 coins when you play 5 coins) for four-of-a-kind.

Following is a full-pay payoff schedule for deuces wild.

PAYOFFS ON DEUCES WILD
9-5 MACHINE

HAND	COINS PLAYED				
	1	2	3	4	5
NATURAL ROYAL FLUSH*	250	500	750	1000	4000
FOUR DEUCES	200	400	600	800	1000
WILD ROYAL FLUSH**	25	50	75	100	125
FIVE OF A KIND	15	30	45	60	75
STRAIGHT FLUSH	9	18	27	36	45
FOUR OF A KIND	5	10	15	20	25
FULL HOUSE	3	6	9	12	15
FLUSH	2	4	6	8	10
STRAIGHT	2	4	6	8	10
THREE OF A KIND	1	2	3	4	5

*Natural Royal Flush–No wild cards as part of the royal flush.

**Wild Royal Flush–The royal flush uses at least one wild card (deuce)

Progressive jackpot machines with larger payoffs for making a royal flush are quite popular among avid video poker players. All payoffs are fixed, as they are in straight machines, except for the royal flush, which pays the accumulated total posted above the machine on the electronic board.

The jackpot total slowly and constantly rises, and can rise into thousands of dollars on quarter and dollar machines in Las Vegas.

WINNING STRATEGY

The big payoff in video poker on jacks-or-better and deuces wild machines is for the royal flush—4,000 units are paid for this score when all five coins are played. You always want to keep yourself in a position to take advantage of this win if you draw the right cards, which is why I keep stressing the importance of playing the full five coins when you sit down at a video poker machine.

On progressive machines, if the full five coins are played, the total could be a great deal higher, possibly as high as $3,000 on a quarter machine. Again, the key phrase is "if the full five coins are played."

Of course, you won't get a royal flush very often. With correct strategy, you'll hit one every 30,000+ hands on average. This doesn't mean, however, that you won't hit one in your very first hour of play. Meanwhile, you'll be collecting wins for straights, full houses and the like, and with proper play, you can beat full-pay video poker machines.

(The 9-6 charts are not applicable to the 8-5 progressives. For full strategy charts on all video poker games including progressives, joker wild, deuces wild and more, order the professional strategy in the back of this book.)

JACKS OR BETTER STRATEGY— 9-6 MACHINES

1. Whenever you get dealt **four cards to a royal flush**, discard the fifth card, even if that card makes a flush or pair on your initial five-card hand.
2. Keep a **pair of jacks or better**, and any higher hand such as a three-of-a-kind or a straight over three cards to the royal. Hold **three cards to a royal** over any lesser hand, such as a low pair or four flush cards.
3. With **two cards to a royal**, keep four cards to a straight or flush, and high pairs or better. Otherwise, go for the royal by keeping the two suited high cards.
4. Never break up a **straight or flush**, unless a one-card draw gives you a chance to make the royal.
5. Keep **jacks or better** over a four straight or four flush.
6. Never break up **quads, a full house, trips and two-pair hands**. The rags, worthless cards for the latter two hands, should be dropped on the draw.
7. Always keep a **pair of jacks or better**, except when you have four cards to the royal, or four to the straight flush.
8. Keep **low pairs** over a four straight, but discard them in favor of a four flush and three or four cards to a royal flush.
9. When dealt an **unmade hand**, a pre-draw hand with no payable combination of cards, save these combinations, in order—four to a royal flush and straight flush, three to a royal flush, four flushes, four straights, three to a straight flush, two cards to the royal, two cards jack or higher, and one card jack or higher.
10. Discard all five cards and draw five fresh ones when **you don't have any of the above combinations** with no card that is a jack or higher.

SIMPLIFIED BASIC STRATEGY CHART

This chart sums up the simplified basic strategy for jacks or better on a 9-6 machine. Keep the hands listed higher in preference to hands listed lower. For example, keep a high pair over three cards to a royal, but throw it away in favor of four cards to the royal.

JACKS OR BETTER STRATEGY 9-6 MACHINE		
HAND TO BE HELD	CARDS HELD	DRAW
ROYAL FLUSH	5	0
STRAIGHT FLUSH	5	0
FOUR OF A KIND	5	0
FULL HOUSE	5	0
FOUR TO A ROYAL	4	1
FLUSH	5	0
THREE OF A KIND	3	2
STRAIGHT	5	0
FOUR TO A STRAIGHT FLUSH	4	1
TWO PAIR	4	1
HIGH PAIR	2	3
THREE TO A ROYAL	3	2
FOUR TO A FLUSH	4	1
LOW PAIR	2	3
FOUR TO A STRAIGHT	4	1
THREE TO A STRAIGHT FLUSH	3	2
TWO TO A ROYAL	2	3
TWO HIGH CARDS	2	3
ONE HIGH CARD	1	4
GARBAGE HAND	0	5

DEUCES WILD STRATEGY

There is no payoff for hands less than three of a kind, so if you're coming from a jacks or better game, you'll need to adjust your strategy accordingly.

The key in deuces wild is to go for the big payouts—the royal flush.

Therefore, when you have three cards toward a royal flush, discard the other two and go for it.

Of course, the same holds true when you have four to the royal. If you have two deuces and a 10 or higher, along with two sub-10 cards of no value, go for the royal.

If you hold one or two deuces with nothing else, dump the junk and hang onto the deuces.

With five unrelated cards, get rid of them all and draw five fresh ones.

Three-card flushes or straights and unmatched high cards are worthless in this game. Discard them.

With two-pair hands (which don't pay in deuces wild games), hang onto only one of the pairs and go for three new cards.

If one of the pairs in a two-pair hand, or a pair by itself is teamed with a wild deuce, keep the three of a kind.

If the deuce forms a pair with a high card, it has no value whatsoever, so keep only the deuce and draw four cards.

Keep a pair unless you have a three-card royal flush, in which case dump the pair and go for the gold.

THE GOLDEN DEUCE

Deuces are gold in this game, so make sure you never discard them by accident. You'll find that many of the hands you're dealt contain nothing worth saving and you'll need to draw five fresh cards. Three-card straights and flushes fit into this category, along with some of the others I've mentioned. In any case, don't be afraid to discard your original five cards if they are nothing of value.

After playing the non-wild versions of video poker that pay you for a pair of jacks or higher, it takes a little while to get used to wild-card video poker. But once you become accustomed to its different payouts and strategies, you should have lots of fun at wild-card machines.

Optimum deuces wild strategy varies depending on how many deuces you are dealt on your starting hand. Beginning with hands where you are dealt no deuces, the following charts give you the best strategy for playing starting hands that contain various amounts of deuces.

DEUCES WILD STRATEGY 9-5 MACHINE		
NO DEUCES		
HAND TO BE HELD	CARDS HELD	DRAW
ROYAL FLUSH	5	0
FOUR TO A ROYAL	4	1
STRAIGHT FLUSH	5	0
FOUR OF A KIND	4	1
FULL HOUSE	5	0
FLUSH	5	0
STRAIGHT	5	0
THREE OF A KIND	3	2
FOUR TO A STRAIGHT FLUSH	4	1
THREE TO A ROYAL	3	2
ONE PAIR (DISCARD 2ND PAIR)	2	3
FOUR TO A FLUSH	4	1
FOUR TO A STRAIGHT	4	1
THREE TO A STRAIGHT FLUSH	3	2
TWO TO A ROYAL	2	3
GARBAGE HAND	0	5

DEUCES WILD STRATEGY 9-5 MACHINE		
ONE DEUCE		
HAND TO BE HELD	**CARDS HELD**	**DRAW**
ROYAL FLUSH	5	0
FIVE OF A KIND	5	0
STRAIGHT FLUSH	5	0
FOUR OF A KIND	4	1
FOUR TO A ROYAL	4	1
FULL HOUSE	5	0
THREE OF A KIND	3	2
FOUR TO A STRAIGHT FLUSH	4	1
FLUSH	5	0
STRAIGHT	5	0
THREE TO A ROYAL	3	2
ONE DEUCE	1	4
TWO DEUCES		
HAND TO BE HELD	**CARDS HELD**	**DRAW**
ROYAL FLUSH	5	0
FIVE OF A KIND	5	0
STRAIGHT FLUSH	5	0
FOUR OF A KIND	4	1
FOUR TO A ROYAL	4	1
TWO DEUCES	2	3
THREE DEUCES		
HAND TO BE HELD	**CARDS HELD**	**DRAW**
ROYAL FLUSH	5	0
FIVE OF A KIND	5	0
THREE DEUCES	3	2
FOUR DEUCES		
HAND TO BE HELD	**CARDS HELD**	**DRAW**
FOUR DEUCES	4	1

PARTING THOUGHTS

I have presented strategies in this chapter for two of the most popular video poker variations, jacks or better and deuces wild. If you want to learn the important differences in strategy between the 8-5 progressive and 9-6 jacks-or-better machines, plus receive the full professional strategy charts for the many other variations, I highly recommend the professional video poker strategy described in the back of this book.

Meanwhile, keep your eye out for the royal flush. It's not as far away as you think. And when you hit it, don't be afraid to scream out those magic words—royal flush!

11 CHO DAI DI

FIVE KEYS TO WINNING AT CHO DAI DI

1. Don't play for money until you get comfortable with the rules of this terrific game and the skill level of your opponents.
2. Your goal is to gain points versus your opponents, not necessarily to go out of a round first.
3. Keep track of the aces and deuces–you always need to know what the controlling cards are.
4. Don't get caught with 10 or more cards in your hand and a double penalty.
5. Usually get rid of your weaker cards first, and hold the strong ones to control rounds.

INTRODUCTION

This exciting card game combines all the elements of a great game—skill, luck and a little just-for-fun backstabbing, with skill being the overriding factor. Cho Dai Di is tremendously popular with the Chinese, but has not yet caught on in other cultures. That's surprising, since the game is not only a lot of fun to play but is perfectly suited to gamblers, especially poker players, as well.

While Cho Dai Di may sound foreign, this unique game uses elements of play that you're already familiar with, and will be fairly easy to learn. It is closely related to poker in that poker hands and values are used in the play of the game; and to other card game variations where players attempt to rid their hand of all its cards.

Cho Dai Di is simple to play, but there is much to learn about its strategy. Take some time to study this chapter and you'll learn how to play a great card game. You and your friends will soon be hooked on Cho Dai Di (the Cantonese D is pronounced like a td together) and you'll start counting the days until the next game begins.

Now, let's get on with the game!

THE BASICS OF CHO DAI DI

Cho Dai Di is played with four players and a standard 52-card deck. Each player plays for himself, pitting his skill and wits against his three opponents.

THE OBJECT OF THE GAME

The object of Cho Dai Di is to discard all 13 cards that you are dealt before your opponents do, or if another player goes out first, to gain points by having fewer cards remaining than the other players.

When the first player goes out, each card that the other players are stuck with counts as one point against them. You gain points from any opponent who is left with more cards than you have.

HAND AND CARD VALUES

Hands that are valid in Cho Dai Di are similar to standard poker hands with two main differences. First, the 2 is the highest value card in Cho Dai Di and not the ace, which is the next in rank. The other difference is that two pair is not a playable hand in Cho Dai Di.

ORDER OF SUITS

Suits play a role in Cho Dai Di. In order of strength, they are spades, hearts, clubs and diamonds. (Note that these rankings are different from the game of bridge, in which diamonds outrank clubs.) The first order of ranking in a card is its numeric value; thus the 4♦ is higher than the 3♠.

However, when both cards are of equal numeric value, such as two fours, their suits determine which is the higher card. Thus, the 4♠ is superior to a four of any other suit since spades are the strongest suit, while the 10♣ is higher ranked than the 10♦.

CHO DAI DI RANKINGS

If you're not yet familiar with poker, here are the best hands, beginning with the lowest ranking hands and going up to the highest ranking. Cards are abbreviated by the commonly accepted abbreviations so that a three will be 3, a jack = J, queen = Q, king = K, ace = A, two = 2 and so on.

CHO DAI DI RANKINGS

High Card: The high card in Cho Dai Di is the 2, followed by the A, K, Q, J, 10, 9, 8, 7, 6, 5, 4 and then the 3, which is the weakest card. Equivalent high-card hands are decided by the order of their suit.

One Pair: Two cards of identical value, such as 4-4 and K-K, form a pair. The highest pair is 2-2, the lowest 3-3. When two pairs of equal value, such as 7♣ 7♥ and 7♥ 7♦, are in competition, the pair with the spade, the highest ranking suit, is the stronger one.

Three of a Kind: Three cards of equal value, such as 9-9-9, form three of a kind. When two players hold a three of a kind, the hand with the higher ranking triplets is stronger. 2-2-2- is a higher ranking hand than A-A-A.

Straight: Five cards in numerical sequence, such as 3-4-5-6-7 or A-2-3-4-5. The ace can be counted as the highest card (A-K-Q-J-10) in a straight, or the lowest card. However, it may not be in the middle of a five-card run, such as Q-K-A-2-3, which is not a straight.

When two or more straights are in competition, the highest ranking card determines the stronger hand. K-Q-J-10-9 is higher than J-10-9-8-7. A straight containing a 2 is higher than any other straight. Thus, A-2-3-4-5 is a higher straight than Q-J-10-9-8. However, if the straights are identical in value, such as K-Q-J-10-9 and K-Q-J-10-9, the strongest suit of the high card–in this example the king–determines the higher ranking hand. A king of hearts straight is higher than a king of clubs straight.

(continued)

CHO DAI DI RANKINGS (continued)	
Flush:	Any five cards of the same suit, such as five hearts. When two players have flushes, the highest ranking card in the flush determines the stronger hand, regardless of suit. If both hands have the same high card, the next highest card determines the stronger hand and so on down to the fifth card. Thus, a 2-A-K-6-4 of clubs is stronger than a 2-K-Q-J-9 of spades. It is only when all five cards are identical that the higher ranking suit makes one flush a higher ranking hand than the other.
Full House:	Three of a kind and a pair together, such as 2-2-2-J-J. When two players have a full house, the higher-ranking full house is the hand with the higher three of a kind. Thus 7-7-7-5-5 is better than 4-4-4-K-K.
Four of a Kind:	Four cards of equal value, such as K-K-K-K. When two players hold a four of a kind, the higher-ranking four of a kind is the higher foursome. J-J-J-J is higher than 3-3-3-3. The four of a kind is played as a five-card hand in Cho Dai Di, with any other card thrown in to make the fifth card.
Straight Flush:	A straight all in the same suit, such as 7♠ 8♠ 9♠ 10♠ J♠. If two players hold a straight flush in the same suit, the highest ranking card determines the more powerful straight flush. If the straight flushes are led by an equivalent high card, the higher ranking suit of the competing straight flushes determines the stronger hand.
Royal Flush:	10-J-Q-K-A, all in the same suit. In the unlikely event that two players hold a royal flush, the higher ranking suit is the dominant hand.

You'll see that the rankings pretty much approximate poker rankings with the noticeable exception that the 2 is the highest ranking card in the deck, and two pair is not considered a Cho Dai Di hand. Also, though four of a kind is a valid hand, it must be played as a five-card hand with any other card thrown in to make the fifth card.

Legitimate Cho Dai Di hands consist of 1, 2, 3 or 5 cards. Again, there are no four-card hands.

LEGITIMATE HANDS BY CARD	
One Card -	Any card may be led.
Two Cards -	The only valid two-card hand is a pair.
Three Cards -	Three of a kind is the only valid three-card hand. A pair with an odd card is not a valid hand for three of a kind.
Five Cards -	In order of strength from the lowest to the highest, these are valid five-card hands: straight, flush, full house, four of a kind with an odd card, straight flush and royal flush.

THE FIRST ROUND DEAL

The dealer for the first round is decided by the random drawing of a card from the deck. Beginning with the person picking the card and going counter-clockwise, right to left, one place is counted off for each number value on the card. For this purpose only, the jack equals 11 places, the queen 12 and the king 13. All other cards are at face value. Thus, if a player picks a 7, he counts his place as 1; to his right, 2; opposite will be 3; to his left, 4; back to himself again, 5; to his right, 6; and again opposite, 7.

Now we have the dealer for the first round—the player opposite the one who picked the card.

Thereafter, the dealer will always be the winner of the previous round, but as you'll see in a minute, the traditional draw is still used to determine which player gets dealt first.

THE TRADITIONAL DEAL

Cards are always dealt counterclockwise in Cho Dai Di. Before the cards are dealt, the traditional draw to determine which player will deal the cards occurs first. Though it has no bearing on the game since the dealer will play first anyway (except for the very first game), this tradition probably arose, like the cut, as a safeguard to the players.

As we did above, the dealer randomly picks a card and counts off one place for each number on the card, starting with himself and proceeding counterclockwise, right to left, around the table.

Then the cards are dealt one at a time, counter-clockwise (right to left), beginning with the player chosen by the traditional draw, and continuing until all players have received 13 face down cards. Since there are four players in the game, the deck should now be exhausted of all cards.

THE DIRECTION OF PLAY

The first round in Cho Dai Di is played in the counterclockwise direction. Thereafter, each round's play will alternate in direction so that on all odd rounds (first, third, fifth, etc.), play will be from right to left, counterclockwise. And all even rounds (second, fourth, sixth, etc.) will be dealt and played clockwise, left to right.

Therefore, if the previous hand was played left to right, the following one will be played right to left.

THE PLAY OF THE GAME

The winner of the previous game is always the dealer of the following game and, except for the first round in the very first game, the dealer will always be the first to lead in a game. He has a choice of whether to play one, two, three or five cards as his opening hand. If he leads with one card, it can be any card he wants, but if he leads with more than one card, it must be a legitimate Cho Dai Di hand to be a valid discard.

Remember that there is no valid four-card lead or hand in Cho Dai Di, as two pair is not a valid hand and four-of-a-kind hands are played as five-card hands with an extra card thrown in. After deciding his move, the dealer lays his hand of 1, 2, 3 or 5 cards face up on the table so that everyone can see what he has played.

The second player to act, the one to the dealer's right, now has two options: He may either pass by announcing "**Dai**," the Cantonese equivalent for pass, or simply say "**pass**," which may also be indicated by rapping your knuckles on the table, waving your hand vertically across the table, or another understood expression just as you would do in poker; or the player may lay down cards in response to the dealer's play.

For the next player to be able to play a hand, he must lay down the same number of cards, no more and no less than what the lead player threw. The card or cards that he plays must not only be a legitimate Cho Dai Di hand, but must be of greater value than the previously played hand. This is true at all times in Cho Dai Di. For example, if the dealer leads with a pair of fours, the next player must play a higher pair than the fours to be eligible to lay down cards. If he cannot beat the pair of fours by either throwing a higher suited pair of fours or a higher pair, or chooses not to, he may not lay down cards and must pass.

His play must be a two-card throw since two cards were led. Thus, a straight or three fives may not be played since they are not two-card hands.

After the second player acts upon his hand, the play moves to the next player in turn who faces the same options—either discarding a higher hand of the same number of cards, or passing. If, for example, the second player played a pair of nines, which he places face up in the middle on top of the fours, the third player must throw a higher suited pair of nines or a higher pair to lay down cards.

Any time a hand is played within a round, the following player must lay down a higher valued hand of the same number of cards to be able to play.

The action in any round, like poker, does not end until three passes in a row are called and the last player to throw cards has had his play unanswered by his three opponents. When a player's throw goes unanswered by three succeeding players, he has the advantage—he or she gets to lead the next round and may lay off any legitimate hand of 1, 2, 3 or 5 cards.

And so the game goes, with one player leading 1, 2, 3 or 5 cards, and the other players answering his lead until three passes in a row have occurred. The last to throw gets to lead, and another round ensues.

The game is over when any player gets rid of his last card. And then it's time to tally the score.

THE FIRST GAME ONLY

In the first round of the first game only, the player holding the 3♦ goes first and must lead that card. The card may be led by itself, or as part of a 2, 3 or 5 card Cho Dai Di hand. Thereafter, the winner of each game leads first in the following game, and is also the dealer.

SCORING

Every card you still have in your hand when an opponent goes out counts as one point against you. But you gain points from any other player who is left with more cards than you have. Thus, strictly speaking, there's usually more than one winner in a round.

However, if a player gets stuck with 10 cards or more when an opponent goes out, he must pay double the points to the other players. Even worse, if a player is unable to get rid of any cards at all, and gets stuck with his original 13 cards, the penalty is triple points to every player, even those stuck with more than 10 cards in their hands.

If two players have more than 10 points, let's say 10 and 11 points, they both must pay the double penalty to the other players, though the one having 11 cards pays just one point to the player having 10 cards.

There is one other scoring rule: the four-deuce bonus. If you are dealt four deuces, immediately turn your cards face up. The four-deuce bonus nets you 39 points from each opponent—the triple penalty times the 13 cards each player holds. Then a new game is dealt.

KEEPING SCORE

Cho Dai Di, like poker, can be played with chips, coins or cash. After each game is played, players settle with each other. The Chinese generally prefer this method because like poker, the instant gratification of touching the winnings is more fun.

If, on the other hand, you're playing just for the challenge of the game or simply prefer using a scorepad to keep track of accounts, Cho Dai Di is best played to a set amount of points—say 150, though you can play for fewer or more points as you wish. Once any player goes over 150 points or whatever amount is set, the game is over; and if you're playing for more than just points, accounts can be settled.

Of course, the idea of the game is to not get points, so the player over the point total first will be the big loser and will have to pay off the difference in the scores to the other three players.

Likewise, the second highest score pays off the two lower scores, and the second lowest score pays off only the low-point total and collects from the two players with more points. The player with the lowest point total, the one who went out first and has no cards remaining, is in the money, since all three of his opponents owe him the difference between their scores and his.

Either keeping score or settling after each game works equally well, and one way is just as valid as the other.

OTHER STYLES OF PLAY

There are different styles of play in Cho Dai Di. However, whatever style you play, it is still basically the same game. For example, some players play that when there is only one card left, opponents must play their highest cards, and may not "feed" a small card to the player with one card remaining and let him go out.

Some games use a different bonus schedule as well. They may penalize a player with double penalties when he's stuck with 8 cards (as opposed to 10), and triple penalties for any point total above 10 (as opposed to 13). They may also disallow the four-deuce instant 39-point bonus from each player, and instead, play the game according to the normal conventions.

You may find games where play always goes in the counterclockwise direction instead of alternating, but whatever the particular rules, Cho Dai Di, for all intents and purposes, is the same game. Once you know how to play, you'll have no trouble adjusting to the nuances of a different style of play.

SAMPLE GAME OF CHO DAI DI

Let's go through a sample game so that you can get a feel for how the game is played. We'll pick up our earlier example where the dealer led a pair of fours to start the game and the next player followed by throwing a pair of nines. Let's put some names on the players to make the game easy to follow. Going counter-clockwise, the direction of play for this round, we have Phil, the dealer, who played the fours, then Quilo, who threw the nines, Marta and finally Chang.

Marta now plays a pair of tens; Chang passes. Play comes back to the dealer, Phil, who also passes, and then on to Quilo, who plays two queens. Marta calls "Dai," pass, as does Chang and Phil, neither of whom have a higher pair, or don't want to play one if they do.

Since his pair of queens went unanswered by three passes, Quilo wins the round and gets to lead the play for the following round.

Quilo now leads with the 4♣ and places it atop the other cards in the center of the table. In Cho Dai Di, cards are played out in the center of the table, and are not collected until the game is over and the cards are ready to be shuffled.

Proceeding counterclockwise, the direction of the game, it is Marta's turn, and since one card is led, she may only play one card as well. She throws the 4♠, which is a higher suited 4.

"Your play, Chang."

Play continues as before, with each player in turn laying down higher ranking hands or passing.

Chang, very quietly plays a 5. Phil throws a 9, then Quilo a higher suited 9, followed by Marta's king and Chang's A♦. Phil passes and

Quilo, still bothered by something about Chang's socks, puts down the 2♠.

He has no need to wait for his opponent's response, because the 2♠ is the highest-ranking card in the deck; no card outranks that deuce.

Now that the 2♠ is out of play, the highest ranking unplayed card is the 2♥. Continuing on, Quilo leads with a five-card diamond flush and promptly announces, "**Bo Do**," the Cantonese expression signifying that he has one card left.

Whenever a player is down to one card, he must announce that fact to the other players.

It is Marta's turn and she must have a higher five-card hand than the flush to play. If she does have one, she had better play it, because Quilo is only one card away from going out. Marta doesn't have anything higher, so she passes, but Chang does have a higher hand and plays a full house. Nobody answers that play, and after three consecutive passes, Chang wins the round and gets the lead.

Chang sees that Quilo has only one card left and would like to feed him that one card and let him go out, because if Quilo goes out, they will both collect points from Phil, who is stuck with 10 cards, and Marta, loaded with 9.

The problem is that Phil plays first, and if he plays a controlling card, or at least one that is higher than Quilo holds, Quilo won't be able to go out and Phil will take control of the lead and maybe turn the game to his own advantage. In any case, the play is clear-cut since Chang has a pair of sevens and plays them. All three opponents rap their knuckles on the table, pass. Nobody has a higher pair, and Quilo can't play against two cards with a one-card hand. Chang leads with another pair, 8-8 this time, and again takes the round.

Chang leads again, plays a 10 and, leaning forward, announces in a whisper, "Bo Do." Chang also has only one card left. He looks over at Quilo, then glances coolly at the money in front of his place, and dreamily awaits the next play.

Phil, holding the 2♥, the highest-ranking card now that the 2♠ is gone, immediately plays it and takes the round. With 10 cards in his hand, he can't play games, not with two players who are one card away from going out.

He leads a small straight, which no player can answer, then leads again with the 2♣, which also takes the round without response. Since the 2♦ had been played earlier as part of a flush, the 2♣ is the highest ranking card remaining. With its removal, the A♠ is the highest card remaining.

Normally, the correct strategy is to save a **controlling card**, the highest ranking card remaining, to win a round and gain the lead, but if a smaller card is led, Phil will never see the chance to do that, not with two players one card away.

Phil is down to three cards, and having little other choice, plays the Q♥. Continuing around the table from right to left, Quilo can't go out with his 10 and passes. Marta plays the Q♠, a higher ranked queen.

Chang hesitates for a few seconds and bowing his head ever so slightly, plays the K♥, and goes out.

SCORING OF THE SAMPLE ROUND

After Chang went out, players were left with the following cards.

CARDS LEFT AT END OF ROUND 1	
Player	**# Cards Left**
Chang	0
Quilo	1
Phil	2
Marta	8

SCORE AFTER THE FIRST GAME

For Chang, who went out first, it's a good win, because the three other players owe him points, one for each card they have remaining. Thus, he wins 8 points from Marta, 2 from Phil and 1 from Quilo.

Quilo doesn't fare badly at all, because he loses only 1 point to Chang, the winner of the round, while he collects points from the other two players, 1 from Phil and 7 from Marta, for an overall gain of 8 points.

Phil loses 2 points to Chang and 1 point to Quilo, but gains 6 from Marta. Despite paying off two opponents, Phil wins enough points from Marta to chalk up an overall win of 3 points.

Marta, uncharacteristically quiet, didn't have the best luck this round, and winds up paying 8 points to Chang, 7 to Quilo, and 6 to Phil for a total loss of 21 points on the round.

In this round, we saw three winners of varying degrees and one loser. Let's see how it works when a player gets caught with penalty points.

THE SECOND GAME

In this next round, Marta goes out first with a flourish of knowing looks, mostly directed at Phil, who mutters about her good luck.

CARDS LEFT AT END OF ROUND 2	
Player	**# Cards Left**
Marta	0
Quilo	4
Chang	4
Phil	11

Marta collects 4 points from both Quilo and Chang, plus a big 22 (2 x 11) from Phil. A pretty good round, she wins 30 points. Quilo loses 4 points to Marta, is dead even with Chang, but gains a hefty 14 points (7 point difference x 2) from Phil thanks to the double penalty that he is paying, and comes out ahead 10 points for the round.

Having the same number of cards remaining, Chang and Quilo neither win nor lose from each other, and Chang's total is also +10 points for the round.

Phil bites the big one in this round. After losing 10 points to both Chang and Quilo and 22 to Marta, who was screeching with delight at the victory, he finds himself with a 42 point loss for the round.

SCORE AFTER THE SECOND GAME

If you're keeping score on paper, this is how the first two games would look.

SCORE AFTER ROUND 2			
Quilo	**Chang**	**Marta**	**Phil**
1	0	8	2
4	4	0	22
5	4	8	24

STRATEGY

The dealer enjoys a distinct advantage over the others since he gets to play his cards first, and thus control the initial tempo of the game. And since the goal is to get rid of cards, the player who acts first certainly has that head start as well.

The worst position in a round is the fourth to act. That's a spot you don't want to be in.

Why?

Because by the time play comes around to you, the cards already played may be stronger than what you hold, and you'll be forced to pass without getting to play any cards at all. Not a good thing!

LAYING DOWN CARDS

Generally speaking, you lay down cards whenever possible. However, there are times when you may find it advisable not to put down playable cards, either because it may break up a bigger hand, or because of future positioning.

CONTROL

Making the first discards in a playing round is advantageous—the player laying down cards first not only controls the number of cards to be played in the round, but also dictates the initial strength of the cards that must be beaten for others to lay down cards. This player controls the tempo of the round and may play into his own strengths in an attempt to rid his hand of all cards. Naturally, you'd love to be able to do that in every game!

The name of the game in Cho Dai Di is control—a lot of your strategy is worked around that. If you can control a round by playing the final cards, you get to lead the next round, which is a big advantage. For example, if you hold the 2♠, the most powerful card in the deck, and the lead is a single card, you know that you can control that round because nobody has a higher-ranking card. Being in control is sweet.

PLAYING FIRST

If you're the player who goes first in the game, you usually, though not always, will want to play a five-card hand, especially if it's a low ranking hand such as a 10-high straight. The straight is unlikely to control the round, but it does quickly get rid of five cards and prevents you from being blocked out of playing your straight later on if another player plays a higher five-card hand.

GAINING POINTS

Your strategy in Cho Dai Di is not so much to be the first one to go out in a round, but to gain points overall against the other players. You can do this by having the next fewest number of cards or sometimes, as we saw in the sample game, even having the third largest number of cards with only one player having more.

Thus, if it's your lead and the player to go next has one card remaining, you might not mind throwing a small one-card lead if a third player will get caught with 10 cards or more and you'll win double points. Of course, you would rather be the player going out first since the wins are larger, but that's not always possible, and it isn't always necessary.

Let's outline some other important winning concepts.

MORE WINNING CONCEPTS

TRY TO LEAD WITH SMALLER CARDS FIRST

Generally speaking, you want to play your low cards first, and get rid of these weaker cards. The weaker the card, the less playable that card is. For example, if a player has two cards remaining, a 4 and a 3, he'll have great difficulty in going out. For one thing, he will have trouble in gaining the lead with a small card, if he can even play it at all; and even if he is lucky enough to get rid of one of them, he will be unable to control a round and unload the second small fry.

However, if one of your two remaining cards is high, you may be able to maneuver that card into a controlling position and win the round. The small card can now be led, and since that's the last card, the game is over.

DON'T GET CAUGHT WITH 10 OR MORE CARDS

If an opponent is within striking distance of going out, the wise move is to break up a good hand so that you don't get caught with a double penalty. It's better to get stuck with eight cards and have to pay three players their dues than risk getting caught with 10 or more cards and have to pay a double penalty to all three opponents.

If you can't control the game, don't take chances if another player gets close to going out—break up your hand and play the game safe.

KEEP TRACK OF THE HIGH CARDS

It is extremely important to know which deuces and aces have been played. When it gets near the end, you need to know if the single lead you play can be followed later by a card that you hold and know to be the highest, thereby giving you control over the next round's start. You always need to know what the current controlling card is.

Remember, the 2♠ is the initial controlling card, and when it has been played, the 2♥ becomes the controlling card, then the 2♣, the 2♦, the A♠ and so on.

Knowing how many aces and deuces have been played also clues you in to the highest possible pairs that can be made. If you know that three aces and all four deuces have already been used, your pair of kings rules as the highest pair left. Or if you hold the remaining ace, you have the highest card left and can control with it.

DEFENSIVE PLAY

If an opposing player has only one card left, do not lead with one card unless you lead with the highest single card remaining. That way, the player cannot go out in his turn and you'll also control the round. On the other hand, you'll also benefit if that one-card player goes out, since you have few cards remaining and the other players have more cards left in their hands that you can get as points.

This strategy also applies when opposing players have two, three, four or five cards remaining before they can go out. If you're stuck with a lot of cards and one player has only two to go, a two-card lead is dangerous because a pair gives that player an opportunity to go out.

PARTING THOUGHTS

I hope you'll give this exciting game a shot. Cho Dai Di has a lot of strategy and lots of challenges. But they're worth it in exchange for the fun and friendly competition you'll get out of playing this terrific game. Let me know how you enjoyed playing your first game of Cho Dai Di. Until then, "Jhoy King"—see you later.

Cjok Lay Ho Wan—Good Fortune!

12 HORSERACING

FIVE KEYS TO HORSERACING

1. The best straight bets for your money are win and show. Avoid place bets.
2. If betting to win, stick with horses that give you odds of 5-1 or better; if betting to place, stick with odds of 5-1 or less.
3. If you really like a horse, go with your instincts and make a play on it. Don't bet horses you don't really like.
4. Avoid horses that are moving up in class. It's one thing to beat up on lesser horses, quite another to beat up on better ones.
5. Your best bets are often with horses that have some winning background, not with ones that are chronic losers and have never crossed the finish line first.

INTRODUCTION

Horseracing draws countless fans every year at tracks across the country. It is also quite popular in numerous other countries around the world. Fans everywhere are enthralled with the thrill of competition and the challenge of analyzing all the relevant data to pick a winner.

The tracks are fervid with the excitement, color and anticipation of the race. Men and women, their faces buried deep into their racing forms, analyze and handicap the races, figuring which horse going off at what odds presents them the best bet. They look at various factors, discuss the possibilities, and watch the tote board to see how the odds are moving.

Others, out to the track for the first time or simply less handicapping-minded, may choose the horse with a name that strikes their fancy—perhaps it's similar to the name of someone they know, a place they've been, or just sounds good to them. Or maybe they like the color associated with that horse.

This section explains the language of the track, the various wagers available to the bettor, different philosophies and strategies of winning, and the odds you face every time you wager on a horse—plus eleven suggestions for winning at the track. With these important factors under your belt, you can have a lot of fun with your friends at the races—and maybe even some profit in your pockets.

THE BETS

STRAIGHT BETTING

The win, place and show bets, called **straight bets**, are the most popular wagers at the horse track. The **win bet** is a wager that a horse will finish first in the race. Any finish other than first is irrelevant, as it is only the first place finish that counts with a win bet.

The **place bet** is a wager that the horse will come in first or second—either way, the bet is a winner. A **show bet** allows you even more leeway—the horse may come in first, second or third for the bet to be a winner.

Of the straight bets, win tickets will pay the best since they are hardest to pick. Place and show bets pay less than win bets because more horses share the betting pool; two in the case of place bets and three in the case of show bets.

EXACTA BETS

The **exacta** is a bet that the two horses chosen in a race come in first and second, in exact order. Many bettors like this type of wager because the payoffs can be pretty good if their exacta ticket is a winner.

QUINELLA BETS

On this wager, the **quinella**, you're betting on the top two finishers in a race, like the exacta, except that with the quinella, you don't care about the order of finish—you only care that your two horses are the first and second place finishers in that race.

The quinella bet is easier to win than the exacta, and consequently pays less.

DAILY DOUBLE

This popular bet is a wager on the winners of the first two races. If you correctly pick the winner of one race only, your bet counts for nothing. To win a **daily double**, you must correctly pick the winners of both the first and second races.

TRIPLES

This bet is similar to the Daily Double except that with the **triple**, you must choose the winner of the three consecutive races designated by the track.

PICK SIX

You can make a fortune correctly choosing a **Pick Six**, but it's not easy—you must pick the winner of six races! Good luck on this one. There is usually a smaller payoff, a type of consolation prize, if you get five winners out of the six

OTHER EXOTIC BETS

Some tracks offer other exotic bets, but these should be clearly explained on the track's programs. You may find bets like a **Pick Nine**, where you have to choose the winners of nine races. Win that one and all your money troubles are over.

SOME TRACK BASICS

THE TOTE BOARD

The big computerized board at the track, called the **totalizer** or **tote board**, displays the amount of money bet on each horse to win, place and show, plus the resultant odds, which constantly change as wagers come in on particular horses. The lines listed on the tote board reflect the betting at the track—the more money bet on a horse, the lower its odds will be. Thus, if many people favor Robert the Grand Hungarian to win and they back him with more bets than any other horse, Robert the Grand Hungarian will be the **favorite**, and will have the smallest payoff of any horse in the race.

Horses that get little action are considered **longshots** and will go off at high odds; 10 to 1 or 17 to 1, for example.

The tote board is important to watch because it shows the odds of each horse and lets you know which horse is the current favorite and which horse is the longest shot (the horse with the least amount of money bet on it and consequently, the highest odds).

The odds continually change as more betting money comes in, and will be reflected on the tote board for all to see. Sometimes a favorite will become a bigger favorite, or even get supplanted by another horse as the favorite as late money comes in.

When the race is ready to begin, no more bets will be accepted and the posted odds become the actual odds of the race on which all payoffs are based. If you were lucky enough to pick the winner, it will be the final odds at post time that determines your payoff, not the odds at the time you placed your bet.

THE MORNING LINE

The initial line at which the odds on competing horses are quoted is set by the track handicapper, and is his estimation of how the horses might be bet by the public. This line is called the **morning line** and has no final bearing on the actual payoff on a horse if it wins.

Once bets start coming in, the odds on the tote board change to reflect the amounts bet on each horse.

Many bettors use the morning line as a rough guide to the comparative strengths of the horses. Horses listed at low odds, say 2 to 1, probably have a good chance of winning the race, while those going off at 25 to 1, considered high odds, probably have little chance of finishing in the money.

BETS AND PAYOFFS

The minimum bet in horseracing is generally $2.00. The amount of money you receive for a winning bet will reflect the winning odds as listed on the tote board plus your original $2.00 bet. For example, if your horse goes off at 5 to 2 odds and is a winner, you'll receive $5.00 for the win plus your original $2.00 bet for a total of $7.00.

The results posted are always based on the $2.00 bet so if you place a larger bet or $10.00, for example, you simply multiply the $2.00 results by 5 ($10.00 is five $2.00 wagers) to come out with the total won. In this example, a $10.00 bet would pay off $25.00 in winnings plus your original bet of $10.00 for a total $35.00 return.

The tote board will read $7.00 on the 5-2 win anyway, already reflecting the $2.00 bet placed.

Let's say that in a particular race, horse #2, Liberty Charles, wins the race at 3 to 1 odds; horse #5, Skidmore Jones, comes in second; and horse # 1, Happy Harry, comes in third.

This is how it may be listed:

POSTED WINNINGS

Horse	Order of Finish	Win	Place	Show
2 Liberty Charles	Winner	8.00	4.80	4.00
5 Skidmore Jones	Second		11.60	4.80
1 Happy Harry	Third			2.60

Only those who bet horse #2 (Liberty Charles) to win collect the $8.00; $6.00 in winnings for the 3-1 odds, plus the $2.00 bet. Players who bet Liberty Charles to place collect only $4.80, and ones who bet him to show get back $4.00.

Players who bet either the #5 or #1 horse to win are losers because those horses didn't win. However, place and show bets on #5, and show bets on #1, will pay the amounts shown on the chart.

HOW TO BET

Horses are identified by **post position** in the racing program, as well as on the tote board and the tickets you buy at the betting windows. Thus, a horse sporting a "1" in the program, will be running out from the first post position, and a horse identified by a "7" will be exiting from the seventh post position.

The tote board also uses the post position numbers to identify horses. To follow the betting line as it progresses, simply track your horse by its post number.

Let's say that you've added up the pros and cons of each horse and are ready to place your bet. The horses on your program are listed as follows:

PROGRAM LISTING	
Squarebacks	1
Bongo Player	2
Rubics	3
Ted the T.	4
Chess	5
Octogon	6
Woodstock	7
Bird in the Cage	8

If you want to bet on Bongo Player to show and Octogon to win, you would identify #2 as the place and #6 as your win bet. Similarly, if you want to pick Octagon (post position 6) and Bird in the Cage (post position 8) as your 1-2 horses in an exacta, you'll identify the ticket as a 6-8 exacta.

THE PARI-MUTUEL POOL

The **pari-mutuel pool** is the total amount of money bet, less the **takeout**—the amount deducted from the prize pool for state and local taxes, purse money, expenses at the track and the track's profit— which is available for the winners to collect. After the government and track take are pulled from the total bets, the rest is proportionately divided among the winners. The higher the odds of a winning horse, the greater the payoff will be if the horse wins or comes into the money. Likewise, the lower the odds (meaning that more bettors wagered on the horse), the smaller the winning payoff will be.

Keep in mind that historically, the higher the odds against a horse, the less chance the horse has of winning.

Let's see just how big a cut is taken from the pari-mutuel pool before the bettors get their share.

THE PERCENTAGES

Betting is as embedded in horseracing as the horses themselves, but it is one of the tougher gambling pursuits to beat. Racing fans face a stiff tax at the horse races, and must overcome this albatross to come ahead a winner. Few do.

Here is why.

All tracks have a takeout that ranges in the 14-20% range, usually nearer the higher amount, which is deducted from the prize pool. This is a gargantuan percentage to overcome. Additionally, fans that make exotic bets such as the Pick Six and Triple get taxed at an even greater rate—as high as 30%!

There is one additional price the horse bettor must pay, and that is called breakage. The track pays out winnings to the dime only, and keeps whatever odd pennies are left over. For example, if the mutuel payoff figures to be $5.78, the bettor would receive only $5.70 back, or a $3.56 win would pay off at $3.50.

So what's the big deal, a few pennies here or there? Plenty. On average, this costs you about another 2% per dollar wagered—more straws on the camel's back.

You have to be a very good handicapper to overcome these percentages. In fact, they'll leave you in a ditch that's hard to shovel your way out of if you're a serious bettor.

It's a lot of fun to watch the horses and jockeys compete, to be part of the colorful track atmosphere, and to study the racing form and figure the winning horses. However, keep the races and the heavy odds in perspective when you hit the mutuels for a little action.

A WORD ON HORSERACE BETTING

Keep in mind that you're bucking big odds when you take on the track. I heartily recommend that you pursue betting on the horses as strictly recreational. If you decide you want to play the track on a more serious level, you should first test your skills on a small scale. If you maintain a winning record at that level, you might move up to bigger stakes.

Don't jump up in bet size until you've proven your skills—the difference between betting small dollars and betting big dollars might end up only with bigger losses. In other words, making bigger bets won't necessarily change your luck.

THE CLASSES OF RACES

There are five basic classes of horseracing. While there is some overlap between the groupings, these classifications will give you a good idea about the relative strength of horses in one group as compared to another.

CLAIMING RACES

Out of the nine or so races you'll see featured in a racing program, the claiming race will be the type of race you most frequently see. The purses for winning horses are the smallest of any of the races; consequently, the horses entered in claiming races are the lowest in quality.

The concept of the claiming race is quite interesting. Any horse entered in a **claiming race** can be bought—in the jargon of the track, **claimed**—by anyone for the **claiming price** listed in the program.

Generally, another stable or horseman will be the buyer, but now and then an amateur out of the stands might pick one up.

A horse must be claimed prior to a race, in writing, and once claimed, is the exclusive property of the new owner. The purse for that race, however, will still belong to the previous owner.

It is more difficult to handicap these types of races because the horses entered, being of the lowest quality, are more inconsistent, and therefore more difficult to predict.

There are varying claiming prices on these horses, and you can figure that a higher claiming price generally indicates a better class of horse. Sometimes you'll see a horse going down in class, being entered at a lower claiming price than previously. This might indicate that the horse was unable to successfully compete at the higher level, and has therefore dropped down, the owner perhaps hoping to catch some purses against lesser class horses, or maybe hoping to unload the horse at a cheaper price. Horses cost a lot of money to maintain, and the owners, business people, need to keep the ship afloat.

The claiming system is clever and is a deterrent against higher-class horses entering a race and stealing the purse, because once a horse is entered, it is open market for another buyer who thinks the horse is worth the claiming price.

Some trainers and owners are good evaluators of talent, and make a nice business out of claiming horses. They are referred to as **claiming trainers** or **claiming owners**.

MAIDEN RACES

These races are clearly a cut above the claiming races, and sometimes the best of horses start out at this level. Horses entered in **maiden races** have not yet won a race and are too valuable to the owner to run in a claimer.

Within this category is the **Maiden Special Weight** race for two-year-old horses that also have not won a race.

ALLOWANCE RACES

A variety of elements are factored into **allowance races**, such as the number of races run and money won previously. The horses are assigned a **weight allowance** to help offset the differences between them and the other contestants in a race. For example, a seemingly superior horse may be assigned five extra pounds on the theory that those extra pounds will put its talents on equal grounds with lesser horses in the race.

Allowance races are run for different ages of horses and for different purse sizes. There are also class levels within the allowance category. You can figure a horse running a $25,000 allowance to be superior to a horse running a $15,000 race.

HANDICAP RACES

Handicap races are for near top-level horses competing for high purses. The track handicapper examines each horse's credentials carefully and assigns weights to each one, in an attempt to equalize the speeds and skills, so that each horse has a fair shot at winning the race.

STAKES RACES

Stakes races feature the cream of the talent, the top thoroughbreds competing for the top prizes. Races such as the Preakness, the Kentucky Derby and the Belmont Stakes, the events of horseracing's famous **Triple Crown**, are all stakes races.

Here is where famous horses such as Secretariat and Seattle Slew cement their fame in horseracing's hall of fame.

These races create the most excitement of all the thoroughbred events because the top contenders in the world are competing horse to horse in a thrilling spectacle that is discussed long before the race is ever run and glorified long after it is over.

HANDICAPPING PHILOSOPHIES

FORM HANDICAPPING

A horse's current form, how it has fared in the last few races, is what racetrackers call **form handicapping**. The proponents of this type of handicapping argue that horses, like humans, are conditioned athletes—they reach peaks of high performance at times, and at other times are simply not as good.

If a horse has not run well lately, form handicapping says that all the other handicapping factors just don't make sense. Plainly, the horse is not in good enough form to win the race.

Form handicappers attempt to bet on horses that, according to recent past performance charts, are in the peak of their form and, on that basis, have the best chances of winning the race.

TRIP HANDICAPPING

Trip handicappers are looking for inconsistency in a horse caused by a track mishap that caused an otherwise strong contender to perhaps finish out of the money. The final result may show that the horse didn't fare so well, but the trip handicapper—noting that the horse started fast, suddenly lost a bunch of lengths, but then finished strong—may conclude that the horse got tripped-up and is really a better horse than the order of finish in the past race might indicate.

CLASS HANDICAPPING

Class handicapping proposes that there is no more important factor than a horse's class. Horseplayers define **class** as a comparison of the quality of a race that a horse has competed in as judged by the level or claiming price of the race, the importance of the race, or the stakes involved. They will look for opportunities where a superior horse, judged on class, will race against inferior horses.

There are many formulas used to judge class. One of the more popular ones is to judge the amount of money earned by a horse over a specified period of time, divide the earnings amount of the horse by the number of races run, and come up with a figure that could be used for comparison.

For example, when a horse attempts to move up in class, the class handicappers will look carefully at the horse's credentials, and if they conclude that it is racing out of class, they consider the horse a poor bet. On the other hand, a horse moving down in class enjoys a marked advantage over the lesser horses and, given the right odds, may indeed be a very good bet.

SPEED HANDICAPPING

Speed handicapping stresses that the speed with which the horse has run its races is the most important variable in picking winners. A general rule of thumb at the track is to assign one second to every five lengths at the track. Thus if a horse finished 10 lengths behind the winner's time of 1.11 in a six furlong race, you would call the speed 1.13.

Horses run races under different conditions and speed handicappers adjust times or give weighting to these factors so that horses with different racing backgrounds can be compared to each other. Speed handicappers adjust for the speed of tracks, the different jockey weights, and the length of the track, among other variables, to find the horse that shows the greatest potential speed for the race to be run—and make their pick accordingly.

PACE HANDICAPPING

Pace handicappers believe that the crucial element in winning races is not so much how fast a horse can run, but how well the horse paces itself during a race. A pure speed horse can have the edge in a sprint race, but when the race is a route, other elements such as pace come into play.

On the theory that a horse cannot run a route at absolute full speed for the length of the track, but must pace itself against the others and save its maximum energy for the stretch run, the pace handicappers spot the horses they think can run the distance at the best pace. Pace handicappers may avoid fast sprint horses, instead opting for horses that have a proven record in routes.

TAKING INTO ACCOUNT MORE INFORMATION

There are numerous other ways that horseplayers figure an angle on the race, not the least of which is a jockey's abilities and a trainer's abilities. Some jockeys and trainers are proven winners with records that are far better than their peers, which is an element that some bettors factor into their analysis.

Let's look at some standard percentages that have held true over many years and then give you a few winning techniques to get you started.

STANDARD WINNING PERCENTAGES

Over the long run, a horse's winning percentage is in direct correlation to its **send-off position**, the relative listing of odds on the horse at race time.

Over the years, certain percentages have held in horseracing:

- Horses going off as **favorites** will win approximately 33% of the time
- **Second choices**, horses with the next lowest odds after the favorite, will win about 20% of the time.
- **Third choices**, the next down in send-off position, will win the race about 15% of the time.
- **Fourth choices**, **fifth choices** and so on will win a smaller proportion of the races in order of send-off position.

Altogether, the top three choices account for almost 70% of all wins. Favorites will place a bit over 50% of the time, while second choices place around 40%, and third choices 30%.

Keep in mind that these figures have stayed fairly constant over the years, but that doesn't mean they'll hold true over a limited period of time at a particular track. As in all forms of gambling, short run anomalies are normal in horseracing, but these figures are good guideposts to go by when formulating your winning approach at the track.

WINNING STRATEGIES

To give you a leg up on many other horse bettors, here are general guidelines that many pros follow.

ELEVEN WINNING STRATEGIES

1. When betting straight, restrict your bets to win and show only.
2. As a general rule, bet horses you like with odds of 5 to 1 or greater to win, and odds of 5 to 1 or less to place.
3. Pay close attention to a horse's recent performances. Form handicapping has a lot of merit, and you face your best chances with a horse in top condition.
4. Horses backed heavily by touting services and computer handicappers may win more, but so many bettors are placing their dollars on them, they give poor value for the money. Try to find the "dark horse," one that has a good shot at the tape but is not overly backed.
5. Be wary of the "smart money," bets placed at the last minute by, supposedly, those in the know. There isn't much smart money at the tracks.
6. Go with your gut feelings. If there's a horse you like, by all means bet that horse. There's no worse feeling than not doing what you felt you should have done, and it working out—without you. And if it doesn't work out, no big deal.
7. Pay special attention to fast starters on off tracks. It's more difficult to maneuver on a muddy or slow track, and these conditions will favor the horse that takes the early lead.
8. Avoid horses moving up in class. They may have looked good against lesser horses, but the move to better competition may reveal some different colors.
9. Avoid horses that have not raced in the past four weeks. They may be recuperating from illness and the owners are using the race as a tune-up. The winning percentages of long-idled horse are way below the average.
10. Bet only winners. If you see a horse that has been around but has never won a race, why figure that today's race will be a reversal of past performance? Instead, choose a horse that has some background of winning.

11. Bet only horses that you think have a good chance of winning. If you had eliminated all the horses you've bet in the past, but have not really believed in, you would be sitting with a much higher winning percentage. If you don't like a horse, don't bet it.

PARTING THOUGHTS

I've provided you with a lot of information on how horseracing works, including five key handicapping approaches and eleven solid winning tips to help you win money at the track. There are many theories on why one horse will outrun another on a given day, at a given race, and on a given track. Adding up and sifting through all the data and the tangible and intangible factors makes the analysis of a horserace both intriguing and mystifying.

What's the best approach when all is said and done? I've given you some food for thought; I'll leave it up to you to figure out the best winning approach to fit your style of thinking.

13 KENO

FIVE KEYS TO KENO

1. Do not play keno as a moneymaking venture. The odds typically range from 20% to 35% against you, way too high to play the game seriously.
2. The optimal tickets to play are the 3 spot to 8 spot tickets. You typically get the best odds on these bets.
3. You'll rarely if ever hear of anyone catching a 12 spot ticket or higher. Get the picture? Don't mark that many spots.
4. Also avoid 1 and 2 spot tickets. The house edge is very high.
5. Shop around for the best payouts. Keno paybacks vary widely from casino to casino, and you want to play at the venue that offers the best return.

INTRODUCTION

The origins of keno go back some 2,000 years to the Han Dynasty in China—quite a long history, and quite a long distance to travel to make it to casinos as far away as Nevada, halfway across the globe.

One of the attractions of this popular casino game is that it's easy to play. The only decisions you need to make are which numbers you want to play and how much to bet. Once your bet is placed, the fun begins as numbers appear one at a time on the keno board, and you anxiously wait to see if you catch enough lucky numbers to bring in the big bucks. And there's always that attraction of the giant win—that a $1.00 wager, or whatever you play, may catch the right numbers and land a $200,000 bonanza.

Keno has that lure—the big win, the myriad possibilities of numbers that can land, the almost wins, the "If I had played those numbers" near misses.

Let's move on now, learn how the game is played, and how best to increase your chances of winning.

THE BASICS OF KENO

HOW TO PLAY

All bets in keno are made and recorded on a **keno ticket**, a preprinted form on which you mark the numbers you want to play. Tickets are readily available in the **keno lounge**, at every seat in the keno area, and at every table in the casino's restaurants. Situated near the tickets will be thick, black crayons that are used to mark keno tickets, plus the casino's **rate card** showing the exact payoffs for tickets played and won.

There are 80 numbered squares on a keno ticket that correspond exactly to the 80 numbered balls in the keno cage. You may choose from one to 15 or even 20 numbers to play by marking an "X" on the keno ticket for each number you pick. The more numbers you choose, the more numbers you need to hit to be a winner—but also the bigger the payout you will receive if your selections were good.

You'll notice some special wording on the keno ticket, such as "Aggregate Keno Limit $100,000," or "Aggregate Keno Limit Posted." This means that if you hit the big prize in the same game as another player, you'll have to split the jackpot. However, the likelihood of this occurring stretches the imagination into far off places, so don't worry about it. It's hard to win one jackpot, but two people hitting it at the same time? It's not going to happen, especially with so few tickets being played simultaneously.

Twenty balls are drawn each game and appear as lighted numbers on the keno screens. As the game progresses, each number will be lit as it is drawn, so that you can easily see how your ticket is faring.

Winnings are determined by consulting the payoff chart that each casino provides. If you pick enough numbers, you have a winner, and the chart will show your payoff. The more numbers that come up, the greater your winnings.

BETTING

Bets are usually made in $1.00 multiples, though other standard bets such as $2 and $5 may also apply. You may bet as many games at a time as you desire. For example, if you want to bet $1 per game and play five games in succession with the same number combinations, you would bet $5.00 and mark "5" in the "Number of Games" (sometimes abbreviated to "No. of Games") square on your ticket.

HOW TO MARK THE TICKET

The amount being wagered on a game should be placed in the box marked **Price Per Game** in the upper right hand corner of the ticket. Leave out dollar or cents signs. You would indicate a $1 bet by simply placing "**1-**" in the box. Of course, you can wager any amount up to the house limit.

There are usually four other boxes on a keno ticket. "Mark Number of Spots" or "Ways Played" is where you mark the number of spots (numbers) you've selected for the game. If you select six spots on the ticket, mark the number "**6**;" if you choose 15 numbers, mark "**15**."

In the **Number of Games** box, you mark how many successive games you want to play. The **Total Price** box is where you mark the total of your wager. For example, if you're betting $1 on one game, you would mark "1-"; and if you're betting 5 games, you would mark "5-".

The other box you'll find on most casino's keno tickets is **Account #** which is where you write your Slot Card Membership number to get credit for your keno action.

Let's show a five-spot ticket that we've marked for a $1 game.

MARK PRICE HERE

1—

1	2	3	4	5	6	7	8	9	10
11	12	13	14	15	16	17	18	19	20
21	22	23	24	25	26	27	28	29	30
31	32	33	34	35	36	37	38	39	40

5

KENO LIMIT $50,000.00 TO AGGREGATE PLAYERS EACH GAME

41	42	43	44	45	46	47	48	49	50
51	52	53	54	55	56	57	58	59	60
61	62	63	64	65	66	67	68	69	70
71	72	73	74	75	76	77	78	79	80

5-spot straight ticket

This type of ticket, which is the most popular among bettors, is called a **straight ticket**—in this example, a five-spot straight ticket. Similarly, if 10 numbers were chosen, it would be called an 10-spot straight ticket.

THE DUPLICATE TICKET

Now you have your ticket filled in and are ready to play the game. You take this **original ticket** or **master ticket** to the keno writer at the window and hand it in with the dollar amount you'll be playing.

The writer will retain your original ticket and give you a **duplicate ticket**. This ticket will show the same numbers you have chosen. In Las Vegas casinos, the ticket writer enters your number onto a computer, which records your choices, the amount you are wagering, and the total numbers you are playing. The computer then spits out a duplicate ticket, which the writer gives to you. In older casinos, the ticket writer uses an inked brush to mark the same information in thick black strokes.

Your ticket will also show some things that were not on your original. The duplicate will have printed on it the date and time of the game, the game's number, and a barcode number used by the casino. You'll also see some words printed at the bottom of the ticket, such as "Winning tickets must be collected immediately after game is called," if that is the casino's policy. In some casinos, you must present your winning ticket before the next game starts, or you will forfeit that payoff.

These rules vary from casino to casino, so you want to carefully read the keno rules where you're playing so you understand the collection procedures. For example, in the Station casinos, you have 48 hours from the time you play your ticket before you must collect your winnings—or forfeit them. The 4 Queens in downtown Las Vegas requires you to present your winning tickets within seven days. Similarly, the Harrahs casinos give you up to seven days to collect on tickets played. However, if you play tickets good for 21 games or more, they allow you up to one year to collect. The 4 Queens allows up to one year as well for multi-game tickets greater than twenty. The Station casinos also allow you up to one year to collect on multiple keno plays, but in that case you must play 10 consecutive games (as opposed to the 21 of the Harrahs group).

In any case, that information will be printed at the bottom of your ticket. Just make sure you don't wander off with a winning ticket and come back when it is too late! Because policies vary, be sure to read the small print and take this piece of writing seriously.

THE KENO RUNNER

Most casinos offer players the chance to play keno from virtually anywhere in the casino. You can play the game while playing your favorite slots or enjoying a meal in the casino's restaurants.

A casino employee, called a **keno runner**, takes keno bets from patrons in various parts of the casino, returns to them a duplicate ticket, and collects their payoff on winning tickets to deliver to them.

Ah, the easy life! If you win, it is customary to tip the runner (the bearer of good tidings) a small amount of your win.

REPLAYING A TICKET

You may have a lucky set of numbers you like to play, or a particular set that has either just won for you, or which you've just played and feel that the same numbers are ready to come home and roost.

In any case, the casino allows you to replay the same numbers again. To save you the trouble of rewriting your ticket, simply hand in your duplicate, which now becomes your original ticket, and the keno writer will issue you a new duplicate.

Easy as that. You can do this all day long if you like.

Or, if you prefer, you can specify a consecutive number of games you would like to be played with your ticket. For example, if you can choose to play 21 games in a row, or even 50. This is called **multi-race keno**. As written earlier, you have up to one year from the time you play your tickets to collect your winnings provided the minimum number of games as specified by the casino is played.

PAYOFF CHARTS

Let's look at two keno payoff charts from two Las Vegas casino groups. One is from the Station Casinos (Palace Station, Boulder Station, Texas Station, Sunset Station, Santa Fe Station, Red Rock, Fiesta Rancho, Aliante Station, Green Valley Ranch and Fiesta Henderson) The other rate card is from the Harrahs casinos (Harrahs, Caesars Palace, Rio, Bally's, Paris, Imperial Palace and Flamingo).

In the Harrahs casinos, the top jackpot is $200,000, but you'll need to hit 14 numbers on a 14-number $2 ticket to hit it. Note that you still get only $200,000 by hitting fifteen numbers on a fifteen number ticket. You can also win the $200,000 on a 8-spot ticket by hitting all eight numbers. But look what happens on the bigger spot tickets. You still get the same $200,000 by hitting nine out of nine, ten out of ten, even up to fifteen out of fifteen. So obviously, if you're going for the big prize, you want to choose the lowest ticket possible as it is much easier to hit.

In the Station Casino group, the top aggregate payout is $100,000. To win this, you need to hit ten out of ten spots playing a $1 ticket, but, as in the Harrahs group, hitting more numbers, which is much more difficult, does not increase the grand prize. If you hit 15 out of 15, you still get the same $100,000. Hitting ten out of ten spots in the Harrahs casinos pays just $80,000—and that's on a $2 ticket.

You'll notice that there are payoff schedules for any amount of numbers picked, 1 through 15 or 20, depending on the casino, and that each one has its own minimum set of numbers needed to win and amount of payoff that you'll get for hitting winning combinations. For example, if you play a 10-spot game with a $2.00 bet at Palace Station, you'll need to **catch** a minimum of four numbers for a payoff. In this case, $2.00 would be returned. You'd get $4 back on five numbers, $20 on six, $200 on seven, $2,000 on eight numbers, $10,000 on nine numbers, and $100,000 if you hit all ten. At Rio, that same $2 10-spot ticket wouldn't pay anything on four or five spots; the first payout would be on six numbers hit, giving winners a $46 payout. Seven numbers hit would win $300, eight pays $2,000, nine pays $10,000, and all ten would pay $80,000.

As you see, there can be significant differences in payouts between one casino and the next. Before playing, you may want to shop around for the various payoffs and see which one suits you best.

KENO PAYOUT SCHEDULE A Harrahs Casinos			
# WINNING SPOTS	$2 PAYS	$5 PAYS	#10 PAYS
PICK 1			
1	6	15	30
PICK 2			
2	24	60	120
PICK 3			
2	2	5	10
3	84	210	420
PICK 4			
2	2	5	10
3	6	15	30
4	240	600	1,200
PICK 5			
3	2	5	10
4	46	115	230
5	1,000	2,500	5,000
PICK 6			
3	2	5	10
4	6	15	30
5	180	450	900
6	3,000	7,500	15,000
PICK 7			
4	2	5	10
5	34	85	170
6	700	1,750	3,500
7	18,000	45,000	90,000
PICK 8			
5	14	35	70
6	160	400	800
7	3,000	7,500	15,000
8	60,000	150,000	200,000
PICK 9			
5	6	15	30
6	88	220	440
7	600	1,500	3,000
8	8,000	20,000	40,000
9	60,000	150,000	200,000
PICK 10			
6	46	115	230
7	300	750	1,500
8	2,000	5,000	10,000
9	10,000	25,000	50,000
10	80,000	200,000	200,000

KENO PAYOUT SCHEDULE A Harrahs Casinos			
# WINNING SPOTS	$2 PAYS	$5 PAYS	#10 PAYS
PICK 11			
6	16	40	80
7	160	400	800
8	740	1,850	3,700
9	3,800	9,500	19,000
10	30,000	75,000	150,000
11	150,000	200,000	200,000
PICK 12			
7	80	200	400
8	600	1,500	3,000
9	1,800	4,500	9,000
10	4,000	10,000	20,000
11	34,000	85,000	170,000
12	150,000	200,000	200,000
PICK 13			
7	34	85	170
8	180	450	900
9	1,460	3,650	7,300
10	8,000	20,000	40,000
11	14,000	35,000	70,000
12	50,000	125,000	200,000
13	150,000	200,000	200,000
PICK 14			
7	20	50	100
8	84	210	240
9	640	1,600	3,200
10	2,800	7,000	14,000
11	8,000	20,000	40,000
12	40,000	100,000	200,000
13	100,000	200,000	200,000
14	200,000	200,000	200,000
PICK 15			
7	10	25	50
8	60	150	300
9	300	750	1,500
10	1,000	2,500	5,000
11	6,400	16,000	32,000
12	18,000	45,000	90,000
13	100,000	200,000	200,000
14	200,000	200,000	200,000
15	200,000	200,000	200,000

KENO PAYOUT SCHEDULE B (1$ Progressive) Station Casinos			
# WINNING SPOTS	$1 PAYS	$2 PAYS	#5 PAYS
	PICK 1		
1	3	6	15
	PICK 2		
2	12	24	60
	PICK 3		
2	1	2	5
3	42	84	210
	PICK 4		
2	1	2	5
3	3	6	15
4	130	260	650
	PICK 5		
3	1	2	5
4	10	20	50
5	750	1,500	3,750
	PICK 6		
3	1	–	–
4	2	–	–
5	70	–	–
6	Progressive Starts at $2,500		
	PICK 7		
0	1	–	–
4	1	–	–
5	15	–	–
6	200	–	–
7	Progressive Starts at $10,000		
	PICK 8		
5	5	–	–
6	75	–	–
7	1,500	–	–
8	Progressive Starts at $50,000		
	PICK 9		
4	1	–	–
5	3	–	–
6	30	–	–
7	300	–	–
8	3,000	–	–
9	Progressive Starts at $60,000		

KENO PAYOUT SCHEDULE B (1$ Progressive) Station Casinos			
# WINNING SPOTS	$1 PAYS	$2 PAYS	#5 PAYS
	PICK 10		
4	1	2	5
5	2	4	10
6	10	20	50
7	100	200	500
8	1,000	2,000	5,000
9	5,000	10,000	25,000
10	75,000	100,000	100,000
	PICK 12		
0	2	4	10
5	1	2	5
6	3	6	15
7	20	40	100
8	200	400	1,000
9	750	1,500	3,750
10	3,000	6,000	15,000
11	25,000	50,000	100,000
12	100,000	100,000	100,000
	PICK 15		
0	10	20	50
1	2	4	10
6	1	2	5
7	5	10	25
8	20	40	100
9	50	100	250
10	250	500	1,250
11	2,000	4,000	10,000
12	10,000	20,000	50,000
13	25,000	50,000	100,000
14	50,000	100,000	100,000
15	100,000	100,000	100,000

"ADVANCED" TICKETS

You are not limited to just straight tickets but may also play as many combinations as you choose. The following tickets are for players that are getting beyond the basics and are comfortable playing these "advanced" tickets.

SPLIT TICKETS

A split ticket allows you to bet two or more combinations in one game—essentially, wagering multiple straight tickets on one ticket.

This is done by marking two sets (or more) of 1-15 numbers on a ticket and separating them by either a line, or by circling the separate groups. Numbers may not be duplicated between the two sets.

On split tickets, in which several games are being played in one, the keno ticket should be marked as follows. In addition to the X that marks each number, and the lines or circles showing the groups, the ticket should clearly indicate the number of games being played.

For example, a split ticket playing two groups of six spots each would be marked 2/6 in the column of white space. The 2 shows that two combinations are being played, and the 6 shows that six numbers are being chosen per game.

If $1 is being bet per combination, put a "1-" and circle it underneath the slashed numbers to show this, and of course, in the Mark Price Here box, "2-", to show that $2 is being bet—$1 on each combination.

Here are two examples of a split ticket, one separated by a line, and the other separated by circles.

Split Ticket • Line Separated

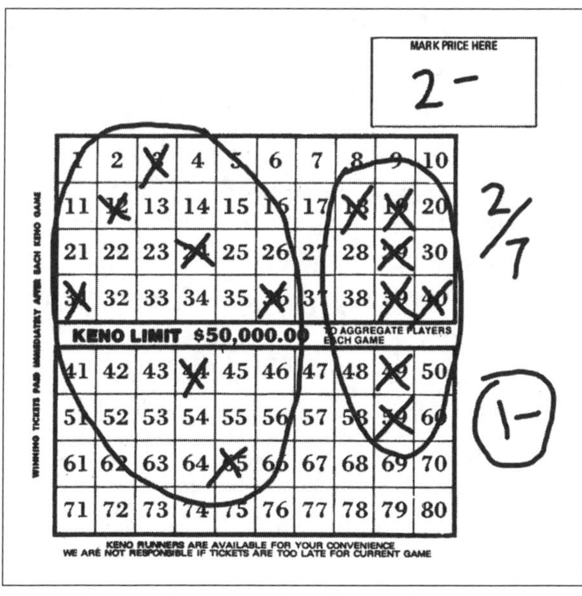

Split Ticket • Circle Separated

You could theoretically play 80 one-spots on one split ticket, or 40 two-spots or 10 five-spots—as long as numbers aren't duplicated.

Remember that on split tickets, each split game is essentially played separately and counts as a separate game. Numbers cannot be combined among different groups to create a winner; the winning numbers must be isolated among one group.

Any odd combination of split groups is allowed on a split ticket. If you desire, for example, you could play two groups of five-spots, one seven-spot, one four-spot and one three-spot on the same ticket. Different amounts of money can be wagered on each group. In the above example, $1.00 could be bet on the five, seven and four-spot groups, while $2.00 could be wagered on the three-spot.

The only restriction to the different dollar amounts you're allowed to bet on one split ticket is that equal groupings of numbers—in the above example, the two five-spots—must be bet with the same amount of money. Otherwise, bet what you will on each grouping as long as it conforms to the minimum and maximum amounts permitted by the casino.

COMBINATION TICKETS

Combination tickets allow you to combine groups of numbers in all sorts of ways with the player betting one unit for each combination possible.

For example, you can indicate groups of two, three and four numbers on a ticket. Using all possible combinations, you can play the game as a 2-spot, 3-spot, 4-spot, 5-spot (2 + 3), 6-spot (2-spot + 4 spot), 7-spot (3-spot + 4 spot) and 9-spot (2-spot, 3-spot and 4-spot) for a total of a seven-unit bet.

Whew—lots of combinations!

The groups bet on combination tickets should all be clearly marked in the white space on the right of the keno ticket. In the above example of a combination ticket, you would mark 1/2, 1/3, 1/4, 1/5, 1/6, 1/7 and 1/9, showing that one combination is being played on each of these groupings.

If $1 was bet per grouping, you would circle a "1-" underneath, just like on the way ticket. Seven combinations by $1 per group, and you have a total bet of $7. This gets marked as "7-" in the "Mark Price Here" area.

Here's one more example, this time a simpler combination ticket. You circle two groups of five. At $1.00 per game, $3.00 total is bet, $1.00 each on two groups of five, and $1.00 on one grouping of ten.

MARK PRICE HERE

3-

1	2	3	4	5	6	7	8	9	10
11	12	13	14	15	16	17	18	19	20
21	22	23	24	25	26	27	28	29	30
31	32	33	34	35	36	37	38	39	40

KENO LIMIT $50,000.00 TO AGGREGATE PLAYERS EACH GAME

41	42	43	44	45	46	47	48	49	50
51	52	53	54	55	56	57	58	59	60
61	62	63	64	65	66	67	68	69	70
71	72	73	74	75	76	77	78	79	80

2/5

1/10

1-

WINNING TICKETS PAID IMMEDIATELY AFTER EACH KENO GAME

KENO RUNNERS ARE AVAILABLE FOR YOUR CONVENIENCE
WE ARE NOT RESPONSIBLE IF TICKETS ARE TOO LATE FOR CURRENT GAME

Combination Ticket

WAY TICKETS

When you want more action than a regular one-bet keno ticket gives you, way tickets are the way to go. A way ticket make it possible to wager more than one bet on a single ticket, for example, you can have three or more "ways" to win in action at the same time, instead of having only one way to win on a straight keno ticket.

Way tickets feature at least three groups of equal numbers that can be combined in several ways. The groupings must be equal and the dollar amount bet must be the same for all groups.

If you pick good, it is fun to have several winners at once on the same ticket.

HOW TO MARK A WAY TICKET

Let's suppose you want to play a 9-spot way ticket. First, mark nine of your favorite numbers with X's. Then separate the X's into three groups of three numbers each by drawing circles around them. The result is that the nine numbers you picked have now become seven bets, or ways to win. In the "Mark number of spots or ways played" box, you would mark "3/3," "3/6", and "1/9." This means that you have three 3-spot bets, three 6-spot bets, and one 9-spot bet in action on the same ticket. If you want to play your 9-spot way ticket for one $1-game, it will cost you $7.00, since you have 7 ways to win. You mark "7-" in the "Total Price" box, turn in your ticket, and you're ready to go.

Most Las Vegas casinos allow you to cut the cost of playing way tickets by offering you the opportunity of paying half-price per way you bet. On a 7-way, $1-ticket like the one explained above, your cost would be $3.50 (50 cents per way). By marking "3.50-" in the "Total Price" box, you automatically inform the casino that you're taking advantage of the half-price way ticket. Of course, you will be paid only one-half the payoff you would receive if you had paid the full $1 for each way. But then, half-price way tickets are one way you can double your fun while waiting for your dinner to arrive.

Now let's show how you might play a three-way, 15-spot ticket. First, choose fifteen numbers you like; then split them into three groups of five numbers each. Let's say that you want to play the odd numbers across the top row: 1, 3, 5, 7 and 9. Then you decide to balance your odd numbers with a group of even numbers in your second group: 28, 38, 48, 58 and 68. Finally, you decide on some double numbers, so you pick them in a diagonal for your third group: 11, 22, 33, 44 and 55.

Your 3-way ticket combines these numbers into three groups of 10-spots. The odd numbers would combine with the evens for one 10-

spot; odd numbers with the doubles for a second 10-spot; and the even numbers and the doubles would combine for the third 10-spot.

In this example, you would mark "3/10" to show that three groups of 10 are being played, and mark your total price as "3-." Give your ticket to a keno attendant and wait for your lucky numbers to show up on the keno board.

This is how the ticket would be marked:

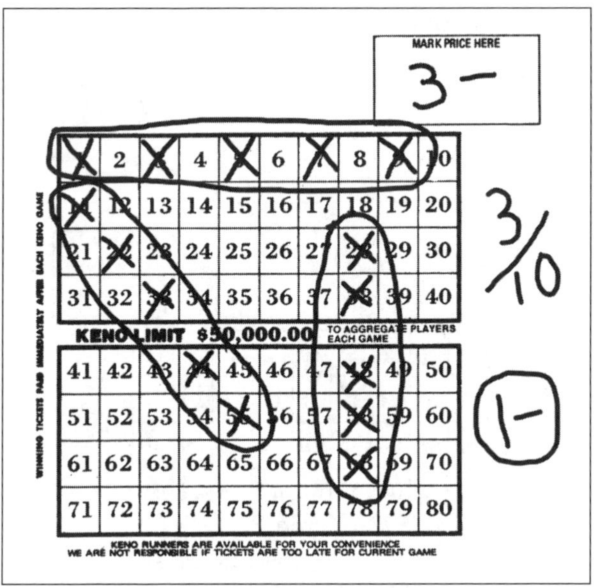

Way Ticket

KING TICKETS

Finally, there is the **king ticket** in which one number is circled by itself, called the **king**, and used in combination with other circled groups on the ticket.

For example, along with the king, you circle a group of two numbers and three numbers. The game can now be played as a 3-spot (king + 2-spot), 4-spot (king + 3-spot), 5-spot (2-spot + 3-spot) and a 6-spot (king + 2-spot + 3-spot) for a total of four ways. If each group cost $1, than this ticket would cost $4 to play.

You can make king tickets complicated by combining the king in all sorts of variations and giving yourself a myriad of possibilities to appease your gods of chance. And then you have the hidden attraction of the ticket: When's the last time you had a chance to play with the king?

King tickets are marked similarly to the way and split tickets, showing the combinations played, the amount bet per grouping and the total bet.

Let's show the above example of a king ticket, using the number 69 as the king.

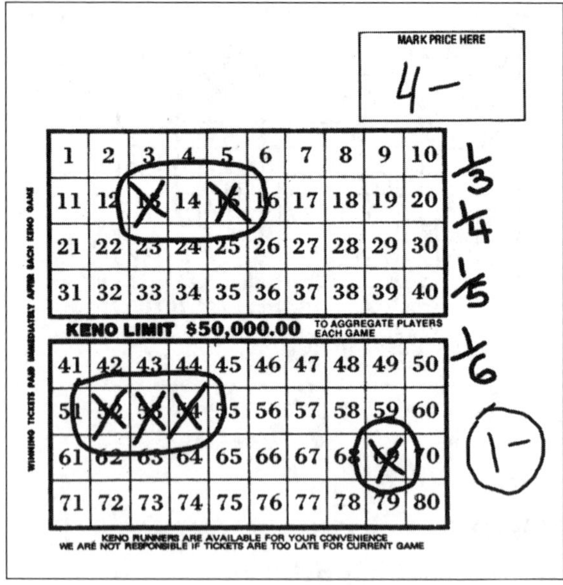

King Ticket

SPECIAL TICKETS

Casinos often promote their keno games in various ways, perhaps through a coupon or special incentive, and in many of these instances they'll present you with a **special ticket**—a keno ticket that must be played a certain way and that will pay according to a different payoff structure—marked on the special payoff chart you will receive.

These tickets generally offer a little better deal than the regular ticket and are an incentive to get you to play a game. However, do check the payoff rate to make sure that indeed the payoff is more attractive than the regular card. When playing a special card, make sure that you mark your ticket "SP" for special on your original ticket, or however the casino requires you to mark it.

Some Las Vegas casinos offer keno progressives as incentives to their patrons. There will be brochures in the keno area advertising these and rate cards showing the basic payouts, in addition to what it takes to win the progressive jackpot. In the progressive games, a certain amount is taken out of every bet and added to the progressive, so that it grows progressively larger and larger—until it hits. Then, there is one very happy keno player.

QUICK PICK GAMES

Many casinos now offer a **quick pick** option, which lets the computer automatically pick numbers for you if you would rather not pick your own. Maybe you feel your luck is running dry and the computer can do better, or you just can't be bothered knocking out your own numbers.

Of course, whether you feel luckier picking your own select numbers or having the computer generate them for your ticket, is up to you.

VIDEO KENO

Video keno is played pretty much like the traditional keno game except, of course, you're making your bets on a machine. The advantage of the video keno game is that you're generally getting more favorable odds—the payout schedules are much better than traditional keno—but there are a few downsides to this seemingly more favorable version.

First, is that you're playing on a machine, so the charm of the keno lounge and the leisurely pace of the game are replaced by the rapidity and coldness of a metal machine. In a live game, you might get about twelve games per hour. But video keno can be played at a pace of eight games per *minute*, depending upon your speed of play! Second, while you're getting better odds on the machine, the speed of the game leads to losses at a greater rate.

This is the rare occasion where I actually recommend a higher house percentage play (on the traditional lounge keno game) over better odds (on the video keno machines). Ironically, my conclusion is that traditional keno actually gives you a better chance of winning!

WINNING STRATEGY

Keno is a game that you should not play as a serious pursuit because the odds against winning are steep. Like, really steep. The house edge is typically well over 20% and can be as high as 35%—daunting odds if you hope to win in the long run, or even in the short run. However, keno can be a fun game—it certainly has been fun enough to last 2,000 years—and the attraction of a big payoff for only a small bet keeps many players entranced. In the old days, $50,000 was the big prize, but nowadays you can win $100,000 or even $200,000 on a lucky draw. That's not necessarily life-changing money like a multimillion dollar lottery win, but it's certainly a big mood enhancer.

Look for casinos that have better payout schedules than others; this will improve your chances of winning money and, of course, improve your winning odds. So you would be well advised to do a little keno shopping to find the payoff schedules that will work best for your plan. For example, downtown Las Vegas casinos generally have a better payoff per dollar bet than the strip casinos, so if you're predominately a keno player and you're in Las Vegas, downtown is where you'd like to be. And if you find a casino offering $100,000 on a big win as opposed to $50,000 for the same number of spots hit—with all else equal—by all means play for the bigger jackpot.

In general, one- and two-spot keno tickets have bad odds and should be avoided. On the other end of the spectrum, trying to catch all of the spots on a nine-spot or greater ticket is astronomical, though that's where the big payouts may come in if you are indeed very, very, very lucky. I could add a few more "verys" into that sentence. Catching 9 out of 9 numbers is well more than one in a million; catching 10 out of 10 approaches one in nine million; and 12 out of 12 approaches one in 500 million! By contrast, catching eight out of eight is "only" one in 230,115. While those odds are long, they are at least in the realm of reachable as opposed to the one-in-many-millions type of tickets.

Your best bets will generally be on tickets that have from three spots to eight spots. They'll give you the highest return for your dollar and a shot at the big prize for those types of tickets.

PARTING THOUGHTS

Keno is a great game to test out your lucky numbers. Picking birth dates, anniversaries, license plate numbers and the like offer a big pool of possibilities to see which ones will really pay off. Perhaps you like the evens, odds and doubles as used in one of our examples, or a progression using every fourth number, or numbers with either a 3 or a 5 in them.

Do you play the same numbers and combinations every game or switch around when one set fails? And what if the original set subsequently wins, or what if you didn't switch and the numbers you would have played won? Oh, the heartaches!

If you have lucky numbers, you might have some fun by giving them a whirl and seeing if you can walk away with a six-figure bonanza.

14 BINGO

FIVE KEYS TO BINGO
1. Play bingo for fun and camaraderie, not as a way to make money.
2. Don't play more tickets at one time than you can comfortably handle.
3. Avoid playing casino bingo everyday–unfortunately, unlike blackjack, the more you play, you more you stand to lose at this fun game.
4. Also avoid putting extra money into longshot gambles such as playing the power-ball number. Those extra dollars can add up fast.
5. Shop around for the best places to play bingo. Look for venues with lively, spacious and friendly games where you can earn credit on your slot card.

INTRODUCTION

Bingo has been an immensely popular game ever since it was legalized in the 1950s in the United States. It's a fun way for millions of players to let loose with an evening of recreational gambling. It is played in numerous countries around the world, in places as far away as Australia and Africa, and has spurred a life of its own in Indian casinos around the U.S., where the game is very big business.

There are many versions of bingo, from the standard five spots across, down, or diagonally, to hitting numbers on all four corners, making a double bingo on the same card, and a multitude of other combinations.

One U.S. county even runs a cow pie bingo game as a fundraiser. A field is parceled off into squares that are bought by players. Where the cow lands its load—bingo! The buyer of the square is the lucky winner.

You can find bingo game anywhere in America. It is probably the most popular nonprofit fundraiser for organizations around the country. Religious organizations, schools, fire departments and a whole slew of charitable, social and fraternal organizations count on their bingo games as an important source of income. Funds are often split three ways. One part goes to the organization running the event, a second part to the professional group running the game itself, and the third part is awarded as prizes to the winners.

Let's move on now and see what this fun game is all about.

THE BASICS OF PLAY

BINGO CARDS

Bingo is played with bingo cards (game cards) that have pre-printed numbers on them. Traditionally, the cards are made of paper on which you mark the numbers when they are called with a crayon or a dobber, a pre-inked marker that covers your numbers with a round ink spot. The game card is no longer valid once the game is finished and can be thrown away.

Another traditional way of marking numbers is by using a hard "permanent" board that also has pre-printed numbers. You can use these game cards, typically made of cardboard or plastic, for multiple games. Each number appears in a tiny window that has a sliding tab. As each number is called, players simply close that window by sliding the tab to cover it.

In today's modern casinos, however, you won't find these traditional ways of marking your bingo card. You're more likely to be looking at a video monitor than a piece of paper and a dobber. Like slot machines, bingo has come a long way.

The standard bingo card has 25 squares arranged in five columns of five boxes each. Each square is numbered with the exception of the middle square, which automatically counts as a number called for all players. You get the square for free. So at the start of a session, you mark the center square before any numbers are called.

The five columns across the top of the bingo card spell out B-I-N-G-O. The first vertical column is headed by the letter B and contains five numbers between 1 and 15. When a number in that column is called, it will be referred to as B-7, for example. The second column (I) has five numbers from 16 to 30; the third column (N) has five numbers ranging from 31 to 45; the fourth column (G) has five numbers from 46 to 60; and finally the fifth column (O) has five numbers from 61 to 75.

The B-I-N-G-O letters above each column serve only as reference points to help players locate their numbers. It's easier to find 56 on your card when you know that it is in column G; in fact, it is called as G-56 to speed up the game. Many different cards may contain similarly numbered squares, but no numbers are ever repeated on the same card: You will never find 56 in two different spots in the G column on the same card.

BINGO BALLS

Bingo is played with 75 ping pong balls that are imprinted with numbers from 1 to 75, one number for each ball, and letters representing the column they fall in. The number 14, for example, will say B14, the number 65 will be O65. This makes it easy for all players to quickly locate the numbers on their card.

The 75 balls are randomly mixed in a spherical wire cage or enclosed blower. When the game is ready to start, balls are drawn one by one, and announced by the caller of the game. As soon as the balls are removed from the cage, the caller takes them out of action by placing them into a separate rack. Called numbers are immediately flashed onto an electric board so that all players can see the numbers that have been picked.

B	I	N	G	O
10	25	33	49	71
3	17	42	55	65
11	23	FREE	60	74
2	21	38	50	69
5	20	36	54	73

Bingo Card

HOW BINGO IS PLAYED

You must be armed with at least one game card to play bingo, though many fanatic bingo players play multiple cards, some as many as twenty or more for one game. In casino games, you can purchase cards with different price tags. For example, you might buy a white card for $1, a blue card for $2, or a yellow card for $5. The higher the price of the card you purchase, the higher the payout for hitting a bingo.

Bingo cards are usually bought in casinos as part of a package that coves many games in the same session. A favorite with bingo players is a six-pack that contains six bingo cards for each scheduled game. Each separate bingo card contains the numbers that may—or alas, may not—turn out to be winners.

In casinos, you purchase as many cards in advance as are needed to play the entire session, which often is ten games. Thus, you might buy ten cards, one for each game; or you might buy a six-pack of sixty cards, six cards for each game. Each casino bingo session lasts about an hour, and new sessions begin every other hour. For example, one casino's bingo sessions start on the odd hours, and others start on the even hours.

When the game is ready to begin, the caller announces the type of bingo game to be played. As the numbers are drawn, one by one, the room grows profoundly silent. Players pore over their cards carefully as numbers are drawn, making the numbers on their cards and checking out which numbers they need to make their bingo card a winner.

The game moves forward as players fill their cards with numbers. A growing buzz of anticipation electrifies the room as players edge just one number away from victory. The tension builds as another number is called, a few players creep forward in their seats, and as soon as one more number is called, you hear BINGO! screamed across the room, sometimes by more than one player.

BINGO! Some lucky player is a winner.

Either an electronic device or an official of the bingo game then verifies that the cards of players claiming bingo have been correctly marked. If indeed, the call is correct, the game is over and the winner or winners collect the prize.

There can be more than one winner on a call, and there often are, particularly when a lot of numbers have been called before anyone scores a bingo. It doesn't matter who calls bingo first—all winning bingos share in the prize. If one winner has bought a card that costs more than the other winners, his higher-priced card will win more money than the lower-priced cards.

WINNING BINGOS

The standard combination needed to win at bingo is the completion of five winning numbers in a line—horizontally, vertically or diagonally. But in addition to these standard bingos, there are a multitude of other ways to score a bingo, limited only by the imagination of the sponsors of the game.

Some venues that are really in tune with the game have upwards of 100 different bingo games in their arsenal to entertain players. The variety of these games runs the gamut of bingo's possibilities.

Let's look at some of the more common winning patterns used in bingo.

HORIZONTAL BINGO

A standard bingo formed by five numbers in a straight horizontal line.

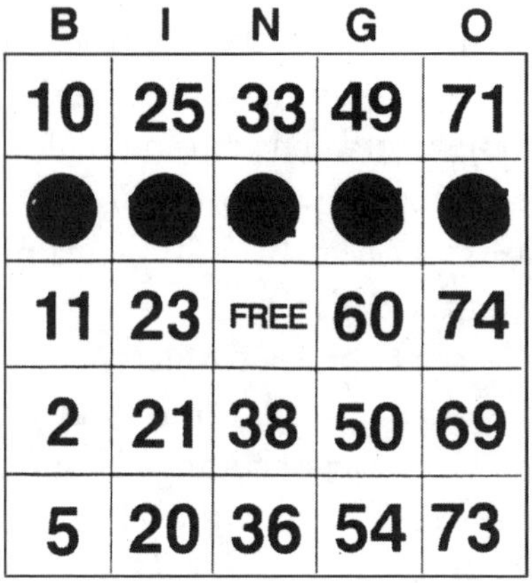

B	I	N	G	O
10	25	33	49	71
●	●	●	●	●
11	23	FREE	60	74
2	21	38	50	69
5	20	36	54	73

Horizontal Bingo

VERTICAL BINGO

A standard bingo formed by five numbers in a straight vertical line.

B	I	N	G	O
10	●	33	49	71
3	●	42	55	65
11	●	FREE	60	74
2	●	38	50	69
5	●	36	54	73

Vertical Bingo

DIAGONAL BINGO

A standard bingo formed by five numbers formed in a diagonal line, which includes the middle "free" square.

B	I	N	G	O
●	25	33	49	71
3	●	42	55	65
11	23	●	60	74
2	21	38	●	69
5	20	36	54	●

Diagonal Bingo

FOUR CORNER BINGO

In this game, the winning bingo tickets have all four corners caught.

B	I	N	G	O
●	25	33	49	●
3	17	42	55	65
11	23	FREE	60	74
2	21	38	50	69
●	20	36	54	●

Four Corner Bingo

COVERALL OR BLACKOUT BINGO

This one takes more work than the others: You need to catch all the numbers on your card to win the blackout or coverall bingo.

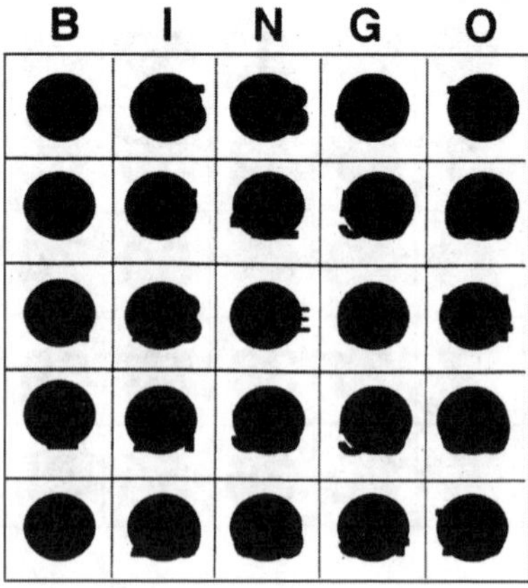

Coverall or Blackout Bingo

DOUBLE BINGO

You need two bingo patterns on the same card to catch a winner.

B	I	N	G	O
10	25	●	49	71
3	17	●	55	65
11	23	●	60	74
2	21	●	50	69
●	●	●	●	●

Double Bingo

LAYER CAKE

You need to hit all the numbers in the first, third and fifth horizontal rows.

B	I	N	G	O
●	●	●	●	●
3	17	42	55	65
●	●	●	●	●
2	21	38	50	69
●	●	●	●	●

Layer Cake

THE PICTURE FRAME

This is a fun one. You need to fill all the outside numbers, making a picture frame, to win.

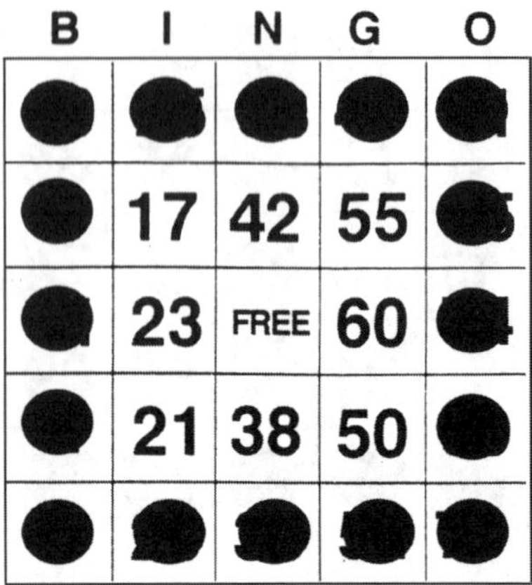

The Picture Frame

There are tons of other bingo patterns with exotic and fun names. But whatever the game called, the caller will make it clear to players exactly what they have to do to win the game. In casinos, the pattern of numbers you must hit to win is flashed on big-screen video displays that you can see from any seat in the room.

PROGRESSIVE BINGO

Progressive bingo games are very attractive to a lot of players. Prizes nowadays run well into the thousands of dollars at many places and even into the tens of thousands of dollars. Now and then, super jackpots even run into the six figures! The higher the bingo progressive prize rises, the more fevered the game. Then again, how would you feel if your bingo card looks like it may catch a grand prize of $200,000?

Pretty good, I'll bet!

To win the progressive jackpot, a player needs to "blackout" his or her ticket and catch all the numbers within a specified period of draws, such as 50 or maybe 52. Many casinos also offer the option of buying an extra bet on the powerball. For example, you might pay $1 in advance of the session in the hope that you will make a bingo by hitting it with the number on the powerball. As soon as the session begins, the powerball number will be posted on the video displays around the room.

BINGO ODDS

The odds you face at bingo varies from place to place, and is a direct function of how much money the bingo room pays back to players in proportion to the amount of money they take in. However, with revenues presumably being split three ways in many bingo games, you can imagine the odds for players are not very good at all.

Each bingo game has its own set of payback schedules, and more often than not, they may not be regulated. The bingo games must return enough prize money to keep players coming back for more, but in any case, don't quit your day job yet and count on making a living as a professional bingo player.

Without knowing the exact cut of each venue and the consequent return to the player, it is impossible to state with certainty the odds that a player faces at bingo—except to say that they're not very favorable.

WINNING APPROACH

Basically, you just need to get lucky to win at bingo. And, as in all other gambling games, you need to practice good money management. Yes, even in bingo. Don't play so often that it pinches your pockets or sends you to the poorhouse. It's surprising how a few $10 or $20 bingo sessions can erode your bankroll. Play bingo for fun, not for profit, and don't spend money you need for necessities on the game.

You may wish to choose your own cards if the option is available, carefully combing over the numbers to see which appear most propitious for the game. Maybe you want to search out some cards that contain your lucky numbers, your birthday or other important dates, or even the way the planets are aligned. Large casinos, however, don't usually offer this option.

In casino bingo games, your fate is up to Lady Luck alone, as you are issued random cards. But hey, she's a fickle lady—sometimes she smiles on you and sometimes she laughs in your face. Good luck! That's all you need to win at bingo.

PARTING THOUGHTS

Bingo is a great leisure game for many people. Groups of friends often play together, toting special bags for their bingo gear. Frequent players are often called **bingo bunnies**, and sometimes wear distinctive shirts or hats monogrammed with their favorite numbers. For some players, the bingo parlor is a place to unwind; for others, it's a place to get wound up.

But hey, as long as you're having fun and enjoying the camaraderie of playing with friends, bingo is good entertainment. With the big money jackpots of modern-day bingo, the game has become more interesting and fun than ever before. One day it may be your turn with a big jackpot at stake to yell out the magic word—bingo!

15 SPORTS BETTING

FIVE KEYS TO SPORTS BETTING

1. There is no such thing as a sure win, no matter how good a bet looks.
2. Shop around for the best payouts.
3. Look for events or games where one side is a fan favorite. That may give you a good "wrinkle" to bet on the other side.
4. Educate yourself before you place a bet. Finding the best percentage plays requires a lot of work.
5. Don't bet money that you can't afford to lose. Too many people have gotten caught up in sports betting and taken a hard turn down the wrong road.

INTRODUCTION

Gambling on sports is a fervent passion in the United States and fuels a tremendous underground economy that runs into the billions of dollars yearly. Sports games are exciting to watch, and for many people, putting their money where their mouths are makes the games all the more intense.

Football, baseball, basketball, boxing, and mixed-martial arts all have their share of aficionados. In this section you'll find out what goes into the making of the sports lines, how to read them, the odds involved, and how to get an edge on the lines so that you'll have a better chance of winning at sports betting.

THE BETTING LINES

There are two types of lines in sports betting—the **money line**, which is used in baseball, boxing, and mixed-martial arts (MMA) and the **pointspread** (the "**spread**"), the line used for football and basketball. The money line penalizes bettors wagering on the **favorite**, the team or individual more likely to win, by making them **lay money**; that is, bet more money than they hope to win back. For example, if a bettor had to lay 6 to 5 odds, it means he would have to lay $6 to win $5.

On the other side of that coin, bettors wagering on the **underdog**, the team or individual more likely to lose, would receive back more than they bet as compensation for betting on the "**dog**." If the odds on a contest are listed as 8 to 5, a $5 bet on the dog would pay back $8 if the bet is won.

The pointspread tries to equalize betting money by awarding the underdog extra points and creating what is called a **spread**. Thus, if the sportsbook creates a spread of 7 points in a football game and you bet the underdog, you can win the wager even if your team doesn't win the game. Either a loss by less than 7 points or an outright victory gives the underdog bettor a winning wager. An underdog defeat by more than 7 points loses the wager.

If you bet the favorite, in this example, your team must win by more than 7 points to win the bet. A three-point victory by the favorite is all well and good for the team, but not for those who bet the favorite. The favorite did not cover the 7-point spread, and therefore, all bets on the favorite are lost.

If the favorite wins by exactly 7 points on a 7 point spread, the bet is a **push**, a tie, and both favorite and underdog bettors receive their wagers back.

Thus, the concept of winning at football and basketball betting, sports where the pointspread line is used, is based on winning against the spread and not necessarily on the raw outcome of the game.

HOW THE LINE IS SET

The main purpose of the betting line is to divide public opinion in such a way that money gets bet equally on both sides of an event. As such, the important consideration in setting a line is figuring out how the public will perceive an upcoming contest.

This is a very important concept to understand. Bookmaking, whether legal as in Nevada casinos, or illegal, is a business that makes money by handling bets and taking a commission on the money wagered. Sportsbooks really don't care which contestant wins a match—they only care that money is bet equally on both sides so that they can collect their **vigorish** or **vig**, the bookmaker's built-in commission, no matter which side wins.

Thus, the betting line represents how fans perceive the game and how they will bet—not the actual match-up of the teams.

For example, a number of years back, the aging Mohammed Ali, in another of his comeback tries, faced his former sparring partner Larry Holmes, who was 30 years old and fighting in his prime. Prizefight experts knew that this match was really lopsided; Ali was clearly over the hill. On the other hand, the betting public was still enamored with the mystique of the once great Ali, and this perception had driven the odds down to 8/5 in favor of Holmes.

If the betting line had been made on the basis of Ali's real chances of winning, Ali would have been fighting as an overwhelming underdog, and most of the money would have come in on Holmes. This would have created a situation called being **sided**—when most of the money gets bet on one side of a gambling proposition and comparatively little on the other.

Being sided is a tremendous risk for sportsbooks because it makes them gamblers. That is not their business. Their business is to collect commissions on gambles that *other* people take. If the sportsbooks had not adjusted the line in the Ali-Holmes fight to reflect how the betting public would bet, an Ali win would have taken them to the cleaners.

As businessmen, sportsbooks attempt to form a line such that they can collect profits regardless of who wins.

The principle of bookmakers trying to divide the betting money holds true in the betting lines for all the sports—football, hockey, basketball, baseball, boxing, mixed-martial arts and other sporting events that attract gamblers.

An astute bettor who realizes this and who follows his sport carefully can use this information to make money at sports betting.

THE FIRST PRINCIPLE OF BEATING THE SPORTSBOOK

Now that you understand how and why the line is made, let's outline the foremost principles of winning money at sports betting. First of all, look for games and sporting events where public opinions, for one reason or another, distort the line and therefore give the sharp and ready bettor an edge in the game.

But having an edge is not enough. The edge must be sufficient enough to overcome the built-in vig that sportsbooks and other bookmakers have. This section discusses each sport in turn to show the exact odds you face with each betting proposition, and how best to overcome those odds.

SPORTS BETTING COMPARISON CHART

SPORT	TYPE OF LINE	PAYOFF	WINNING % NEEDED TO BREAK EVEN
BASEBALL	Money Line	Variable	Variable
BASKETBALL	Pointspread	10-11	52.38%
BOXING	Money Line	Variable	Variable
FOOTBALL	Pointspread	10-11	52.38%
MMA	Pointspread	10-11	52.38%

FOOTBALL BETTING

INTRODUCTION

Every year, as constant as the seasons, sports fans gear up for the gala opening of NFL and collegiate football. Even before opening day, football fever spurs the frantic analysis and heated discussions that accompany every season, and helps fuel the mammoth underground economy of football betting. When it's that time of year, football owns weekends and Monday nights for many Americans, a good portion of whom could not conceive of life without this staple of excitement.

Betting is very much a part of football for fans, and the wagers that many bettors make add a lot of spice and enjoyment to the gridiron wars they watch on the field.

Let's see just what is involved in setting the line, what odds you're up against, and how best to play ball.

THE FOOTBALL LINE

Whether college or pro, football betting works according to the pointspread. The sportsbooks handicap opposing teams in a way that offers them the chance to get equal betting action on both teams, and thus earn their vigorish without risk. As such, football contests have a pointspread, with one team playing the favorite and the other playing the underdog.

Bettors wager according to these lines, giving points when they bet favorites, and taking points when they bet the underdog.

Here is how a typical line may look.

San Francisco	MIAMI	+3

You may also see that line listed as follows, but either way means the same thing.

San Francisco	-3	MIAMI

The lines will always list the favorite first and show the home team in capital letters. In the above example, San Francisco is the favorite and as such is listed first, while Miami, listed in capital letters (the home team) is the underdog. The number shown indicates the number of points that the favorite is favored by. It makes no difference whether the number shows up as a + next to the underdog or a – next to the favorite.

In the above examples, we see the San Francisco 49ers listed as 3-point favorites over the Miami Dolphins.

THE BOOKMAKER'S VIGORISH

To bet on NFL or college football games, you have to lay 11 to 10 on all bets, whether betting the favorite or the underdog. To win $10, you have to give the bookmaker $11. For example, if you want to bet $50, you must give the bookie $55.

This difference between the 11 to 10 wager that bettors must lay with the bookmaker and the true odds of 10-10, even money, is the bookmaker's profit margin, his vig, which allows him to conduct business.

For example, if you lay $11 to $10 on a game and win the bet, you'll get paid $21—the $11 bet, plus the $10 in winnings. If you bet $110, you'll get back $210 from the bookmaker, your original $110 bet plus $100 in winnings.

Let's see what happens when you bet $110 per game, and you win one game and lose one game laying 11 to 10 odds.

LAYING 11 TO 10: 2 BETS

	Result	$ Results
Wins	1	+$100
Losses	1	-$110
Net	**Even**	**– $10**

You have an even win percentage, but yet have lost money. As you can see, winning half your games isn't good enough to make money at football betting. If you win only half of the time, you're going to be a loser at a rate of $1 for every $22 bet, an edge to the bookmaker of 4.54%.

This 4.54%, the bookmaker's vig, is the figure you must overcome to show a profit on the gridiron.

Let's carry these figures over a 16-game season with a $110 bet to see how a 50% win rate would work out. Remember, we have to lay 11 to 10 on every game.

LAYING 11 TO 10: 16 BETS

	Result	$ Results
Wins	8	+$800
Losses	8	-$880
Net	**Even**	**– $80**

Though we won 8 out of 16 games, which is not too bad, the bookmaker's vig has eaten away at our stake, and we show a loss of $80.

What winning percentage is needed to overcome the house vig?

Here's your magic number: 52.38%. As a football bettor, this is the figure that must be foremost in your betting mind. To be a winner, you must win greater than 52.38% of your bets. A winning percentage less than that and you will be a net loser.

LINE CHANGES

As the week progresses, the line might change up or down a little to reflect the bets coming in. For example, if the Giants are playing the Cowboys and are favored by +3 points, and more money is coming in on the Cowboys than the Giants, the sportsbook might move the line to +4, and then if necessary, move it to maybe +5 to encourage more money to be bet on the Giants.

However, once your bet is made, it is committed to the pointspread at which it was placed, regardless of how the line moves later on. If your bet was placed when the line was +3, and the line moves to +5, your bet is committed to the +3.

TEASERS

The **teaser** bet is an inducement for bettors to wager two games or more as a group with the condition that both teams chosen must win. If one of the teaser teams loses, the whole bet is lost. Also, a tie against the spread on either game loses the teaser as well.

The sportsbook allows 6, 6 1/2 or 7 points, depending upon the wager made, as the tease incentive for the bettor to use in any way desired on the match-ups chosen.

On a two-team tease, a 6-point bonus gets an even money bet instead of the usual 11 to 10 lay. If 6 1/2 points is taken, the regular 11 to 10 bet is laid, and if a 7-point tease is chosen, the bettor must lay 6 to 5.

Let's look at a teaser with the following two teams:

Chicago Bears	New England Patriots	+6
New York Giants	Green Bay Packers	+3

On a 6-point tease you may elect to take the underdog Patriots at 6 points more for a +12 spread, and the favorite Giants, who now have a 3-point spread with the 6 points added.

You could also choose those games the other way around, or play both favorites or both underdogs. Wagering any of these 6-point tease combinations allows your bet to be made at even money instead of the usual 11 to 10.

You could also play the teaser taking 6 1/2 points and lay 11 to 10, or take 7 points and lay 6 to 5.

PARLAY BETS

A **parlay** bet is similar to a teaser in that the results of more than one game's results are tied together. With a parlay bet, you must pick a minimum of three teams, and all of these teams must win. A loss or tie in any of the contests spells a loss for the entire bet.

However, unlike a teaser, your teams are not given extra points—they must beat the spread straight out. The payoffs are big and that attracts a lot of bettors, but the odds are so atrocious that you would be better off throwing your money away.

A typical parlay card might pay as follows:

TYPICAL PARLAY CARD		
Teams	**Payoff**	**True Odds**
Three	$6 for $1	7 to 1 (8 for 1)
Four	$11 for $1	15 to 1 (16 for 1)
Five	$20 for $1	31 to 1 (32 for 1)
Six	$40 for $1	63 to 1 (64 for 1)
Seven	$80 for $1	127 to 1 (128 for 1)
Eight	$150 for $1	255 to 1 (256 for 1)
Nine	$300 for $1	511 to 1 (512 for 1)
Ten	$500 for $1	1023 to 1 (1024 for 1)

You may notice the "for" in the Payoff column, which is a subtle gambling expression telling you that you're getting less. A payoff of $6 for $1 means that you get back $6 total on a won bet, your original $1 plus $5 in winnings, as opposed to the word "to," as in $6 to $1, meaning that you win $6 for every $1 you bet, and will get back a total of $7.

As you can see by the chart, parlays are sucker bets, and I advise you to avoid them, unless you happen to be the one booking other people's parlays, in which case, you'll make lots of money.

OVER & UNDER BETS

When you place an *over* or *under* bet in football, you have two choices. You can bet that the two teams combined will score more than a prescribed number of points set by the sportsbook, in which case you are betting the **over**. Or you can bet that they will score less, or the **under**. Over and under bets work just like that of the pointspread betting in football. You still have to lay 11 to 10 on all your bets and will need a 52.38% winning percentage to beat the house.

TOUTS

Tout services or **touts** are services that offer betting advice for a fee. Be careful with them. Generally speaking, they are scam operations. These businesses are often started by gamblers who have gone belly-up with their own money and are now passing along their worthy experience to others at $50 a pop—or more.

You might see an advertisement that reads "65% win against the spread," for example, or "3 out of our 4 best bets won last week," or any of a myriad of other enticing numbers. The problem is that these figures represent only a small slice of the truth, if it is even the truth. How about the week before or last year, facts that conveniently go unmentioned. Any bettor in any game can have a run of luck and presenting just that slice of the whole picture can make anyone or anything seem real good at making picks, even a chicken pecking at corn.

It's easy to describe a segment of time and make it sound appealing, which is what most of these services do. Let's say that I run a two-man race and my opponent beats me at the finish line. Well, I comment, "I finished second, right behind the winner while my opponent finished next to last." Little does the listener know that only two people ran in the race.

In any case, be careful with tout services. Instead, I recommend putting your money into learning more about winning and how to place your bets.

BASEBALL

THE BASEBALL LINE

Betting on major league baseball is done according to the money line. Whenever you bet the favorite in baseball, you must lay odds, bet more that the amount you hope to win. And when you bet the underdog, you will win more than you bet if the dog wins.

Let's see how a game may be listed and show how the money line will work.

YANKEES	Tigers	6 1/2	7 1/2

The favorite, in this example the Yankees, is listed first, and is capitalized because it is the home team.

The line in baseball is listed to reflect all payments to $5.00. The first number, 6 1/2, represents the amount that a Detroit bettor, the underdog, will win for every $5.00 bet. Thus, on a won bet, the Tigers bettor will receive $11.50—the original $5.00 wager plus $6.50 in winnings. The second number, 7 1/2, is the amount of money that a Yankee bettor must lay to win $5.00. A Yankee win will return to New York bettors $12.50—the original $7.50 wager plus $5.00 in winnings for every $7.50 wagered.

This style of listing can be confusing, so we'll show you an easy way to remember which number goes with what team and just what the line means to you as a bettor.

The favorite, which is always listed first, belongs to the larger number—what the bettor must lay to win $5.00—while the underdog, listed second, belongs to the lower number—what the bettor will win with a $5.00 bet.

Just use word-association—favorite, larger number; underdog, smaller number. And remember, all bets are to $5.00.

You might also see that same line on the Yankee-Tiger game expressed as follows:

YANKEES	-1.30	Tigers	+1.50

It is the same exact line, just written differently to reflect bets based on $1.00 as opposed to $5.00 in the example above. Casinos usually list the line this way. If you bet on the Yankees, you need to lay $1.30 to win $1.00, and on the Tigers, a $1.00 bet will win $1.50. Multiply these numbers by $5.00 and you have the same numbers as the 6 1/2 and 7 1/2 figures discussed above.

This line is called a **20¢ line** for the 20¢ difference between the underdog and favorite's bet when worked out to the dollar; and it represents the bookie's take on each set of bets. This 20¢ line is the standard baseball betting line, the one that most bettors will face when betting on the "bigs."

PAYOFF CHARTS AND HOUSE EDGE

The following chart shows the house edge on the various lines.

20¢ OR 1 POINT LINE			
QUOTE	TRUE ODDS	% EDGE UNDERDOG	% EDGE FAVORITE
11-10	1-1	4.55	4.55
5-6	11-10	4.76	3.97
5 1/2-6 1/2	6-5	4.55	3.50
6-7	13-10	4.35	3.11
6 1/2-7 1/2	7-5	4.17	2.78
7-8	3-2	4.00	2.50
7 1/2-8 1/2	8-5	3.85	2.26
8-9	17-10	3.70	2.06
8 1/2-9 1/2	9-5	3.57	1.88
9-10	19-10	3.45	1.72
9 1/2-10 1/2	2-1	3.33	1.59
10-11	21-10	3.23	1.47
10 1/2-11 1/2	11-5	3.13	1.36
11-12	23-10	3.03	1.26
11 1/2-12 1/2	12-5	2.94	1.18
12-13	5-2	2.86	1.10
12 1/2-13 1/2	13-5	2.78	1.03

Quote–The line quoted by the sportsbook or bookmaker.

True Odds–The actual odds between the quoted numbers for favorite and underdog, which would give the house no edge at all.

Sportsbook's % Edge: Underdog–The house edge on underdog bets at the line quoted.

Sportsbook's % Edge: Favorite–The house edge on favorite bets at the line quoted.

You'll notice that in all cases the edge is lowest when betting favorites, except in the 11-10 quote where the edge is equivalent for underdog or favorite bettors. This does not necessarily mean that favorites are the best bets. This is the bookmaker's edge against what he figures the true odds to be. That doesn't translate to a superior wager. We get a different view in the next chart.

PAYOFF CHART

THE VEGAS LINE	TAKE ODDS	PROFIT TO $1.00
+220	11-5	2.20
+200	2-1	2.00
+180	9-5	1.80
+170	8 1/2-5	1.70
+160	8-5	1.60
+150	7 1/2-5	1.50
+140	7-5	1.40
+130	6 1/2-5	1.30
+120	6-5	1.20
+110	5 1/2-5	1.10
Even	1-1	1.00
-110	5-5 1/2	.91
-120	5-6	.83
-130	5-6 1/2	.77
-140	5-7	.71
-150	5-7 1/2	.67
-160	5-8	.62
-170	5-8 1/2	.59
-180	5-9	.55
-200	1-2	.50
-220	5-11	.45
-240	5-12	.42
-260	5-13	.38
-280	5-14	.36
-300	1-3	.33

The Vegas Line–The line coming out of Vegas, though it could represent any standard line.

Take Odds–The first column equivalent in a different format.

Profit to $1.00–The amount a won bet will return for every $1.00 bet.

On the Payoff Chart, we see the profit that you will make every time you wager $1.00 and win your bet. The + numbers on the top half of the first column indicate the payoff amount for underdogs, while the minus numbers below show the payoff on favorites. Thus, a Vegas line of +220 means that a winning underdog bet of $1.00 pays $2.20, while a Vegas line of -220 indicates the opposite, that a winning $2.20 bet pays $1.00 to a favorite bettor.

Let's go back to our Yankee-Tiger game where the line reads +130 - 150, and see what the Payoff Chart shows us. If we bet on the Tigers beating the Yankees, the favorite, we'd have to lay $1.50 to win $1.00. Looking at the column "Profit to $1.00," we see that we'd win only 67¢ for every dollar bet. If instead we bet on the Tigers, the dog, we'd get $1.30 for every dollar bet, for a net profit of $1.30.

Betting on the favorite and laying $1.50 forces you to win 60% of the time just to break even. There's a big penalty betting on favorites. At a certain point, the winning percentage needed to show a profit on big favorites becomes too high to realistically show a profit.

BREAK-EVEN POINTS: FAVORITES AND DOGS

The next table is very important because it shows the break-even point for all bets in which odds are being laid as a favorite bettor or are taken on the underdog side.

BREAK-EVEN POINT AGAINST THE LINE			
THE LINE	UNDERDOG % NEEDED TO WIN	THE LINE	FAVORITE % NEEDED TO WIN
110 Pick	52.4	110 Pick	52.4
Even	50.0	-120	54.6
+110	47.6	-130	56.5
+120	45.5	-140	58.5
+130	43.5	-150	60.2
+140	41.7	-160	61.7
+150	40.0	-170	62.9
+160	38.5	-180	64.5
+170	37.0	-200	66.7
+180	35.7	-220	69.0
+200	33.3	-240	70.4
+220	31.3	-260	72.5
+240	29.4	-280	73.5

You can see that the bigger the favorite, the greater and more intimidating a win percentage will be needed just to break even. Let's say that you make a series of 100 bets laying –1.50/1 on the favorite at $7.50 a crack, and you win 60 of these wagers.

Here's how it would look.

-1.50 TO 1 ON THE FAVORITE LAYING $7.50 TO WIN $5.00: 100 BETS		
	Result	**$ Results**
Wins	60	+$300
Losses	40	-$300
Net		**Break Even**

There is no gain and no loss. The bets have broken exactly even. To win 60% of the time is a gargantuan effort. If you could sustain that winning percentage in football betting, you'd be virtually minting your own money. But against very big favorites, as in the above example, you don't even make a penny! For a big-league team to win 60% of its games in a 162-game schedule, it must win 97 games! That's usually enough to take a division title. With anything less than a 60% win ratio while laying -1.50/1, you will show losses in your wagers.

The question is, how many teams that you bet on will be good enough to do that for you? That's the real problem in betting big favorites in baseball. As you can see, even though the bookie's edge is lower when you bet on favorites, your chances of winning are not necessarily less since you have to score a big percentage of wins just to cover the odds you lay.

Let's now look at an example where you're pursuing an even bigger favorite, at -1.70/1. As the chart shows, you need to win at a 63% clip just to break even. If you win 58% of the time, that is not good enough to come out ahead at a -1.70/1 line.

Let's see how this looks. Laying -1.70 equates to 8 1/2 to 5, or in dollars, betting $8.50 to win $5.00.

-1.70 TO 1 ON THE FAVORITE
LAYING $8.50 TO WIN $5.00: 100 BETS

	Result	$ Results
Wins	58	+$290
Losses	42	-$357
Net		**-$67**

That's a rough loss to take, especially when you've scored 58%, which is a pretty good win rate. Let's now look at the previous betting situation from the other side of the coin. We'll assume that 100 $5.00 bets are made on the underdog half of the +1.30/–1.50 (6 1/2 – 7 1/2) odds; 44 of those bets win and 56 lose.

Here's how it looks:

-1.30 TO 1 ON THE UNDERDOG LAYING $5.00 TO WIN $6.50: 100 BETS		
	Result	**$ Results**
Wins	44	+$286
Losses	56	-$280
Net		**+$6**

Obviously, it's a whole different smoke betting on underdogs. Even with a terrible losing percentage, a profit was shown betting the underdog position at +1.30. But then again, don't run to the sportsbook with your pockets stuffed with money—it's not so easy. Big underdogs are big underdogs for a reason. Just as underdogs can be good bets, favorites can be good bets as well.

Look at each situation separately and judge it on its unique merits.

BETTING STRATEGIES

You should avoid betting favorites that call for a line of -150 or more. A winning percentage of 58%, which would show you good profits in football or basketball—and get your baseball team pretty close to a pennant—would leave you in the hole betting against a +150 line. That's a big wall to climb.

On the other hand, you may find some good spots betting as the underdog part of a 1.50/1.00 line because, as the chart shows, you need only a 40% win rate to break even.

However, you must pick your games carefully, keeping in mind that there's always a reason why a team is listed as a big underdog. For example, former MLB pitcher Randy Johnson of the Seattle Mariners was virtually unbeatable when he was on his game, once going more than 20 straight decisions without a loss. That may be a match-up you wouldn't want to bet against. Aces at the top of their game are tough to bat against and equally tough to bet against.

What I've shown you are the cold hard numbers you face in baseball betting. Now use your baseball knowledge and handicapping skills, combined with prudent money management, to come out of the season as a winner at baseball betting.

BASKETBALL

THE POINT LINE

Betting on the hoops is done according to a point line. If you bet on the favorite, you need to give points, and if you take the underdog, you receive them. As in football, you really don't care if the team you're betting on wins or loses, only that it covers the spread.

For example, if the Los Angeles Lakers are favored by 7 points over the Boston Celtics, the Lakers must win by 8 points to cover the spread. Even if Los Angeles wins the game by 4 points, it is still a loss for Lakers *bettors*—the team has not covered the spread.

GREAT BETTING OPPORTUNITY

This was exactly the situation in the 2010 NBA Finals. I sensed a great opportunity with the spread. Boston, a championship team just two years earlier, had been blown out in Game 6, and while I felt the Lakers were in stride, I felt either team could win in Game 7. In Las Vegas, everybody was talking about the Lakers. When I heard LA was a 7 point favorite, I immediately made a sizeable bet on the Celtics. I felt that the game would be close and all those points were too good to pass up. Early in the game, Boston had the upper hand and looked like they might win outright, but in the end, it didn't matter—at least for me. I had Boston plus 7, and while LA won, it was only by 4 points, 83-79.

If the Lakers won the contest by exactly 7 points, the game would have been a push and the sports book would have returned underdog and favorite wagers to the bettors without any loss at all. No commission is made on tie bets.

EXAMPLE OF A BASKETBALL LINE

Following is an example of a basketball line:

KNICKS	Bulls	+3

The favorite is listed first and the underdog second, and the home team is listed in capital letters. The points listed show how many points the underdog, Chicago in this example, is being given.

Thus, we see that the Knicks, listed first, are the favorites by 3 points, and they're playing in New York since their heading is capitalized. Or if you want to look at it the other way, Chicago is a 3-point underdog and is playing an away game.

THE BETTING ODDS

As in football, you have to lay 11-10 on all bets, regardless of whether you're betting the favorite or underdog. The bookmaker's profit comes from the difference between the 11 and the 10, which works out to a vig of 4.54%. As a bettor trying to beat the odds, the break-even point against the vig is 52.38% no matter whether you bet the favorite or the underdog. Anything less than the 52.38% and you're in the red; anything better and you'll make a profit.

Basketball can also be bet as an **over/under** bet, also known as a **totals bet**. The bookmaker sets a number and bettors can wager whether the total points in the game will exceed the listed number or go below. The final winner is unimportant in this type of bet—it's only the total combined point count of the teams that matters.

Thus, if the Chicago-New York game has an over/under number of 195, and the final score is 95 to 93, bettors wagering under will win since the total points equal only 188. Should the score be 100-95 for a total of 195 points, the bet is a push and nobody wins.

Over/under bets are also laid at 11-10, and the break-even point for bettors is the same 52.38%.

TEASER BETS

Sportsbooks offer teaser bets in basketball, where two or more team are chosen and both must win for the wager to pay off. Bettors are usually given 4 points extra per game as an inducement to bet the teaser; however, all games wagered in the tease must be won. If just one game is lost or tied, the wager is lost.

The extra points can be used to bet on the favorite or underdog and are added to the current pointspread at the time of the wager. Thus, if the Knicks are 5-point favorites at home against the Bulls, you can take the 4-point tease to bet the Knicks as 9-point favorites. Or maybe you think that the Bulls with those extra points are a great bet against the Knicks, and you take them as a 1-point underdog using the teaser points against the spread.

The teaser bet is laid at 11 to 10 odds like the regular wagers. The main problem with teasers is that it's tough enough to win one game at a time against the spread without having two games tied together where both contests are must wins. One win and one loss won't do here—that's a loser on the tease. Both bets must be won.

If you're a pretty tight handicapper, those extra points may make the difference and turn good bets into very good bets.

Certainly though, stay away from teasers involving more than two games. It's just too difficult to call three wins. Keep your chances of winning within the stadium.

KEEPING RECORDS

The most important part of winning at basketball betting, as in the other forms of sports betting, is keeping good records. All handicappers stress this point, and with good reason. To know what is going on, you need the facts at hand. If you're a serious bettor, there is no better way to actually see in black and white just what is happening with the calls you are making.

BOXING

The big marquee fights create tremendous excitement and big-time betting, not only in the United States but worldwide as well. Millions of people anticipated great bouts such as Ali-Frazier, Leonard-Duran, and Hagler-Hearns and were ready to splash down some major cash if the odds were right. Fights such as Tyson-Holyfield, or ones involving some of the many retreads, occasionally generate some excitement too.

In recent years, Manny "Pac Man" Pacquiao bouts have flooded Las Vegas with thousands of avid boxing fans, and any bout featuring Floyd "Money" Mayweather Jr. causes a frenzy among boxing aficionados.

And of course, new stars are always emerging and drawing interest among the betting public.

THE MONEY LINE

Prizefight betting is based on the money line, as in baseball, but at a greater disadvantage to the bettor. While baseball bettors wager against a 20¢ line, the bettor in boxing is generally up against a **30¢ line**, a bigger hurdle to overcome.

As in baseball, the boxing quotes are based on a $5 bet. The bigger number is the amount you must wager to win $5 and the lesser number is the amount you will win if you wager $5.

A fight listed at 6-8 means that you must lay $8 to win $5 if you bet the favorite, odds of 8-5, and that you will win $6 on a $5 bet if you take the underdog. Of course, you can bet any amount permitted by the bookmaker, but it will be based on that line. Thus, a $100 bet on the underdog wins $120 if the underdog comes through, while the favorite bettor must lay $160 to win $100.

Let's call the underdog "Smith" and the favorite "Jones" and look at that line expressed in "+" and "-." You might see that same line expressed as follows:

SMITH	+120	Jones	-160

"Smith +120" means you would win $120 for every $100 you bet, and "Jones -$160" means you would have to bet $160 on Jones to win $100.

The underdog in a fight is always indicated by a "+" and the favorite is always indicated by a "-." Word-associate the minus with the concept of you having to put more money on the boxer than you will get back, and the plus with you getting back more than you wager.

WINNING STRATEGY

Boxing matches should be viewed on a fight-by-fight basis, as each match must be judged on its own merits. Over the years, betting on prizefights has lost some of its luster, as wary bettors tire of the unpredictable and questionable quality of the officiating as well as the undertones of tainted fights. Too many times, a boxer has been robbed of a clear victory in the ring by judges who seemed to watch a different fight than what fans saw in the ring.

Then you have fights such as the Buster Douglas-Evander Holyfield match of 1990. Douglas came into the fight bloated and clearly unmotivated, essentially just laying down and closing his eyes in what many fans viewed as a non-bout. This further discredited boxing to the public.

With all these problems, boxing is fairly tough to pick, but now and again some real opportunities come along that allow an astute bettor to pick up good action.

I would look for fights where an aging but popular champion who should be retired is coming back for a last hurrah against a young, proven star. By popularity alone, the old champion gets a lot of money bet in his corner, but has little chance of winning—as in the Ali-Holmes example earlier. Almost all champions go one fight too many, or a few fights too many, so these opportunities present themselves over and over again.

Boxing upsets often register more shock among fans and bettors than in other sports. When a highly touted boxer loses, it seems unfathomable, primarily because some boxers have such a fearsome reputation that when they lose, spectators are left in shock. In perhaps the greatest upset in boxing history, Buster Douglas, a whopping 42 to 1 underdog, scored a KO in the tenth round against Mike Tyson in 1990. No one saw that upset coming.

One may often find profitable spots near fight time when a contender appears to be without motivation. For example, sharp bettors made some money betting against Douglas in the Holyfield fight when the one-fight champion showed up for the weigh-in looking like a beached whale, clearly out of shape.

No matter how good a fight looks, it is poor money management to put all your eggs in one basket because you never know what might happen.

MIXED MARTIAL ARTS

INTRODUCTION

In recent years, mixed martial arts (MMA) has become huge, eclipsing boxing in popularity and, of course, becoming huge sports betting events. Huge MMA stars have emerged and with these stars come big fights and betting opportunities.

MMA betting is just like boxing; it is based on a 30¢ money line, and if you follow the sport closely, you'll find good betting opportunities.

WINNING STRATEGY

You can do well in MMA betting, especially going against popular fighters who are overvalued because they are on the downside of a big career or because they are American with a big following, fighting against a foreigner who hasn't yet become a fan favorite. Look for skilled opponents, especially Brazilians, who seem to dominate the sport, when going against a popular fighter who may be good, but whose betting odds are propped up based more on popularity than good sense.

But like everything else in sports betting, nothing is a given. Upsets can happen—all it takes is one big strike or submission, or lightning coming out of the bottle, and a fighter who looks to be unbeatable might be seeing stars. Which means, you should never bet the farm—or a good portion of it—on any one fight. For example, Georges St. Pierre, who looked unbeatable, got floored by underdog Matt Serra in UFC 69, in the biggest upset ever in UFC history. In another example, considered the biggest MMA upset ever, the seemingly invincible Fedor Emelianenko was submitted by Fabricio Werdum, a huge underdog, in just 69 seconds of round 1, in their June 27, 2010 match. Fedor came into the fight overconfident, which was not hard to imagine after being unbeaten in ten years, and carelessly allowed himself to be beaten by a triangle submission.

BEWARE THE "LOCK"

Let me say this one more time, because sports bettors keep falling into the trap of the "sure thing." There is no such thing as a lock, especially in MMA, so keep your bets within an acceptable range.

SEVEN PRINCIPLES OF WINNING AT SPORTS BETTING

1. FIND SITUATIONS WHERE EMOTIONS RUN HIGH FOR A PARTICULAR CONTEST AND HAVE DRIVEN UP (OR DOWN) THE ODDS BEYOND WHAT THE REAL ODDS SHOULD BE

Generally speaking, hometown fans bet with their hearts and will willingly bet against lopsided odds to support their team. Excellent bets can be found in these situations since fans tend to ignore realities and bet blind. A good example was the Ali-Holmes match-up discussed earlier. Ali was every bit as much the people's champion as he billed himself, and his fans supported him right to the end. Fine as a fan, foolish as a bettor. Smart bettors made lots of money on that fight. Look for those situations.

2. DON'T BET ON GAMES YOU'RE EMOTIONALLY INVOLVED WITH

If your game plan is to win money, and I assume it is since you're reading this section on smart betting, you cannot wager as a fan. Betting emotionally clouds your judgment and leads to stupid and costly mistakes.

If you're a diehard fan, you could probably watch your team lose six out of seven and yet still feel that it will win its eighth game, knowing full well that your team just doesn't have what it takes. Lay off those games—find other ones where you can see the game for what it is.

3. ALWAYS BET WITHIN YOUR LIMITS

No game or situation in life is a lock. You never know what can happen, no matter what the situation appears to be. Of course, if you feel strongly about a bet, by all means make that bet. However, never bet money that is above your means or is out of line with your normal stakes. It would be idiotic to have one bad loss destroy a whole season of steady wins. Many foolish and greedy gamblers know that story only to well.

For those of you who believe in the game that can't miss, think of the Oakland A's versus the Los Angeles Dodgers in the 1988 World Series. Nobody gave the Dodgers a chance but they rolled over the big, bad A's. There are many examples in all the sports.

Even more illustrative, let's look at a boxing match between Julio Cesar Chavez and Frankie Randall in 1994. This bout between Randall, the 15-1 underdog, and Chavez, who had been undefeated in 90 fights, looked like a lock if there ever was one. Basically, you had to be crazy to bet against Chavez, who was seemingly invincible. But in a fiercely contested fight, Randall dropped the iron-jawed Chavez for the first time ever, going on to win a split decision—a classic upset for the records book.

Another example of the big upset occurred in October, 2007, when the mighty Trojans of USC played an unheralded Stanford team in Palo Alto. Oddsmakers favored USC by 41 points—a whopping 7 touchdowns and 6 extra points. Yikes! But that didn't daunt Stanford fans from betting their team, giving the sportsbooks action on the game even at such lopsided odds. Actually, these underdog bettors didn't look too silly after the game ended. With one rather amazing catch in the fourth quarter, Stanford pulled off what many touts consider the greatest upset in college football history with a 24-23 win that drowned USC's hopes of winning another national title.

If you find betting situations you really like, by all means take advantage of them and make a bet. But always keep money management principles foremost in mind whenever money is at stake.

4. BET ONLY ON GAMES WHERE YOU THINK YOU HAVE THE EDGE

Stay away from marginal games that don't fit your winning formula. Many good handicappers have been brought down by making bets on teams that they didn't feel strongly about. Cut out the bad bets, the ones you know you shouldn't make, and your good bets may keep you a winner.

5. MAKE YOUR OWN RATING SYSTEM FOR TEAMS

Most professional handicappers advise you to thoroughly study your game and keep your own personal rating system of teams' comparative strengths. When there's a significant difference between the way that you would handicap a game and the bookmaker's line, you may have a good bet.

6. BET ON CONSISTENCY

Don't let one bad week or one excellent week in a team's performance cloud your estimate of a team's true ability. Every team has good and bad days, but one day doesn't make a team or a player.

If a proven consistent winner looks bad in one game, you may find a great betting opportunity the following week as public perception sours on that team's capabilities—and vice versa with bad teams having good days.

7. BE FLEXIBLE IN YOUR WINNING APPROACH

There is no one tried and true way of beating the bookmaker, so don't be conned into thinking there is one. There are many angles that can give you an edge. Look at them all before making the proper decision.

PARTING THOUGHTS

Betting on sports is a great passion for many fans, and if you do your homework and are good at the analysis needed to be a winner, it can be very profitable as well. I've discussed how the lines are made, why they exist, and how to beat the sports books and make money at football, baseball, basketball, boxing and mixed martial arts. Now it's up to you to find good opportunities, wager on them sensibly, and see if you can build up a big bankroll from your profits.

16 THE MONEY WHEEL

FIVE KEYS TO THE MONEY WHEEL
1. This carnival-inspired game has poor odds, requires no skill, and offers little else other than a quick, usually losing thrill. In other words, don't lose too much time or money at this game.
2. Given that the odds start at a "low" 11.11% against, I would recommend the fun level be kept to minimum bets.
3. The $5 wager is your best bet on a typical wheel.
4. The $1 wager is your second-best bet on a typical wheel.
5. If you somehow manage to get ahead in this game, immediately leave! Get out a winner and move on to something with better odds.

INTRODUCTION

The big spinning wheel, called the **Money Wheel** or the **Big Six** is not frequently found in casinos outside the United States, and even within the U.S., the wheel barely gets any play. But apparently it gets some action since the Big Six is still operating in numerous casinos. People seem to drop by, drop some quick money, then move on a touch lighter in the wallet after a few mild thrills.

The Money Wheel is fairly popular at county fairs, "Las Vegas Nights," carnivals, and other such events. And, probably because of a lack of competition from other gambling games and a beer drinking and festive crowd, they get pretty good play—and I might add, very few winners.

The wheels vary in the amount of slots that can be landed upon, generally around 54. They're filled with $1, $2, $5, $10, $20 and sometimes other denominations that can be won. Some wheels might even feature prizes in the slots.

Almost without exception, this quick and boring game, has poor odds, and very little to cheer about. In Nevada casinos, the odds range from 11% against the player on the $5 bet to as high as 24% on others. Very steep.

PAYOFFS AND ODDS

Following are the typical odds of a Nevada-type 54 slot wheel on a $1 bet.

THE MONEY WHEEL • PAYOFFS AND ODDS

WAGER	# OF WINNING SPINS	# OF LOSING SPINS	PAYOFF	CASINO'S ADVANTAGE
$1	23	31	$1	14.81%
$2	15	39	$2	16.67%
$5	8	46	$5	11.11%
$10	4	50	$10	18.52%
$20	2	52	$20	22.22%
$40*	1	53	$40	24.07%

*The $40 bet is usually indicated by a joker or a "flag." In Atlantic City, the payoff on this bet is generally 45 to 1, which drops the odds on the wager to 14.81%

The overall average of all the bets combined comes out to just under 20%, not the most enticing figure for discriminating bettors.

PARTING THOUGHTS

The odds can be even worse in carnivals and fairs than in the casinos, depending on how the payoffs are set, so don't lose any sleep if the Money Wheel isn't offered the next time you're at a county fair or a casino.

With odds like you see in the Payoffs and Odds chart, you can see why I'm not a big fan of the "Little Thrill."

17 CARIBBEAN STUD POKER

FIVE KEYS TO CARIBBEAN STUD POKER

1. Odds of 2.56% against aren't too steep but they'll get worse and burn a hole in your pocket quickly if you don't learn the proper strategies.
2. Always call when holding a pair.
3. Call with hands of A-K-J or higher, otherwise fold and get out.
4. Stay far away from the $1 Progressive unless the jackpot is more than $200,000. The house edge is abysmal on this bet, sometimes as high as 75%.
5. Walk away with your winnings when luck is going your way and make a hasty retreat when Lady Luck isn't smiling on you.

INTRODUCTION

As its name suggests, Caribbean stud poker first caught on and became popular in Caribbean casinos, but it has since spread and now can regularly be found in Las Vegas casinos and other casinos around the world. In shape and size, the tables resemble blackjack tables, with a dealer and cards. When you sit down, however, you see that a different game is being played.

While Caribbean stud poker shares the same hand rankings as standard poker games—which makes it even easier for players familiar with poker to learn the game—the similarity ends there. For one, the game is played against the casino, not against other players, which is a huge difference. Also, there is no bluffing, and payoffs come as a result of having achieved a predetermined poker hand, not having outmaneuvered or outlasted other players.

Caribbean stud poker is simple to play. Five cards are dealt to each participating player and there are no draws. Your only playing decision in this game is whether to make an additional bet after you have seen your cards or fold your hand and forfeit your original wager. Caribbean stud poker also features an additional $1 bet that is tied in with a progressive jackpot that awards bonus payouts for winning hands—even as much as hundreds of thousands of dollars if you hit a royal flush.

You can use certain strategies to shave the house edge to the smallest possible percentage, and give you the best chance to beat the casino. We'll talk about all this in this section.

Let's move on now and see what the game is all about.

THE BASICS OF PLAY

THE SETTING

Caribbean stud poker can be played with just one player against the dealer or with a full complement of seven players. In either case, the strategy and play of the game is the same since you play against the house, not against fellow players. The game is played on a table that closely resembles a blackjack table, with the players seated around the curved side of the table, and the dealer standing along the flat side facing the players. In front of the dealer is a chip rack that holds the table's bankroll. From this stash of chips, the dealer will pay off winning hands, or deposit losing bets that he has collected.

The minimum and maximum bets allowable are usually posted on the corner of the table. In most casinos, $5 is the minimum bet and ante allowed. You may also choose to make the **progressive bet** by putting $1 into the drop slot.

Caribbean stud poker uses one standard 52-card deck with 13 cards of each rank, ace to king, and four suits, spades, diamonds, clubs, and hearts.

THE OBJECT OF THE GAME

Your goal in Caribbean stud poker is to draw a five-card poker hand that is not only stronger than the dealer's, but which is of a high enough ranking to qualify for a bonus payout. The higher the rank of your hand, as long as your hand is stronger than the dealer's, the greater the bonus you will win according to a preset payoff schedule. However, there is one caveat: The dealer must hold a hand containing an ace and a king, or at least a pair or higher—that is, a **qualifying hand**—for the bonus to count.

When placing the $1 optional progressive wager in Caribbean stud poker, your goal is to draw a flush or better to receive additional bonus payouts. In particular, you would like to get a royal flush, a hand that can win hundreds of thousands of dollars.

Before we look at qualifying hands and how they affect the game, let's review the poker hands that are used to determine the payoffs in this game.

HAND RANKINGS

If you're a poker player, you'll notice that the hand rankings are exactly the same ones used in standard high poker games, except for the A-K hand, which is given value in Caribbean stud poker. The hands below are listed in descending order of strength, from the most powerful, the royal flush, to the least powerful hand that still pays out money to players, the A-K high.

CARIBBEAN STUD POKER: HAND RANKINGS	
Royal Flush:	An A-K-Q-J-10, all of the same suit, is called a royal flush. It is a rare sight, one that you may never see in a lifetime of play.
Straight Flush:	Five cards of the same suit in numerical sequence, such as the J-10-9-8-7 of clubs, is called a straight flush. This particular example is called a jack-high straight flush since the jack is the highest-ranking card. In a straight flush, an ace can be used as either the highest card–forming an ace-high straight flush, which is actually a royal flush–or the lowest card, as in the A-2-3-4-5 of diamonds. The Q-K-A-2-3 of clubs is not a straight flush, just an ace-high flush.
Four of a Kind:	Four cards of identical rank, such as 6-6-6-6-3, are called four of a kind. The unmatched card in this example, the 3, is irrelevant and has no bearing on the rank of the hand.
Full House:	A full house consists of three cards of identical rank and two other cards of identical rank, but different from the rank of the first three cards. Two examples of full houses are 8-8-8-J-J and K-K-K-7-7.
Flush:	Any five cards of the same suit constitute a flush. The A-K-7-3-2 of spades is an ace-high flush, and the Q-10-7-5-3 of hearts is a queen-high flush.
Straight:	A straight consists of five unsuited cards in sequential order, such as 10-9-8-7-6. In a straight, an ace can be used as either the highest card in the run, such as the ace-high straight A-K-Q-J-10, or the lowest card, as in the 5-high straight 5-4-3-2-A. The hand made up of the Q-K-A-2-3 is not a straight. It is merely an ace-high hand and will be beaten by any pair.

CARIBBEAN STUD POKER: HAND RANKINGS	
Three of a Kind:	Three cards of identical value along with two unmatched cards are called a three of a kind. An example of three of a kind is 7-7-7-Q-2.
Two Pair:	Two sets of equivalently valued or "paired" cards, along with an unmatched card is a two-pair hand. Examples of two-pair hands include 4-4-3-3-A and K-K-3-3-J.
One Pair:	One pair of identically valued cards along with three unmatched cards is called a pair. The hand 2-2-8-4-A is referred to as "a pair of twos." Pairs are ranked in order of value from aces, the highest, down to deuces, the lowest. Thus, a pair of aces beats a pair of kings, and a pair of nines wins over a pair of sixes.
Ace-King:	In Caribbean stud poker, a hand lacking all the above combinations but led by an ace and a king, such as A-K-J-5-3, ranks below a one-pair hand. This is the weakest hand that qualifies as a dealer hand. If both the dealer and the player hold this hand, the highest-ranked of the remaining cards decides the winner.
All Other Hands:	Any hand not including any of the above combinations is a non-qualifying hand and has no value in Caribbean stud poker.

ODDS OF DRAWING HANDS

The following table shows the odds of being dealt the above hands in Caribbean stud poker. These are the same odds as in regular draw poker for the first five cards dealt.

ODDS OF DRAWING QUALIFYING HANDS	
Royal Flush	649,739 - 1
Straight Flush	72,192 - 1
Four of a Kind	4,165 - 1
Full House	693 - 1
Flush	508 - 1
Straight	254 - 1
Three of a Kind	46 - 1
Two Pair	20 - 1
One Pair	1.37 - 1

RESOLVING TIES

Should both the dealer and player be dealt equivalently ranked hands, the normal rules of poker rankings are used to determine the winner. This involves using the higher ranked unmatched cards to determine the better hand when there are one pair and two pair hands, or in the case of flushes and straights, using the highest cards leading those hands. Let's take a closer look at these situations.

THREE OF A KIND AND FULL HOUSE TIES

When two players hold three of a kind or full houses, the hand with the higher ranking three of a kind wins the pot. For example, K-K-K-7-7 is a higher-ranking full house than Q-Q-Q-A-A, and 9-9-9-3-4 beats 8-8-8-Q-5.

FLUSH TIES

When the dealer and the player both hold flushes, the flush led by the highest card wins. If those cards are tied, the next highest cards are compared, and so on down the ranks. In the unlikely event that both flushes contain identically valued cards, the outcome is a tie or a **push**.

STRAIGHT AND STRAIGHT FLUSH TIES

The lead card also determines the winner of straight and straight flush ties. An ace-high straight beats any other straight, and ties against another ace-high straight. Similarly, a king-high straight is stronger than a queen-high.

TWO PAIR TIES

The same holds true for two-pair hands. For example, J-J-7-7-K beats out 10-10-9-9-A, and 8-8-4-4-10 loses to 8-8-5-5-9. When both pairs are evenly matched, the higher-ranking fifth card, the unmatched card, determines the victor. If all cards are equally ranked, such as 5-5-3-3-2 and 5-5-3-3-2, the hand is a tie.

ONE PAIR AND A-K TIES

If the player and the dealer hold the same pair or an unpaired hand led by A-K, the hand with the highest unmatched card wins. Should the highest unmatched card in each hand be of equal rank, the next highest ranking cards are compared. If all cards are identical in value, the hand is a tie. For example, if the dealer has a 9-9-K-J-5 and the player has a 9-9-K-Q-4, the player wins by virtue of his queen beating the dealer's jack. Similarly, A-K-Q-7-2 beats A-K-J-10-9.

PLAYING THE GAME

In front of you will be three betting spots, one for each of the three wagers you can make. The bet and the ante wagers are adjacent to one another in a design that looks like a treasure chest. The spot closest to the dealer, and where you will place your initial wager, is marked "**Ante**." It is rectangular in shape. The betting spot just below it, which is closer to you and enclosed in a circle, is marked, "**Bet**." These are the areas where you will do the majority of your betting.

The final betting area, closest to the dealer, is actually a drop slot, a "hole" in the table where you can make an optional and separate $1 wager on the progressive jackpot.

You begin by placing your bet in the area marked "Ante." You may also choose to make the progressive bet by dropping $1 into the drop slot. For now though, no money can be wagered in the area marked "Bet." When all players have placed their bets, the dealer's first action will be to push a button that automatically collects the $1 progressive bets that were made. These bets will drop out of sight into the table, and a red light will go on in front of each player who made the bet. The ante bets remain on the table

The dealer is now ready to distribute the cards. Five cards will be dealt face down to each player. The dealer will also deal himself five cards, four face down and one face up to be viewed by all players. This exposed card is known as an **upcard**. No further cards can be drawn by either player or dealer.

If you think that your five-card hand can beat the dealer or qualifies for a bonus payout, you can **call**. You do so by placing an additional wager in the box marked "bet" and placing your cards face down on the table. This wager is double the ante bet. Thus, if the ante bet was $5, you must place $10 in the bet area. Similarly, if $25 was the ante, $50 is the additional wager you must place in the bet area. In the first case, you would have total ante and call bets of $15, and in the second case, adding $25 to $50, $75 would be the total.

If you do not wish to place this additional bet, you **fold** by returning your cards to the dealer. Your ante bet will be forfeited and collected by the house. You can no longer participate in the hand and no additional money is at risk.

Each player in turn must decide whether to play by placing the additional double bet in the bet box, or fold and forfeit his ante bet. Play proceeds clockwise, beginning with the player at the dealer's left and continuing to the player positioned at the dealer's immediate right, the position at the table known as **third base**. Calling or folding is the only playing decision you will make once the cards have been dealt. When all players have played their hands, the dealer will turn over his remaining four down cards to reveal his final five-card hand. These cards will be compared to your hand to see whether you have won or lost on your bets.

The dealer's first action once his cards are revealed is to determine whether he has a qualifying hand, the minimum hand required by the rules of the game for bonuses and extra payouts to occur for players holding stronger hands.

Let's see what it means to have a *qualifying hand.*

THE QUALIFYING HAND

A dealer's qualifying five-card hand contains at least an ace and a king or a higher total such as a pair or better. For example, A-K-4-3-2 (ace-king high), 3-3-7-9-Q (pair of threes), and 7-8-9-10-J (straight), are all qualifying dealer hands, while A-Q-3-4-7 is not.

Why is a qualifying hand so important?

Let's take a look at that now.

WHEN THE DEALER DOES NOT HAVE A QUALIFYING HAND

If the dealer does not have a qualifying hand, all players who have remained in the game automatically win their ante bet, regardless of whether their hand is stronger than the dealer's. For example, if the dealer holds A-J-10-8-2, a non-qualifying hand, and you hold Q-9-8-6-2 or even 7-6-4-3-2, you win. The dealer cannot win if his hand doesn't contain at least an A-K, nor can any player who has folded win—that money is already collected and gone.

That's the good news. The bad news is that if the dealer does not have a qualifying hand, you win only your ante bet. The call bets, the ones placed in the bet area, are returned. They are not eligible for bonus payouts or even 1-1 payoffs regardless of the hand drawn.

Thus, if $5 was wagered on the ante and $10 in the bet circle, and you have three jacks when the dealer holds 2-3-7-9-K, a non-qualifying hand, your total win would be only the $5 paid at even money on the ante bet. The non-qualifying dealer hand negates the 3 to 1 bonus that would have been paid for your three of a kind. In this example, the $10 wager in the bet circle is returned to you.

Let's see what happens when the dealer does have a qualifying hand.

WHEN THE DEALER HAS A QUALIFYING HAND

When the dealer does have a qualifying hand of at least an A-K or better, he will compare his hand to each of the players to determine who has the stronger hand.

As opposed to the non-qualifying situation, both the ante bet and the call bet (the wager in the "bet" area) are at stake now. You will either win both bets or lose both bets, depending upon who has the stronger total. For example, if you had put in $5 for the ante and $10 on the call bet, and the dealer held 8-8 to your 2-2, you would lose both bets since you have the weaker hand.

However, if you have the better hand, say, a pair of tens, you win both bets. Each wager, the ante bet and the call bet, is paid differently. Ante bets are paid at even money, 1 to 1, while call bets are paid according to the bonus schedule shown below. Note that no bonus payout is awarded for an A-K hand.

BONUS PAYOUTS ON THE CALL BET

BONUS PAYOUTS ON THE CALL BET	
Royal Flush	100-1
Straight Flush	50-1
Four of a Kind	20-1
Full House	7-1
Flush	5-1
Straight	4-1
Three of a Kind	3-1
Two Pair	2-1
One Pair	1-1

Let's look at an example hand to make the bonus payouts perfectly clear. Let's say that you have a $5 ante bet and a $10 call bet and hold 9-9-9-5-3 against the dealer's Q-Q-J-4-2. Because the dealer has a qualifying hand, you qualify for the bonus payout on your three of a kind hand. Thus, you'll win even money on the ante bet, $5, plus 3 to 1 on the call bet, for $30 more. The dealer would push $50 over to you, $35 in winnings plus the original $15 in bets.

In the unlucky event that the dealer does not hold a qualifying hand, your three of a kind would go to waste and you would only win the ante bet. You also don't qualify for bonus payouts if your hand is weaker than the dealer's. For example, if he held a pair of jacks and you held tens, your ante and call bets would be outright losers.

Note that the dealer only wins at even money, regardless of the strength of his hand. The most you could lose is what you bet, while the house could lose a lot more, according to the payout schedule.

HELPFUL HINT

To qualify for a bonus payout, three things must occur:

1. The dealer must have a qualifying hand.
2. You must have a better hand than the dealer.
3. You must have at least a one-pair hand or better.

THE MAXIMUM BONUS PAYOUT

Be aware that casinos have a limit on the maximum amount they'll pay in bonus payouts. Some limits may be as low as $5,000, while others may go as high as $50,000 or more. There is no standard so you'll need to check the limit posted on the table.

How does this maximum payout affect you?

Well, not in a good way if you have bet more than you can win, because in that case, you will be denied the full amount of the payout on a big hand if your winnings exceed the table limit for bonus payouts.

Here's an example to make this concept perfectly clear. Let's say that you wager $150 on the call bet and draw a straight flush in a casino that has a $5,000 maximum limit bonus payout. Normally, you would be entitled to $7,500 —50 to 1 multiplied by the $150 bet. However, since the maximum bonus payout is only $5,000, you would lose out on an extra $2,500. That's a very big hit to take. Your loss would be even greater if that hand had been a royal flush paying 100 to 1 on the bonus—you would only get $5,000 of the $15,000 and lose out on the extra $10,000!

So you see, being aware of the maximum bonus payout and adjusting your bets accordingly is a key factor in your strategy considerations for this game. You don't want to get caught in a situation where you have to forego big winnings simply because you weren't properly prepared to bet the correct amount. To protect against this happening, always make sure that the maximum call bet multiplied by 100 does not exceed the bonus payout. I use the number "100" because the largest bonus, the royal flush bonus, pays at 100 to 1. If 100 times the call bet is greater than the casino's limit, you will not get the full payout for a royal flush.

To calculate the maximum bet that won't be penalized if you are dealt a royal flush, divide the casino's maximum payout by 100. For example, if the maximum payout is $5,000, your maximum call bet should not exceed $50—$5,000 divided by 100. And if the call bet were $50, the ante, which is always half that amount, would be $25.

You can also divide the maximum payout by 200 to reach the maximum ante that will be paid off in full.

THE PROGRESSIVE JACKPOT

The optional wager, the progressive bet, is made by placing $1 in the drop slot, also known as the **progressive slot**, before the cards are dealt. The goal of this bet is to earn additional bonus payouts by drawing a flush or higher ranked hand. While a flush, full house, or other powerful hand would be great, what you ideally would like to hit is a royal flush, a hand that will pay you the full progressive amount.

On or near every Caribbean stud poker table will be a jackpot meter that goes up in value each time $1 is placed into the drop slot at any table linked to that meter. Depending upon the casino, this jackpot can be as little as $5,000 or $10,000, the general starting point after a royal flush is hit, or as high as hundreds of thousands of dollars. Obviously, in the latter case, this is where the possibilities of this wager become a lot more interesting for you.

Before each hand is dealt, the dealer will push a button that causes the dollar bets to drop into the holding area below the table, and at the same time, causing the progressive jackpot to rise. The amount that each progressive bet increases the jackpot varies from casino to casino. Some casinos put in only 49¢ of each dollar played, while others, particularly larger, more forward-thinking casinos that understand the ability of larger jackpots to draw players, may put in as much as 75¢ per dollar played to boost the jackpots faster. Obviously, the smaller the amount of money put back into the progressive, the slower the jackpot will grow.

However, the actual percentage of money that gets put back into the jackpot is not really a concern for you unless you plan on camping out and adding to the casino coffers with endless progressive bets to help build the jackpot. What really matters is which casino has the highest jackpots. You want to win the thing when it has a lot of money waiting for you. How it got that high is neither here nor there. As that jackpot grows, so should your interest. Just like the lottery, you don't really care about the details of the big prize; you just want to know, "How many millions of dollars can I win if I pick the right numbers?"

What does it take to win the full amount of the progressive?

Why, nothing less than the big sandwich with all the dressings—the royal flush. While drawing this hand would certainly be nice, don't hold your breath. It's a long shot—1 in 649,739, to be exact. But playing long shots is what much of gambling is about. And meanwhile, you have other big hands that will give you payouts while you dream about that big salami being delivered into your hands.

The following charts contain payout schedules for progressive jackpots. The first schedule, which would more likely be found at a larger casino aggressively targeting Caribbean stud poker players, is liberal in its payout structure, which obviously benefits you if you can find this good paytable. The second schedule is more common and pays much less on four of a kind, full houses, and flushes. However, note that in all cases, the royal flush pays the full 100% shown on the progressive meter, and the straight flush pays 10% of the meter.

Note that the three numbers following the name of each schedule show the payoffs given on four of a kind, full house, and flush hands.

PAYOUT SCHEDULE A (LIBERAL) 500/250/100	
Royal Flush	100% of the jackpot
Straight Flush	10% of the jackpot
Four of a Kind	$500
Full House	$250
Flush	$100

PAYOUT SCHEDULE B (COMMON) 100/75/50	
Royal Flush	100% of the jackpot
Straight Flush	10% of the jackpot
Four of a Kind	$100
Full House	$75
Flush	$50

In between the 500/250/100 liberal and 100/75/50 common schedules shown above, you may find 500/150/75, 500/100/75, 500/100/50, 500/75/50, 300/100/50, 250/100/50, and 150/100/50.

Keep in mind that the progressive is a separate bet and is not affected by the results of the ante or regular call bet. For example, if you are dealt a full house and the dealer miraculously—I should say, disastrously—has a four of a kind, you would still win $250 on the $1 progressive bet—assuming Schedule A is in play—even though your call and ante bets are losers.

By the same token, you would get the full bonus payout on the $1 progressive bet even if the dealer doesn't have a qualifying hand. Therefore, when the dealer has a non-qualifying hand, you must be careful to alert the dealer to flushes and better hands before he accidentally removes the cards without checking for progressive winners.

Finally, there is no maximum limit on a progressive payout like there is on the bonus payout. If you hit the royal flush, you'll get paid the full amount of the progressive meter. If that occurs, I'm sure you'll be one very happy camper.

THE AGGREGATE PAYOFF ON PROGRESSIVES

On the progressive bet, one other casino rule comes into play. The bonus payout is limited to an aggregate payoff on the straight flush and the royal flush. This means, for example, that on a straight flush hand, a total of 10% will be paid out. If two players hold a straight flush on the same deal, they would split that 10%, getting only 5% each.

For example, if the meter showed $12,000, the total pool of $1,200 for the straight flush would be divided evenly between the two winners at $600 each. This applies only to straight flush and royal flush hands on progressive wagers, not to the bonus payouts on the four of a kind, full house, and flush hands, where each player receives the full amount listed.

The chances of two players holding a straight or royal flush on the very same hand is so unlikely—quantum degrees more than one hundred million to 1 against (the exact odds depending upon how many other players are at the table)—that this rule shouldn't be of great concern to you.

HOUSE PERCENTAGES

THE BASIC GAME

The house advantage in Caribbean stud poker on the regular ante and call bets, if the proper strategy is followed, is 2.56%, which is not too bad compared to other games or bets within games that can be found in the casinos. For example, American-style double zero roulette will have you bucking odds of 5.26%, which is steep, but not as bad as proposition bets in craps, which are over 11% against you. On the other hand, the good bets in craps have you competing against a house edge of well less than 1%, and in blackjack, with proper play, you have an actual advantage over the house.

So, how you view the house edge in Caribbean stud poker is relative. If you like the game and have a good time playing it, you can feel much better here than at keno tables and at many slot machines, where the house edge is much more significant. When you put the house edge at Caribbean stud poker into perspective with the other games available in a casino, the percentages aren't all that bad. You still have to keep in mind that whenever the house has an edge, you have the expectation to lose more than you will win in the long run. In the short run, however, you can get on a roll and take their money.

When you play the basic game in Caribbean stud poker, making the call and ante bets, your job is to keep the house edge at the minimum possible because the lower the casino's edge, the better your chances of winning their money. And that's why you always want to play your best game.

PROGRESSIVE BET

The house edge on the progressive bet is relative to how much money is in the pool itself, but generally speaking, you're looking at an edge in excess of 25%. The greater the pool, the lower the house edge on the $1 bet. But keep in mind that your chances of being dealt a royal flush don't change whether the jackpot is $10,000 or $100,000. You don't get the best odds making the progressive wager, but you want to get a big payoff if you hit.

A CLOSER LOOK AT THE ODDS

On average, when you utilize proper strategy, you will make a call bet on just over half of your hands—about 52% of the time. In other words, every other hand will involve a call bet, which is double the size of the ante bet. If you think in terms of units, on one hand you'll have a one-unit bet, and on the next hand you'll bet three units—one unit on the ante and two units on the call. If we simulate a progression, the first hand will be one unit, the second will be three units, the third will be one unit, and the fourth will be three units again. That's an average of two units bet per hand that you will make in Caribbean stud poker.

Thus, if your ante bet is $5 (one unit), you will average about $10 in bets per hand.

If you never made the call bets, which would be foolish, and only made the ante bet, you would lose at a 5.25% clip, which is very steep. However, when the call bets are averaged in—and they should be—the overall house odds drop to 2.56% of the money wagered if you play the proper strategies.

You will sometimes see the house percentage for the game quoted at that same 5.25% edge, but it is misleading since it only accounts for the ante bet—before you make the advantageous call bet. It would be like quoting the house edge at blackjack without including the doubling and splitting opportunities, which would again mislead you as to the true house edge you face at blackjack. As stated above, playing the proper strategy on the ante and call bets, the house edge in Caribbean stud poker is 2.56%. That's the number to keep in your head.

The call bets in Caribbean stud poker are similar to double downs in blackjack or odds bets in craps. You will place these bets only when you either have an even game against the house, which will bring down the overall house edge on a bet, or when you actually have an edge. You never want to increase the size of a wager or risk additional money when the odds are against you. That, of course, is not a winning approach. But when the call bets give you a chance to put more money on the table when you have the edge, that's where you reduce the house edge and where you can make more money.

PLAYING & BETTING STRATEGY

INTRODUCTION

In this section, we'll go over the playing and betting strategies that optimize your chances of winning at Caribbean stud poker. We'll discuss the ante, call, and progressive bets, the best way to approach call or fold decisions, and an overall winning approach to putting some green in your pockets.

PLAYING STRATEGY

You have one crucial decision to make in Caribbean stud poker—whether to make the call wager at double the ante size, or fold and forfeit the ante without risking additional money. In some cases, for example, when you have a strong hand such as three of a kind or two pair, the strategy is fairly obvious: You want the additional money out on the table. On the other hand, when your cards are weak and you don't even have an ace and a king—cards that will at least compete with a qualifying dealer total—the strategy is also clear cut: You want to fold.

The basic strategy outlined below will have you playing at a near optimal level. Playing the absolute perfect optimal strategy will help your chances of winning by only a few hundredths of a percentage point. This gain is so tiny that the extra effort needed to learn a complicated playing strategy is not worth it.

The strategy presented here is all that you need to know to play a near-perfect game with no practical loss of profit.

The correct playing strategy divides hands into two categories: those that are stronger than the dealer's qualifying total of A-K, which you'll generally keep; and hands that are weaker than the minimum A-K, which you'll throw away.

The general strategy in Caribbean stud poker is to minimize losses in bad situations. For example, holding a small pair will show long term losses, but you'll play it because you'll lose less by hoping the dealer is weaker or doesn't qualify. This is better than tossing the pair and automatically losing your ante wager. At the same time, you'll maximize winnings when your cards are strong, for example, when you have a hand of two pair or higher, a situation where you're a big favorite and get a good payout. Very simply, when you have the edge, you want to get more money on the table, and when the house has the edge, you want less money out there.

Let's look at the specific starting hands that should be played, beginning with the strongest hands you can hold and working down to the weakest hands.

TWO PAIR, THREE AND FOUR OF A KIND, STRAIGHTS, FLUSHES, FULL HOUSES, STRAIGHT AND ROYAL FLUSHES

Two pair, three and four of a kind, straights, flushes, full houses, and straight and royal flushes are all very strong hands that not only are heavily favored to win, but which qualify for bonus payouts. The strategy for these hands is very clear even to beginning players: Get more money out there—make the call bet!

PAIRS

Pairs are dealt 42% of the time in five-card poker, so this is a hand you'll see on a regular basis. The correct strategy when holding a pair—any pair—is to call, regardless of the dealer's upcard. This is a clear gain in all situations.

This doesn't mean that you'll win money in the long run playing all pairs, because you won't. Do not confuse gaining—that is, making more money doing something than not doing anything—with profit, which means that you expect to win money over the long term in a given situation. Your chances of winning a hand are tied in to the rank of your pairs; essentially, the higher the pair, the more hands you will win in the long run. The stronger pairs—tens, jacks, queens, kings and aces—have a positive expectation of winning against all dealer upcards. You can look at them as an excellent profit center.

However, with the smaller pairs, you may or may not have an edge against the dealer, depending on the upcard he is showing. Overall, when you are dealt twos, threes, fours, fives, sixes and sevens, your long-term expectations are negative; that is, you expect to show a loss. However—except for the lowest of pairs, twos through fours—if your pair is higher than the dealer's upcard, you will always have a positive winning expectation. For example, let's say that you hold 7-7 and the dealer shows a 6. You already know that the dealer's 6, if it is paired, but is not improved with another 6 or a second pair, is a loser to your sevens, so that's a big edge. You have a long-term expectation of winning, not only here, but when the dealer shows any upcards of 2-6 in this situation.

Small pairs may be weak, but it would be a huge mistake to throw them away. Keeping them is more profitable than discarding them and forfeiting your ante bet without a fight. While the dealer may have a pair 42% of the time, 58% of the time he won't and you'll win that ante bet—but not the call bet, which will be returned to you. You're putting more money on the table by making the call bet, but of course, the times the dealer does make that bigger pair, you will lose the ante bet and the call bet. Overall, however, it works out to your advantage. Players who throw away small pairs give up anywhere from 5 to 10%, depending on the pairs they discard and the situation. That's a bad loss to take.

Compare the above hand to a situation where you still hold the sevens, but the dealer holds an 8 (or higher) instead. If he pairs that 8, you're now on the losing end of the pairs. So you see, what the dealer holds as an upcard has a big effect on your winning chances. You should still put more money on the call bet in this situation, because it is still to your advantage, but it isn't as much to your advantage as it would be if the dealer had a smaller upcard to your pair.

In summary, play all pairs, even small pairs, and make that call bet. Sometimes you'll have the expectation to win in the long run, and sometimes you won't, but in all cases you will come out ahead by making this play.

A-K

When you hold A-K, you have a borderline hand and your strategy will depend on the other three cards that you hold and the dealer's upcard.

WHEN YOUR THIRD-HIGHEST CARD IS A JACK OR QUEEN, CALL THE DEALER

For example, the hand A-K-J-9-4 should be played against all dealer upcards, including the ace. The thinking here is that if the dealer makes a qualifying hand of A-K-x-x-x (where "x" stands for any card other than those that would give the dealer a pair or another higher hand), the A-K-J or better hand is strong enough to win, thus making the call bet a profitable play.

WHEN YOUR THIRD HIGHEST CARD IS LOWER THAN A JACK, CALL THE DEALER ONLY IF HIS UPCARD MATCHES ONE OF YOUR FIVE CARDS

Examples: Call with A-K-10-5-2 versus an ace, and A-K-10-5-2 versus 2, but fold A-K-10-5-2 versus a queen, and A-K-8-7-6 versus a 5.

The A-K hands are almost 50-50 in terms of long-term gain. In order for calling to be the correct play, you need to have a little extra edge to push the A-K hand into your favor. In the situation where one of your cards matches the dealer's upcard, the dealer is less likely to have a pair. That's one less card that can help the dealer defeat your hand, and it gives you the extra edge needed to make this a profitable play.

If your A-K hand doesn't have a jack or a queen to back it up and none of your five cards pair up with the dealer's upcard, the correct play is to fold.

A-Q OR LESS

Any hand that doesn't have any of the above combinations—that is no A-K-J or better, or A-K-duplicated card—should be folded. Thus, if the best you're looking at is an unpaired hand with no straights or flushes, and an A-Q or less, you have an automatic fold. For example, fold A-Q-J-10-9, A-Q-8-7-6, K-Q-J-10-6, and 10-8-4-3-2.

The problem with these hands is that they're worthless. Hands that are led by A-Q are no better than jack-high or even 8-high hands. In all cases, if the dealer qualifies, these hands will lose, since by definition a qualifying dealer hand contains an A-K or better.

THE DISADVANTAGE OF PLAYING A-Q OR LESSER HANDS

There is one constant in Caribbean stud poker that makes playing A-Q or less hands disastrous: The dealer will make a qualifying hand approximately 56% of the time. At first glance, you might think that the loss is $12 for every $100 bet—56 losses less 44 wins. That's a very convincing argument not to make this play. Giving up 12% is a foolish play. But the loss is actually much worse. When the ante bet is figured in, your disadvantage comes out to more than 10 times that, about 125%! Let's take a closer look at the math behind this.

We'll use a $10 ante bet for this example. In 100 hands, the dealer will fail to qualify 44 times, and you'll win a total of only $440. Since the dealer didn't qualify, the $20 call bet is returned and only the ante bet is paid off. That's $10 for each winning hand at 1-1, even money. The other 56 times that the dealer qualifies, you'll not only lose the $10 ante bet, but the $20 call bet as well. That's $1,680 in losses against only $440 in wins for a net loss of $1,240.

Thus, for every $1,000 made in ante bets, you'll lose $1,240. That's a very heavy loss to overcome in this game, or in any game. An approximate 125% house edge is way too much to give up in any betting proposition.

The moral of the story: Don't play A-Q or less, no matter what kind of hunch you have. You should never, ever think about playing these hands. To be a winner at Caribbean stud poker, you absolutely must avoid any situation that gives the house an exorbitant edge.

PROGRESSIVE BET STRATEGY

Generally speaking, unless the jackpot is in the hundreds of thousands, the progressive $1 wager is a complete sucker bet that gives the house an edge of anywhere between 50 to 75%. Ouch!

Even when the jackpot is $250,000, for example, you still may be giving the casino an enormous advantage by making this bet. The exact edge the casino enjoys is a function of several factors: the bonuses paid on four of a kind, full houses and flushes, which vary from casino to casino; the size of the jackpot itself; and equally important, the size of the ante bet.

This last factor, the size of the ante bet, is important because the progressive bet cannot be made as an independent wager. To play Caribbean stud poker, you must place, at a minimum, an ante bet; only then can you make the progressive bet as well. Since each bet gives the casino roughly a 5.25% edge, the larger the average bet, the higher the jackpot must be to compensate for these wagers. Thus, if $5 were wagered on the ante, a break-even for the progressive would be far lower than if $10 were the average ante bet.

For example, if you're playing in a casino with liberal payouts, say $500 for four of a kind, $250 for a full house, and $100 for a flush, and the average ante bet is $5, the break-even on a progressive jackpot would be around $200,000. However, if there are less liberal payouts of $100 for four of a kind, $75 for a full house, and $50 for a flush, which are found at many casinos, the break-even progressive jackpot pops up closer to $350,000 on that average $5 bet.

But if that average ante was $10 in a game with liberal payouts, the break-even jackpot jumps almost $100,000 to $300,000. A $1 average ante bet would yield better overall odds on the $1 progressive, but that will rarely be found. Most casinos have a $5 minimum ante bet.

Thus these three important factors—average ante size, jackpot size, and bonus payout schedule—influence the house edge you're up against when making a progressive bet in Caribbean stud poker.

In rare cases, you will find a monster payout that has built up, and the progressive bet may actually be advantageous. It's always nice to dream of the big hit, hence the millions and millions of people who play the lottery consistently and the many players who donate the $1 to the progressive pool in Caribbean stud poker. However, my approach to gambling is to stick to the bets that offer the best chances of winning in the long run. And unless the progressive jackpot is in the hundreds of thousands of dollars, you would be better off avoiding the progressive bet altogether.

If a you feel the pressing need to make that $1 dream bet, you might consider playing the lottery. Lousy odds, but if you do hit, the payout is not a measly five figures, it's a two-year cruise around the world, a dream home, instant retirement, and the most expensive cigars money can buy.

But then again, my advice is always to play rationally. Make the best bets the games can give you, and if you're winning, walk away with the casino's money in your pocket.

BETTING STRATEGY

If you find a situation where the progressive jackpot gets into the hundreds of thousands of dollars, and you're going to play Caribbean stud poker strictly for the purpose of taking a shot at the jackpot, you would want to keep the ante bet as small as possible in order to minimize the combined effect of the house edge on the ante and call bets.

Other than the advice given on the $1 progressive bet above, there is no particular betting strategy on the ante and call bets in Caribbean stud poker that will give you an advantage, as there is in blackjack. Your best betting strategy is to bet intelligently according to your bankroll and your comfort level. We'll discuss more about money management later on, but the most important rule of all rules when deciding on bet size and the amount to put at risk is the following: Never risk money that you cannot afford to lose. That is the cardinal guideline for any betting proposition.

WINNING STRATEGY

The main thing to keep in mind with most games offered by the casino, including Caribbean stud poker, is that the game is a negative expectation gamble. The casino has an advantage of 2.56% on the call and ante bets when the proper strategy is followed, which is not too bad by casino standards. The progressive $1 wager, on the other hand, can give the casino as much as a 75% edge, which by any standards is a hard nut to crack.

If you want to get the best odds possible, meaning that you give yourself the best chances of winning money, your first order of business is to avoid the progressive bet. Unless the jackpot is enormous, at least $200,000 or more under normal circumstances, this bet gives too much away to the casino. Avoiding this wager will avoid a constant $1 drain on your bankroll.

Secondly, you must study the playing strategy so that you make the correct moves and optimize your chances of winning. As we saw earlier, there is a lot of information to remember, but successful players learn the strategies and use them all the time, not just when the mood strikes them. There is no substitute for correct play. Hunches only build the casino's profits and make players poorer. Don't be among the crowd of losers. Prepare yourself and play a tough game.

PARTING THOUGHTS

To win at Caribbean Stud Poker, you must not only play the correct strategies, you must also make intelligent money management decisions at the tables. When things are going poorly, which they sometimes do, you must limit your losses. Avoid taking a bad beating in any one session. And when you're on a hot streak, make sure that when the dust settles, you leave a winner.

Caribbean stud poker is like all gambling games—you will have good streaks and bad streaks. With a little luck and smart money management, you can get more from the house than they get from you.

18 LET IT RIDE

FIVE KEYS TO LET IT RIDE

1. Play only good three-card hands–a pair of tens or better, three-straight flushes, three-flushes with at least two tens or better, or one 10 with a one-gap straight, and either a 10, J, Q or a J, Q, K.
2. Similarly, do not play pairs lower than tens, low straights or flushes, and other poor three-card hands.
3. Holding four cards, Let it Ride only with tens or better, four-card flushes and open-ended straights.
4. Avoid the $1 bonus bet (lousy odds). Better to play $1 in the lottery.
5. Learn the correct strategies. Don't give the house any extra edge at all.

INTRODUCTION

Let it Ride was first introduced to Las Vegas casinos in 1993 and immediately became a rousing success. The game has continued to maintain its relevance on the casino floor and is now a mainstay of action in casinos across the country and around the world.

Let it Ride is a simple game to play. To start, you make equal-sized bets on the three betting circles in front of your position. So, if you bet $5 on one circle, for example, you must bet $5 on the other two circles as well. There is also an optional $1 bonus bet that can be made. After bets have been placed, the dealer deals three cards to each player. He then deals two community cards face down into the boxes in front of his position. You combine the two community cards with your three cards to form your final five-card hand.

Winning hands are paid based solely on their strength and the paytable that is posted at the table. You do not compete against fellow players; your only goal is to get a high enough hand to qualify for a payout. For example, you want at least a pair of tens, which pays 1 to 1, while higher ranked hands will pay even more.

The unique twist to Let it Ride, which is a very attractive feature, is that you have the option to remove one of your three bets after you've seen your three-card hand. Then the dealer turns over the first of the two down cards in front of him. Now you have the opportunity to remove the second of your three bets, or let it ride if the hand is profitable. The third bet, however, cannot be removed. When all players have made their choices, the dealer will turn over the second community card. Your five-card hand is now revealed. If you have made a pair of tens or better, you will get paid on the third bet, at the least, plus each of the other bets you let ride. And if your hand does not qualify for a payout, you lose only the bets that you let ride.

Let's take a closer look to see how the game of Let it Ride works.

THE BASICS

THE SETTING AND LAYOUT

Let it Ride is dealt on a blackjack-style table with a single standard deck of 52 cards. From afar, you wouldn't know that it wasn't a blackjack game unless you glanced up and saw the sign announcing "Let it Ride."

Once you approach the table, however, you'll see that an entirely different game is being played. On the layout in front of each player are three betting circles. From left to right, they are marked **$**, **2**, and **1**, respectively. These are the spots where your basic bets will be placed before each deal. There will be one additional bet spot in front of you, a red button where the **$1 bonus bet** can be made. The table also features the Shuffle Master, a device that automatically shuffles the cards after each deal.

In front of the dealer will be two card-sized rectangles, where the two community cards will be dealt. There will also be a see-through plastic discard rack, where unused cards are placed after all the cards have been dealt. On the layout itself, you will see the words, "Shuffle malfunction voids all plays and pays," and "$25,000 aggregate payouts per round," though casinos may choose different amounts to limit their aggregate payout. We'll talk more about this later.

The dealer stands on the flat side of the table with a chip rack in front of his position, while across the layout and along the rounded edge, are as many as seven players trying their hand at lady luck.

THE OBJECT OF THE GAME

In Let it Ride, the winning hands are based on standard poker rankings, with your goal being to draw one that is strong enough to qualify for one of the winners in the payout schedule. These payoffs range from even money on a pair of tens to 1,000 to 1 on a royal flush.

On the $1 optional bonus bet, which is a separate wager, you are trying to get a hand of at least one pair, which will pay 1 to 1, though you would really like to see a big hand such as a straight flush, or even a royal flush, which will pay substantially more according to paytables that vary from casino to casino.

You do not compete against other players, as in regular poker, or against the dealer, as in Caribbean stud poker. Though other players may form better hands than you, it is of no relevance to your winning chances: The strength of other players' hands have no bearing on your chances of getting a payout, nor does the strength of your hand help affect their chances. You only need to be concerned with your own cards. So, even though Let it Ride shares the same ranks as regular poker, it does not resemble it in any way except for the hand rankings.

In Let it Ride, your only goal is to qualify for a payout by drawing a strong enough hand.

Let's take a look at those hands now.

WINNING HANDS

Following are the hands recognized in Let it Ride, in descending order of strength, from the most powerful, the royal flush, to the ones that aren't any good at all and thus do not qualify for payouts.

LET IT RIDE: WINNING HANDS	
Royal Flush:	An A-K-Q-J-10, all of the same suit, is called a royal flush, the most powerful and rarest hand in poker.
Straight Flush:	Five cards of the same suit in numerical sequence, such as the J-10-9-8-7 of clubs, is called a straight flush. In a straight flush, an ace must be used as either the highest card–forming an ace-high straight flush, which is actually a royal flush–or the lowest card, as in the A-2-3-4-5 of diamonds. The Q-K-A-2-3 of clubs is not a straight flush, just an ace-high flush.
Four of a Kind:	Four cards of identical rank, such as the 6-6-6-6-3, is called a four of a kind. The unmatched card in the above example, the 3, is irrelevant and has no bearing on the rank of the hand.
Full House:	A full house consists of three cards of identical rank and two other cards of identical rank, but different from the rank of the first three cards. Two examples of full houses are 8-8-8-J-J and K-K-K-7-7.

LET IT RIDE: WINNING HANDS	
Flush:	Any five cards of the same suit consti tute a flush. The A-K-7-3-2 of spades is an ace-high flushand the Q-10-7-5-3 of hearts is a queen-high flush.
Straight:	A straight consists of five unsuited cards in sequential order, such as 10-9-8-7-6. If a straight contains an ace, the ace may serve as either the highest card in the run, such as the ace-high straight A-K-Q-J-10, or the lowest card, as in the 5-high straight 5-4-3-2-A. The hand made up of the Q-K-A-2-3 is not a straight. It is merely an ace-high hand and will be beaten by any pair.
Three of a Kind:	Three cards of identical value along with two unmatched cards is called a three of a kind. An example of a three-of-a-kind hand is 7-7-7-Q-2.
Two Pair:	Two sets of equally valued or "paired" cards along with an unmatched card is a two pair hand. Examples of two-pair hands include 4-4-3-3-A and K-K-3-3-J.
One Pair:	One set of identically valued cards along with three unmatched cards is called a pair. The hand 2-2-8-4-A is referred to as "a pair of deuces." Pairs are ranked in order of value from the highest, aces, down to the lowest, deuces. Thus, a pair of aces beats a pair of kings, and a pair of nines wins over a pair of sixes.
All Other Hands:	Hands with none of the above combinations are losing hands. Since they don't qualify for payouts, they have no value in Let it Ride.

ODDS OF DRAWING WINNING HANDS

Below is a table showing the odds of being dealt winning hands in Let it Ride. These are the same odds as those in regular draw poker and Caribbean stud poker for the first five cards dealt.

ODDS OF DRAWING WINNING HANDS	
Royal Flush	649,739 - 1
Straight Flush	72,192 - 1
Four of a Kind	4,165 - 1
Full House	693 - 1
Flush	508 - 1
Straight	254 - 1
Three of a Kind	46 - 1
Two Pair	20 - 1
One Pair	1.37 - 1

PAYOUTS

A pair of tens is the lowest ranked hand that qualifies for a **payout**. If your hand is smaller, say a pair of nines or threes, or an ace-high hand, there is no payoff and bets that are still active will be lost. On the other side of the coin, while all pairs of tens or better pay 1 to 1, higher combinations such as two pair and three of a kind pay even more.

The best hand, the royal flush, will pay 1,000 to 1 in most casinos that offer the game. However, you must check each time you play, as paytables and regulations can change at any time and may be different from one casino to another. (Note that gaming commissions in some jurisdictions have mandated that casinos cannot pay more than 500 to 1 for the royal flush, and some casinos have adopted this pay scale on their own.)

STANDARD PAYOUTS

The following paytable is considered standard and is commonly found in casinos. It features a 1,000 to 1 payoff on a royal flush, higher payouts for big hands, and smaller payouts for full houses and flushes.

STANDARD PAYOUT SCHEDULE (TABLE A)	
Royal Flush	1,000-1
Straight Flush	200-1
Four of a Kind	50-1
Full House	11-1
Flush	8-1
Straight	5-1
Three of a Kind	3-1
Two Pair	2-1
Pair of Tens or Better	1-1

ALTERNATE PAYOUTS

In this less commonly found paytable, there are smaller payouts on the higher-ranked but less frequent hands—flush, straight flush, royal flush, and four of a kind hands—with larger payouts on the more frequently hit hands, full houses and flushes.

The individual payouts balance each other out in the two paytables, A and B, giving you equivalent odds overall, no matter which schedule is used.

ALTERNATE PAYOUT SCHEDULE (TABLE B)	
Royal Flush	500-1
Straight Flush	100-1
Four of a Kind	25-1
Full House	15-1
Flush	10-1
Straight	5-1
Three of a Kind	3-1
Two Pair	2-1
Pair of Tens or Better	1-1

PLAYING THE GAME

OVERVIEW

Before any cards are dealt, all players must put their bets down on the felt. There are three betting circles in front of each player, marked "1," "2," and "$." The amount of the bet on one spot must be the same on all three of them. For example, if you bet $5 on the circle marked "1", you must also bet $5 on the other two circles, the one marked "2" and the one marked "$." And if you bet $25 per spot, your total bet will be $75.

There is an additional wager that can be placed, the $1 bonus bet, which we'll cover in detail later in this chapter.

Normally, $5 is the minimum allowable bet on each circle, although smaller casinos may offer minimums as low as $3. Whatever the minimum limit, it will be clearly posted on the table, along with the maximum limit.

After all bets have been made, the dealer distributes three downcards to each active player. The Shuffle Master machine automatically spits out three cards at a time. The dealer will gather them up, and push the cards face down to the first active player to his left. Then he will take the next set of three cards and give it to the next player in order, until all players have received a three-card hand. The dealer then takes the next set of three cards, places two of them in the card-shaped rectangular boxes in front of him, and places the extra third card in the discard tray to his left. All players will use these two community cards to form their five-card hands.

There are two rounds of play in Let it Ride. First you receive your three cards and choose whether to let your bet in the "1" spot ride. The second round starts after the dealer has revealed the first community card, at which time you must decide on the bet in circle 2—keep it, or let it ride.

Beginning with the player on the dealer's left and proceeding in a clockwise direction, each player in turn must make these decisions. When the last player, the one in the **third-base seat** (closest to the dealer's right) has acted, the round is over and it is time to see who won and who lost.

The dealer will turn over each player's hand in turn, one by one—from the player's perspective, left to right—either collecting lost bets or paying off the winners. Thus, he will start in the third-base position, and go around paying off or collecting bets from the first-base position. Note that the payoff sequence is exactly opposite the order from which the cards were dealt.

A CLOSER LOOK AT THE TWO ROUNDS OF PLAY

Once your bets have been placed and it is your turn to play, you have a decision to make. Let's take a closer look at the mechanics of keeping or removing your bets.

DECISION 1

After looking at your three down cards, you have the option of playing for the bet in circle 1. You must decide whether to let your bet ride or withdraw that bet from play and return it to your bankroll. If you decide to let a bet ride, you place your cards under or in front of the chips in the first circle. The dealer will understand this to mean that you want to keep your bet in play, and he will move on to the next player.

If you are unhappy with the cards you're dealt and wish to remove your bet in circle 1 from play, you do so by scraping the table with the cards. This motion will prompt the dealer to remove your bet from the first circle and return it to you.

You should not take back your bets; you must let the dealer perform that function.

DECISION 2

After all players have made their decisions on bet circle 1, the dealer turns over one of the two community cards in front of him. You now know four of the five cards that will be used to form your final hand.

Again, as in the first round, you must decide whether to let your bet ride or to take it down and put it back into your bankroll. The motions are the same as they were in the first round; the only difference is that now you are deciding about the bet in circle 2. If your decision is to let your bet ride, slide your cards under the bets in the second circle. And if you wish to remove your bet, scrape the table with your cards. Your bet will be removed from circle 2 and returned to you by the dealer.

Your action on circle 1 has absolutely no bearing on your decision about circle 2. The two actions are independent of each other, so don't feel pressured to make a play one way or the other way based on what you did on the first round of play. For example, you may remove the bet in circle 1 and let the bet in circle 2 ride; while another player may let it ride in circle 1 but remove it in circle 2; a third may remove a bet in each of the two rounds; and a fourth may let both bets ride. All these combinations are permissible.

When all players have made their decisions on the bets in circle 2, it is time for the showdown.

THE SHOWDOWN

The dealer now turns over the second and final community card. You can now see your final five-card hand by combining the two community cards with your three individual cards. Unlike the previous two rounds, the bet in the third circle, marked "$," cannot be removed. This bet is for keeps and will now be settled by the dealer along with the other bets, if any, that you have in the other betting circles.

SETTLING THE BETS

Going from his right and proceeding to his left, the dealer will turn over each player's cards and settle the wagers. Players who hold a pair of tens or any higher-ranked poker hand qualify for payouts according to the payout schedule shown earlier.

Winning hands pay out on all spots that still contain bets. For example, let's say you hold a pair of jacks, which pays 1 to 1, and have a $5 bet on each of the three spots. You would win a total of $15, $5 for each of the spots. Thus $30 would be returned to you, $15 in winnings plus the original $15 wagered. If only spots 2 and $ contained $5 bets, then $20 would be returned, $10 of which would be winnings.

By the same token, players whose hands didn't qualify for the payoff will lose on all spots where they had bets. At the very least, that would be one losing spot, since bets on the $ circle cannot be removed. Players can lose a maximum of three bets each if they let all bets ride. If a player had $5 on each of the three circles and let all the bets ride, but lost in the showdown, a total of $15 would be lost. However, if the player had removed the bets from circles 1 and 2, then only $5 would be lost.

Now let's see how the $1 bonus bet works.

THE $1 BONUS BET

You have the option to make a separate $1 bet that will go toward an additional payout pool. This wager is placed into the bonus betting circle and must be made before the cards are dealt. On the table, there will be a spot marked "bonus" to accommodate this wager. The amount you can win will be determined according to the strength of your hand.

The $1 bonus side bet was introduced in 1997, after the original inception of the game, to replace the original $1 tournament wager. What sets the bonus apart from the tournament is that the bonus payouts are set according to a fixed schedule and are paid out on the spot. There are no tournament playoffs and no million-dollar bounty as there was earlier in the tournament format.

However, the bonus paytable is actually much better for the average player. Rather than building a large pool of money that gets distributed to a few players, the million-dollar payouts are now circulated back into the regular paytables and get distributed among many players. This concept is similar to that of progressive slot machines. The super jackpot machines pay out less to the regular players as money is saved for the big jackpot winner, while the smaller progressives keep the money flowing.

There are six common paytables for the Let it Ride bonus, but payout philosophies in casinos are always in flux, so the charts below may vary from those you'll find in your casino. Game makers are always adjusting their formulas and concepts to find the best mix of casino profitability and popularity among its players. The paytables used in a particular casino may be determined by the local gaming commission or be at the behest of management. Some jurisdictions allow multiple paytables, while others allow only one. If multiple paytables are allowed, it is up to casino management to choose which ones they'll put up for play on the floor.

Depending on the table used, payouts for the best hand, the royal flush, can range from $10,000 to $25,000, while full houses can range from $75 to $200. And while some paytables give bonuses for tens or better, others don't start paying out unless a player holds at least a two-pair hand. Still other games require a minimum strength of three of a kind.

These payout schedules directly affect your overall return and, of course, the house edge on the bet. With the most liberal payouts allowed, you will face a 2.14% house edge on the bonus bet. The least liberal can give the casino an edge as high as 7.28% or more, which is considerably higher. Unfortunately, this unfavorable schedule tends to be the most common one offered.

Keep in mind that the amounts paid on all winning hands is what determines your overall chances of winning, not necessarily how easy it is to get a payout on a hand. For example, a schedule that pays out for tens or better does not necessarily have overall better odds than a paytable that pays out beginning at three of a kind.

THREE PAYOUT SCHEDULES

Schedules A, B, and C show the most common payouts.

BONUS PAYOUT SCHEDULE A	
Royal Flush	$20,000
Straight Flush	$2,000
Four of a Kind	$200
Full House	$75
Flush	$50
Straight	$25
Three of a Kind	$5
Two Pair	$4
Tens or Better	$1

BONUS PAYOUT SCHEDULE B	
Royal Flush	$20,000
Straight Flush	$2,000
Four of a Kind	$100
Full House	$75
Flush	$50
Straight	$25
Three of a Kind	$9
Two Pair	$6
Tens or Better	No Payout

BONUS PAYOUT SCHEDULE C	
Royal Flush	$20,000
Straight Flush	$2,000
Four of a Kind	$400
Full House	$200
Flush	$50
Straight	$25
Three of a Kind	$5
Two Pair	No Payout
Tens or Better	No Payout

WINNING STRATEGY

INTRODUCTION

In this section, we'll go over the third and fourth card playing strategies, house percentages, and the overall strategy for winning at Let it Ride.

The main strategy considerations in Let it Ride have to do with the bets in the first two betting circles, 1 and 2. You must decide whether to let these bets ride or bring them down and play only for the mandatory bet in the third circle. These are the two decisions to make, one for each circle.

Once you've looked at your three downcards, you must make your first decision: Let the bet in circle 1 ride or bring it down? The strategies you use to make this decision will be referred to as the **Third Card Betting Strategy**. After the dealer exposes a community card—your fourth known card—you must make the same decision about the bet in circle 2. We'll call this the **Fourth Card Betting Strategy**.

Let's take a closer look at both decisions.

THIRD CARD BETTING STRATEGY

Your first three cards give you a good indication of where your hand may be headed. You know three-fifths of the cards that will comprise your final hand and can easily determine the best way to play the bets.

Sometimes, as with three of a kind or a pair of tens or better, the strategy decision is obvious: You're sitting with winners and should let the bet ride. A payout is already guaranteed and with a little luck, that hand may improve to a stronger rank and larger payoff. You'll also play strong hands that don't yet have a guaranteed payoff, but which give you a positive expectation of winning.

Conversely, weak hands with negative expectations of winning call for a strategy of minimizing losses, and the correct play will be to take down the bet in circle 1.

Below are the six categories of Let it Ride poker hands where the optimal play is to let the circle 1 bet ride. Hands are listed from the strongest to the weakest. Remember that tens, jacks, queens, kings, and aces are considered high cards. When they are paired, these hands are winners.

HANDS THAT YOU WILL PLAY

Let your bet ride with the following three-card hands:

1. **Three of a Kind**
   This is fairly obvious. You have an automatic winner that guarantees you at least a 3 to 1 payoff on all your bet spots.
2. **Tens or Higher Pair**
   Another obvious play. You already have a 1 to 1 payoff and can't lose. Improving the hand will give you an even larger payout.
3. **Three to a Royal Flush**
   You have all sorts of shots here for a payoff: a flush, a straight, a high pair—even three of a kind and two pair—and of course, the hand you would really like to get, a royal flush.
4. **Three to a Straight Flush**

Ditto above. There are good possibilities for improvement. You should let the bet ride.

5. **Three to a Flush with Two Cards 10 or Higher, and a Straight Possibility**
   It is not enough to have the flush chance alone, because you still need two additional suited cards to make the flush. In order to let the bet ride, you must also hold two high cards, which you hope to pair. There is also the possibility of making a straight, which adds more value. If all of the above conditions are met, you can let your circle 1 bet ride. Examples of this type of hand include Q-J-9 of clubs and K-J-9 of hearts.
6. **Three to a Flush with J-9-8, 10-9-7, or 10-8-7**
   Unlike the previous grouping, which can be played with a two-gap straight possibility, these three hands have only one high card and are more marginal. In order to let your bet ride with a hand like this, you need the greater straight possibility that the one-gap hand provides, compared to the two-gap straight in the previous category.
   For ease of remembering, these hands can also be thought of as a three-card flush with one high card and one gap.

HANDS THAT YOU WON'T PLAY

Unless you have one of the hands listed in the six categories above, remove your bet from the first circle. While there are always winning possibilities with any three starting cards, the cost of playing low percentage hands is too high to justify letting the bet ride. When you have a chance to remove a bet with inferior cards, you should always do so. That's the smart way to play.

Now let's look at some particular hands that you're not going to play. Though similar to some of the playable hands mentioned above, A-K-Q is a hand you won't play. It can only be filled one-way and is therefore a more difficult straight possibility to fill. And J-10-9 is not worth playing since it has only two high cards that can pair into a payoff. On these marginal hands, you just don't have enough strength to justify the bet in circle 1, and the best percentage play is to take the bet down.

Low pairs, pairs less than tens, should not be played either. For example, with 7-7-Q, you should take down your bet. While it's possible that you'll catch the third 7 or another queen, the number of times that you don't will far outweigh the number of times you do, with a negative long-term result. That's exactly what you're trying to avoid.

FOURTH CARD BETTING STRATEGY

After the dealer exposes one of the two community downcards, you know four of the five cards that will make up your final hand. You're now faced with your final strategy decision: Should you let your circle 2 bet ride, or should you reclaim it for your bankroll?

As with the third card betting strategy, you'll play hands that give you a positive expectation of winning, and take down bets in the second circle when your expectation of winning is negative. In the obvious cases where you already have a winning combination, the clear-cut play is to let the bet ride. However, in many cases, you won't be quite as thrilled with your prospects, and you'll be more than happy to take down your bet.

Following is the correct strategy for letting bets ride or taking them down on circle 2.

HANDS THAT YOU WILL PLAY

You'll let your bet ride with the following four card hands:

1. **Four of a Kind**
   This is an obvious winning hand paying 50 to 1. Let 'em ride!
2. **Three of a Kind**
   This is also an obvious winner, paying 3 to 1 on all betting circles. Let 'em ride!
3. **Two Pair**
   You already have a guaranteed 2 to 1 payoff with possibilities of improving to a full house for an 11 to 1 yield.

4. **Pair of Tens or Higher Pair**
   You've already got a winner paying 1 to 1 and can improve to two pair or three of a kind with a good draw on the final card.
5. **Four to a Royal Flush**
   One more card and you're there with a big payoff. There are also the possibilities of making a flush or straight, and an excellent chance of catching a high-paying pair since any of your four high cards, if matched, becomes a winner.
6. **Four to a Straight Flush**
   This is not as strong as four to a royal flush, but it still holds excellent possibilities.
7. **Four to a Flush**
   If you draw the flush, the payoff is 8 to 1, which is greater than the odds of filling the flush. Here's why: Of the 48 unseen cards in the deck, nine of them will make the flush and 39 will not, odds of 4.33 to 1. Being paid 8 to 1 on odds of about 4.33 to 1 is always a great bet in my book.
8. **Four to an Open-Ended Straight**
   If you aren't holding any high cards, this bet is a wash. Of the 48 unseen cards, eight of them will make the straight, and 40 will not—odds of 5 to 1. Since the payoff is exactly 5 to 1, you have an even chance. There is no theoretical loss or gain on the play, so you can choose whether to let your bet ride or take it down.
   If you are holding at least one high card, you gain the advantage on the four-card open-ended straight draw, since the last community card may pair with your high card for a winner.
9. **Four to a High Straight**
   The hands 10-J-Q-A, 10-Q-K-A, 10-J-K-A, and J-Q-K-A, have two things in common: (1) The ability to match any of the four high cards into a paying winner; and (2) The possibility of filling to an inside straight. Neither factor by itself gives you enough strength to make the third bet, but

taken together, you have the percentages to let the second bet ride. This is due in part to the sensitivity of the single-deck game to particular card removal.

HANDS THAT YOU WON'T PLAY

You don't let your bet ride on circle 2 when holding a one-way or inside straight, such as J-10-9-7, as the chances of making these one-way straights climb to 11 to 1. Since straights only pay 5 to 1, this is not a good percentage bet. The one exception is the four-card high straight, such as A-K-Q-J, because all four cards have pairing possibilities. Small pairs (nines and under) are not worth chasing anymore since these hands promise no payoff. Therefore, the best play in the long run is to take down the bet in circle 2 when you hold one of these hands.

If your hand lacks any of the nine combinations listed above—in other words, if you're holding various degrees of junk—then you have a negative expectation on the fourth card, and the strategy is clear: Take down the bet and have it returned to your bankroll.

HOUSE PERCENTAGES

OVERVIEW

The best percentage that can be achieved at the Let it Ride table games is about 3.5% in favor of the house for the basic bets. This is assuming that you use the optimal basic strategy presented here and that you don't make the $1 bonus bet.

Making poor percentage bets will raise the overall house edge higher than 3.5% and cost you multiple percentage points. How much you give back to the house is based on the number of mistakes or poor decisions you make. For example, if you don't let your bets ride on automatic winning hands, or you do let them ride on terrible starting cards, the house edge will rise precipitously. The more of an edge you give the house, the more money you will lose in the long run.

Another factor that affects the overall house edge is the average bet size you make if you are also making the $1 bonus bet. The smaller the average bet, the higher that house percentage would be. For example, a poor percentage $1 bet has a greater overall negative effect on a $5 bettor than on a $25 bettor.

Players who make bets on the optional $1 bonus spot may be giving the casino a larger edge that the 3.5% for the basic game, an edge that varies depending upon the payouts offered by the casino for the bonus.

MORE PERCENTAGES OF PLAY

In Let it Ride, as in blackjack, the general playing strategy is to minimize losses when you're dealt poor cards and maximize gains when your cards are strong. Thus, while many weak two-card totals in blackjack will be played from a perspective of losing the least amount of money, strong hands will be doubled down whenever possible to take advantage of strong situations. The same holds true for Let it Ride.

Most starting hands in Let it Ride have losing expectations for the player. In fact, in almost 85 out of 100 hands—84.5% to be precise—the correct playing strategy dictates that both the first and second bets should be removed. It is the other 15% of the time, when your hand is in an advantageous situation, that you should let the second or third bets ride.

You take advantage of profitable situations by making sure money is bet on your profitable hands. In these favorable occasions, when all three bets are riding, you are able to win back the money you've lost on the other 85% of the hands. Those second and third bets allow you to make up for lost ground.

Using the proper playing strategy, a total of two bets will stay in action about 8.5% of the time, and the full three bets will stay in action 7.0% of the time. When all three situations are added up (the wagers with one bet, the wagers with two bets, and the wagers with three bets) the house edge at Let it Ride ends up at 3.5% if you follow the proper playing strategy.

FREQUENCY OF WINS

Using either of the two basic Let it Ride paytables, you can expect to win a payout 23.88% of the time, or about one time in four hands. On the bonus paytables, the frequency of winning will range up to the same 23.88% if the same number of payoffs are given, and less, of course, when there are fewer payoffs to be had.

CONCLUSION

When you play perfect basic strategy, the 3.5% house edge in the Let it Ride basic game is higher than the overall house edge of 2.56% in Caribbean stud poker, but certainly far more favorable than American roulette, with its 5.26% odds, and games such as keno, the big wheel, and many of the slot machines spread around the casino. In Let it Ride, like many of the casino games, the house edge is totally dependent on the strategy decisions you make. If you play it well, you give up 3.5%. If you play it poorly, you give the house much more of an edge, which is never a good idea.

One of the big draws for the original versions of Let it Ride was the hope of hitting a monster hand on the $1 tournament bet. However, the house edge on this wager was much worse than the 3.5% edge of the basic game, giving players a bigger hill to climb to emerge a winner. The newer bonus wager, with that same $1 bet, offers more favorable odds than the tournament versions, again depending on how generous the paytable is for the player.

A word on betting limits and understanding the amount of money you put at risk in this game: Whether betting $5 or $100 per betting spot, don't let these amounts deceive you into thinking that you are betting only $5 or $100—you aren't. For example, at a $5 minimum table you're not just betting $5, you're betting $15, $5 on each of the three required betting spots. And if you're laying out $100 per betting spot, you actually have $300 in wagers on the felt. This is an important consideration because you don't want to have more money at risk than you are comfortable with or can handle.

I recommend going after the best odds you can get in any game. Of course, if you really like to play a game, go for it, regardless of its odds. But do so making the best percentage plays you can, thus giving yourself the best chances of winning. In other words, play a tough game, giving the casino as little as you possibly have to. It is a mathematical truth: The greater the house edge, the less chance you have of winning. And the converse rings just as true: The lesser the house edge, the greater the chance you have of winning.

If you like the big payoffs with small bets, the overall attraction of the extra bonus bet is that it gives you a chance to win large sums of money with just a $1 wager. While the bonus bet may not have the glamour of the million-dollar jackpot offered by lottery games, it does offer odds that are worlds better than the lottery hustles.

With much better chances of winning something good for just a little money, the Let it Ride bonus bet is popular among players. And since fun is what gambling is supposed to be about, at least you have a much better shot at winning something at Let it Ride than throwing a buck away on a numbers game such as bingo, keno or the lotto.

PARTING THOUGHTS

Let it Ride offers the unique feature of allowing you to remove one of your three initial bets if you don't like your starting cards, and then allows you to remove a second wager if you don't like your next card! Removing bets when the house has the edge is a fun concept, but to maximize your advantage in these situations, you need to play the correct third- and fourth-card playing strategies. This will bring the house edge down to the lowest possible figure.

Remember to set table bankroll limits before you start playing and, on the other hand, be sure to walk away with the casino's money when you're winning. There is no better feeling in the casino than that!

19 POKER

FIVE KEYS TO POKER
1. Know the house rules for the game you are playing.
2. Learn the best hands to play.
3. Fold your cards when you think you are beaten.
4. Pay close attention to opponents' body language and mannerisms.
5. Play the right size game for your wallet and skill level.

INTRODUCTION

Poker is an American tradition, an exciting game where people of all classes gather around a table and play for stakes ranging from mere pennies to thousands and even millions of dollars. No other gambling game offers you the combined challenges of skill, luck and psychology—and the drama of the bluff—in such a fascinating weave. In this chapter, you'll find out how to conquer these challenges and become a winner at poker!

You'll learn the basic strategies of each of the major variations of poker—Texas hold'em (limit and no-limit), seven-card stud (high, high-low and razz) and Omaha high-low. We discuss all the fundamentals of poker—the ranks of hands for high, low, and wild card poker; the rules of the games; your options as a player; how to bet; the jargon of poker; and everything else you need to be an informed player—plus the differences between casino and private games.

You'll find out how to apply the five winning strategies of poker to get an edge on your opponents and turn that edge into winnings. You'll learn to recognize strong, marginal and weak hands and adjust your strategy accordingly; how to play position at the table; how to use pot odds to determine the soundness of a bet; how to read the playing styles of your opponents and cash in on that information; how to play against loose opponents, tight opponents, and aggressive ones who like to bluff.

It's all here in this section. Now let's go out there and win!

OVERVIEW

Poker is a betting game requiring two or more players. It is played with a standard pack of fifty-two cards consisting of thirteen ranks in each of four suits (hearts, clubs, diamonds, spades). The ace is the best and highest card, followed in descending order by the king, queen, jack, 10, 9, 8, 7, 6, 5, 4, 3 and then the deuce or 2, which is the lowest ranked card. The king, queen, and jack are known as **picture cards** or **face cards**.

The four suits in poker have no basic value in the determination of winning hands. Cards are referred to in writing by the following commonly used symbols: ace (A), king (K), queen (Q), jack (J), and 10 through 2 by their numerical value.

THE FOUR SUITS	
♣ = clubs	♦ = diamonds
♥ = hearts	♠ = spades

When the cards are held together in various combinations, they form hands of different strengths. These are called **hand rankings**.

All variations of poker have these four things in common:

1. Players receive an equal number of cards to start.
2. There will be a starting wager after these cards are received; players that match the wager can continue playing the hand, players that don't match it have to sit out of the hand. You have to pay to play!
3. More cards are usually dealt, with players having an option to wager more money following each round of cards.
4. The winner of each hand is the player with the best hand or the last one standing because all opponents have refused to match his bets.

Each player in poker plays by himself and for himself alone against all other players. Playing partners is illegal and is considered cheating.

OBJECT OF THE GAME

Your goal in poker is to win the money in the **pot**, the accumulation of bets and antes in the center of the table. You can win in two ways. The first way is to have the highest-ranking hand at the **showdown**—the final act in poker, where all active players must reveal their hands to see who has the best one. The second way is to be the last player remaining when all other players have dropped out of play. When this occurs, there is no showdown, and you automatically win the pot.

TYPES OF POKER GAMES

If you're new to the game, the wide variety of poker games can be bewildering. Not only are there different variations of each game, there are different formats for playing them. For example, you have your choice of playing straight high poker, low poker, or high-low poker. Then there are cash games and tournaments, as well as limit, no-limit, and pot-limit betting structures.

How do you make sense of them all? Here's a down and dirty guide to understanding all the varieties of poker games.

BASIC GAME FORMATS

Poker can be played in two basic forms—cash games and tournaments. While tournaments get all the television coverage, the more popular versions being played in cardrooms are actually the cash games. Let's take a quick look at each one.

CASH GAMES

In a **cash game**, the chips you play with represent real money. If you go broke, you can always dig in to your pocket for more money. If you give the poker room $100 in cash, you get $100 worth of chips in return. If you build it up to $275, you can quit and convert your chips to cash anytime you want. Your goal in a cash game is to win as much money as you can, or minimize your losses if things are going poorly.

TOURNAMENTS

Tournaments are a competition among players who start with an equal number of chips and play until one player holds all the chips. Unlike a cash game where the chips are the equivalent of cash money, **tournament chips** are only valuable in the tournament itself and have no cash value. Players are eliminated from the tournament when they have lost all their chips.

Your goal is to survive as long as you can. At the very least, you want to stay in action long enough to earn a share of the prize pool. In the best-case scenario, you win it all, become the champion, and take home the biggest prize.

BETTING STRUCTURES

Poker has three different types of betting structures: limit, pot-limit, and no-limit. These structures don't change the basic way the games are played, only the amount of money that can be bet. The big difference between the three structures is game strategy. The amount you can bet influences the hands that you should play, when you should play them, and how much you should risk in any given situation.

Let's take a brief look at each betting structure.

LIMIT POKER

In **limit poker**, all bets are divided into a two-tier structure, such as $1/$2, $3/$6, $5/$10, $10/$20 and $15/$30, with the larger limit bets being exactly double the lower limit. On the preflop and flop in hold'em variations, and on third and fourth street in stud poker, all bets and raises must be at the lower limit; on the turn and river, all bets double and must be made at the higher limit. In a $5/$10 limit game, for example, when the lower limit of betting is in effect, all bets and raises must be in $5 increments. When the upper range is in effect, all bets and raises must be in $10 increments.

One form of limit poker, called **spread-limit**, allows you to bet any amount between the minimum and maximum amounts specified for the game. Spread limit is typically played in very low stakes games. For example, in a $1 to $5 game, you may bet or raise $1, $2, $3, $4 or $5 on any betting round. There is also a $1-$4-$8 spread-limit format where all bets in the early betting rounds can be any amount from $1 to $4, and in the later betting rounds, from $1 to $8.

In the sections on the individual games, we will go over exactly when the upper level of betting comes into effect and how that works.

NO-LIMIT POKER

No-limit hold'em is the exciting, no-holds barred style of poker played in the World Series of Poker main event and seen on television by millions weekly on the World Poker Tour and channels such as ESPN and GSN. The prevailing feature of **no-limit poker** is that you can bet any amount up to what you have in front of you on the table anytime it is your turn to act. When a player announces "**All in**," it signals his intention to put all his chips on the line. No-limit is usually associated with Texas hold'em, but this style of betting can be played in any variation of poker.

POT-LIMIT POKER

Pot-limit is most often associated with hold'em and Omaha, though this betting structure, like no-limit, can be played in variation of poker. The minimum bet allowed in **pot-limit** is set in advance while the maximum bet allowed is defined by the size of the pot. For example, if there is $75 in the pot, the maximum bet allowed is $75. The pot sizes in pot-limit quickly escalate to large amounts. Like no-limit, this betting structure is not for the timid.

HAND RANKINGS & WINNING COMBINATIONS

Poker is typically played as **high poker**; that is, the player with the highest five-card combination at the showdown wins the money in the pot. But there also are variations where the low hand wins, and there are some games where players compete for both ends of the spectrum—the best high hand and the best low hand.

In each variation, a player also can win the pot if all of his opponents fold their hands at any point before the showdown, leaving only one player to claim the pot—even though he may not actually have the best hand!

HIGH POKER

The best poker hand you can hold is a royal flush, followed by a straight flush, four of a kind, full house, flush, straight, three of a kind, two pair, one pair, and the best high-card hand. The order in which cards are dealt, or how they are displayed, is irrelevant to the final value of the hand. For example, 7-7-K-A-5 is equivalent to A-K-7-7-5.

Poker hands are ranked in this way because of one cold, hard fact: The more rare the probability of being dealt a particular poker hand in five cards, the higher it ranks on the scale. Note that all poker hands eventually consist of five cards, regardless of the variation being played.

HAND RANKINGS

High-Card Hands—A hand that contains five unmatched cards—that is, one that lacks any of the combinations shown below—is valued by its highest ranked card. 3-9-K-7-10 is a "king-high" hand. When the highest ranked cards are identical, the next highest unmatched card wins. A-K-J-10-4 beats A-K-J-3-2, for example.

One Pair—Two cards of equal rank and three unmatched cards. Example: 5-5-8-J-K. If two players are competing with one-pair hands, the higher ranked of the pairs—aces highest, deuces lowest—wins the pot. And if two players have the same pair, the highest side card is used to determine the higher-ranking hand. 5-5-A-7-6 beats 5-5-K-Q-J, since the ace is a higher card than the king.

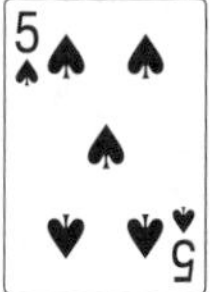

Two Pair—Two pairs and an unmatched card. Example: 6-6-J-J-2. The highest pair of competing two-pair hands will win, or if the top pair is tied, then the second pair determines the winner. If both pairs are equivalent, the fifth card decides the winner. K-K-3-3-6 beats J-J-8-8-Q and K-K-2-2-A, but loses to K-K-3-3-9.

Three of a Kind—Three cards of equal rank and two unmatched cards. Also called trips or a set. Example: Q-Q-Q-7-J. If two players hold a set, the higher ranked set will win, and if both players hold an equivalent set, then the highest odd card determines the winner. 7-7-7-4-2 beats 5-5-5-A-K, but loses to 7-7-7-9-5.

Straight—Five cards of mixed suits in sequence, but they may not wrap around the ace. For example, Q-J-10-9-8 of mixed suits is a straight, but Q-K-A-2-3 is not—it's simply an ace-high hand. If two players hold straights, the player with the higher straight card at the top end of the sequence wins. A player holding J-10-9-8-7 beats an opponent holding 5-4-3-2-A, but ties any other player who also holds J-10-9-8-7.

Flush—Five cards of the same suit. Example: K-10-9-5-3, all diamonds. If two players hold flushes, the player with the highest untied card wins. No suit is superior to another suit in determining the value of a flush; the rank of cards is the only factor that counts. Thus, Q-J-7-5-4 of diamonds beats Q-J-4-3-2 of spades because the ranks of the diamond flush are higher.

Full House—Three of a kind and a pair. Example: 5-5-5-9-9. If two players hold full houses, the player with the higher three of a kind wins. J-J-J-8-8 beats 7-7-7-A-A.

Four of a Kind—Four cards of equal rank and an odd card. Also called **quads**. Example: K-K-K-K-3. If two players hold quads, the higher ranking quads win the hand. K-K-K-K-3 beats 7-7-7-7-A and K-K-K-K-2.

Straight Flush—Five cards in sequence, all in the same suit. Example: 7-6-5-4-3, all spades. If two straight flushes are competing, the one with the highest card wins.

 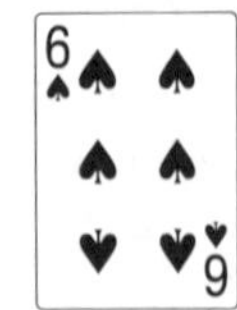   

Royal Flush—The A-K-Q-J-10 of the same suit, the best hand possible. No royal flush is higher than another.

POKER PROBABILITIES

There are a total of 2,598,960 five-card combinations possible with a 52-card deck. The chart below shows the chances of receiving each type of hand in the first five cards dealt.

PROBABILITIES OF FIVE-CARD POKER HANDS		
Hand	**Number**	**Approximate Odds**
Royal Flush	4	649,740 to 1
Straight Flush	36	72,192 to 1
Four of a Kind*	624	4,164 to 1
Full House	3,744	693 to 1
Flush	5,108	508 to 1
Straight	10,200	254 to 1
Three of a Kind	54,912	46 to 1
Two Pair	123,552	20 to 1
One Pair	1,098,240	1.37 to 1
No Hand	1,302,540	1 to 1

*Though there are only 13 four-of-a-kind combinations, to be accurate, this calculation must include the total number of possibilities when the fifth card is figured in to make a five-card hand.

LOW POKER

In **low poker**, the ranking of hands is the opposite to that of high poker, with the lowest hand being the most powerful and the highest hand being the least powerful. There are two varieties of low poker games: ace-to-five and deuce-to-seven.

In **ace-to-five**, the ace is considered the lowest and therefore most powerful card. The hand 5-4-3-2-A is the best low hand possible with 6-4-3-2-A and 6-5-3-2-A being the next two best hands. Straights and flushes are not considered high hands so they don't count against low hands.

In **deuce-to-seven** low poker, also known as **Kansas City lowball**, the 2 is the lowest and best card and the ace is the highest and worst card. The hand 7-5-4-3-2 is the best possible hand, followed by 7-6-4-3-2 and 7-6-5-3-2. Unlike ace-to-five low, straights and flushes count as high hands, so you don't want to end up with 7-6-5-4-2 all in hearts, or 8-7-6-5-4.

HIGH-LOW POKER

In **high-low poker** (and its variant, **high-low 8-or-better**), players compete for either the highest-ranking or lowest-ranking hand, with the best of each claiming half the pot—with some restrictions that we'll go into in the individual game sections. With two different ways to win, these games tend to produce a lot of betting. The best high hand and the best low hand split the pot. However, if one player is fortunate enough to have the best high and the best low hand, he wins it all, called **scooping the pot**.

High-low games are sometimes played with a **qualifier**, a requirement that a player must have five unpaired cards of 8 or lower to win the low end of the pot. If no player has an 8-or-better qualifier, the best high hand wins the entire pot. For example, if the best low hand at the table is 9-6-5-4-2, there is no qualified low hand and the best high hand wins the entire pot. This version of high-low is called **8-or-better**. Popular 8-or-better games include Omaha high-low 8-or-better and seven-card stud high-low 8-or-better.

THE BASICS OF POKER

PLAYERS AND DEALERS

Poker can be played with as few as two players to as many as the 52-card deck can support, usually anywhere from eight to ten players, depending on the variation.

The **dealer** is responsible for shuffling the cards after each round of play so that they are mixed well and in random order. Casinos and cardrooms employ dealers. They do not participant in the betting or play of the game. Their job is simply to shuffle the deck, deal the cards, and direct the action so that the game runs smoothly. They point out whose turn it is to play and pull bets into the pot after each round of cards. And at the showdown, the dealer declares the winner and awards the pot to the winning player. Then he reshuffles the cards and gets ready for the next deal.

In casino poker games in which the "dealer" enjoys a positional advantage, such as hold'em, lowball, and Omaha, a **button,** a circular disc labeled "dealer," is utilized to designate the dealer's imaginary position. The button rotates around the table, one spot at a time in clockwise fashion, so that each player has a chance to enjoy the advantages of acting last.

THE CARDROOM MANAGER OR TOURNAMENT DIRECTOR

In a cardroom, the employee responsible for the supervision of poker games is the **cardroom manager**, or the **tournament director** if a tournament is being played. When a dispute arises, the dealer or any player may ask the supervisor (called a **floorperson** or more commonly, **floor**) for a ruling. If a player gets out of line, the floorperson may ask the player to act more appropriately and let that serve as a warning. If the situation warrants it, or if the abuse or infractions of the rules or decorum of the game continues, the player may be given a "time out," and will be disallowed from play for ten or twenty minutes, twenty-four hours, or even permanently.

THE POKER TABLE

In a cardroom, the players and dealer sit around a table built to accommodate the game of poker. The dealer sits in the middle of the long side where there is an indentation cut into the table to facilitate access to the players. He usually has a small rack in front of him where he keeps an extra deck of cards, chips, cash, and a few other items. In a cash game, he may also have a **drop box** where he deposits money taken out of the pot as the house commission, known as the **rake**.

MONEY AND CHIPS

Poker is almost always played with **chips** that are assigned specific values, such as $1, $5, $25, or $100. To receive chips in a cardroom, give the dealer cash, and he'll give you back the equivalent value in chips. This exchange of cash for chips is called a **buy-in** and can be done either at the table or at the poker room "window," where a cashier sells chips. Dealers and poker room cashiers accept only cash for chips, so if you have traveler's checks, credit cards, or other forms of money, you need to exchange these for cash at the Casino Cashier before you make your buy-in.

CUTTING THE CARDS

The casino dealer cuts the cards, using a blank **cut card**, a colored plastic card that is not a part of the deck. He uses the cut card to separate the deck into two stacks so that the top and bottom of the stacks can be reversed, and then places the cut card on the bottom of the deck. Cutting the cards helps protect against cheating, while the cut card covers the bottom card of the deck so that it is not accidentally exposed.

MANDATORY STARTING BETS

In poker, one or more players are typically required to put a bet into the pot before the cards are dealt. There are two types of mandatory bets: blinds and antes. **Blind bets**, or **blinds**, are used in hold'em, Omaha, and some draw variations. They are generally required of the first two players to the left of the dealer position. An **ante**, also known as a "sweetener," is a uniform bet placed into the pot by all players before the cards are dealt. The house sets the sizes of the blinds and antes.

Players frequently play aggressively in the first betting round, hoping to force opposing players out of the pot and pick up the antes and blinds without going further into a hand. In games with blinds, this is called **stealing the blinds**. In ante games, it is called **stealing the antes**.

THE PLAY OF THE GAME

If the game requires antes or blinds, you must place the appropriate bet into the pot before the cards are dealt. After the dealer shuffles and cuts the deck, he starts the deal. The dealer begins by distributing cards to the player on his immediate left. He deals cards one at a time in a clockwise rotation until each player has received the requisite number of cards for the poker game being played. Like the dealing of the cards, play always proceeds in a clockwise direction. The player sitting to the immediate left of the blinds in flop games opens the play of the round. In seven-card stud games, the player with either the high or low card opens the play. Play continues around the table until each player in turn has acted.

In later rounds, the first player to act will vary depending on the poker variation being played. The particulars of play are covered under the sections on the games themselves.

PLAYERS' OPTIONS

The following options, which apply to all forms of poker, are available to you when it is your turn to play:

1. **Bet:** Put chips at risk; that is, wager money if no player has bet before you on that round.
2. **Call:** Match a bet if one has been placed before it is your turn.
3. **Raise:** Increase the size of a current bet, forcing opponents, including the original bettor, to put additional money into the pot to stay active in a hand.
4. **Fold:** Give up your cards and opt out of play if a bet is due and you do not wish to match it, thus forfeiting your chance to compete for the pot.
5. **Check:** Stay active in a hand without making a bet and risking chips. This is only possible if no bets have been made before you on that round.

The first three options—bet, call, and raise—are forms of putting chips at risk in the hope of winning the pot. If a bet has been made, each **active player**—one who has not folded—is faced with the same options: call, fold, or raise. That is, once someone has bet, you must either match the bet to continue playing for the pot, raise the bet, or fold your hand. Checking is not an option when someone has bet in front of you. However, if no chips are due, you can remain active without cost by checking.

After a bet has been made, it no longer belongs to the bettor; it becomes the property of the pot, the communal collection of money that is up for grabs by all active players.

Betting continues in a round until the last bet or raise has been called by all active players, at which point the betting round is over. A player may raise only another player's bet or raise; he may not raise his own bet after everyone has acted.

PLAYING TIP

Never fold a hand, no matter how bad, when you can check and remain active for free.

THE SHOWDOWN

The **showdown** is the final act in a poker game where remaining players reveal their hands to determine the winner of the pot. It occurs when two or more players remain at the conclusion of all betting in the final betting round of a poker game.

The player whose last bet or raise was called—if all players checked, the first player to the left of the dealer position—turns over his cards first and reveals his hand. The player with the best hand at the showdown wins all the money in the pot. Players holding losing hands at the showdown may concede the pot without showing their cards.

In the event of a tie, or if there are two winners—as may be the case in high-low games—the pot is split evenly among those players.

If only one player remains after the final betting round, or at any point during the game, there is no showdown. The lone remaining player automatically wins the pot.

BETTING FUNDAMENTALS

WHAT BETTING IS ALL ABOUT

You bet for one of three reasons:

1. You believe your hand has enough strength to win and you want to induce opponents to put more money into the pot.
2. You want to force opponents out of the pot so that the field is narrowed, since having fewer opponents increases your chances of winning.
3. You want to induce all your opponents to fold so that you can win the pot uncontested.

LIMIT POKER: MINIMUM AND MAXIMUM BETS

The minimum and maximum bets in limit games are strictly regulated according to the preset limits. For example, $3/$6 and $5/$10 are two common limits. The number of raises allowed in a round are also restricted, usually limited to three or four total according to the house rules for the cardroom. In other words, if there is a three-raise limit and the action goes bet, raise, reraise, and reraise, the raising would be **capped**. No more raises would be allowed for that round.

The exception to this rule is when players are players heads-up, in which case, there is no cap to the number of raises that can be made.

NO-LIMIT POKER: MINIMUM AND MAXIMUM BETS

In no-limit cash games and tournaments, there is typically no cap to the number of raises allowed, though there are cardrooms that still impose the three- or four-raise rule. There is also no limit to how high a bet or raise can be, as long as the player has those chips (or cash) on the table in front of him. Players may raise as often as they like and for all their chips.

The minimum bet in no-limit must be at least the size of the big blind. The minimum raise must be at least equal to the size of the previous bet or raise in the round. For example, a $10 bet can be raised $30 more to make it $40 total. If the next player reraises, he has to make it at least $30 more—since that is the size of the last raise—for $70 total.

HOW TO BET

A bet is made by either pushing chips toward the pot—an action that speaks for itself—or by verbally calling out your intention, and then pushing the chips out. Simply announce, "I call," "I bet," "I raise," or whatever clearly indicates your desired action, and then push your chips out on the felt. Note that if you announce a check, bet, raise, or a fold, it is binding and you are committed to your announced action.

Your bet should be placed at least six inches toward the middle, but not so far that your chips mingle with those already in the pot and cannot be distinguished from them. That is, your chips should be far enough away from your own stack and the pot so that they are clearly seen not only as a bet, but as *your* bet.

Do not throw your chips into the actual pot, which is called **splashing the pot**. This rule protects all players from an opponent intentionally or unintentionally miscalling a bet. It also allows the amount of the wager to easily be verified, while making it clear to all players that a bet or raise has been made.

To check, simply tap the table with your fingertips or announce, "I check" or "Check." To fold, push your cards or face down toward the dealer. It is illegal to show your cards to active players who are competing for the pot.

BETTING ETIQUETTE

You must wait for your turn to play before announcing or revealing to any opponents the decision you will make. And if you fold, pass the cards to the dealer face down so that no other player can view them. If a player reveals any of his cards to another player, he is required to show them to everyone at the table so that all players are kept on equal footing.

It is improper and illegal to discuss your cards or another player's cards while a hand is in progress. It is also very poor form to criticize other players, no matter how poorly they appear to be playing. Having opponents that play poorly is good news for you: Go win their chips.

TABLE STAKES GAMES, TAPPED-OUT PLAYERS, AND SIDE POTS

Table stakes means that you may only bet or call bets up to the amount of money you have on the table in cash games. You are not allowed to withdraw money from your wallet, borrow from other players, or receive credit while a hand is in progress. Getting extra cash or chips is permissible only before the cards are dealt.

For example, if someone bets $25 and you only have $10, you may only call for $10. If you call with your last $10, you are **tapped out** since you have no more money on the table to wager. The remaining $15 and all future bets during the hand—except for bets by opponents to equal the $10 you called—are separated into a **side pot**. As a tapped-out player, you can still receive cards until the showdown and play for the main pot. However, you can no longer bet in the hand and you have no interest in the side pot. The other active players can continue to bet against each other for the money in the side pot. They also remain in competition against you for the **main pot**.

At the showdown, if the tapped-out player has the best hand, he receives only the money in the main pot. The player with the best hand among the remaining players wins the side pot. Should one of the other players hold the overall best hand, that player wins both the original pot and the side pot. If only one opponent remains when a player taps out, there is no more betting. The cards are simply dealt to the showdown, where the best hand wins.

THE RAKE

In casino games the house gets a cut of the action, called a **rake**, as its fee for hosting the game. In low-limit games, the rake can be anywhere from 5% to 10%, usually with a cap of $3 to $5 per pot. In high-limit games, the house typically charges players by the amount of time they remain active in the game.

SEVEN-CARD STUD: HIGH, LOW (RAZZ), AND HIGH-LOW

Seven-card stud's three main variations—high, low, and high-low—pack five exciting betting rounds into play. In each variation, players form the best five-card combination out of the seven dealt to produce their final hand.

In **seven-card high stud**, the highest-ranking hand at the showdown wins the pot. In **seven-card low stud**—**razz**—the lowest hand claims the gold. And in **seven-card stud high-low 8-or-better**, players vie for either the highest ranking or lowest ranking hand, or both, with the best of each claiming half the pot—with some restrictions, which we'll go into.

Players receive a total of seven cards if they play through to the end. After the first three cards are dealt (two **face-down**, or **closed**, and one **face-up**, or **open**), the first betting round commences. The following three cards—the fourth, fifth, and sixth—are dealt open, one at a time, to each active player. A betting round occurs after each new card is dealt. The last card, the seventh, comes "down and dirty," facedown.

All players who have not folded hold three hole cards and four open cards at the end of the deal. A final round of betting follows the seventh card, and then the showdown occurs with the best hand (or hands, as may be the case in high-low) claiming the pot. In each variation of seven-card stud, a player can also win the pot before the showdown by forcing out all opponents through bets and raises that opponents do not choose to match.

THE PLAY OF THE GAME

All antes, if required, must be placed into the pot before the cards are dealt. Once an ante is placed, it is like any other wager: It is the property of the pot and will be awarded to the eventual winner of the hand.

The dealer distributes the cards in a clockwise direction beginning with the player to his immediate left and continuing around the table until all players have received their initial three cards. Either the lowest open card or the highest open card on the table, depending on the stud variation, is forced to make a **bring-in bet**, an opening bet that starts the action.

Play proceeds in a clockwise direction beginning with the player to the bring-in bettor's left and moving around the table until all bets and raises have been called. If no player chooses to call the bring-in, the play ends right there and the pot is awarded to the bring-in bettor. This first round of betting is called **third street**, so named for the three cards that each player holds.

The bring-in bet is usually less than the size of the smaller bet in a limit game. For example, in a $5/$10 game, the bring-in might be $2. In seven-card stud high and high-low games, the player holding the lowest open card makes the bring-in. If two players have identically ranked cards, the player with the lower ranked suit plays first. For this purpose only, the suits are ranked the same way they are in the game of bridge: spades being the highest, followed by hearts, diamonds and clubs.

In seven-card razz games, the player with the highest-ranking open card starts the betting. If two or more players hold equivalent values, the high-card player closest to the dealer's left must make the mandatory bring-in bet. You cannot check on third street.

The first player to the bring-in's left goes next. He must either complete the bring-in, raise the completed bring-in, or fold his hand. **Completing the bring-in** means bringing it up to the lower limit of the betting structure. In a $5/$10 game with a $2 bring-in, the bettor must make it $5 (increasing the $2 bring-in by $3 more). In that case, all subsequent players must call the completed bring-in, the $5 in this example, to remain active in the hand.

Bets and raises in this first betting round are at the lower limit of the betting tier. If you're playing a $5/$10 game in which someone has completed the bring-in before it is your turn, you and all bettors after you must call the $5 bet. If you want to raise the pot after someone has completed the bring-in bet, you must raise $5 more, making it $10 to any player who wishes to remain active in the hand.

When third-street betting is completed, each active player receives a face-up card. Everyone now holds a total of four cards, two open and two closed. Play in this round, called **fourth street**, and all the following rounds begins with the best open hand and moves clockwise around the table. In high and high-low seven-card stud, the best hand is the highest ranked. In razz, the best hand is the lowest ranked. When two or more players hold identically ranked cards, the player closest to the dealer's left plays first.

For example, in razz, a player showing 8-6 on fourth street, called an "8-6" hand, must act before a player showing 9-5. Similarly, a 6-4 board would open against a 7-3. And if players held K-K, A-Q, or 6-6 on fourth street in a high or high-low game, the pair of kings would lead off the betting.

Beginning on fourth street, which is the second betting round, and continuing through the last betting round, the first bettor to act may check to open the betting since there is no bring-in bet to meet. It is only on third street that an opening bet is required for players to stay in active competition for the pot. All bets and raises on fourth street are in the lower limit of the betting structure unless an open pair shows on board, in which case players may elect to open with a bet from the upper limit of the betting. Thus, on fourth street in a $5/$10 game, bets are $5 unless an open pair forms on board, in which case $10 can be bet in high seven-card stud.

Once fourth-street betting is concluded, another open card is dealt to each active player. Players now have a total of three upcards in addition to their two downcards. This round is called fifth street. All bets and raises on **fifth street** and on the following two rounds, are in the upper tier of the betting limit. In a $5/$10 game, bets and raises must be in increments of $10; in a $3/$6 game, $6; and in a $15/$30 game, $30.

After the fifth-street round of betting closes, active players receive their fourth open card. This is **sixth street**. Again, the highest (or lowest) ranking open hand acts first. The round ends either when all bets and raises have been called, or when all opponents fold, ceding the pot to the last remaining player.

Seventh street is the final betting round. Each remaining player receives his seventh and final card facedown. There is one last round of betting followed by the showdown if two or more players remain active.

THE SHOWDOWN: HIGH STUD AND RAZZ

In straight high stud and in razz, each player chooses five cards out of the seven total he holds to form his best hand. In seven-card high stud, the best high hand wins, and in razz, the five best low cards will claim the pot.

THE SHOWDOWN: HIGH-LOW STUD 8-OR-BETTER

The main difference between high-low stud and straight high or low versions, is that you're actually playing for two parts of the pot: Half the pot goes to the player with the best high hand and the other half goes to the player with the best low hand.

High-low seven-card stud is played as **cards speak**. That is, players simply reveal their cards at the showdown. The dealer announces the best high hand and the best low hand, and those two hands split the pot. However, if one player is fortunate enough to have both the best high and low hands, he wins the entire pot.

Seven-card high-low stud is played with a qualifier, a requirement that a player must have five unpaired cards that are 8 or lower (better) to win the low end of the pot. For that reason, seven-card stud high-low is often called seven-card stud 8-or-better, or simply 8-or-better. If no player has an 8-or-better qualifier, the best high hand wins the entire pot. For example, if the best low at the table is 9-6-5-4-2, there is no qualified low hand and the best high hand is awarded the whole pot.

STRATEGY FOR SEVEN-CARD STUD: HIGH POKER

The first three cards you receive in seven-card stud lay the groundwork for the future possibilities of your hand. Therefore, you should only stay in with cards that have the right winning ingredients.

Starting and staying with promising cards is especially important in seven-card stud, since the five betting rounds of this game add up to a lot of bets and raises. With all these chips at stake, you want to give yourself every chance of winning.

These are the minimum starting cards you should have to enter the betting in seven-card stud:

SEVEN-CARD STUD • MINIMUM STARTING CARDS
Three of a kind
Three-card straight flush
Three-card flush
Three-card straight
Pair of tens or higher
Low or middle pair with ace or king kicker*
Concealed pair with face-card kicker
Three high cards, two of them suited

*A **kicker** is the highest side card to a hand of one pair, two pair, three of a kind, or rarely, four of a kind.

Three of a kind is a powerful starting hand that is heavily favored to win. With these cards, you want to keep as many players as possible in the pot. Play low key on third and fourth street, calling bets but not raising. If your opponents start showing threatening signs of flushes or straights on fifth street, bet as much as you can. You want to either force them out or make them pay for the privilege of trying to buy their hands. However, if your trips turn into a full house, you have nothing to fear from straights or flushes. You want them to make their straights and flushes—and how!

With three-card flushes and straights, call third-street betting, but do not raise. In general, it is prudent to raise only if you either have the goods or are bluffing (and only under the right circumstances). If your three-card straight or flush doesn't improve by fourth street, it's time to say goodbye. Fold the hand. The odds against completing it are getting too steep for the cost of calling bets and chasing cards for three more betting rounds.

One interesting thing about three-card flushes that most players don't realize is that when you end up winning with these cards, your winning hand often is not the flush you were drawing to, but a lesser combination. Along the way, you may make a two-pair hand, three of kind, a straight, full house, or perhaps a high pair. So it's important to remember that you prefer your three-flush starting hand to contain high cards. Holding a 10-7-4 flush draw is not as valuable as a K-J-2 flush draw.

For example, suppose the highest exposed card on board is a queen. If you pair your king in the hand K-J-2, you will have a more competitive hand. If the showdown ends up pitting pair against pair or two pair against two pair, your high pairs will often win.

As you can see, pairing big cards is much more valuable than pairing a 10, 7, or 4, weaker cards that form weaker one-pair and two-pair hands that often lose to bigger one-pair and two-pair hands. Of course, there are other considerations to take into account, but the high-card factor is one that must be considered from the get-go. Bigger is better.

Having a big kicker (side card) to low and medium pairs is critical, which is why you don't want to enter the pot without an ace or a king to support your lower pairs. If you pair the ace or king, you will have a good chance to outlast opponents with smaller two-pair hands than yours. Of course, if there is an ace on board, your king could be playing second best, so you need to be aware of that. But if you have an ace and pair it, you have at least the top pair, and are in pretty good shape. If your small and medium pairs haven't improved by fourth street, you'll probably want to toss the hand if an opponent raises the pot before your turn, or if he bets with a higher pair on board. It's best not to chase hands when you're probably beat.

A key factor to winning at seven-card stud, or at any poker game, is making sure that you lose as little as possible in the pots you don't win. Fold hands that have not panned out or have become underdogs. Avoid the temptation to play "just one more card." One more card costs money and if it's not a sound call, it's a bet deducted from your overall winnings. To be a winner, you must wager with the odds, not against them. And those odds are defined by the cards you hold versus those of your opponents—not on the hopes of what might happen. Again, when a promising hand's possibilities wither and look to be second best, bury it.

Betting intensity can indicate the strength of your opponents' hands. If betting is heavy, with raises and reraises, expect to see strong cards at the showdown. However, if the betting is relatively light, then the opposite applies: Expect the average winning hand to be weaker.

Pay attention to all the open cards in seven-card stud. Cards in play cannot be drawn and therefore greatly impact the chances that you or your opponent will improve your hand. For example, if an opponent holds an open pair of kings and you saw two kings folded earlier, you know that there's no way he can buy a third king no matter how lucky he gets. Further, your chances of completing a four-card club flush draw are greatly diminished if you see that six clubs have already been dealt to your opponents.

What if you hold a marginal hand and are unsure of how to proceed? Lean toward folding if some of the cards you need are already in play, and lean toward playing if they are not.

STRATEGY FOR SEVEN-CARD RAZZ (LOW STUD)

In seven-card low stud, or razz as the game is commonly called, you use your best five cards to form the lowest possible hand. Strategic thinking is different in razz than in standard seven-card stud. Unlike high poker, where players start with strong cards that sometimes can win without improving, good lowball hands always start out as drawing hands that need improvement to develop into winners.

Your first four cards may be A-2-3-4, a golden start, but if the next three cards you receive are J-J-K, your hand melts into nothing. In contrast, seven-card high stud presents situations where you're dealt big hands for starters such as Q-Q-Q, and regardless of the next four cards, these trip queens are heavily favored to win because subsequent draws cannot diminish their inherent strength. But lowball hands that don't improve die on the vine and become worthless.

To be competitive in razz, you must enter the betting with low starting cards that can win the pot with adequate improvement. Here are the minimum opening or calling hands for razz.

RAZZ • MINIMUM STARTING CARDS
Three-card 7-high or better (lower)
Three-card 8-high with two cards valued 5 or lower
Three-card 9-high with an ace, 2, or 3
An ace plus a 5 or lower card, and an odd card (a high card)

If you don't hold one of the above combinations, you should fold. You don't want to play underdog cards and contribute to other players' wins. However, if you're the bring-in and no one completes the bet after you, you're already in, so take the free card on fourth street.

Hands with relatively low supporting cards are called **smooth** hands. For example, in the starting hand 7-3-2, the 3-2 makes it a *smooth 7*; and the 8-4-3-2-A is a *smooth 8*. Hands where the supporting cards are relatively high are called **rough**, such as the 7-6-4, called a *rough 7*, or the 8-7-5-4-3, a *rough 8*. Smooth hands have greater possibilities of winning than rough hands, and should be played more aggressively. If you make an 8-high hand or a smooth 9 on fifth street, you're in a strong position. You should bet and raise forcefully against players still holding drawing hands. You're the favorite, so you want to either force them out of the pot or make them pay for every card they try to catch.

Play aggressively against weak players when you've got the goods. They'll stay in too long with inferior hands. Why not make your winning pot that much larger?

STRATEGY FOR SEVEN-CARD STUD HIGH-LOW

The splitting of the pot into two parts, half for the best high hand and half for the best low, makes seven-card stud an action-packed and exciting game. An astute player can win healthy sums against loose opponents, while a weak player can get buried.

Though there are more ways to win at high-low stud, don't let this tempt you into playing too many hands. The same winning principle applies here as in all poker games: Enter the betting only with strong starting cards that have a good chance of winning. Staying in pots with hands that hold both high and low possibilities, but are mediocre in both directions, is costly.

Look for hands that give you possibilities of winning both the high and low ends of the pot, "scooping the pot." The problem with playing one-way hands in high-low is that your bets lose half their value because you're going after only one end of the pot. If you get shut out, you lose all your chips. And if you win, you get only half of the pot.

And what if you get caught in a pot where one player has a lock on one part of it? You may get whipsawed for a lot of bets, making your pursuit of 50% of the action very costly. The math is not favorable for you in many one-way pots. Therefore, when you are playing for one-half of the pot, you need a hand that is very strong in one direction.

The best starting hand in high-low stud is three suited cards 8 or below (A, 2, 3, 4, 5, 6, 7, or 8), particularly if one of them is an ace. And if three of them are suited and connected to form a draw to a straight flush, you have a great hand with excellent high and low potential, so you want to build the pot. If you're the first one in the pot, raise to build it up, but if there are raisers before it's your turn, just call to disguise the strength of your hand.

Another big hand is a three of a kind, especially if the trips are low. This is a very deceptive hand. A pair of aces with an 8 or lower to go with it, giving it two-way potential, is also a strong hand. Other big pairs such as kings and queens are almost worthless against an aggressive player with an ace showing, as their scooping potential is limited and their high potential is vulnerable. In 8-or-better, big pairs take on more value because if low hands don't qualify, the high hand scoops the pot. However, you should never play a high hand that is not shaping up to be the best hand. This is an extremely important concept in high-low poker.

Other strong two-way starting hands are three-straights that are 8 or lower (A-2-3, 2-3-4, 3-4-5, 4-5-6, 5-6-7, and 6-7-8); three straights 8 or lower with only one gap (such as 4-5-7 or 2-3-5); and three cards 8 or lower that include an ace (such as A-4-5, A-3-5, and A-3-8). You can play these hands strong on third street, raising or calling a few bets in front of you. You have a great shot at low, and if your ace pairs when no other ace is showing, you have a good shot at the high as well.

Even if you don't pair, the ace by itself is sometimes enough to win the high. For example, a player holding K-Q-K would have to consider folding against your upcard ace if you bet aggressively, since his one-way high hand is looking at a possible bigger pair.

If your three-straight 8 or lower has two gaps and doesn't include an ace, such 4-6-8 and 2-4-6, it has some value but should be folded against heavy betting. If you have a four-card low topped by 8-7 or 8-6 on fourth street, you can't handle any action if another player appears to be going for low as well—he's showing a 5-3 or 6-5 on his board, for example. Remember that an 8-low hand is vulnerable against other players going low, particularly if you see no eights on their boards.

You shouldn't play middle pairs without high kickers; three-flushes that don't have three cards 8 or lower; three-card straights with high cards (no scoop potential and only a draw to a high hand); or random cards that don't fit in with the starting hands discussed above. Keep in mind that high hands cannot turn into low hands, but low hands can turn into high ones if you catch the right cards.

The nature of high-low stud calls for some aggressive play. When you have a chance to scoop the pot or you have a lock on either the high or low end of the pot, bet forcefully. You want to create big pots and make your winnings that much sweeter.

TEXAS HOLD'EM

Texas hold'em, or **hold'em** as the game is commonly known, is played as high poker; that is, the player with the highest five-card combination at the showdown wins the money in the pot. You can also win the pot if all of your opponents fold their hands at any point before the showdown, leaving you alone to claim the chips in the middle—even though you may not have the best hand!

Hold'em is played with three types of betting structures: limit, no-limit, and pot-limit. In limit hold'em, bets are preset at two levels. In a $5/$10 limit hold'em game, you must bet in increments of $5 during the first two betting rounds, and $10 during the last two betting rounds. In no-limit hold'em, you may bet any amount equal to or higher than the big blind (the opening forced bet), up to the amount of chips you have in front of you. In pot-limit, you must bet at least the amount of the big blind up to the total amount of chips in the pot.

In all forms of hold'em, your final five-card hand is made up of the best five-card combination of the seven total cards available to you. These include the **board**, the five cards dealt face-up in the middle of the table that are shared by all players, and your **pocket cards** or **hole cards**, the two cards dealt face-down that can be used by you alone. For example, your final hand could be composed of your two pocket cards and three cards from the board, one pocket card and four from the board, or simply all five board cards.

The progression of play is the same for all forms of hold'em. At the beginning of a hand, each player is dealt two cards face down. Then each player gets a chance to exercise his betting options. Next, three cards are dealt simultaneously on the table for all players to share. This is called the **flop**, which is followed by another round of betting. A fourth board card, called the **turn**, is then dealt, followed by a round of betting. One final community card is dealt in the center of the table, making five cards total. This is the **river**. If two or more players remain in the hand, the fourth and final betting round follows. When all betting has been completed, there is a showdown in which the highest-ranking hand in play wins.

HOW TO READ YOUR HOLD'EM HAND

You have all seven cards available to form your final five-card hand—any combination of your two hole cards and the five cards from the board. You can even use all five board cards. Let's look at an example.

YOU HOLD

YOUR OPPONENT

THE BOARD

FLOP TURN RIVER

Your best hand, three jacks, is made using your two pocket cards and one jack from the board. This beats your opponent's pair of aces, formed with one card from his hand and one from the board. In both instances, the other cards are not relevant. For example, there is no need to say three jacks with an ace and a king versus two aces with a king, queen and jack—simply, three jacks versus two aces.

If the river card, the last card turned up on the board, had been a K♦ instead of a K♣, your opponent would have made a diamond flush—using his two pocket diamonds and the three diamonds on the board—which would beat your three jacks, called a set.

THE PLAY OF THE GAME

All play and strategy in hold'em depends upon the position of the button. The player who has the button in front of him, who is also known as the "button," will have the advantage of acting last in every round of betting except the preflop round. After each hand is completed, the disk rotates clockwise to the next player.

The two players to the left of the button are required to post bets, called **blinds**, before the cards are dealt. The player immediately to the button's left is called the **small blind** and the next player to small blind's left is called the **big blind**. The big blind is typically the same size as the lower bet in a limit structure. For example, if you're in a $3/$6 game, the big blind would be $3; in a $5/$10 game, it would be $5. The small blind will either be half the big blind in games where the big blind evenly divides to a whole dollar, or two-thirds of the big blind when it doesn't. For example, the small blind might be $2 in a $3/$6 game, and $10 in a $15/$30 game.

Typical blinds for no-limit cash games might be $2/$5, $3/$5 or $5/$10 for the small blind and big blind respectively. Bigger blinds mean more action and larger games.

In cash games, the amount of the blinds is preset and remains constant throughout the game. In tournaments, however, the blinds steadily increase as the event progresses, forcing players to play boldly to keep up with the greater costs of the forced bets.

ORDER OF BETTING

Play always proceeds clockwise around the table. On the **preflop**, the first betting round, the first player to the left of the big blind goes first. He can call the big blind to stay in competition for the pot, raise, or fold. Every player following him has the same choices: call, raise, or fold. The last player to act on the preflop is the big blind. If no raises have preceded his turn, the big blind can either end the betting in the round by checking (he already has his bet in the pot), or he can put in a raise.

However, if there are any raises in the round, the big blind and other remaining players must call or raise these bets to stay active, or they must fold.

On the other betting rounds—the flop, turn and river—the first active player to the button's left acts first and the player on the button acts last. If the button has folded, the player sitting closest to his right acts last. When all bets and raises have been met on the flop and turn, or if all players check, the next card will be dealt. After all betting has been completed on the river, players must reveal their cards to see who has the best hand.

Betting in a round stops when the last bet or raise has been called, and no bets or raises are due any player. Players cannot raise their own bets or raises. At any time before the showdown, if all opponents fold, the last active player wins the pot.

PLAYING TIP

Never fold the big blind unless the pot has been raised. If no one raises, there is no further cost to play so you can see the flop for free.

LIMIT HOLD'EM SAMPLE GAME

Let's follow the action in a sample $3/$6 limit game with nine players so that you can see how hold'em is played.

In limit poker, the betting structure has two levels. The lower level is the amount you must bet or raise on the preflop and flop ($3 in a $3/$6 game). The higher level is the amount you must bet or raise on the turn and river ($6 in a $3/$6 game). The small blind and the big blind must post their mandatory bets before the cards are dealt. The dealer then distributes cards one at a time to each player, beginning with the small blind and proceeding clockwise until all players have received two cards face down.

PREFLOP

The player to the big blind's left acts first. He has the option of calling the $3 big blind bet, raising it $3 more, or folding. Checking is not an option on the preflop as there is already a bet on the table—the $3 big blind bet. Let's say this player folds. The next player is faced with the same decision: call, raise, or fold. He calls for $3. Since this is a $3/$6 game, all bets and raises in this round must be in $3 increments. The next three players fold. The following player raises $3, making it $6 total—the $3 call plus the $3 raise.

It is the button's turn, the player sitting in the dealer position. He thinks about his cards and calls the $6. Now it is up to the small blind. The small blind has already put in $2 so he must put in $4 more to play. If there had been no raise, it would cost him just $1 more to meet the $3 big blind bet and stay active.

The small blind folds and it is the big blind's turn to act. The big blind always has the option to raise on the preflop. The dealer will say "option" when it is the big blind's turn to let him know that he can raise. If there have been no raises and the big blind opts not to raise, the preflop betting is finished for the round. If the big blind raises, the other active players must meet that raise to stay active. If all players fold on the preflop, the big blind wins the hand by default.

In our game, the big blind considers reraising the raiser, but instead just calls the $3 raise. Play now moves back to the original caller. Since he has put only $3 into the pot, he must meet the $3 raise to stay in the hand. He calls the raise.

Now that all bets and raises have been matched, the round is over. We'll see the flop four-handed.

FLOP

At the conclusion of betting, the dealer pulls the blinds and bets into the pot. He takes the top card off the deck and **burns** it; that is, he removes it from play. Then he deals the three card flop face-up in the center of the table. Bets and raises during this round are still at the $3 level. The first active player to the button's left goes first. Since the small blind has folded, it is the big blind's turn. There are no bets that have to be met—the forced first-round blind bet only occurs on the preflop—so the big blind may check or bet. The big blind has no reason to fold, which would be foolish, as it costs him nothing to stay active.

The big blind checks, the next player checks, the preflop raiser checks, and now it is the button's turn to act. He pushes $3 into the pot forcing the other three players to put up $3 if they want to see another card. The big blind, who checked first in this round, is the next active player. He must call or raise the bet to continue with the hand—or he must fold. He decides to call for $3 and the other two players fold.

Since all bets have been called, betting is complete for the round. We're now heads-up, the big blind versus the button.

TURN

The dealer burns the top card and then deals a fourth community card face up on the table. This is known as the turn or fourth street. Betting moves to the upper limit, so all bets and raises must be in $6 increments. Since the big blind is the first active player on the button's left, he goes first and checks. The button checks as well. Since all active players have checked, the betting round is over.

RIVER AND SHOWDOWN

After the top card is burned, the fifth and final community card is turned over and placed next to the other four cards in the center of the table. Players now have five community cards along with their two hole cards to form their final five-card hand.

At the **river** (fifth street), as this round is called, there is one final round of betting. The big blind goes first and leads out with a $6 bet. The button calls, concluding the betting since the big blind cannot raise his own bet. We now have the showdown. The big blind turns over K-Q, which combines with a board of K-Q-10-7-5 for two pair, kings and queens. The button's K-10 also gives him two pair led by kings, but his second pair is tens. The big blind has the superior hand and wins the money in the pot.

Had the button simply folded, the big blind would have won by default, since no other players remained to contest the pot.

On the showdown, the last player to bet or raise (or if there has been no betting in the round, the first person to the left of the button) has to show his cards first. Losers can simply **muck** their hands—fold them, without showing their cards.

The dealer pushes the chips in the pot over to the winner, collects and shuffles the cards, and prepares to deal a new hand. The button moves clockwise, so the big blind is now the small blind, and the small blind becomes the button.

SEVEN KEY CONCEPTS OF HOLD'EM

The following key concepts apply to all forms of hold'em.

1. **Respect Position**
   Where you sit relative to the button is called your **position** in hold'em. In a nine-handed game, the first three spots to the left of the button are known as **early position**; the next three, **middle position**; and the last three, **late position**. In a ten-handed game, early position is the four spots to the left of the button. The later the position, the bigger the advantage, because you get to see what your opponents do before deciding whether to commit any chips to the pot. The earlier the position, the more vulnerable your hand is to being raised and thus the more powerful your hand must be for you to enter the pot.
   In late position, you have more options and leverage, so you can play more hands. If the early betting action is aggressive, you can fold marginal hands without cost. If the betting action is weak, you can be more aggressive with marginal hands and see the flop in the best position at the table.
2. **Play Good Starting Cards**
   You must start with good cards to give yourself the best chance to win. While this seems obvious, you'd be surprised at the number of players who ignore this basic strategic concept and take loss after loss by chasing with inferior and losing hands. If you play too many hands in poker, you'll soon find yourself without chips. Enter the pot with good starting cards in the right position and to give yourself the best chance of finishing with winners.
3. **Observe Opponents**
   By watching how an opponent plays, you get all sorts of information on how to take advantage of his playing tendencies. For example, when a player seldom enters a pot, he is called **tight**, and you can often force him out of hands

even when he may have better cards than yours. Give him credit for big hands when he's in a pot, and get out of his way unless you have a big hand yourself.

An opponent who plays a lot of hands is **loose**, and you usually can figure him for holding weaker cards. You also need to adjust for **aggressive** players who often raise when they get involved in a pot; and **passive** players that you can play against with little fear of getting raised.

4. **Be the Aggressor**

   Hold'em is a game where aggression reaps the best returns. It's almost always better to raise than to call. Raising puts pressure on opponents who will often fold right there, unwilling to commit chips to their marginal hands. Or they may see the flop but be ready to drop out against further bets if it doesn't connect strongly enough with their cards—which happens most of the time.

5. **Win Chips, Not Pots**

   You want to win chips. To do that, you need to win pots, particularly big ones if you can. So keep this in mind: It is not the quantity of pots you win, but the quality of them that matters.

6. **Fold Losing Hands**

   Part of winning is minimizing losses when you have the second-best hand. This means not chasing pots when you are a big underdog, especially longshot draws against heavy betting. You can't win them all. Save your chips for better opportunities. Cutting losses on hands you lose adds to overall profits.

7. **Patience**

   Hold'em is a game of patience. You will often endure long stretches between good hands. Winning players patiently wait for situations where they can win chips. Your good hands will come. If you haven't blown yourself out trying to force plays, you'll be able to take advantage of them and win some nice pots for yourself.

LIMIT HOLD'EM STRATEGY

The three main factors to consider when deciding how to play a hand in limit hold'em are:

1. The strength of your starting cards.
2. Where you are sitting relative to the button.
3. The action that precedes your play.

Other considerations also enter into the mix, including the cost of entering the pot and the aggressiveness or tightness of the table, but you should always consider the three fundamental factors first.

STARTING CARDS

Playing too many hands is the biggest mistake that novices and losing players make in hold'em. Each call costs at least one bet. Losing players compound their mistakes when they catch a piece of the flop—but not enough of it—and make inadvisable bets and raises when they are holding a losing hand, thus making the situation even more costly. These lost chips add up quickly and set the stage for losing sessions.

The foundation of winning hold'em is starting with solid cards; that is, playing the right cards in the right positions.

We'll divide the starting hands into four different categories: Premium, Playable, Marginal, and Junk.

PREMIUM STARTING HANDS

Aces, kings, queens, jacks, and A-K are the best starting hands. They are strong enough to raise from any position at the table and should be played aggressively. You hope to accomplish two things with the raise. First, you want to get more money into the pot on a hand that you're probably leading with; and second, you want to protect your hand by narrowing the field of opponents.

The greater the number of players who stay in the pot, the greater the chances that a weaker hand will draw out and beat your premium hand.

If a player raises ahead of you or reraises behind you, reraise with aces and kings, and just call with the other premium hands and see how the flop goes. Jacks are weaker than the other big pairs because there is about a 50% chance that an overcard, a queen, king, or ace will come on the flop, making your hand vulnerable.

If an overcard flops when you have J-J, Q-Q, or even K-K, or if you miss entirely with A-K, you have to think about giving up on these hands if an opponent bets into you or check-raises. For example, if the flop is Q-7-6 and you have A-K or J-J, and an opponent leads into you, you're probably donating chips. A better flop would be K-10-3 for A-K, or 10-8-2 for J-J.

It's also tough to play high pairs against an ace flop since players will often play starting cards containing an ace. And in low-limit games, you'll get players seeing the flop with all sorts of hands, so if there are a bunch of players in the pot, you have to be concerned about an ace flopping when you have a big pocket pair such as K-K or Q-Q. If you have A-K, however, an ace on the flop puts you in a strong position, especially in a game where opponents like to play ace-anything.

You're also concerned with flops of three connecting cards such as 8-9-10 and three suited cards if you don't have the ace of the same suit for a powerful nut flush draw. These are not good flops for big pairs or an A-K.

PLAYABLE STARTING HANDS

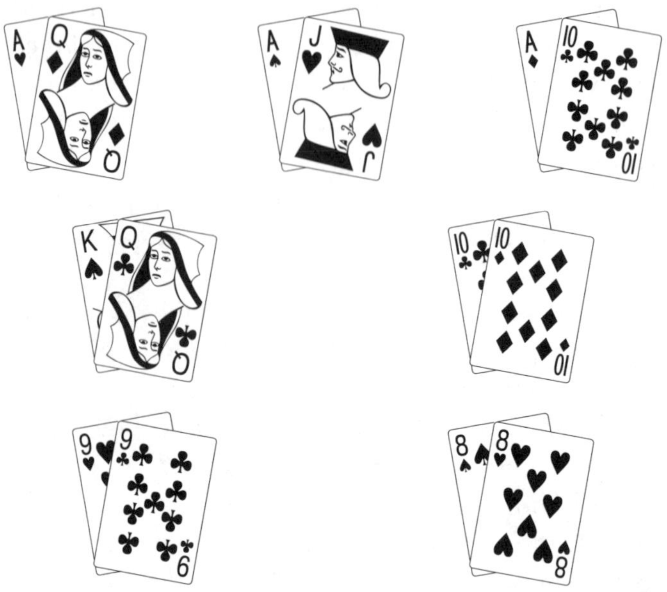

These starting hands should be folded in early position. They should also be folded in middle or late position if the pot has been raised from early position, which suggests strength, unless you think the raiser is loose and you can see the flop for just that one bet.

If players **limp** into the pot before you—that is, if they just call the bet—you can limp in as well with a playable hand. Sometimes a raise will be good if you can force out players behind you and isolate the limper. However, if you're in there against loose players who are not easily moved off a pot, which is usually the case in low-limit games, you might consider calling. When you're up against opponents who cannot be chased away by raises, you'd prefer to see the flop for one bet with these hands.

If you enter the pot and it gets raised after you, you have to make a decision. If the raise comes from a loose player in late position, you have more reason to call then to fold for just one bet. However, if it's raised twice and costs you two more bets, or if it looks like you might be trapped between a bettor and a raiser, get away from these hands while it's still cheap. There is probably too much strength against you. The problem with A-Q, A-J, A-10, and K-Q in raised pots is that when you do connect with the flop, your ace-big hands could be out-kicked by ace-bigger hands, leading to a lot of trouble. Always suspect opponents for premium cards, especially when they come into the pot from early position.

If you can see the flop with a pair in four-handed action, you have enough value to call a raise, but only if you're confident that you won't be stuck between bettors and raisers when you're holding a less-than-premium hand.

What if no one has entered the pot before you? If you're in middle or late position, you can raise coming into the pot and try to limit the field or, even better, win the blinds.

MARGINAL STARTING HANDS

A-x (ace with any other card)

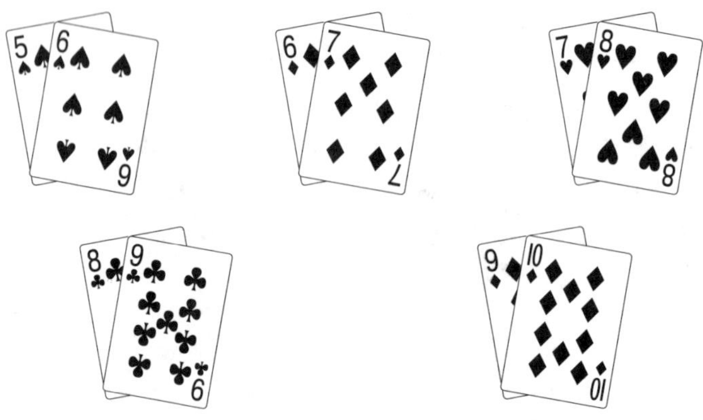

Suited connectors

Play marginal hands in middle and late position only if you can get in for one bet—but not at the cost of two bets—which means that you'll fold these hands in raised pots or when you are vulnerable to being raised. The exception is with the small pairs (2-2 through 7-7), where quantity equals quality. If you have reason to believe that the pot will be played four-handed, you will be getting the right odds to call a raise in the hope of catching a set and winning lots of chips.

In late position, call in an unraised pot. However, if the pot has been raised from early or middle position, or if you are between a bettor and a raiser, these marginal cards become unprofitable and should be folded.

If there is a raise after you enter the pot, you can call with these marginal hands—when the cost is only one bet—but fold in the face of a double raise or in situations where yet another raise can follow.

PLAYING LATE POSITION

You can play many more hands from late position. You've had a chance to see the betting before it reaches you. If the action is heavy, fold all non-premium hands. If the action is light and the cost is cheap, you can get more creative. And if no one has entered the pot, you should often raise, as there is a good chance that no one will call and you'll win the blinds.

If everyone has just limped, you can add **suited connectors**—cards that are consecutive in rank, such as 5-6 or 8-9 and in the same suit—to your list of starting hands. Suited connectors are best played in a pot with three or more players to give you the proper odds to draw to your hand. You want multiple opponents in the pot so that you can win a bunch of chips if you hit your hand. If the pot is raised and it would cost you two bets to play, call only if it looks like there will be enough players in to see the flop.

Pairs of twos through sevens are played similarly to connectors before the flop. You want to play them in late position when you can see the flop cheaply and the pot will be multiway. If there are several callers, you should call, but if the pot has been raised and it will cost you two bets to play, you can quietly muck your small pair. If you've already bet and the pot gets raised, you can call that extra bet if you feel that you won't get trapped and raised again.

Though a pair will only improve to trips (three of a kind) about one time in eight, you'll be sitting with a big hand that can trap opponents for a lot of chips when it does. If it doesn't improve and there are overcards on the flop, you probably have the worst of it and should fold against an opponent's bet. One rule of thumb here—no set, no bet.

JUNK HANDS

All other hands that are not in the above categories should be folded. They are heavy underdogs with little chance of winning. If you're in the big blind and the pot is unraised, by all means take the flop for free. But if it costs you to see the flop, fold immediately. It's cheaper to watch a raised pot as a bystander.

PLAYING THE BLINDS

If you can get in the pot cheaply from the small blind for just a few chips (you already have some chips in the pot), it is often worth expanding your starting cards to see if you can catch a lucky flop. And again, if you're in the big blind and the pot is unraised, be careful never to fold.

OTHER CONSIDERATIONS

If you miss the flop and think that a bet will cause your opponent to fold, make the play. Otherwise, don't throw chips at long shots. Save them for better spots.

Be careful playing flush and straight draws unless you are drawing to the **nuts**—the best hand possible given the cards on board. A **flush draw** is four cards of one suit needing one more card of that suit to complete a flush, while a **straight draw** is four cards to the straight needing one more to complete the straight. For example, you don't want to play a straight draw if there is a flush draw on board, or if you have 6-7 on a board of 7-8-9-10-X, as someone holding a jack might bust you. Many players like to play J-10, so that 7-8-9 flop is dangerous to your hand from the get-go.

If you think you have the best hand, bet or raise. Do not give opponents a cheap or free ride. You want to narrow the field and build the pot. If you have a huge hand, however, you want players to stay in the pot, but don't give away your hand by playing different than you usually would in the situation. If opponents expect you to bet, then bet.

In limit hold'em, as in all forms of poker, if you don't have the winning hand or a draw to it with enough money in the pot to go for, get out. Every bet you save is worth the same as a bet you win.

Minimize your bad bets and you're more likely to win money in any poker game.

NO-LIMIT HOLD'EM STRATEGY

In no-limit hold'em, your entire stack of chips is at risk on every single hand—as are those of your opponents. One big mistake and say goodbye to your stack. In limit hold'em, one bet is only one bet, but in no-limit, that one bet could be the defining moment of your game because it could be for all your chips. And that changes the way you play hands.

No-limit hold'em appears deceptively simple at first glance, but as you get deeper into its strategies and situations, you start to understand the many complexities of the game.

STARTING HANDS

If you're the first player coming into the pot before the flop, you usually want to enter the pot with a **standard raise**, three times the size of the big blind. If the big blind is $5, make your raise $15; and if it's $10, make your raise $30. The reason you don't raise only two times the big blind is that you make it too easy for your opponents, particularly the big blind, to enter the pot cheaply with marginal hands, and thus subject you to lucky draws by opponents who might not otherwise see the flop.

You want to consistently make your preflop raises three times the size of the big blind so that opponents get no extra information about the strength of your hand. Players that vary their preflop raises may inadvertently announce the strength of their hands.

If your opponents limp in to see the flop and you have a raising hand, make it four times the big blind. There is more money in the pot and you want to make it unprofitable for them to call with marginal cards.

The big bet or the all-in bet—the **hammer** in no-limit hold'em—puts a lot of pressure on opponents who hold marginal or strong hands in which they don't have confidence. Even when opponents think you're bluffing, it costs chips for them to find out for sure, which is often a greater amount than they're willing to risk.

EARLY POSITION

The best starting cards in no-limit hold'em are the **premium hands**—A-A, K-K, Q-Q, J-J, A-K and A-Q. In an unraised pot, bring these hands in for a standard raise in early position. Your goal is to either win the pot right there when all players fold, or narrow the field to one or two callers, thus reducing the number of players who will see the flop.

If you have aces or kings, hopefully you'll get a caller or two, or even better, a raiser. Then you can reraise the size of the pot, or go in for all your chips if you get reraised. With Q-Q and A-K, you can stand a raise to see the flop, but if the raise is for all your chips and you're not short-stacked, you may need to let these hands go. If you don't want pocket queens to finish your day, you certainly don't want to go out on jacks or A-Q! If an opponent goes all-in or puts in a big raise when you hold J-J or A-Q, you have ample reason to fold.

If a player comes in raising before you, pocket aces and kings are automatic reraises, while the non-premium hands are automatic folds. Lean toward just calling with A-K and Q-Q. If the raiser is tight, fold with A-Q and J-J; if the raiser is loose, raising or calling are both viable options. Remember, no play is set in stone in no-limit hold'em. You need to judge hands situation by situation.

Fold all other hands from early position, especially against an aggressive table. If the table is tight, or if it's early in a tournament and there's little cost to enter the pot, you may take a flier on a hand now and then to mix up your play.

MIDDLE POSITION

In middle position, you can play more hands because there are fewer players behind you who can raise your bet. If there is a raise before your turn, consider folding all non-premium hands. You don't want to go into the flop as a big underdog, which you may be doing if an early position player raises in front of you. And if the raiser is tight, fold J-J and A-Q as well. If you have A-A or K-K, reraise and have no fear of getting all your chips in the middle. You can also reraise with Q-Q and A-K, or you could just call.

If no one has raised in front of you, you will still play the premium hands for a raise and can add the second tier hands—10-10, 9-9, and 8-8, along with A-J, A-10, and K-Q—to your list of raising hands. If someone reraises behind you, consider throwing second tier hands away. These hands have value, but they are chip burners against heavy betting.

Of course, if your opponent is low on chips and moves in before the flop, especially in a tournament, give him credit for holding lesser quality cards. Be prepared to play all premium hands—but again, use judgment. When in doubt, go with your gut feeling.

LATE POSITION

In late position, if the pot has been raised in early position, reraise with A-A, K-K, Q-Q, and A-K. If you get reraised, consider just calling with Q-Q and A-K. If the raiser is tight and goes all-in, you probably want to release these hands. And you certainly do not want to be in that reraised pot with J-J, A-Q or anything less. With aces and kings, you're always ready to play for all the marbles preflop.

If the pot is raised in middle position, reraise with the top four hands, A-A, K-K, Q-Q and A-K. How you play J-J and A-Q is a judgment call, but it may be safer just to call and see the flop.

If the pot has not been raised, you can expand your starting hands to any pair, an ace with any other card, and any two cards 10 or higher; for example, Q-10 or K-J. Generally, it's best to come in raising. Most of the time, you'll win the blinds, which is good. If you get callers, the pot is offering you some extra value to see the flop.

If you have A-A or K-K in late position and you think you'll get a caller, raise. If not, it might be better to limp in. You don't get aces or kings often, but when you do, you want to make money on them.

If you can see the flop cheaply, you can also play suited connectors such as 6-7, 7-8, 8-9 and 10-J.

BLINDS

The blinds have the advantage of going last in the first round of play but the big disadvantage of going first in all other rounds. Play the blinds according to the advice in the early-position strategy section.

If a late-position bettor continually raises you out of the pot when you're the big blind, you have to take a stand at some point to keep him in line. You'd like to have two big cards or ace-anything to reraise with, but you can also reraise with garbage. If you read him correctly, he'll fold and you'll get his chips. Do this once or twice and you'll get his attention and respect too.

If everyone folds to you in the small blind and you can see the flop cheaply, it's not a bad play to call the big blind. You may flop something pretty or check to the showdown and win with better garbage than your opponent.

If you're in the big blind and no one has raised, always see the flop for free—don't make the mistake of folding.

FLOP

If you came in raising preflop, you want to continue playing aggressively. If you're first, bet regardless of what flops. Your opponent will probably fold and you'll win the pot. If he calls and you don't improve, you might consider checking on the turn. If he raises you on the flop, it's a tough call, but you'll have to consider folding unless you think you have a better hand. If you are the second to act and your opponent checks in front of you, bet.

What if he bets into you? If you miss the flop, give him the pot. Since you've shown strength preflop, his bet on the flop means you're probably second best.

When you have what you think is the best hand, your goal is to take the pot immediately, particularly when there are straight and flush draws possible; for example, two cards of the same suit are on the board. You don't want opponents playing for another card cheaply, making their hands, and then destroying you when they shouldn't even have seen another card. If opponents are going to beat you, make them pay to do it.

However, if you have an absolute monster like a full house or quads, you want to keep players in and extract more bets from them. Often, that means checking and hoping that a free card improves them just enough to continue playing against you.

TURN

If you've played aggressively on the preflop and flop and your opponent hasn't budged, you have to figure him for possible strength. It's time for you to look at what you think he thinks you have. If you're representing strength and playing tight, you have to give him credit for a strong hand and slow down your betting unless you're confident that you have a better hand. If he checks, you check. And if you're first, check to him and see how he reacts.

The turn is a time to put the brakes on a bluff that didn't work and possibly ease your way to the river with a hand that can't weather much more betting. If your opponent is weak, he may check along with you. His check may be a clue that you can zap him out with a bet on the river, or simply check and see who shows down the better hand.

You can always push your bluff one more bet, but if your opponent called you on the flop, continuing the bluff could be dangerous.

You've felt your opponents out on the flop. How they played on the flop greatly influences the types of hands you think they may be playing. Use your best judgment and go with it. If you think a bet may push a weak opponent out of the pot, betting is a strong option. If you're not sure, checking is not a bad option. But if you think you have the best hand, put more chips into the pot.

THE RIVER

When you have a big hand that you're confident is the best, you want to get more chips into the pot. If you're last to act and no one has bet, put the amount of chips in the pot that you think your opponent will call. If you're first, you have two options: check or bet. If your opponent is very aggressive or has been leading at the pot, consider checking and letting him bet, then going over the top of him with a raise to try to get more chips in the pot. You want to be careful not to move an opponent off a pot with a bet. Let your knowledge of how your opponent plays guide you.

When you have a strong hand but have doubts whether it's the best one, it's often better to check at the river rather than bet and risk a big raise that you won't call. If your opponent checks, you can see the showdown at no further cost. If he bets, you must decide what you want to do. Be careful about betting in an attempt to get an opponent to fold. He might raise you back or put you all in, and you'll be forced to muck your cards and give up your chips.

If you're going to bluff at the river, however, make sure it's for enough chips so that your opponent will be faced with a tough decision on whether to call.

OMAHA

Omaha is played with two types of betting structures: limit and pot-limit. In **limit Omaha**, bets are preset at two levels. In a $5/$10 limit Omaha game, you must bet in increments of $5 during the first two betting rounds, and $10 during the last two betting rounds. In **pot-limit Omaha**, you must bet at least the amount of the big blind up to the total amount of chips in the pot.

Omaha is played exactly like hold'em, except for two things:

1. Players get four cards to start with, as opposed to just two as in hold'em.
2. Each player must use exactly two of his pocket cards, no more and no less, together with three from the board, to form his final five-card hand.

Omaha poker has two variations, high and high-low. In high Omaha, the highest five-card hand wins the pot. In Omaha high-low (8-or-better), the highest hand and the lowest hand split the pot, as in stud high-low. In this section, we discuss only the high-low version of Omaha the more popular version commonly dealt in cardrooms.

In **Omaha high-low**, the best low hand and the best high hand split the pot. However, if no hand qualifies for low—five unpaired cards that are 8 or lower—the best high hand scoops the entire pot. Players can choose two different five-card combinations to make their final hands, one for the high hand and one for the low hand. Therefore, it is possible for one player to hold both the best high hand and the best low hand. When that happens, he scoops the pot. As in hold'em, Omaha is played with a button, as well as a small blind and a big blind.

The dealer starts by giving each player four cards face down. The first betting round proceeds exactly as in hold'em, with the player to the left of the big blind acting first.

When the betting action has been completed on the preflop round, the flop of three community cards is turned face up in the center of the table. After another round of betting, the turn and river are dealt, each followed by a betting round. At the showdown, the highest and lowest qualifying hand split the pot. If no hand qualifies for low, the highest hand wins the entire pot.

Omaha high-low is usually played in a limit format. All bets in the first round must be in the lower increment: $3 in a $3/$6 game, $5 in a $5/$10 game, $15 in a $15/$30 game, and so on. Betting on the turn and the river are at the higher level of the betting structure. For example, $6 in a $3/$6 game, $10 in a $5/$10 game, and $30 in a $15/$30 game.

HOW TO READ AN OMAHA HIGH-LOW HAND

It is easy to misread your hand in Omaha high-low. For example, if you are dealt four aces in the hole, you don't have quads because only two of the aces count toward your final hand. Three cards have to come from the board in forming your best five-card hand.

Look at this example to see how you form a high and low hand in conjunction with the board. If you hold A-A-J-4 with a board of A-J-7-6-2, two aces from your pocket cards are used to form the high hand, A-A-A-J-7. The ace and 4, combined with the 7-6-2 on the board, form a A-2-4-6-7 for your low hand.

Note that in both instances, you must use two of your downcards and three community cards to form your final poker hand.

BOARD

YOUR FINAL HIGH HAND

YOUR FINAL LOW HAND

Note that you don't have a full house of aces over jacks for the high hand because you can only use two of your hole cards. If your opponent holds 3-3-3-J, he would lose on the high end since he only has a pair of jacks! Since he must use his jack as part of the hand, he does not have a 7-6-3-2-A low, so he would lose on the low end as well.

GETTING QUARTERED

In Omaha high-low 8-or-better, players often split the pot at the showdown. In fact, there can be multiple split pots. For example, if two low hands are tied for best and there is a high-hand winner, the high hand will take half the pot, and the two low players will get **quartered**—meaning that each of them will split the low half, with each getting just one fourth of the total pot.

If there are three low winners, they split the low end three ways, getting one-sixth of the pot each, with the high winner taking sole possession of the high half of the pot. Ties for the best high hand are divided the same way—all winners get an equal portion from the high half of the pot, or from the whole pot if no player qualifies for low.

To qualify for winning the low half of the pot, a hand must be no worse than five unpaired cards that are 8 or lower. For example, the hand 8-7-5-3-A qualifies for low, but the hand 8-7-5-2-2 does not because of the paired deuces. A hand of 9-7-3-2-A would not qualify either, even though it may be the lowest hand, because a 9-high hand doesn't meet the 8-or-better qualifier. In this case, the high-end winner or winners get all the spoils.

STRATEGY FOR OMAHA HIGH-LOW

With both a high half and low half to go after, many players remain in the pot to the river, especially in low-limit "no fold'em" games. Loose players often chase hands in the false hope that the river card will dramatically transform their hand. Don't get sucked into the rampant betting that often occurs in low-stakes Omaha high-low games unless your hand is worthy of all the action. Speculation and loose play can lose you a bunch of chips in a hurry.

Your hole cards play an all-important role in Omaha high-low. As in all poker variations, you must start out with solid cards to give yourself the best chances of winning.

There are great starting cards, good starting cards, and poor starting cards, but what appears to be a good or bad preflop hand may change in a flash when the flop throws three more cards into the mix.

And the final two community cards open up even more possibilities that could make or break your hand.

With such a wide range of possibilities, hopes stay high and betting can be fierce. Unlike hold'em, where the starting hand combinations are fewer and not as many players see the flop, Omaha high-low pots usually have multiple players in them who bet and raise liberally with a wide variety of hands. This brand of poker can get expensive if you play hands that aren't good enough to stand the action. You must play solid poker to survive Omaha high-low with your chips intact.

Your position at the table is also a major factor in which hands you choose to see the flop with and how you play your cards. Before we touch on these points, let's take a look at the four key winning concepts of Omaha high-low.

FOUR KEY CONCEPTS IN OMAHA HIGH-LOW

1. **Key Concept: Scooping**
   In all high-low poker games, one guiding principle is the foundation of winning strategy: Play hands that have a chance to scoop the pot. That is, play cards that can win both the high and low half of the pot. This is especially true in Omaha high-low.
2. **Key Concept: Aces**
   The best card in Omaha high-low is the ace. If you don't have one, you're usually better off not getting involved in the pot because the cost of playing to see the flop, turn and river is too expensive without one. Although there are ace-less hands that have good potential to make money, beginners can still play a profitable game without playing any of them.
   The ace is so important in Omaha high-low because it is the best low card and the best high card. An ace is the boss card that gives you a big edge over any opponent who doesn't have one. Your goal is to scoop the pot, and when you hold an ace, you have a chance to improve to the top pair, top two pair, top set, top straight, top flush and top

full house, as well as the best low hand. Since most of the cards get dealt in a full Omaha game, if you don't have an ace, you can count on one of your opponents having one and holding that boss-card advantage over you.

3. **Key Concept: Play Good Starting Hands**

   An ace, a 2, or a 3 and one more unpaired card 5 or below is a strong starting low. The best starters in Omaha high-low have both high and low possibilities, so along with the ace plus a 2 or 3 and third low card, you'd like to have another ace (A-A-2-5) or two suited cards, preferably led by the ace, so that you have a shot at the nut flush. A king is a good card to accompany the ace, for example A-2-5-K, because it's the top kicker to an ace hand, giving you nut-high and nut-low straight possibilities.

   Four low cards with two suited cards, like A-2-3-4, A-2-3-5 or A-2-4-5, give you a great chance of making a perfect low, a wheel—A-2-3-4-5—or making a flush for the best high hand.

   When competing for the high end of the pot, hands with A-K and A-A have more strength against fewer players but less value against a larger field of opponents since more players stay to the end with draws to straights, flushes, and full houses. You can start with some high-only hands, but if you do, all four of the cards must be **coordinated**, that is close in rank to one another. Thus, a hand like K-K-Q-J would be good, but K-K-Q-7 would not. The 7 is a **dangler**, it doesn't coordinate with the other cards.

4. **Key Concept: Playing for the Nuts**

   With so many players seeing the flop and playing to the river, it is important that you start out with hands that have the potential to be the nuts, the best hand possible given the cards on board. In other words, if you make a flush, it should be the best flush (one led by an ace), and if it's a straight, you don't want to make the **ignorant**, or low, end of the straight. When you're going for low, your hand should have the potential to be the best possible low.

STARTING HAND REQUIREMENTS

If you had a choice, you'd rather be dealt a low hand than a high hand for one very simple reason: a low hand can develop into a high hand (by forming a low straight, an ace-high nut flush, two pair, trips, full house, or quads) and still be the nut low hand. But a high hand can never develop into a low hand.

Three low cards give you a strong starting position in Omaha high-low, so along with your ace, you'd like to have a 2 or a 3 and one more card 5 or below. You need the third low card because the three-card flop will often **duplicate** or **counterfeit** one of your good low cards, that is pair it and render it useless. For example, if you hold A-2-K-K, and the flop is 2-6-8, your 2 is counterfeited and useless to you since you must use two hole cards to form your low hand. You would need two more low cards that are not an ace or 2 to make a qualified low.

But if you held a third low card, say A-2-5-K, your low draw contains four cards, since you can use the A-5 from your hand to help form a low. You only need one more non-pairing low card to be dealt to make your low hand. Thus, with a third low card, you stay very much in the hunt.

The best starters in Omaha 8-or-better have both high and low possibilities, so along with the ace plus 2 or 3 and third low card, you'd like another ace (A-A-3-5), or two suited cards, preferably led by the ace, so that you have a shot at a nut flush. A king is a good card to accompany the ace, for example A-2-5-K, because it's the top kicker to an ace hand with nut-high and nut-low straight possibilities. Four low cards, like A-2-3-4, A-2-3-5, and A-2-4-5, with two suited cards, give you a chance of going low and wheeling (making a perfect low, a wheel—A-2-3-4-5) or flushing to a strong high hand.

When competing for the high end of the pot, hands with A-K and A-A have more strength against fewer opponents and less value against more opponents, since straights, flushes, and full houses are more common as more players stay to the end. You can start with some high-only hands, but if you do, all four of the cards must be coordinated, that is close in rank to one another. Thus, a hand like K-K-Q-J would be good, but K-K-Q-7 would not. That 7 is a dangler that doesn't coordinate with the other cards.

FLOP AND BEYOND

When the three-card flop hits, it's important to reevaluate your situation. The more players remaining to see the flop, the better your hand must be. You need to have either the nuts or a draw to the nuts, because with the loose action common in many low-limit games, it takes the nuts to win the pot.

When you're unsure of how to proceed with a hand, take your table position into account before you act. If you're in early position, you're vulnerable to raises behind you so have an easy fold. If you're in late position, you can call and see what develops on the next community card.

High starting hands of A-A-K-Q and A-A-K-K remain strong if the flop comes with three high cards, preventing low hands from taking half the pot. This is a key concept that players going for the high end of the pot must consider in Omaha high-low. Also, for any player to qualify for a low hand, three low cards (8 or below) must be on board at the river.

KEY TIP FOR THE HIGH END OF THE POT

If only one or two low cards are on board at the river, no low hand is possible, and the best high hand will win the whole pot.

When deciding how to play a high hand, you must consider that the pot is only worth half of what you might normally expect if a low possibility is on board. The dilution of the pot is something that regular high or low players often overlook, but it affects betting and playing strategy. That is why hands with the strength to go both ways are so valuable in high-low games.

If you don't connect with the flop, especially with high-only cards, drop your hand. If you do connect, make sure you are drawing to the nuts, not second best. With more betting rounds to come, you don't want to put in a lot of chips unless you have a hand that can go all the way.

TOURNAMENT POKER

Tournaments are a great way to have fun and, hopefully, win lots of money. You can enter a tournament for as little as $10 or as much as $50,000 in the big events.

Tournament games are quite different from cash games. In cash games, you're not worried about blinds because they're usually small. Nor are you concerned with antes because there aren't any. Your goal in a cash game is simply to win chips. You don't care whether you have more or less chips than other players: You just want to finish playing with more of them than you started with to end up winning money. When you have a good session and win lots of chips, you can take them off the table and leave any time you want.

In contrast, tournaments are set up as a process of elimination. As players lose their chips, the remaining competitors are consolidated into fewer tables. Eventually, only one table of players remains in action—the **final table**. The final table is where the prestige and big money is earned. Those last players will compete until one player holds all the chips—the **champion**.

Tournaments are divided into **levels** or **rounds**. Each level is marked by an increase in the blinds. After a few levels, antes are required in no-limit hold'em events, putting more pressure on players to either make moves or lose their chips to inactivity. Tournament levels may be as short as fifteen minutes in low buy-in events that are designed to be completed in as little as a few hours. Or a level may last for as long as ninety minutes to two hours in major events requiring several days to complete.

There are two types of tournaments—freeze-outs and rebuy tournaments. A **freeze-out tournament** is a do-or-die event: Once you run out of chips, you are eliminated. In a **rebuy tournament**, you can purchase additional chips during the first few rounds of play. After that, your tournament is over when you lose all your chips.

TOURNAMENT PRIZE POOL

Most tournaments are set up so that approximately 10 to 15% of the field (and sometimes 20%) will win cash prizes. The tournament's organizers decide in advance the number of places that will be paid; that is, the percentage of players who will finish **in the money**. For example, if the size of the starting field is 300, the organizers might limit the cash payouts to the top 10%. Often, the payout will be rounded down to the number of full tables remaining so that, if a 300-person tournament is played nine-handed, the event may pay the last three tables (twenty-seven players).

The worst feeling you can have in a tournament is getting eliminated on the **bubble**—that is, being the last player eliminated before the money payouts begin. If you're player number twenty-eight in the example above, you're the **bubble boy** (or girl) and are very unhappy going home empty when every other player remaining wins money.

The payouts are usually posted soon after the tournament begins, as soon as the organizers add up the total number of entrants and figure out the amount that will be paid to each money-winner.

If the tournament's structure will affect your decision to play, you can ask the tournament director how many players he expects—this will give you a good estimate of the size of the prize pool. Once the tournament begins, most players simply wait until the prize-pool announcement is made or is posted on television monitors that are typically placed in an easily visible location, to see how the various finishes will be paid. The monitors will usually list the total number of entrants, the number of places paid, and the amount of money each finisher will win.

You can determine if the event is right for you by the entry fee and the potential prize pool. The greater the number of players, the bigger the prize pool. When the tournament is large, such as the $10,000 buy-in events, the prize pool often gets into the millions. These tournaments draw the top players you see on television, along with amateurs trying their hand at winning the big money.

STARTING CHIP COUNTS

The tournament director determines your starting tournament chip total in advance. In low-limit events, a $30 buy-in might give you $500 in starting chips, though the tournament director could just as easily give you $200 or $1,000. In high-limit events, you typically receive the same number of chips as the amount of the buy-in, though lately, it is more in vogue to give players two or three times the buy-in amount in chips, to give players more play.

For example, in World Series of Poker preliminary events that cost $1,000, players get $3,000 in chips. In the no-limit hold'em Main Event at the WSOP, players get $30,000 in starting chips for their $10,000 buy-in.

Of course, whether you receive $200 in chips, $1,000 in chips, or $10,000 in chips, you begin on a level playing field with your competitors because in a tournament, everyone starts with the same amount of chips.

TOURNAMENT CHIPS

Unlike a cash game, where chips are the exact equivalent of money, tournament chips have no cash value. They may just as well be Monopoly money, because no one is going to give you anything for them outside the tournament. Thus, if you have accumulated $150,000 in chips and try to cash them out, all you'll get from the casino is a strange look and an explanation that your tournament chips have no intrinsic value outside the tournament.

TOURNAMENT STRATEGY

YOUR CHIP STACK

To be a winner in no-limit hold'em tournaments, you must understand the concept that every professional player intuitively knows: It is not how you play your cards, but *how you play your chips*, that matters. The number of chips you have relative to the size of the big blind and how many chips your opponents have are factors in every decision you make. When you're short on chips, you are under greater pressure to make moves to stay alive—and your opponents are aware of this. But when you're awash in chips, you can exert greater pressure on opponents who want to stay out of confrontations with you that can take them out of the tournament. You have the luxury of being patient and choosing the spots that best suit your situation. A few rounds of attrition from the blinds and antes won't make a serious dent in your stack.

Ideally, you would like your stack of chips to be at least twenty-five times the size of the big blind. This is your **minimum ideal stack size**. You have enough chips to play pressure-free poker without worrying too much about getting blinded out. Sometimes your chips get low and put you in the pressure cooker on the stove. Or worse, your chip stack might get so low that you slip into a critical situation. Other times, you'll have a big stack with the advantage of leverage against smaller stacks just trying to survive.

KEY TOURNAMENT CONCEPT

It is not how you play your cards, but how you play your chips!

PLAYING SHORT STACKS

If you have less than ten times the size of the big blind in your tournament stack, you have a **short stack** and must play more aggressively to build your stack. You don't have the luxury of waiting for good cards forever. By doing nothing except folding, every set of deals around the table costs you the equivalent of about two big blind bets. If your starting stack is only the size of ten big blinds, you will be reduced to about eight big blinds after one round of play; and after two rounds, your stack will be cut almost in half to about six big blinds.

Beginners with short stacks make the mistake of limping in pots or calling all-in bets with inferior hands. As a low stack, you want to make the big move first to put the decision to your opponents. Limping in with a third of your chips allows opponents to call with hands they may have folded against a bigger bet. Make the big move when you have to make it—it's your only chance of surviving. And by moving in with all your chips, you maintain enough leverage to give opponents pause in considering whether to call your hand.

PLAYING WITH AN EMERGENCY SHORT STACK

When your chip count is five times the size of the big blind or less—what I call an **emergency short stack**—you're in trouble. You must be ready to pounce with all your power at your first decent opportunity. You have to **pick up the blinds** (win the blinds) and antes to stay alive. It's your food for survival. To give yourself the best chance of getting those chips, you need to use all the leverage you have available. You cannot afford to play passive in this situation—calling is not an option, nor is a standard raise. The all-in bet is your only move.

If the pot has not been raised and you are dealt any pair, ace-anything, or any two cards 10 or higher, push in all your chips and hope for the best. Quite often you'll get no callers, and the blinds and antes that you win will give you enough fuel for another round of play.

If you have to, you'll make your move with any two cards. Keep this in mind: If you have 7-2 and go head-to-head against an opponent with an A-K, you're only about a 2 to 1 underdog—which is not too bad—so you always have a chance to survive.

PLAYING AVERAGE STACKS

Having an **average stack**—about equal to the average amount of chips held by all players—means that you're right in the center of things. You have enough chips to be patient and wait for good opportunities. In other words, you can play your best poker without excess pressure. Just like the big stacks, you want to avoid major confrontations against other average stacks or big stacks unless you think you have the best hand. Good players with chips will avoid confrontations with you as well, so there may be opportunities to bluff. But don't lose chips to foolish moves.

Smaller stacks are your targets. Push them around and win chips from them. If bigger stacks play passively, don't be afraid to exert pressure on them as well. Look for chips wherever you can get them, and from any player who will give them to you.

PLAYING BIG STACKS

Having a **big stack** means that you have more than double the average amount of chips in play. You have a major advantage as a big stack. You can afford to lose big pots and still have enough chips to play, particularly against small stacks. This doesn't mean that you want to risk losing big pots—which can come as a result of a huge mistake or from a bad beat that can't be avoided—only that you can afford a bad break and still stay alive. Having that kind of clout is a luxury that smaller stacks do not enjoy.

As a big stack, you can pressure players trying to stay alive by betting aggressively, especially against those who are playing scared or are short-stacked. You want to avoid other big stacks unless you think you have the best hand. This strategy applies to average stacks as well, because a big confrontation with an average stack can elevate him to a big stack and demote you to an average one or smaller.

Players fear big stacks, especially aggressive big stacks that are willing to push chips into the middle. When you sense weakness in an opponent, pounce on it. Stealing blinds, betting aggressively on the flop, and reraising are very effective weapons. However, do not foolishly throw away chips just because you have a lot of them. Continue playing the way you played to win your big stack to maintain and increase your position. A big stack has leverage, but use that leverage wisely.

STACK SIZES		
CHIP STACK	**STACK SIZE**	**STRATEGY**
EMERGENCY SHORT STACK	5 times big blind	All-in first good situation
SHORT STACK	10 times big blind	All-in is only bet
MEDIUM (AVERAGE) STACK	Average chip stack	Play to style
MINIMUM IDEAL STACK	25 times big blind	Play to style
LARGE STACK	2 times average stack	Step up aggression. Find opponents who play scared and pound them

THE FOUR STAGES OF A TOURNAMENT

EARLY ROUND TOURNAMENT STRATEGY

In the first few rounds of a no-limit hold'em tournament, the **early rounds**, the blinds are generally small, and the antes won't kick in until the third or fourth level. During these early rounds, there is little pressure on you to make any moves as paying the blinds won't make too much of a dent in your stack, at least not a critical dent. Your strategy is to play conservatively, trying to win little pots when possible and avoiding big pots unless you're reasonably convinced that you have the winner. You don't want to risk your tournament on a foolish bluff.

Your goal is to increase your chips stack as the tournament progresses, hopefully doubling up after three rounds.

MIDDLE ROUND TOURNAMENT STRATEGY

The **middle rounds** of a tournament, around levels four to eight, is when players start getting eliminated at a more rapid pace. The blinds and antes are more expensive, which means that you have to play more hands and take more chances.

If you're low-stacked, aggressive play and stealing blinds becomes more important to keep up with the costs of feeding blinds and antes into the pot. If you're big-stacked, you want to push around the weak players and small stacks and get more chips. You're looking to position yourself for the final table.

LATE ROUND TOURNAMENT STRATEGY

If you've lasted into the **late rounds**, you've either made it into the money or are getting very close. Now you look forward, hoping to get to the final table and the bigger money. You want to pick up your game and play your best poker. Avoid facing off in big pots or all-in bets against stacks that can take you out unless you've got the goods. But, as in all tournaments, keep pushing your weight around against players that can be bullied.

FINAL TABLE

If you get to the final table, you have a real shot at winning, but you still have to get through the last players. If you're among the big stacks, avoid going to war against another big stack that can bust you or demote you to one of the small stacks. Use your big stack to put pressure on smaller stacks struggling to stay alive.

If you're low-stacked, the blinds and antes are exerting tremendous pressure, leaving you with little choice but to find your best opportunity and then go after it for all your chips. Calling is not an option.

Think before you make your moves, keeping in mind that every player eliminated means a big jump in prize money.

ONLINE POKER

Playing poker on the Internet has become hugely popular. Millions of players from around the world are competing daily against one another on hundreds of sites. With a few clicks of your mouse, you can get in on the action too.

It's easy to get started playing online. Begin by choosing a site and going to its homepage. From there, the instructions will guide you through all the basics: how to set up a unique account and password, how to play for free, and how to deposit funds into your account so that you can play for real money.

Online poker offers some advantages. Let's take a look and see what they are.

SEVEN ADVANTAGES OF PLAYING ONLINE POKER

1. **It's Convenient**
   At any time of the day or night, all you have to do is log on to your poker site of choice, and off you go. You're playing! There is nothing easier than that. It doesn't matter what you are wearing—or not wearing—or how you look. You don't have to travel to a cardroom and search for the right game. With thousands of players online at any time, a game with the stakes you want to play is always waiting for you.
2. **It's Good Social Fun**
   Poker fires up that competitive spirit, and is a great social outlet as well. You may not be able to see your opponents live, but that won't stop you from being able to communicate with them. Just as in a live game, you can interact with your tablemates. The chat windows in online sites allow you to type messages back and forth to other players.
3. **You Can Make Friends Around the World**
   Internet poker is a worldwide phenomenon: It is common to see players at your table from a variety of countries.

Many great friendships have started online. And you never know, you may soon be visiting some of your Internet poker buddies—or receiving them in your hometown.

4. **It's Great Practice**
   Online poker moves much faster than regular live games, so you get to see lots of hands and situations. You can practice skills that you can apply to your regular tournament or cash games.
5. **You Can Play for Money or Play for Free**
   You can play poker for free on almost every site. Playing with "play money" is a service that online poker rooms offer their customers to get them acclimated to the software. Or if you prefer, you can play for real money.
6. **Online Poker Can Be Profitable**
   Online players are generally much weaker than competitors you'll find in casino cash games, especially in the low-limit games, which makes online games very profitable for good players. If you're a really skilled player, it's more than a good way to make money—it's a way to make a living!
7. **Play Multiple Games**
   One of the great advantages of online poker is that you can play multiple tables simultaneously. For professional players, this is a great way to increase profits. And for players who like more action, multi-tabling definitely fits the bill!

ONLINE STRATEGY TIPS

Online players tend to play too many hands and see too many showdowns. You can profit from this tendency by playing solid, straightforward poker, extracting maximum value from your good hands and minimizing losses with your weak and marginal hands. With more players seeing the flop on average, you want to tighten up a little on the selection of hands you play.

Aggressive betting becomes even more important online, especially in no-limit hold'em. You need to limit the field to protect your premium hands. Avoid bluffing—you can't bluff players who won't fold.

Like poker played in any form and in any setting, learning how your opponents play and adjusting your strategy accordingly will bring you the most profits. Give loose opponents less credit for having strong hands; give tight opponents more credit when they are in a hand with you.

One unique feature of online poker sites is the option that players have to make an advance playing decision by using the **early-action buttons** before play reaches their position. While there are no physical tells in online poker, the frequent use of these early-action buttons can give you information about an opponents' hands. For example, if you see almost instant checks or raises when the action reaches a player, it often indicates that the player has pre-selected his action. A check probably means that he is weak, while a raise probably means that he is either strong or he has decided to bluff at the pot regardless of the action that precedes him.

The key element here is that the player decided in advance what his play was going to be, without considering how the betting might go. So, a player with garbage may select the Check/Fold button, which will fold his hand if there is a bet or check if there is not.

Also look out for players who frequently use the pre-select options and then break the pattern by taking time in a situation. That could be useful information, but at the same time, it could also be indicative that the player was busy doing something else—on the phone, checking email, or in another game. But do pay attention to the timing of an opponent's reactions, and you can pick up online tells that you can use to your advantage. And pay attention to your own tendencies as well. You're not the only one watching!

Once you get comfortable online, you may find it profitable to play two games at the same time, which will allow you to receive lots of hands and have lots of possibilities. Some action junkies (and pros), looking to maximize the number of hands they receive, may play up to twenty games simultaneously! If you are considering playing multiple games, which can get confusing, remember one key tip: Avoid playing tricky marginal hands that show little long-term profit. The concentration you need to finesse victories with these marginal hands will be difficult to maintain when you're flying back and forth between multiple games. Profits in the other games may suffer when your concentration is focused on the marginal hand.

If you're a tournament player, there are an endless number of choices, some that are for straight prize money and some that award seats to the main events in the World Series of Poker and World Poker Tour tournaments as prizes for the top finishers.

PLAYING ONLINE SAFELY

For the most part, playing online poker is safe. Many new players are concerned with being cheated by the online software. While this is possible, and I certainly cannot guarantee or vouch for the integrity of anyone else's business practices, online poker rooms would enjoy no benefit in offering games where they manipulated the software or altered the random distribution of cards. This would be foolhardy on the part of online casinos. Online rooms make their money through the rake and want nothing more than the most honest game possible. And believe me, they make so much money dealing a legitimate game that there is no possible gain they could get from cheating.

This does not mean there isn't cheating. However, it's not so much the online poker rooms you need to be wary of—it's the players. There is collusion in certain games; sometimes by multiple players working together against unaware opponents, and sometimes by an individual who acts as more than one player at a table by having multiple online identities. In either case, this is cheating. Online poker rooms would have you believe that it never happens or that their software protects against this, but the truth is that it does occur. They do their best to prevent collusion, but they have not yet perfected all the safeguards. Your best protection, as in any live face-to-face game, is to trust your instincts. If you're ever uncomfortable in a game, stop playing. Either switch tables, or if you feel uncomfortable playing on a particular site, switch to a different site.

MORE PRINCIPLES OF WINNING POKER

Following are a few more winning concepts you need to have in your arsenal of poker knowledge.

POT ODDS

Pot odds is the amount of money in the pot including what your opponent has already bet—that money is in the pot and he can't take it back—against what it will cost you to call the bet. For example, if $50 is in the pot and you need to call a bet of $10 to play, you are getting pot odds of 5 to 1. In this situation, you can win $50. The question is: Are your winning chances better than 5 to 1, which would be giving you good pot odds and make this a good bet, or worse than 5 to 1, which would be giving you bad pot odds and make this a bad bet?

Suppose $300 is in the pot and your opponent bets the size of the pot, another $300. Now there is $600 available to be won. It will cost you $300 to see the raise and have a chance to win that $600, so you are getting pot odds of 2 to 1. If you're on a flush draw or straight draw with one card to come and are figuring your hand to be about a 4 to 1 or 5 to 1 underdog, you are not getting enough of a return to make this a profitable call. But if you figure your hand has about an even-money chance of winning, you're getting good enough odds to make the call.

Here's another way to look at pot odds: Let's say that you are offered a proposition where you have to bet $20 on a coin toss but could only win a total of $1. You'd turn it down. You'd be getting incorrect odds—and how! The risk isn't worth the reward. However, if you would get $20 for every win, you'd have an even-money shot—a fair proposition. But if you could win $40 on that same flip of the coin, you'd be very happy to risk $20 to win $40. You have one chance in two of winning (1 to 1 odds)—the same as on the other two propositions—but you would be getting a 2 to 1 payoff. If you made this bet all day long, you would make a fortune, provided your host didn't wise up or run out of money.

Use pot odds to determine whether going for the pot is justified by the amount you might win. If the bet will make you money in the long run, it's a good bet. Whenever you have a hand that is favored to win, the pot odds will always be favorable.

But it is also correct to play hands even though you are not favored to win—provided there is enough of a payoff for the risk. So, when you play second-best hands, it should be because they give you good value, that is, your long-term expectation is to win money in that particular situation even though you may lose a majority of the times. If playing a hand gives you more profits than losses in the long run, you should play it. And that, in a nutshell, is what pot odds is all about.

IMPLIED ODDS

The amount currently in the pot (pot odds) is one thing; the amount that might get into the pot with further betting is another thing altogether. This concept is commonly called implied odds, though potential gain is an appropriate term as well, since the amount that might get into the pot is not implied but speculated.

By incorporating the concept of potential gain into your thinking, you increase the number of hands you might play in any form of poker but particularly in no-limit because of the large amount of chips that can be won in a pot. Whenever you play a hand, you must always consider the amount you stand to gain if you hit your cards and can induce an opponent to continue further into the hand—or he induces you, where, on that side of the coin, you need to figure out your risk! For example, in a tournament, if an opponent's stack is $5,000, you may consider that potential gain to be worth a certain amount of risk. On the other hand, if his stack is just $1,000, or if it is say $20,000, that may make a big difference in how you play your cards in a given situation.

So if a pot currently has $50 in it and you have a shot at getting $500 more by sneaking in there with a longshot hand and hitting it, it would be profitable to play more cards in the right circumstances. In other words, the cost is cheap and your hand would have a surprise value if it hit the board, giving you a chance to get lots of chips out of an opponent who couldn't accurately guess the strength of your cards—that is, in poker talk, he couldn't put you on a hand.

SEVEN PRINCIPLES OF WINNING POKER

1. **Play with players you can beat.** Don't be a patsy for players who are just too good for you.
2. **Play at stakes you can afford.** You can never go wrong playing at stakes within your means.
3. **Fold when you're beat.** Being an overall winning player has more to do with losing less when your cards are second best than it has to do with the pots you win when you have the best hand.
4. **Play with starting cards that can win.** The object of poker is to have the best hand at the showdown, which means that to win you must enter the betting with hands that have a reasonable chance of winning.
5. **Play aggressive poker.** Betting and raising often causes opponents to fold, giving you a "free" pot, or makes them more them cautious playing against you on later betting rounds or hands.
6. **Respect position.** Your position is an important consideration in whether and how to play your starting cards and how to proceed in future betting rounds. The deeper your position, the more playable a marginal hand.
7. **Vary your play.** If you're unpredictable, opponents can't get a read on you, which gives you leverage that you can turn into profits.

BLUFFING

The bluff! The beauty, romance and drama of poker lies in the **bluff**, an aggressive bet with a weaker hand that is unlikely to win if called, hoping to cause opponents to fold better hands and winning the pot by default. Bluffing is an integral part of poker and is an art that matures with experience. There are two advantages to successful bluffing. The most obvious advantage is that you can **steal pots** from better hands and win money you otherwise would not have won. The second reason is that when you are caught bluffing, you are more likely to get called on the occasions when you do have the goods, and will therefore win bigger pots.

The more you keep your opponents guessing, the better off you are. A player who is never known to bluff will win smaller pots, for when he has a strong hand, players with weak and marginal hands will not challenge him for the pot.

FIVE POINTERS ON BLUFFING

1. Avoid bluffing in low-limit games. The bluff may be too small to scare anybody out.
2. Don't bluff for small pots by making overly large bets. The small gain possible isn't worth the large risk. However, do bluff for small pots. There is money to be made by stealing blinds and unwanted pots; just keep the amount of your bluff bet within reason.
3. It's easier to bluff a good player than a weak one. Good players respect scare cards. Weak players tend to call with garbage, and almost nothing will get them out of a pot.
4. Bluffs are most effective against one player. The more players in the pot, the greater the chance that at least one player will call the bet.
5. Pick your spots carefully. Successful bluffing is a matter of proper timing and circumstance.

PARTING THOUGHTS

Poker is one of the most exciting gambling games ever invented, one that is sure to challenge you. In this section, I've given you a very brief introduction to the strategies of play. If you're interested in becoming a stronger poker player, I suggest you further your studies by reading more about the poker games you most enjoy playing.

To continue growing and improving as a poker player, you'll need to reevaluate your play at the tables on a constant basis, learning from both your mistakes and strong moves, and from the play of your opponents. Poker is a constant learning process for good players. Every hand is a challenge and every game is a classroom with gems of knowledge you can store away for future hands. Be smart, keep your eyes open, and you will become a better player every time you sit down at a poker table.

20 MONEY MANAGEMENT

FIVE KEYS TO MONEY MANAGEMENT
1. Never bet money you cannot afford to lose, either financially or emotionally.
2. Once you're a big winner, always walk away a big winner. Create a slush fund of winnings that never gets dipped into.
3. Set loss limits before you sit down to play, and never dig in deeper than you originally planned. Never hurt yourself by suffering one big loss.
4. Accept your losses, you can't always win. The practical application of this advice is not to chase losses with big bets that can turn a session into a disaster.
5. Gambling can be fun. Smart money management will keep it that way.

INTRODUCTION

To be a winner at gambling, you must not only gamble intelligently, you must also make proper use of your bankroll and keep your emotions under control. The tendency to ride a winning streak too hard in the hope of a big killing, or to bet wildly during a losing streak attempting a quick comeback, have spelled doom to many a session which otherwise may have been a good win. Wins can turn into losses, and moderate losses can turn into a nightmare.

Winning and losing streaks are a very real part of gambling. It is how you deal with the inherent ups and downs at the table that determines just how well you will fare at the tables. In this section, you will find the sage advice that every gambler should and must take to heart, because money management is a vital part of the winning formula.

You may be playing at an advantage or disadvantage to the house, but just because you're playing at an advantage doesn't mean that you'll win in the short run, and conversely, just because you're playing at a disadvantage doesn't mean that you'll lose. Anything can happen in the short run.

And that's why money management is so important. When you're winning, you have to stretch those winnings to the maximum safe level and make sure you finish a winner. And when things go the other direction, you must restrict losses to affordable amounts and protect yourself from ever getting badly hurt at the tables.

If you follow the advice in this section, you'll be following the advice of professionals and making the best use of your monetary resources. You'll always keep losses under control—and control is always a key concept in gambling—while winning sessions always end up as winning sessions.

You'll be on your way to successful gambling and when your luck falls right, you'll be a winner.

THE RISKS OF OVERBETTING

Sharp gamblers have one thing in common—they know how to manage their money. Superior playing skills alone does not make one a winning player. The concept here is self control, the ability of a player to keep the game in check and never to lose sight of the winning strategies.

OVERBETTING EXAMPLE

Let's show a simple example of how overbetting can quickly change a big winning session into a disaster. Let's say a bettor starts out with a bankroll of $250 and has been betting $5 to $20 a shot. After two hours of skillful play, he has ridden a surge of luck to $225 in winnings. Now he has $475 in front of him.

Getting greedy and caught up in the excitement of the game, the gambler now really wants to put the squeeze on, and fast. So he goes against his pre-planned strategy, if he even has one, and now goes for $50 to $100 a bet. He figures that with a little luck and a few big wins in a row, he'll be on easy street.

However, after three straight losses at $100 a pop, he gets frantic and goes for one more play at $175, pushing all his money on the wager. Make or break. Another loss.

Suddenly, a careful strategy that netted $225 metamorphosed into an, "If I can get lucky on this play, please" strategy, and the gambler is out $250!

Madness.

Here was an example of perhaps a technically skillful player losing control, betting over his head, and taking what by all rights was a tremendous winning session and finishing four bets later losing all his bankroll!

And what if the sequence had gone a little differently, with more of those big bets being won rather than lost, so that instead, the gambler sat with $500 in winnings. We all know that type of player. We also know that he wouldn't have left until the game had broken him. He would've raised his bets again and then he would have been bankrupted—or certainly the next session would have done the job.

ESSENTIAL CONCEPTS

To win, you must want to win, and want to win bad enough that you won't give that money back to the casino.

I'm going to present a very important concept. Once you have won money from a casino, that money is *yours*—it is not the casino's money.

If you have $150 in winnings in front of you, you are not playing with the casino's money. It is your money now! If you think of your winnings as the casino's money, you won't feel bad giving it back. That's a dangerous attitude. Think of the money as being in your wallet, and you won't want to hand it back. And maybe you'll walk away from the table with those winnings.

Let's move on to the most important money management concept.

MONEY MANAGEMENT'S MOST IMPORTANT CONCEPT
Never gamble money that you cannot afford to lose, either financially or emotionally.

Do not gamble with needed funds no matter how "sure" the bet seems. The possibilities of taking a loss are real, and if that loss will hurt, you're playing with fire. Don't come into town, as they say, in a $20,000 Cadillac and leave in a $100,000 Greyhound bus.

Gambling with needed funds is a foolish gamble. Gambling involves chance, and the short term possibilities of taking a loss are real, no matter how easy the game may appear or how well the odds are stacked in your favor. Unexpected things happen in gambling—that's what makes it so interesting. But if you never play over your head, you'll never suffer.

GAMBLING AS ENTERTAINMENT

Gambling is a form of entertainment. If you can't afford the possibility of losing, don't gamble at the stakes you were considering. Either play at lower levels or don't gamble at all. If the larger wagers of your gambling game make your adrenalin rush out of control, you're over your head and need to find a game with lower limits.

Don't overlook the emotional side either. If playing the game causes you undue anxiety, for whatever the reason, it ceases to be a form of entertainment—you need a break. You need to take some time away from the game, be it a coffee break or a month's rest. Playing under anxiety not only ruins the fun of the game but also adversely affects your play and can influence you to make decisions contrary to what smart strategy dictates.

Your goal in gambling is not just to win—you also need to get satisfaction out of the game. Keep that in mind and you can never go wrong.

THE NATURE OF THE GAMBLE

In any gambling pursuit where luck plays a role, fluctuations in fortune are common. It is the ability of a player to successfully deal with the ups and downs inherent in the gamble that separates the smart gamblers from the losers.

You can't always win—even when the odds favor you—and you won't always lose, even when the odds are against you. In the short run, anything can happen and usually does. But over the long run, luck evens itself out, and it is skill in the bets you make and how you play the game that will determine whether you are a winner or a loser.

Smart players bide their time, remain patient, and keep their game under control. As a result, smart players can win when the odds are in their favor.

OVERBETTING AND UNDERCAPITALIZATION

Overbetting (or being undercapitalized) can leave you vulnerable in two ways. First, a normal downward trend can wipe out a limited money supply. Second and equally important, you may feel pressured by the shortage of capital and play less powerfully than smart play dictates.

For example, psychology and bluffing play an important part in poker, but if you're undercapitalized and are playing with "scared money," your opponents will have a field day forcing you out of pots.

If the amount staked on a bet is above your head, you're playing in the wrong game. Play in a lower limit game—at levels of betting that you feel comfortable with.

KNOW WHEN TO QUIT

What often separates the winners from the losers is that when they are winning, the winners leave the table a winner; and when losing, winners restrict their losses to affordable amounts. Smart gamblers never allow themselves to get destroyed at the table.

Minimizing losses is the key. You can't always win. If you're losing, keep the losses affordable—take a break. You only want to play with a clear head.

MINIMIZING LOSSES

The key concept in minimizing losses during a bad gambling run is to set a stop-loss limit. Before sitting at the table and making your bets, you must decide on the amount of money you'll put at stake. If luck turns against you, you must restrict your losses to that amount only.

Do not go against this rule and you can never take a big beating. If things go poorly at first, take a break—simple as that.

PROTECTING YOUR WINS

Once you've accumulated a sizable win at the tables, the most important thing is to walk away a winner. There is no worse feeling than skulking away from a table after having lost all your winnings back.

The general guideline that I recommend is to put away one half to two thirds of your winnings into a "protected" area that you won't touch under any circumstances. That money is bankable, for you won't play it. Keep playing with the rest of the winnings, putting more aside as your wins accumulate. Once the streak stops and the tides of fortune go against you, you'll leave the table a guaranteed winner because you've played it smart.

For example, let's say you're up 20 units. (A **unit** is the bet size you're using as a standard and could be $1, $5, $10, $25, $100, $500 or any other value you want to assign.) Let's say that your unit-bet size is $5, so you're up $100. Put aside $50 (10 units) of your winnings into the protected zone and play the other $50 (10 units).

Set no limits on a winning streak. When you've got a hot hand, ride it for all its worth.

INCREASING BETS WHEN WINNING

If you want to risk more to win more, go for it—but in moderation. Increase your bets gradually when winning, never becoming overzealous.

For example, if your bet size is a flat $10 in a game, and your winnings are rapidly accumulating, jump up to $15, and if all goes well, move up to $20. This way if you keep winning, your wins get larger. If however, a sudden losing streak ensues, it's no problem, for you have protected yourself.

If you're playing in a game such as blackjack where you use a betting range, take a $5 to $20 range up to $10 to $30 gradually, and then slowly higher if you're still winning.

And as you gradually increase bets in your gambling game, continually sock away won bets into your "don't touch" pile, so that by the time the streak ends, you've already got plenty in the bank and can walk away a big winner.

21 THE WINNING WORD

FIVE KEYS TO WINNING
1. Prepare for the games you will be wagering on by reading the appropriate section carefully and practicing in the comfort of your home.
2. Protect your wins, limit your losses, and you're on the way to winning.
3. Make the correct strategy move on every play, all the time. Hunches and feelings are for losers. There is only one correct move for every situation and it is the winner who makes that move.
4. Never gamble with money you cannot afford to lose, either financially or emotionally.
5. Think and play like a winner.

THE WINNING WORD

Okay, this is my last chance at you in this book. I want to make you a winner. I want you to beat the casino. But to be successful at gambling, you must want to win, and like anything else, you have to work at it. Prepare for your games and play them like you want to win money. If you take your gambling money seriously, you'll find that you'll leave casinos with more of it on the good days, and leave a ton less behind on the bad ones. You'll also find more good days than bad days if you follow the advice I have given you in this book.

The winning attitude goes a long way in life and it goes a long way in gambling too. Behind the will to succeed is an approach that keeps you on the proper course. What you wish for may not occur, but by thinking right and playing right, you give it every chance. And that is all I can ask you to do.

Play smart and be smart about your money—that's the winning formula.

G GLOSSARY

BACCARAT

American-Style Baccarat

Also NEVADA-STYLE BACCARAT, PUNTO BANCO, or simply BACCARAT.

Baccarat

The gambling card game of French origin. Also, the score of zero.

Baccarat a Tout Va

Variation of baccarat where there is no maximum limit on bets.

Baccarat Banque

Variation of CHEMIN DE FER.

Banco

The BANKER position; In CHEMIN DE FER, a bet by a player covering the entire bank.

Bank

Position on table where BANKER bets are placed.

Banker

One of the two betting positions.

Banker Rules

The rules by which the banker position must draw cards or stand pat.

Burned Cards

Cards removed from play without being used.

Caller

The dealer who controls the pace and runs the game

Chemin De Fer
The European version of BACCARAT.

Cover
See FADE.

Croupier
DEALER, in French.

Dealer
Person dealing the cards; casino employee running a gambling game; *Also* CROUPIER.

Fade
In Chemin de Fer, describing the act of betting against the bank. *Also* COVER.

Le Grande
A total of 9 points.

Le Petit
A total of 8 points.

Mini Baccarat
BACCARAT which is played on a blackjack-style layout, with a capacity to seat around six to seven players.

Natural
A two-card count of 8 or 9.

Player
One of the two betting positions. *Also* PUNTO. Any bettor wagering in a game.

Player Rules
The rules by which the player position must draw cards or stand pat.

Punto
The PLAYER position.

Punto Banco
In Europe and other international locations, the name for the standard form of baccarat.

Scorecard
See TALLY SHEET.

Shill
Casino employee hired to sit at a game and make it look busy.

Tally Sheet
Sheet of paper used to record wins by either the BANKER or PLAYER position, and other data from a game. *Also* SCORECARD, TABLE DE BANQUE CARD.

Tie Bet
A wager that the player and banker will tie; pays off at 9 for 1 (8 to 1) giving the casino an edge of 14.10%.

BINGO

Bingo
The winning cry; the name of the game.

Bingo Card
The playing card containing the numbers needed to win. *Also* CARD.

Blackout Bingo
Bingo combination where all numbers are covered. *Also* COVERALL BINGO.

Blower
The compressed air apparatus used to circulate the ping pong balls.

Cage
Hand operated wire enclosure used to manually mix the bingo balls.

Called Numbers
Numbers which are drawn at a bingo game.

Caller
The bingo official who draws the balls and calls the results.

Card
See BINGO CARD.

Checker
Bingo official whose job it is to verify winning bingo tickets.

Coverall Bingo
See BLACKOUT BINGO.

Covered Square

See FREE SPACE.

Diagonal Bingo

A bingo formed by five numbers formed in a diagonal line, which includes the middle "free" square.

Dobber

A pre-inked marker used to mark numbers on a keno card.

Double Bingo

A bingo requiring two patterns to win.

Early Bird

Games played before the regular session begins.

Fingertip Card

Plastic or metal bingo card where called numbers can be tracked by closing the shutters.

Four Corners Bingo

A winning bingo ticket requiring all four corners to be caught.

Free Space

The middle square in the bingo card (in the middle of the N column), which is automatically counted as a hit for the player. *Also* COVERED SQUARE.

Hard Card

A reusable, more solid type of bingo card.

Horizontal Bingo

A bingo formed by five numbers in a straight horizontal line.

Indian Bingo

Refers to bingo on the American Indian reservations.

Late Bird

Bingo games played after the regular session.

Layer Cake

A bingo requiring all the numbers in the first, third and fifth horizontal rows to be hit.

Masterboard
The rack where played bingo balls are placed after being drawn. *Also* RACK.

Picture Frame
A bingo requiring all the outside numbers, making a picture frame, to win.

Powerball
An extra bingo bet on a number that, if it makes the bingo, wins a big prize.

Rack
See MASTERBOARD.

Six-Pack
A set of six bingo cards.

Sleeper
Player who suddenly realizes he had a bingo on a previous number called.

Soft Card
Disposable paper cards used in bingo.

Superjackpot
You'll know what this means if you ever hit one.

Vertical Bingo
A bingo formed by five numbers in a straight vertical line.

Wire Cage
The cylindrical wire apparatus used to randomly mix bingo balls.

BLACKJACK/SPANISH 21

Anchorman
See THIRD BASE.

Barring a Player
The exclusion of a player from the gaming tables.

Basic Strategy
The optimal playing strategy for a particular set of rules and number of decks used, assuming the player has knowledge of only his own two cards and the dealer's upcard.

Blackjack
An original two-card holding consisting of an ace and ten-value card; the name of the game. *Also* NATURAL, 21.

Bonus Hand
A hand that awards players extra payouts for making specified card combinations.

Bonus Options
In Spanish 21, options that allow players to increase their bet, generally in favorable situations.

Break
See BUST.

Burn Card
A card, usually from the top of the deck, that is removed from play. The top card is traditionally burned after a fresh shuffle and before the cards are dealt.

Bust
Also BREAK. To exceed the total of 21, a loser.

Card Counter
A player that keeps tracks of cards already played and adjusts his strategies to take advantage of the depleted deck.

Card Counting
A method of keeping track of the cards already played so that knowledge of the remaining cards can be used to adjust strategies. A player that counts cards is called a CARD COUNTER.

Composition Change
A situation where, as cards are removed from the deck, the normal proportion of certain cards to other groups of cards change.

Composition of the Deck
A term used to describe the particular makeup of cards remaining in the deck.

Conceptual Strategy
The thinking process and reasoning involved in making correct strategy decisions.

Dealer
The casino employee who deals the cards, makes the proper payoffs to winning hands and collects lost bets.

Double, Double Down
A player option to double the original bet after seeing his original two cards. If the player chooses this option, one additional card will be dealt.

Doubling after Splitting
Option offered in only some United States and international casinos, whereby players are allowed to double down after splitting a pair (according to normal doubling rules).

Downcard
A card that is dealt with its rank and suit value facing the felt and can only be viewed by the player holding it—as opposed to UPCARD.

Draw
See HIT.

Early Surrender
An option to forfeit a hand and lose half the bet before the dealer checks for a blackjack—as opposed to SURRENDER (LATE SURRENDER).

Even Money
A bet that pays $1 for every $1 wagered.

Exposed Card
See UPCARD.

Eye in the Sky
Refers to the mirrors above the gaming tables where the games are constantly supervised to protect both the player and the house from being cheated.

Face Card
A jack, queen or king. *Also* PAINT.

First Base
Seat closest to the dealer's left. The first baseman acts upon his hand first.

Five Card 21
In Spanish 21, a player's seven-card hand which is less than or equal to 21 points.

Flat Bet
To bet the same amount on every hand—no bet variation.

Floorman
A casino supervisor.

Hard Total
A hand without an ace or if containing an ace, where the ace counts as only 1 point (10, 6, A).

Head-to-Head
Playing alone against the dealer.

High Roller
A player that wagers big money.

Hit
The act of drawing (requesting) a card from the dealer. *Also* DRAW.

Hole Card
The dealer's unexposed DOWNCARD.

House
A term to denote the casino.

Insurance
A side bet that can be made when the dealer shows an ace. The player wagers up to half his original bet and gets paid 2 to 1 on that bet if the dealer shows a blackjack. If the dealer does not have a blackjack, the insurance bet is lost.

Late Surrender
See SURRENDER.

Multiple Deck Game
Blackjack played with two or more decks of cards, usually referring to a 2-, 4-, 6-, or 8-deck game.

Natural

See BLACKJACK.

Nickels

$5 chips, usually red in color.

No-Hole-Card Rule

A blackjack procedure where the dealer takes his second card after all the players have acted upon their hands or, in some cases, where the dealer gives himself the card, but does not check a 10 or ace for blackjack until after the bettors have finished playing their hands. On hands that are doubled or split, the additional bet will be lost if the dealer has a blackjack.

Paint

See FACE CARD.

Pat Card

A dealer upcard of 7 through ace, which tends to give the dealer pat hands.

Pat Hand

A hand totaling 17-21.

Pit Boss

Casino employee who supervises play at the tables.

Push

A tie between the dealer and the player.

Quarters

$25 chips, usually green in color.

Seven Card 21

In Spanish 21, a player's seven-card hand which is less than or equal to 21 points.

Shoe

An oblong box used to hold multiple decks of cards for dealing.

Shuffle

The mixing of cards by a dealer prior to a fresh round of play.

Silver

$1 tokens or dollar chips.

Single Deck Game
Blackjack played from a single pack of cards.

Six Card 21
In Spanish 21, a player's six-card hand which is less than or equal to 21 points.

Soft Hands, Soft Total
Hand in which the ace counts as 11 points.

Split, Splitting Pairs
A player option to split two cards of identical value so that two separate hands are formed. A bet equal to the original wager is placed next to the second hand.

Stand, Stand Pat
To not draw additional cards—staying with the original two cards dealt.

Standees
Players who are not occupying a seat and betting spot at the table, but are allowed to place bets in the boxes of players already seated.

Stiff Card
A dealer upcard of 2 through 6, giving the dealer a high busting potential.

Stiff Hand
A hand totaling hard 12, 13, 14, 15, or 16; can be busted if hit.

Super Bonus
In Spanish 21, an extra bonus for a hand which contains three sevens, all of the same suit.

Surrender
A player option to forfeit his original hand and lose half the bet after it has been determined that the dealer does not have a blackjack—as opposed to EARLY SURRENDER. *Also* LATE SURRENDER

Table Bankroll
The amount of money needed or recommended for a single session of gambling.

Ten Factor
Refers to the concentration of tens in the deck.

Ten-Value Card

A 10, jack, queen, or king.

Third Base

Position closest to the dealer's right. The third baseman makes the last play before the dealer's turn. *Also* ANCHORMAN.

Three 7s

In Spanish 21, a bonus given for a player's hand whose three cards are all sevens.

Toke, Tip

A gratuity either given or bet for the dealer.

21

See BLACKJACK.

Unit

Bet size used as a standard of measurement.

Upcard

A card that is dealt with its rank and suit value facing up and can be viewed by all participants in the game—as opposed to DOWNCARD.

CARIBBEAN STUD POKER

Ace-King

A hand containing both an ace and a king, but no higher combinations such as a pair or straight. This is the weakest hand that qualifies as a dealer hand.

Ante Bet

The initial bet made before the cards are dealt. Also, the area where the bet is placed.

Bet

An area on the layout where the CALL bet is placed.

Bonus Bet

An optional $1 bet that can be made by players.

Bonus Payout

A winning combination.

Call

To make an additional wager two times the size of the ante bet, after the cards are dealt.

Drop Slot

Place where players can make the $1 BONUS BET.

First Base

Seat closest to the dealer's left. The first baseman acts upon his hand first.

Flush

Five cards of the same suit.

Fold

To give up one's cards and forfeit the ante bet.

Four of a Kind

Four cards of identical rank, plus an odd card.

Full House

Three cards of identical rank plus two cards of a different identical rank.

Maximum Bonus Payout

The most the casino will pay in total for a big winning combination, even if the stated payout is higher.

Non-Qualifying Hand

A dealer's hand that does not contain at least an ace and a king, or higher combination.

One Pair

One pair of identically valued cards along with three unmatched cards is called a pair.

Progressive Bet

A $1 wager that makes the bettor eligible for a PROGRESSIVE JACKPOT.

Progressive Jackpot

A winning pool of money that gets progressively higher every time a progressive $1 bet is made until a royal flush is drawn, whereupon the progressive jackpot will return to a stated level and begin accumulating anew.

Qualifying Hand
A dealer's hand containing at least an ace and a king, or higher combination.

Royal Flush
An A-K-Q-J-10, all of the same suit.

Straight
Five cards in sequential order, such as 10-9-8-7-6, containing at least two suits.

Straight Flush
Five cards of the same suit in numerical sequence, such as the J-10-9-8-7 of clubs.

Third Base
Position closest to the dealer's right. The third baseman makes the last play before the dealer's turn.

Three of a Kind
Three cards of identical rank along with two unmatched cards.

Two Pair
Two sets of equivalently valued or "paired" cards, along with an unmatched card.

Upcard
The dealer's face up (exposed) card.

CHO DAI DI

Bo Do
An announcement that a player has one card left in his hand.

Controlling Card
The highest-ranking card remaining.

Dai
The Cantonese equivalent of PASS.

Flush
Any five cards of the same suit, such as five hearts.

Four of a Kind
Four cards of equal value, such as K-K-K-K.

Full House
THREE OF A KIND and a PAIR together.

High Card
The high card in Cho Dai Di is the 2, followed by the A, K, Q, J, 10, 9, 8, 7, 6, 5, 4 and then the 3, which is the weakest card.

One Pair
See PAIR.

Pair
Two cards of identical value, such as 4-4 or K-K.

Pass
To not be able to lay down cards when it is a player's turn, or elect not to, and cede the option of playing to the next player in turn. The Cantonese word for this is "DAI."

Royal Flush
10-J-Q-K-A, all in the same suit.

Straight
Five cards in numerical sequence, such as 3-4-5-6-7 or A-2-3-4-5.

Straight Flush
A STRAIGHT all in the same suit, such as 7♠ 8♠ 9♠ 10♠ J♠.

Three of a Kind
Three cards of equal value, such as 9-9-9. The higher raking three of a kind is 2-2-2, the lowest 3-3-3.

CRAPS

Any Craps
A bet that the following roll will be a 2, 3, or 12.

Any Seven
A bet that the following roll will be a 7.

Back Line
Refers to the DON'T PASS area.

GLOSSARY

Bar the 12

A term found in the DON'T PASS and DON'T COME areas which makes the roll of a 12 (in some casinos the 2) a tie.

Big 6 & Big 8

A bet that the 6, or the 8, whichever is bet on, will be thrown before a 7 is rolled.

Boxman

Casino executive who supervises the craps table from a seat between the two standing dealers.

Buy Bets

A player option to buy a point number and get paid at the correct odds. However, a 5% commission must be paid to buy the number.

Call Bet

A verbal bet that a wager is working. Disallowed in many casinos by the indication "No Call Bets" on the layout.

Center Bets

See PROPOSITION BETS.

Come Bet

A bet that the dice will win, or PASS. Works just like a PASS BET except that it can only be made after a point is established.

Come-Out Roll

The roll made before any point has been established.

Coming Out

A term to designate that a new come-out roll is about to happen.

Correct Odds

The mathematical likelihood that a bet will be a winner, expressed in odds.

Crap Out

The roll of a 2, 3, or 12 on a come-out roll, an automatic loser for pass line bettors.

Craps

Term used to denote a 2, 3, or 12. Also the name of the game.

Craps-Eleven

A one roll bet combining the ANY CRAPS and 11.

Dealer

The casino employee who works directly with the players and who handles all monetary transactions and bets.

Dollar

A $100 chip.

Don't Come Bet

A bet made against the dice. The bet works just like the DON'T PASS except that it can only be made after a point is established.

Don't Pass

A bet made on the COME-OUT ROLL only, that the dice will lose.

Double Odds Bet

A FREE-ODDS BET that allows the player to bet double his line wager as a right bettor, and double the line payoff as a WRONG BETTOR.

Easy, Easy Way

The throw of a 4, 6, 8, or 10 other than as a pair, such as 1-5, *6 the easy way.*

Even-Money

The payoff of $1 for every $1 bet.

Field Bet

A one-roll bet that the next roll will be a number in the FIELD box 2, 3, 4, 9, 10, 11, or 12.

Free-Odds Bets

Also ODDS BET. A bet made in conjunction with the line, come and don't come bets, which is made after the establishment of a point. The house has no advantage on these wagers.

Front Line

See PASS LINE.

Hardway

The throw of a 4, 6, 8, or 10 as a pair, such as 3-3; *6 the hardway.*

Hardway Bet

A sequence bet that the HARDWAY number, the 4, 6, 8, or 10, will come up in doubles before it comes up *easy*, or before a 7 is thrown.

Hop Bet
A bet that the next roll will be a specific combination. Usually not found on the layout.

Horn
The numbers 2, 3, 11 and 12 on the layout.

Horn Bet
A one-roll bet that the next throw will be a 2, 3, 11, or 12.

Horn High Bet
A five-chip wager that the next roll of the dice will hit one of the HORN numbers—2, 3, 11, or 12.

Inside Numbers
The PLACE numbers 5, 6, 8, 9.

Lay Bet
A wager made by wrong bettors that a 7 will show before the POINT is thrown.

Lay Odds
To put more money on a bet than will be won. For example betting $12 to win $10.

Line Bet
A pass or don't pass bet.

Marker Buck
Round disk used to mark either the point or to indicate that no point is yet established. *Also* PUCK, or MARKER PUCK.

Nickels
$5 chips.

Odds Bet
See FREE-ODDS BET.

Off
A designation that a bet is not working on a particular roll.

On
A designation that a bet is working on a particular roll.

One Roll Bet
A bet whose outcome is determined on the very next throw of the dice.

Outside Numbers
The numbers 4, 5, 9, and 10.

Pass
A successful roll for PASS-LINE bettors.

Pass Line
A bet made on the come-out roll only, that the dice will PASS, or win. *Also* FRONT LINE.

Payoff, House Payoff
The amount of money the casino pays players on a winning bet.

Pit
A central area formed in the middle of a group of craps tables.

Pit Boss
A casino supervisor.

Place Bet
A wager that a particular number, the 4, 5, 6, 8, 9, or 10, will be rolled before a 7.

Point, Point Number
The throw of a 4, 5, 6, 8, 9, or 10 on the come-out roll becomes the point.

Proposition Bets
The bets located in the center of the layout. *Also* CENTER BETS.

Puck
See MARKER BUCK.

Quarter
A $25 chip.

Right Bettors
Players betting that the dice will PASS—PASS and COME BETTORS.

Sequence Bet
A bet whose outcome may take a succession of rolls to be determined.

Seven-Out

The roll of a 7 after a point has been established, a loser for PASS LINE bettors.

Shoot

A progression of rolls ending in either an immediate decision on the COME-OUT ROLL, or the SEVENING-OUT after a point had been established.

Shooter

The player throwing the dice.

Silver

A $1 chip.

Single Odds

A FREE-ODDS BET that allows the player to bet equal to his line wager as a RIGHT BETTOR, and equal the payoff as a WRONG BETTOR.

Stickman

Casino employee who controls the dice with a hooked stick, calls the game and controls the PROPOSITION BET area.

Toke, Tip

A gratuity given or bet for the dealer.

Unit

Bet size used as a standard of measurement.

Working

Designation that a bet is on or in play.

Wrong Bettors

Players betting that the dice DON'T PASS. DON'T PASS and DON'T COME bettors.

Yo-Leven

Slang term for the roll of an 11.

HORSERACING

Allowance Race

A type of horse race where the horses are assigned weight allowances to help equalize the various contestants.

Being in the Money
A horse that comes in first, second or third.

Breakage
The odd pennies kept by the track on bets when they round down to the nearest ten cents.

Claimed
A horse purchased in a CLAIMING RACE.

Claiming Price
The price at which a horse can be bought in a CLAIMING RACE.

Claiming Race
A type of horse race where the horses entered may be purchased by anyone for the price listed.

Class
The quality of a race a horse has competed in as judged by the level or CLAIMING PRICE of the race, the importance of the race, or the stakes involved.

Class Handicapping
To HANDICAP a race based mostly on a horse's class.

Daily Double
A bet on the winners of both the first and second races.

Exacta
A bet that the two horses chosen in a race come in first and second, in exact order.

Favorite
The horse considered most likely to win a race.

Form Handicapping
To HANDICAP a race based on how the horse has performed in the last few races.

Handicap
To figure the likelihood and odds of a horse's perceived chances of winning a race.

Handicap Race
A type of horse race ran by near top-level horses.

Longshot
A horse that is considered a big UNDERDOG to win.

Maiden Race
A type of horse race where no animal has yet won a race.

Morning line
The initial line at which the odds on the horses are set.

Pace Handicapping
To HANDICAP a race based on how well a horse paces itself during previous races.

Pari-Mutuel Pool
The total amount of money bet, less the management fees and government taxes, which is available for the winners to collect.

Pick Nine
A bet on the winner of nine races.

Pick Six
A bet on the winner of six races.

Place Bet
A wager that a horse will come in first or second

Post Position
The rail position from which horses begin a race.

Quinella
A bet that the two horses chosen in a race come in first and second, in either order.

Second Choice
The horse considered to be the second most likely to win a race.

Show Bet
A wager that a horse will come in first, second or third.

Speed Handicapping
To HANDICAP a race based on the speed with which the horse has run its previous races, adjusted for different conditions and factors.

Stakes Races
The top level of horse races, which include races such as the Preakness, Kentucky Derby and Belmont Stakes.

Straight Bet
Making any of the WIN, PLACE and SHOW bets.

Takeout
The amount deducted from the prize pool for state and local taxes, purse money, expenses at the track, and the track's profit.

Third Choice
The horse considered to be the third most likely to win a race.

Totalizer
See TOTE BOARD.

Tote Board
The big computerized board at the track that displays the amount of money bet on each horse to WIN, PLACE and SHOW, plus the odds. *Also* TOTALIZER.

Trip Handicapping
To HANDICAP a race based on track mishaps that caused an otherwise strong contender to perhaps finish worse than it should have in its previous races.

Triple
A bet on the winners of the three consecutive races designated by the track.

Weight Allowance
The weight assigned to horses to help equalize them in ALLOWANCE RACES.

Win Bet
A wager that a horse will finish first in the race.

KENO

Aggregate Limit
The total amount the casino will pay to all winners on a jackpot.

Basic Ticket
See STRAIGHT TICKET.

Caller
Casino employee who calls each number as it's drawn

GLOSSARY

Catch

To match one or more numbers on a ticket with those drawn.

Combination Ticket

A ticket combining groups of numbers to form two or more winning possibilities.

Draw

The random drawing of 20 numbers in a game.

Draw Ticket

See PUNCH-OUTS.

Duplicate Ticket

The ticket marked in dark ink by the keno writer reflecting the numbers bet and returned to the player.

Inside Ticket

See ORIGINAL TICKET.

Keno Balls

The 80 numbered balls, 1-80, of which 20 are randomly drawn in a keno game.

Keno Board

The lit board that indicates the 20 numbers drawn in a game.

Keno Lounge

The area set aside for keno in a casino.

Keno Runner

A casino employee who roams the casino area outside the keno lounge and take bets on keno games.

Keno Writer

The employee who processes keno bets and issues DUPLICATES. *Also* WRITER.

King Ticket

A combination type ticket using the KING NUMBER. *Also* TICKET.

King, King Number

The roaming number on a KING TICKET which is combined with other groups or kings to make combinations in a game.

Master Ticket
See ORIGINAL TICKET.

Multi-Game Ticket
A ticket recorded once and played unchanged for one or more games.

Original Ticket
The original ticket filled out by the player and held by the casino. *Also* INSIDE TICKET and MASTER TICKET.

Punch-Outs
Special ticket with holes punched-out reflecting the 20 drawn numbers in a game. *Also* DRAW TICKET.

Quick Pick Game
An option to have the computer automatically pick the numbers of a keno ticket.

Rate Card
The booklet issued by a casino showing the bets and their payoffs.

Special Tickets
Tickets with different prices and payoffs from those on the rate card.

Split Ticket
A combination-type ticket with two or more groups of numbers.

Spots
The marked numbers on a ticket.

Straight Ticket
A ticket where 1-15 spots are selected without combinations. *Also* BASIC TICKET.

Ticket
See KENO TICKET.

Video Keno
Keno played on a slot-like machine.

Way Ticket
A combination-type ticket with at least three different groups of equal numbers.

Writer
See KENO WRITER.

LET IT RIDE

Bonus Bet

A separate $1 bet made before the cards are dealt, where players qualify for payouts based on the strength of their hand.

$

The betting circle where the player makes a bet that cannot be withdrawn—unlike the other two betting circles, "1" and "2."

Flush

Five cards of the same suit.

Four of a Kind

Four cards of identical rank plus an odd card.

Fourth Card Playing Strategy

The playing strategy used after the first community card is revealed.

Full House

Three cards of identical rank plus two cards of a different identical rank.

1

The betting circle where a player chooses, after the first three cards are dealt, whether to let his bet ride or withdraw it.

One Pair

One pair of identically valued cards along with three unmatched cards.

Royal Flush

An A-K-Q-J-10, all of the same suit.

Showdown

After the dealer turns over the second and final community card, when all bets are settled.

Straight

Five cards in sequential order, such as 10-9-8-7-6, containing at least two suits.

Straight Flush

Five cards of the same suit in numerical sequence, such as the J-10-9-8-7 of clubs.

Tens or Better
Referring to two tens or a higher-ranking hand that is required to win a payout in Let it Ride.

Third Base
Position closest to the dealer's right. The third baseman makes the last play before the dealer's turn.

Third Card Betting Strategy
The playing strategy used after the player sees his three-card hand.

Three of a Kind
Three cards of identical rank along with two unmatched cards.

2
The betting circle where a player chooses, after the first community card is revealed, whether to let his bet ride or withdraw it.

Two Pair
Two sets of equivalently valued or "paired" cards, along with an unmatched card.

POKER

Ace-to-Five
Low poker, where the ace is the lowest and best card and the king the weakest.

Act
To bet, raise, fold, or check.

Active Player
Player still in competition for the pot.

Aggressive
A player who frequently bets and raises.

All in
A bet of all one's chips.

Ante
Mandatory bet placed into the pot by all players before the cards are dealt.

GLOSSARY

Average Stack

To have about equal to the average amount of chips held by players in a tournament.

Bet

Money wagered and placed into the pot.

Big Blind

The larger of two mandatory bets made by the player two seats to the left of the BUTTON.

Big Stack

In a tournament, to have more than double the average amount of chips in play.

Blind

A mandatory bet made on the first round of betting; also, the player making that bet.

Bluff

To bet or raise with an inferior hand for the purpose of intimidating opponents into folding their cards and making the bluffer a winner by default.

Board

See COMMUNITY CARDS.

Bring-In

Forced opening bet in seven-card stud, or the amount required to open betting.

Bubble

In a tournament, to be the last player eliminated before the money payouts begin.

Button

The player occupying the dealer position; also the disk used to indicate this position.

Buy-In

A player's investment of chips in a poker game or the actual amount of cash he uses to purchase chips for play.

Call

To match an amount equal to a previous bet on a current round of betting.

Cap

Limit to the number of raises allowed in a betting round.

Cardroom Manager

The supervisor of the cardroom.

Cards Speak

A rule stating that the value of a hand is the final arbiter in a hand, not a player's call or miscall of it.

Cash Game

Poker game played for real money—as opposed to TOURNAMENT.

Check

The act of "not betting" and passing the bet option to the next player while still remaining an active player.

Check and Raise

A player's raising of a bet after already checking in that round.

Chip

Circular token used as currency in poker games.

Closed Cards

See FACE DOWN.

Community Cards

In hold'em and Omaha, the face-up cards shared by all players. *Also* board.

Completing the Bring-In

In seven-card stud, the player that enters the pot in the first round of betting must bring the opening bet up to the lower limit of the betting structure.

Counterfeit

In low poker, when a key card in a player's hand is duplicated by a second card of the same rank being dealt, rendering that card useless to the player.

Cut Card

A colored plastic card used to separate a deck into two parts and to cover the bottom card of a deck so that it is not accidentally viewed.

Dangler

In Omaha, a card that doesn't coordinate with other cards.

Dealer

The house employee responsible for shuffling and dealing the cards after each round of play and directing the action so that the game runs smoothly.

Deuce-to-Seven

Low poker, where the deuce is the best card and the ace the weakest.

Downcards

See FACE DOWN.

Draw

The exchange of cards allowed after the first round of betting in draw poker variations.

Drop Box

A container below the playing surface of the poker table where money taken out of pots as house commission are deposited.

Early Position

Approximately the first third of players to act in a 9- or 10-handed game.

Early Rounds

The first three or four levels in a tournament.

Early-Action Buttons

In online poker, the option players have to make an advance playing decision by using the action buttons available on their screen.

8-or-Better

In high-low poker, a requirement that a player must have five unpaired cards of 8 or less to win the low end of the pot.

Emergency Short Stack

To have less than five times the size of the big blind in a tournament.

Face Card

Any jack, queen, or king. *Also* PICTURE CARD.

Face Down

A card positioned such that its rank and suit faces the table and cannot be viewed by competing players. *Also* DOWNCARDS, CLOSED CARDS.

Face Up

A card positioned such that its rank and suit faces up and is therefore visible to all players. Cards dealt this way are also known as UPCARDS or OPEN CARDS.

Fifth Street

In seven-card stud, the third betting round, so named for the five cards held by each player. In hold'em and Omaha, the fifth community card and its betting round.

Final Table

The last table of players in a tournament, where the prestige and big money are earned.

Floor

See FLOORPERSON.

Floorperson

A supervisor who helps run a poker room or tournament and settle disputes. *Also* floor.

Flop

In hold'em and Omaha, the first three cards simultaneously dealt face-up for communal use by all active players.

Flush

A hand of five cards of the same suit.

Flush Draw

Four cards to the flush needing one more to complete the flush.

Fold

Get rid of one's cards, thereby becoming inactive in the current hand and ineligible to play for the pot. *Also* MUCK.

Four of a Kind

A hand containing four cards of identical value, such as K-K-K-K (four kings). *Also* QUADS.

Four-Card Flush

Four cards to a flush needing one more to fill.

Four-Card Straight

Four cards to a straight needing one more to fill.

Fourth Street

In seven-card stud, the second betting round, so named for the four cards held by each player. In hold'em and Omaha, the fourth community card and its betting round.

Freezeout Tournament

A tournament played as do or die—when a player runs out of chips, he is eliminated—as opposed to a REBUY TOURNAMENT.

Full House

A hand consisting of three of a kind and a pair, such as 7-7-7-K-K.

Hammer

In no-limit and pot-limit hold'em, a big bet or an all-in.

Hand

The cards a player holds; the best five cards a player can present.

High Poker

Poker variations in which the highest hand wins.

High-low

Poker variation in which players compete for the best high and low hands, with the winner of each getting half the pot.

Hole Cards

Cards held by a player, the value of which is hidden from other players. *Also* POCKET CARDS.

Ignorant End

The low end of the straight—as opposed to the high and stronger end.

Implied Odds

The amount that might get into the pot with further betting, compared to the cost of a bet to stay active in a hand.

In the Money

In a tournament, to finish among the top players and win cash.

Kansas City Lowball

See DEUCE-TO-SEVEN.

Kicker
The highest side card to a hand of one pair, two pair, three of a kind, or rarely, four of a kind.

Late Position
Approximately the last third of players to act in a 9- or 10-handed game.

Late Rounds
In a tournament, the rounds of action after players get into the money and work their way towards the final table.

Level
In a tournament, a fixed period of play that ends with increased blinds or antes, or both. In any poker game, one complete turn of hands around a table. *Also* ROUND.

Limit Poker
Betting structure in which the minimum and maximum bet sizes are set at fixed amounts, usually in a two-tiered structure such as $5/$10.

Loose
A player that plays well more than the average number of hands.

Low Poker
A form of poker in which the lowest hand wins.

Middle Position
Approximately the middle third of players to act in a 9- or 10-handed game.

Middle Rounds
In a tournament, after the early rounds and before the late rounds, the levels of play before players get in the money.

Muck
To FOLD.

No-Limit
Betting structure in which the maximum bet allowed is limited only by the amount of money the bettor has on the table.

Nuts
The best hand possible given the cards on board.

One Pair
Hand containing two cards of the same rank, such as Q-Q or 7-7.

Online Poker
Poker played on the Internet.

Open Cards
See FACE UP.

Overcard
In hold'em and Omaha, a hole card higher in rank than any BOARD card. For example, a jack is an overcard to a flop of 10-6-2.

Passive
A player who rarely raises.

Pick Up the Blinds
To win the blinds through aggressive play.

Picture Card
See FACE CARD.

Pocket Cards
See HOLE CARDS.

Position
A player's relative position to the player acting first in a poker round.

Pot
The sum total of all antes and bets placed in the center of the table by players during a poker hand and collected by the winner or winners of that hand.

Pot Odds
A concept which examines the cost of a bet against the money to be made winning a pot and compares that amount to a player's chances of winning that pot.

Pot-Limit
Betting structure in which the largest bet can be no more than the current size of the pot.

Preflop
The first betting round in hold'em, when each player has only his two pocket cards.

Premium Hands
The top tier of starting cards.

Quads
See FOUR OF A KIND.

Qualifier
In high-low games, a requirement that a player must have five unpaired cards of 8 or less to win the low end of the pot.

Quartered
To split one half of one half the pot in high-low games—get only 25% of the total pot.

Raise
A wager that increases the size of a current bet.

Rake
The amount of money taken out of the pot by the house as its fee for running the game.

Razz
Seven-card stud played for low only.

Rebuy Tournament
A tournament played where additional chips may be purchased during the first few rounds of play when a player's stack goes below a stated amount
as opposed to a FREEZEOUT TOURNAMENT.

Reraise
A bet equaling a previous bet and raise, plus an additional bet
a raise of a raise.

River
The last card dealt or its betting round.

Rough
In lowball, hands with relatively high (less strong) supporting cards.

Round
See LEVEL.

Royal Flush
An A-K-Q-J-10 of the same suit. The highest-ranking hand in high poker.

Scoop
In a high-low game, to win both the high and low ends of a pot.

Set
In hold'em and Omaha, a three of a kind formed by a pocket pair with a third card of the same rank on board.

Seventh Street
In seven-card stud, the fifth betting round, so named for the six cards held by each player.

Short Stack
To have less than ten times the size of the big blind in a tournament.

Showdown
The final act of a poker game, where remaining players reveal their hands to determine the winner of the pot.

Side Pot
When one player has bet all his chips and two or more opponents remain, a segregated pot created for, and that can only be won by, players who still have chips to bet.

Sixth Street
In seven-card stud, the fourth betting round, so named for the six cards held by each player.

Small Blind
The smaller of two mandatory bets made by the player sitting immediately to the left of the dealer button position.

Smooth
In lowball, hands with relatively low (strong) supporting cards.

Splashing the Pot
Tossing bets into the pot where the amount bet is not clearly distinguished, as opposed to placing chips in a clearly segregated area in front of the player.

Spread-Limit
A form of LIMIT POKER where players may bet any amount between the minimum and maximum amounts specified for the game.

Standard Raise
In no-limit and pot-limit, a raise of two-and-a-half to three times the size of the big blind.

Steal a Pot
To win a pot by bluffing, or through getting lucky and outdrawing an opponent.

Stealing the Antes
To raise with an inferior hand for the purpose of winning the antes uncontested.

Stealing the Blinds
To raise with an inferior hand for the purpose of winning the blinds uncontested.

Straight
A sequence of five consecutive cards of mixed suits, such as 4-5-6-7-8.

Straight Draw
Four cards to the straight needing one more to complete the straight.

Straight Flush
A sequence of five consecutive cards in the same suit, such as 8-9-10-J-Q of spades.

Suited Connectors
Cards that are consecutive and of the same suit, such as 8-9 of spades.

Table Stakes
A rule stating that a player's bet or call of a bet is limited to the amount of money he has on the table in front of him.

Tell
An inadvertent mannerism or reaction that reveals information about a player's hand. In hold'em and Omaha, the third community card and its betting round.

Third Street
In seven-card stud, the first betting round, so named for the three cards held by each player. In hold'em and Omaha, the third community card and its betting round.

Three of a Kind
Poker hand containing three cards of the same rank, such as 4-4-4. *Also* TRIPS.

Tight
A player that plays much fewer than the average number of hands.

Tournament
A competition among players who start with an equal number of chips and play until one player holds all the chips
as opposed to CASH GAME.

Tournament Chips
Chips used only for tournaments that have no cash value.

Tournament Director
The house employee in charge of a tournament.

Trips
See THREE OF A KIND.

Turn
In hold'em and Omaha, the fourth community card on board.

Two Pair
Poker hand containing two sets of two cards of the same rank, such as J-J-5-5.

Wild Cards
Cards designated as "wild" can be given any value, even as a duplicate of a card already held, by the holder of that card.

WSOP
World Series of Poker.

ROULETTE

A Cheval
SPLIT BET, in French.

American Roulette
Roulette as played in the United States, featuring wheels with both the zero and double zero.

American Wheel
0 and 00 roulette wheel

Ball
Spherical ball spun against wheel's rotation.

Biased Wheel
An imperfect casino wheel that creates a bias in the expected numbers.

Carré
FOUR-NUMBER BET, in French.

Colonne
COLUMN BET, in French.

Columns Bet
A bet on a "column" of 12 numbers.

Combination Bet
Any bet combining two or more individual numbers at once.

Corner Bet
See FOUR-NUMBER BET.

Croupier
The French term for DEALER.

D'Alembert
See PYRAMID SYSTEM.

Dealer
The casino employee who handles all the functions at the table. He changes money into chips, spins the wheel, collects losing bets, and pays off the winner.

Douzaine
DOZENS BET, in French.

Dozens Bet
A wager on either the first, second or third dozen numbers.

En Plein
SINGLE NUMBER BET, in French.

En Prison

A European option on even-money bets, that allows players, when a 0 gets spun, to either give up half their bet or go for another spin and keep the original bet intact.

European Roulette

Roulette as played in Europe, featuring wheels with only the zero and offering EN PRISON and PARTAGE.

European Wheel

Roulette wheel using the 0.

Even-Money Bets

The HIGH-LOW, ODD-EVEN and RED-BLACK bets which pay off at even money.

Five-Number Bet

In American roulette, the bet covering the 1, 2, 3, 0 and 00.

Four-Number Bet

A bet covering four numbers. *Also* SQUARE BET, CORNER BET.

Grand Martingale

A betting system used at roulette.

High-Low

An even-money bet on numbers 1-18 (low) or 19-36 (high).

Impair-Pair

ODD-EVEN BET, in French.

Layout

The betting cloth on which players make their bets.

Marker Button

A coin or chip which is used by the dealer to indicate the value of roulette chips used by a player betting that color.

Martingale

A betting system that attempts to win one unit on every sequence by doubling up after every loss, and betting one unit after every win.

Odd-Even Bet

An even-money wager on either the ODD or the EVEN numbers.

Outside Bet
A wager on either the EVEN-MONEY, DOZENS or COLUMNS BETS.

Partage
Similar to EN PRISON in that players forfeit only half their wager when an even-number bet is made and a zero (or double zero) is spun, and different in that there is no option to let the entire bet ride for another spin. *Also* SURRENDER, in some U.S. casinos.

Passe-Manque
HIGH-LOW BET, in French.

Pyramid System
A betting system that increases bets by one unit after each loss. *Also* D'ALEMBERT.

Quatre Premiere
Bet covering the 0, 1, 2, and 3, in French.

Red-Black Bet
An even-money bet on either the red or black numbers.

Rouge ou Noir
RED or BLACK, in French.

Roulette Wheel
See WHEEL.

Single Number Bet
A wager on one of the thirty-six numbers, 0 or 00.

Sixaine
SIX-NUMBER BET, in French.

Six-Number Bet
A bet covering six numbers.

Split Bet
A wager covering two numbers.

Square Bet
See FOUR-NUMBER BET.

Surrender
See PARTAGE.

Tourneur
The DEALER, in French.

Transversale
TRIO BET, in French.

Trio Bet
A bet covering three numbers.

True Odds
The actual mathematical likelihood of an event occurring.

Wheel
A circular apparatus containing 36 grooved slots numbered from 1 to 36, with half the numbers red and half black, plus either a 0 or a 0 and 00 are used. This wheel is spun and a tiny ball is used to determine the numbers that will be in play. *Also* ROULETTE WHEEL.

Wheel Checks
Colored chips which are valid only at the roulette table which issues them.

Zero-Double Zero
The numbers on the wheel which account for the casino's edge over the player.

SLOTS

Action
The total amount of money played measured by the sum of all bets placed.

Bank of Machines
A group of machines connected together in a structure as a design unit.

Bar
A popular symbol on the slot machines. This symbol is often found as one bar, two bars, and three bars.

Big Bertha

The gigantic slot machine of many reels, usually eight to ten, that are strategically placed by casinos near their front entrance (usually, but not always) to lure curious players into their casinos for a pull or two.

Bill Acceptor

A slot machine device that accepts and converts money into credits.

Blank

The stop on a REEL which contain no symbols, thus, blank stops, or blanks.

Buy-Your-Pay

A machine with a single payout line that will only pay on certain symbols if enough coins are played.

Cage

The cashier's cage, where players can exchange chips for cash, or change traveler's checks.

Carousels

An oval or round-shaped area containing a BANK OF MACHINES.

Cash Back Club

SLOT CLUBS that offer cash rebates to players enrolled in their program.

Cashout Button

This button, when pressed, issues a ticket, redeemable at the cashier's cage or inserted into another machine for equal credits; in older machines, pressing this button releases all the coins that were held as credits.

Change Booth

A booth set up for the specific purpose of changing bills into coins, or coins into bills.

Changeperson

The casino employee responsible for changing player bills into coins.

Cherry

A popular symbol on slot machines.

Cold

A machine that pays out less than expected; a player on a losing streak.

Comp

Short for complimentary. Freebies given out by the casino, usually as a reward for play.

Credits

The amount of units a player has available to play, either through putting money into the machine, or by winning them.

Criss-Cross Machine

See FIVE LINE CRISS-CROSS.

Denomination

The minimum bet amount needed to play a particular machine.

Five Line Criss-Cross

Also CRISS-CROSS MACHINE. A multiple payline machine that has five winning directions—three horizontal and two diagonal.

Hold

The percentage or actual dollar amounts a casino wins from its players.

Hot

A machine that pays out better than expected, or a player on a winning streak.

Jackpot

The big win on any machine—the jackpot!

Lemon

A symbol found on the slot machines.

Liberty Bell

The original slot machine invented by Charles Fey. Also, the symbol on the reels of many slot machines.

Long Run

The concept of what certain results are expected to be when occurring over many trials, thus, *in the long run.*

Loose Payer

A loose machine.

Loose, Loose Machine

A slot machine marked by frequent winners, with a high percentage payback to the players—as opposed to a TIGHT MACHINE which has a low percentage payback.

Max Bet Button
See MAX COIN BUTTON.

Max Coin Button
The button that plays all credits allowed, usually three or five, when pushed. *Also* MAX BET BUTTON.

Mega-Progressive Machines
A progressive slot machine with enormous, usually million-dollar jackpots.

Mills Machines
An early machine, manufactured by Mills, an early slot innovator and producer, that was the first to use the fruit symbols and have a jackpot.

Money Management
The strategy used by smart players to wisely manage their money while gambling.

Multi-Game Machine
A slot machine that features multiple games on the same device. Players can switch back and forth between the various games offered without changing machines.

Multiple Payline
A slot machine with more than one winning payline.

Multiple Progressives
A machine which contains more than one progressive jackpot.

Multiplier
A multiple coin slots which pays proportionately more on winning combinations for each coin played, though often the jackpot pays much more if all coins are played than if a lesser amount is deposited.

One Credit Button
The button that plays one credit for the player when pushed.

One-Armed Bandit
A colorful (and dated) term used for slot machines.

Payback or Payout Percentage
The expected return percentage for money wagered.

Payline
The line on the glass over the reels of the machine behind which the symbols need to line up to be a winning combination.

Payout Meter
The display on the machine that shows the number of coins played and won on a spin.

Penny Slots
Slots that play in 1¢ denominations.

Progressive Slots, Progressives
Progressives feature a jackpot which increases each time a credit is played on a machine hooked up to the progressive. When the jackpot does hit, the lucky player wins the total accumulated in the jackpot.

Random Number Generator
A computer chip that generates numbers in a random order. *Also* RNG.

Rating
The evaluation received by a player from the casino stating the level of action this player gives the casino.

Reel
The spinning mechanism containing the symbols on a slots machine. *Also* STEPPER REEL.

RNG
See RANDOM NUMBER GENERATOR.

Seven
A popular symbol on the slot machines, generally showing up in the number form "7."

Short Run
A brief sequence of trials, where anything can happen, even though the odds say they may not be likely to.

Slot Club
A casino marketing program that allows players to earn rewards for their slot and video poker machine play.

Slots Host
The person responsible for taking care of the slots players and their needs.

Slots Palace

A casino that only contains slot machines.

Start

On some machines, pushing this button will spin the reels if credits are already bet.

Step

A place where the slot reel can land and display a symbol. *Also* STOP.

Stepper Reels

See REELS.

Stop

See STEP.

Straight Slots

Slots that pay winning combinations according to the schedule list on the machine.

Symbols

The various markings on a slot machine reel.

Ticket-in, Ticket-out Machine

Slot machines that generate paper tickets showing the amount that a player has won. These tickets can be cashed in at the casino cashier.

Tight Machine

A slot machine marked by infrequent winners with a low percentage payback to the players—as opposed to a LOOSE MACHINE, which has a high percentage payback.

Touch-Screen Machines

Slots where the options can be activated by touching the video screen as opposed to pressing buttons.

Video Slots

Modern slots which are essentially computer devices (no moving reels) that generate the winning symbols and display them on a video screen.

Well

The bottom metal area of the machine where winning coins fall.

Wild Play Machines

Slot machines that use WILD SYMBOLS to multiply the winning payouts.

Wild Symbol

The symbol earmarked as "wild" by a slot manufacturer, could be designated as any winning symbol for the benefit of the player, or in addition, can increase the normal winning payout by a multiple.

Window

The glass area in the front of the machine where the player views the symbols and reels.

SPORTS BETTING

AL

American League.

Bigs

Slang for the "Big Leagues," the major leagues. Used primarily for baseball.

Bookie, Bookmaker

The individual or business that sets the line and books the bets in sports, whether legal or illegal.

Crease

See DISTORTION.

Distortion

A situation where overwhelming fan support for one of the contestants creates an unbalanced line favorable for the astute bettor. *Also* CREASE.

Dog

See UNDERDOG.

Favorite

The team or individual more likely to win, or at least perceived that way by the betting public.

Home Field Advantage

The advantage a team inherently enjoys by playing before its fans on its own field.

Hoops

Slang for basketball.

Laying Money

Betting more money than one hopes to win back.

Laying Points

A situation where favorite bettors must give the underdog extra points in a game to equalize the contest.

Line

The points or odds set by the bookie which determine the conditions under which a bet is placed.

Lock

A sure bet to win, a fallacy in sports betting
no sports contest is ever for sure.

MMA

Short for mixed martial arts.

Money Line

The line in baseball and boxing where FAVORITE bettors lay money, that is, bet more than they hope to win, while UNDERDOG bettors, take odds, win more than the amount they wager.

NBA

National Basketball Association.

NFL

National Football League.

NL

National League.

Over-Under

Wagers that a team will score either more, "OVER," or less "UNDER," than the points listed. *Also* TOTALS BET.

Parlay

A bet combining two or more teams together in which all the teams in the parlay must win for the bet to win.

Pointspread

The line used for football and basketball where FAVORITE bettors lay (give) points and UNDERDOG bettors take points. *Also* SPREAD.

Push

A bet that is a tie, with the bettor receiving his original wager back (with no commission taken out).

Sided

When a lot more money gets bet on one side of a contest, forcing bookies to gamble, rather than earn their sure commission by having money evenly bet on both sides.

Spread

See POINTSPREAD.

Straight-Up

Betting a game without taking or giving points.

Taking Odds

A wager on the UNDERDOG where a winning bet pays more than originally wagered.

Taking Points

A situation where UNDERDOG bettors receive extra points in a game to equalize the contest.

Teaser

A wager which ties two or more games together by giving bettors incentives in the way of extra points or better odds. All games "teased" must be won for the teaser to win.

30¢ Line

A 30¢ spread between the FAVORITE and the UNDERDOG the bookie's VIG. Used in boxing and MMA.

20¢ Line

A 20¢ spread between the FAVORITE and the UNDERDOG the bookie's VIG. Used in baseball.

Totals Bet

See OVER/UNDER.

Tout

A service that offers betting advice for a fee.

Underdog

The team or individual more likely to lose, or at least perceived that way by the betting public.

Vig

See VIGORISH.

Vigorish

The bookmakers commission on sports bets. *Also* VIG.

THREE CARD POKER, FOUR CARD POKER

Aces Up Bet

In four card poker, a wager that the player's hand will be a pair of aces or better (similar to the PAIR PLUS bet in three card poker, where a player must make *any* pair or better to win).

Ante Bet

In three card poker and four card poker, a wager that the player has a better hand than the dealer.

Ante Bet Bonus Payout

In four card poker, a bonus paid out if a player's hand is a three of a kind or better.

Ante Bonus

In three card poker, an ante bonus will be paid on a hand of a straight, three of a kind, or straight flush.

Ante/Play Bet

In three card poker, a combination of the ANTE and PLAY BETS part of the game.

Ante/Play Game

In three card poker, a combination of the ante and play bets part of the game—as opposed to the PAIR PLUS GAME.

Call

See PLAY

Flush

Four cards of the same suit, such as K-7-6-2 all hearts.

Fold

In three card poker, to forfeit the ANTE BET and not continue on with the hand.

Four of a Kind

Four cards of the same rank, such as 9-9-9-9.

Full Ante Bet Bonus Payout Schedule

In three card poker, the optimum bonus pay schedule on the ante bet, paying 5 to 1 on a straight flush, 4 to 1 on a three of a kind, and 3 to 1 on a straight.

High Card

A hand containing no pair or better hand, just odd cards such as Q-7-3-2 in different suits.

Non-Qualifying Hand

In three card poker, when the dealer holds a hand that is less than a queen-high hand, for example J-9-3.

One Pair

One pair of equally ranked cards, such as J-J-9-2.

Original Paytable

In three card poker, the original paytable on the PAIR PLUS as developed by inventor Derek Webb which is distinguished by a 40 to 1 payoff on a three of a kind, a 6 to 1 payoff on a straight, and a 4 to 1 payoff on a flush.

Pair Plus

In three card poker, a wager that the player will have a hand of a pair or better.

Pair Plus Game

In three card poker, betting on the pair plus part of the game as opposed to the ANTE/PLAY GAME.

Play

In three card poker, to increase the ante wager when a player thinks he has a better hand than the dealer. *Also* RAISE, CALL; in four card poker, to increase the ante wager by up to three times when a player thinks he has a better hand than the dealer. *Also* RAISE.

Qualifying Hand

In three card poker, a dealer holding at least a queen-high hand.

Raise

See PLAY.

Shuffle Master

The company that licenses and distributes three card poker and four card poker, among other games.

Straight Flush

Four cards of the same suit in sequence, such 10-9-8-7, all diamonds.

Straight

Four cards of mixed suits in sequence, such as J-10-9-8.

Three of a Kind

Three cards of the same rank, such as 5-5-5.

Two Pair

Two cards of identical rank and two other cards of identical rank, such as 8-8-3-3.

VIDEO POKER

A

The ace.

Action

The total amount of money played measured by the sum of all bets placed.

Bank of Machines

A group of machines connected together in a structure as a design unit.

Bill Acceptor

A slot machine device that accepts and converts money into credits.

Bonus Quads

A jacks or better machine that offers special bonus payouts on specified four-of-a-kind hands.

GLOSSARY

Bonus Royal
Type of video poker machine that gives a large bonus payout on a specified royal flush if hit.

Cage
The cashier's cage, where players can exchange chips for cash, or change traveler's checks.

Cashout Button
This button, when pressed, issues a ticket, redeemable at the cashier's cage or inserted into another machine for equal credits; in older machines, pressing this button releases all the coins that were held as credits.

Change Booth
A booth set up for the specific purpose of changing bills into coins, or coins into bills.

Changeperson
The casino employee responsible for changing player bills into coins.

Cold
A machine that pays out less than expected, or a player on a losing streak.

Comp
Short for *complimentary*. The freebies given out by the casino, usually as a reward for play.

Credits
The amount of units a player has available to play, either through putting money into the machine, or by winning them.

Denomination
The size of coin (or bill) used to play a particular machine.

Deuces Wild
A video poker variation where all deuces are WILD CARDS, that is, they can be used as any card that would most benefit the player, even though that card may already be used.

Deuces and Joker Wild

A video poker game dealt from a 53-card deck, the regular 52-card deck plus a wild joker. All deuces are WILD in this game too, for five wild cards.

Discard

A card that a player chooses not to keep, instead drawing a new one.

Double Card Option

This feature, found on some video poker machines, uses a 53-card deck to deal the game.

Double Down Stud

A video poker variation that deals four cards and gives players the option to either double their bet and receive the fifth card, or fold and give up their bet.

Draw

To take cards as a replacement for discarded ones.

Double or Nothing Button

A feature on some machines that allows winning hands to double their bet at the risk of losing it all in a one-card showdown draw—high card wins—against the machine.

Draw/Deal Button

This button, when pressed, deals the cards.

Five of a Kind

A hand containing five cards of the same rank, for example, 4-4-4-4-4 (one or more of these cards could be a wild card).

Five Deck Frenzy

The progressive variation of FIVE DECK POKER.

Five Deck Poker

This video poker variation assigns one deck of cards to each video poker position so that, in theory, a player could hold five cards of the same suit and value.

Flat-top Machine

A machine with set payoffs—as opposed to a PROGRESSIVE. *Also* STRAIGHT machine.

Flush

Five cards of the same suit.

Full House

A hand containing three cards of the same value (three of a kind) and two cards of another identical value (a pair). Q-Q-Q-K-K would be a full house.

Full Pay Machines

Video poker machines that have the ideal, or maximum, payout schedule for its type.

Hand

The player's five cards.

High Card

In JACKS OR BETTER, a jack, queen, king or ace. In TENS OR BETTER, the ten as well.

Hold

The action of keeping a card (not discarding it), or the button marked as such that is used for this purpose. Also, the percentage or actual dollar amounts a casino wins from its players.

Hold Button

The button that, when pressed, tells the machine to keep the card. When it is pressed again, it releases the "hold" and directs the machine to discard the card.

Hot

A machine that pays out more than expected, or a player on a winning streak.

Inside Straight

A four-card straight that can only be filled in the inside, not on either end. For example, 5-6-8-9 is an inside straight since only a 7 will fill the straight.

J

A jack.

Jackpot

A very big winning combination.

Jacks or Better

The standard video poker machine that pays out for any poker hand of at least jacks or higher. Also, refers to a hand of at least the strength of jacks, that is, jacks, queens, kings, or aces, or any higher combination.

Joker Wild

A video poker machine dealt from a 53-card deck, the regular 52-card deck plus a joker which serves as a wild card.

K

A king.

Long Run

The concept of what certain results are expected to be when occurring over many trials, thus, *in the long run.*

Low Pair

A pair that doesn't qualify for a payout. In JACKS OR BETTER, that would a hand of tens or worse.

Max Bet Button

See MAX COIN BUTTON.

Max Coin Button

The button that plays all credits allowed, usually five when pushed. *Also* MAX BET BUTTON.

Mega-Progressive Machines

A progressive video poker machine with an enormous, usually million-dollar jackpot.

Money Management

The strategy used by smart players to wisely manage their money while gambling—to preserve their capitol, avoid big losses, and manage their wins.

Multiple Progressives

A machine which contains more than one progressive jackpot.

9-5 machines

A deuces wild payout schedule, so named for the 9-coin payoff on a straight flush, and the 6-coin payoff for the four of a kind.

9-6 Machines

A jacks or better payout schedule, so named for the 9-coin payoff on a full house and the 6-coin payoff for the flush.

One Credit Button

The button that plays one credit for the player when pushed.

Pair

Two cards of the same rank, such as two fives or two jacks.

Payback

See PAYOUT PERCENTAGE.

Payout Percentage

The expected return percentage for money wagered. A 97% payback states that the expected return on every dollar bet will be 97¢, for a loss of 3¢.

Paytable

The display on the video poker machine showing winning combinations and their payouts.

Payout Meter

The display on a machine that shows the number of coins played and won on a spin.

Progressives

Progressives feature a jackpot which increases each time a coin is inserted into a machine hooked up to the progressive meter. When the winning combination hits, usually a royal flush, the lucky player wins the total amount posted. The jackpot total will be reset to a predetermined starting point.

Q

A queen.

Quad

A specified four-of-a-kind hand that pays a bonus amount if drawn.

Rating

A casino evaluation of a player stating the level of action he gives the casino.

Royal Flush

The A-K-Q-J-10, all of the same suit.

Second Chance

A video poker feature, sometimes found, that allows players to receive a sixth card in an additional "second draw" if the drawing of that one card would give the player a chance to make a straight or better hand.

Sequential Royal Flush

A royal flush that must be hit in an exact order by position. For example, the royal may need to be in order with the 10 being in the leftmost position, then consecutively, the jack, queen, king, and finally the ace in the rightmost position.

Short Run

A brief sequence of trials, where anything can happen, even though the odds say they may not.

Slots Club

A casino club set up to reward frequent slots and video poker players with comps and rewards.

Slots Host

The casino employee responsible for taking care of the slots and video poker players.

Straight

Five consecutive non-suited cards, such as an 8-9-10-J-Q. If an ace is contained in a straight, it must be either the highest or the lowest card of the sequence, or the hand is not a straight. Q-K-A-2-3 is not a straight.

Straight Flush

Five consecutive cards all in the same suit, for example, the 4-5-6-7-8 of clubs.

Straight Machine

See FLAT-TOP MACHINE.

Suit

Any of one of the following groups of cards—hearts, diamonds, spades, or clubs.

Tens or Better

A video poker variation that pays out for any poker hand of at least tens or higher.

Three of a Kind

Also TRIPS. Three cards of the same value, such as 9-9-9.

Triple Play

A video poker variation that features the simultaneous play of three poker hands.

Trips

See THREE OF A KIND.

Two Pair

A five-card hand that contains two sets of identically valued cards (two pairs) such as 7-7-A-A.

Two Pairs or Better

A video poker variation that requires a minimum hand of two pairs for a payout.

Well

The bottom metal area of the machine where winning coins fall.

Wild

See WILD CARD.

Wild Card

Cards designated as WILD can be given any value or suit, even as a duplicate or triplicate of a card already held.